'This book truly reflects the changing nature of HRD in the complex world of the
21st century. It provides insight and critique of the main aspects of HRD and how
they enhance the quality of the workforce and thereby organisational competitive
advantage.' – **Associate Professor Peter Holland, Director of Post-Graduate Human
Resource Management Programs, Monash University, Australia**

'This book will appeal to reflective and reflexive practitioners who want a deeper
insight into core concepts and constructs in order to challenge and develop the theorizing and practice of HRD. The book brings together influential scholars in the field
of HRD who offer critical reviews of HRD theory and practice. In doing so, they challenge many taken for granteds and provide a deeper insight into contemporary HRD.' –
Dr Aileen Lawless, Senior Lecturer in HRM, Liverpool John Moores University, UK

'This book brings together through critical reflection a wealth of references and theoretical links in the area of Human Resource Development. For a serious student of
this field there will be both additional writers to explore and new ideas. The book is
very clearly written and readable. An excellent grounding in key theories in this area of
making learning work.' – **Derek Miles, Professor of Human Resource Development,
Middlesex University, UK**

'A thought-provoking text drawing on a range of theoretical and methodological
perspectives, encouraging a critical, reflexive interpretation of key contemporary challenges within the field of HRD. An accessible book entirely appropriate to MBA and
Masters student as well as practitioners seeking alternative perspectives in consideration of HRD.' – **Darren Caudle, Principal Lecturer in HRM, University of
Gloucestershire, UK**

'Adopting an insightful and critical approach to HRD concepts, practices and
orthodoxies, this text is a timely contribution for students, teachers and practitioners in the field.' – **Dr Karin Mathison, Lecturer in Human Resource Development,
University of Tasmania, Australia**

'Walton and Valentin have assembled a treasure-trove of exquisite ideas that is capable
of unleashing the full potential of professionals to open their minds further to the
mysteries of human learning, development and performance within global contexts.' –
Professor Francesco Sofo, University of Canberra, Australia

MANAGEMENT, WORK & ORGANISATIONS SERIES

Series editors: **Gibson Burrell**, School of Management, University of Leicester, UK
Mick Marchington, Manchester Business School, University of Manchester and Strathclyde Business School, University of Strathclyde, UK
Paul Thompson, Strathclyde Business School, University of Strathclyde, UK

This series of textbooks covers the areas of human resource management, employee relations, organisational behaviour and related business and management fields. Each text has been specially commissioned to be written by leading experts in a clear and accessible way. The books contain serious and challenging material, take an analytical rather than prescriptive approach and are particularly suitable for use by students with no prior specialist knowledge.

The series is relevant for many business and management courses, including MBA and post-experience courses, specialist masters and postgraduate diplomas, professional courses and final-year undergraduate courses. These texts have become essential reading at business and management schools worldwide.

Published titles include:

Stephen Bach and Ian Kessler
THE MODERNISATION OF THE PUBLIC SERVICES AND EMPLOYEE RELATIONS

Maurizio Atzeni
WORKERS AND LABOUR IN A GLOBALISED CAPITALISM

Emma Bell
READING MANAGEMENT AND ORGANIZATION IN FILM

Paul Blyton and Peter Turnbull
THE DYNAMICS OF EMPLOYEE RELATIONS (3RD EDN)

Paul Blyton, Edmund Heery and Peter Turnbull (eds)
REASSESSING THE EMPLOYMENT RELATIONSHIP

Sharon C. Bolton
EMOTION MANAGEMENT IN THE WORKPLACE

Sharon C. Bolton and Maeve Houlihan (eds)
SEARCHING FOR THE HUMAN IN HUMAN RESOURCE MANAGEMENT

Peter Boxall and John Purcell
STRATEGY AND HUMAN RESOURCE MANAGEMENT (3RD EDN)

J. Martin Corbett
CRITICAL CASES IN ORGANISATIONAL BEHAVIOUR

Susan Corby, Steve Palmer and Esmond Lindop
RETHINKING REWARD

Ian Greener
PUBLIC MANAGEMENT (2ND EDN)

Keith Grint
LEADERSHIP

Irena Grugulis
SKILLS, TRAINING AND HUMAN RESOURCE DEVELOPMENT

Geraldine Healy, Gill Kirton and Mike Noon (eds)
EQUALITY, INEQUALITIES AND DIVERSITY

Damian Hodgson and Svetlana Cicmil (eds)
MAKING PROJECTS CRITICAL

Marek Korczynski
HUMAN RESOURCE MANAGEMENT IN SERVICE WORK

Karen Legge
HUMAN RESOURCE MANAGEMENT: ANNIVERSARY EDITION

Patricia Lewis and Ruth Simpson (eds)
GENDERING EMOTIONS IN ORGANIZATIONS

Patricia Lewis and Ruth Simpson (eds)
VOICE, VISIBILITY AND THE GENDERING OF ORGANIZATIONS

Alison Pullen, Nic Beech and David Sims (eds)
EXPLORING IDENTITY

Jill Rubery and Damian Grimshaw
THE ORGANISATION OF EMPLOYMENT

Hugh Scullion and Margaret Linehan (eds)
INTERNATIONAL HUMAN RESOURCE MANAGEMENT

John Walton and Claire Valentin (eds)
HUMAN RESOURCE DEVELOPMENT

Colin C. Williams
RETHINKING THE FUTURE OF WORK

Diana Winstanley and Jean Woodall (eds)
ETHICAL ISSUES IN CONTEMPORARY HUMAN RESOURCE MANAGEMENT

For more information on titles in the Series please go to **www.palgrave.com/business/mwo**

Series Standing Order

If you would like to receive future titles in this series as they are published, you can make use of our standing order facility. To place a standing order please contact your bookseller or, in case of difficulty, write to us at the address below with your name and address and the name of the series. Please state with which title you wish to begin your standing order.

Customer Services Department, Macmillan Distribution Ltd,
Houndmills, Basingstoke, Hampshire, RG21 6XS, UK

HUMAN RESOURCE DEVELOPMENT

Practices and Orthodoxies

Edited by

John Walton

Claire Valentin

palgrave
macmillan

First published 2014 by
PALGRAVE MACMILLAN

Palgrave Macmillan in the UK is an imprint of Macmillan Publishers Limited,
registered in England, company number 785998, of Houndmills, Basingstoke,
Hampshire RG21 6XS.

Palgrave Macmillan in the US is a division of St Martin's Press LLC,
175 Fifth Avenue, New York, NY 10010.

Palgrave Macmillan is the global academic imprint of the above companies
and has companies and representatives throughout the world.

Palgrave® and Macmillan® are registered trademarks in the United States,
the United Kingdom, Europe and other countries.

ISBN 978–0–230–29227–7

This book is printed on paper suitable for recycling and made from fully
managed and sustained forest sources. Logging, pulping and manufacturing
processes are expected to conform to the environmental regulations of the
country of origin.

A catalogue record for this book is available from the British Library.

A catalog record for this book is available from the Library of Congress.

CONTENTS

v

FIGURES AND TABLES

FIGURES

TABLES

ABOUT THE EDITORS

John Walton

John Walton was until his retirement in 2010 Professor in Human Resource Development (HRD) in the Business School at London Metropolitan University, UK, where he was Director of the Management Research Centre. He was also responsible for the MA in Human Resource Strategies which is targeted at seasoned HR practitioners studying both in the UK and in Russia who have a significant responsibility for facilitating policy development and change initiatives in their own or client organizations; and launched the first professional doctorate in Personnel and Development in the UK. He is a Fellow of the Chartered Institute of Personnel and Development, for whom he has been involved for over 15 years in the design and development of advanced national professional qualifications. He is a founder member and former Chair of the University Forum for HRD, whose aims include developing international research and consultancy activities which bridge the academic-practitioner divide in the human resource development field. He is also the first person from the UK to have served on the Board of the Academy of Human Resource Development. Research and consultancy projects have included a UK Cabinet Office consortium project seeking to assist a number of governmental departments and agencies to develop HRD strategies which contribute to the overall strategic direction. He is the author of the Financial Times/Prentice Hall publication on *Strategic Human Resource Development*, which has received international acclaim and in 2000 received the Academy of Human Resource Development Book of the Year award. Current research interests include (1) the role of HRD in facilitating scenario forecasting and strategic visioning for organizations, (2) the growth of the corporate university and (3) critical discourse analysis of HRD texts.

Claire Valentin

Claire Valentin lectures at the University of Edinburgh, Scotland. She was responsible for setting up one of the first HRD Master's programmes in the

UK. Currently, she has responsibility for development, delivery and management of postgraduate programmes leading to professionally validated awards in HRD. Prior to entering academia in the mid-1990s, she worked in the voluntary sector in development and training, as a training officer in a local authority, and as a training and OD consultant and researcher. She is a Fellow of the Chartered Institute of Personnel and Development (CIPD), for which she was until recently on the national examining team for awards in Learning and Talent Development. She is a former Vice-Chair of the University Forum for HRD, and chaired the Committee for Programmes and Qualifications. She was leader of the Higher Education Academy Business Management and Finance subject centre Special Interest Group for teaching and learning in HRD. Her current research interests include (1) critical perspectives on human resource development practice, research and education, (2) teaching and learning in HRD, (3) employee engagement and (4) HRD and sustainability. Her research has been recognized in the UK and internationally, through contributions to conferences and symposia, and to books and journal special issues.

ABOUT THE CONTRIBUTORS

Rod Githens is Assistant Professor & Programme Director in Organizational Leadership and Learning at the University of Louisville, USA. His primary interests surround the fostering of humane, accessible and diverse workplaces through workforce and human resource development. His publication record includes work dealing with older workers' use of technology and older adults and e-learning. His practitioner experience includes an active consulting practice and experience as an HR Manager in a large division of a major logistics services provider in the US.

Jeff Gold is Professor of Organization Learning at Leeds Business School, Leeds Metropolitan University, UK, and Visiting Professor at Leeds University, UK, where he co-ordinates the Northern Leadership Academy. He has led a range of seminars and workshops on leadership with a particular emphasis on participation and distribution. He is the co-author of *Leadership and Management Development, Strategies for Action* (with Richard Thorpe and Alan Mumford), published by the Chartered Institute of Personnel and Development in 2010, and *Human Resource Management* (with John Bratton) published in 2012 with Palgrave Macmillan

Linda M. Hite is Professor and Chair of Organizational Leadership and Supervision at Indiana University-Purdue University Fort Wayne, USA. Her publications include journals and book chapters primarily focused on career development and workplace diversity. She is Book and Media Review Editor for *New Horizons in Adult Education and Human Resource Development* and serves on the editorial boards of *Advances in Developing Human Resources* and *Human Resource Development Quarterly*. Prior to joining the faculty at

IPFW, she worked in corporate training and development and in academic administration.

K. Peter Kuchinke, PhD, is Professor of Human Resource Development at the University of Illinois at Urbana-Champaign, USA. A native German, he holds a doctoral degree from the University of Minnesota, USA, in Human Resource Development and Strategic Management. His current research interests include the role of work in overall life design, self-directed career behaviours, and cross-cultural differences in career preparation and development. He has published over 125 scholarly articles and book chapters and presented his research at more than 50 national and international business and education conferences. He is the past Editor for *Human Resource Development International* and Director of a US-Brazilian University Consortium funded by the US Department of Education and the Brazilian counterpart. His current service appointments include Director of Graduate Studies for the Department of Education Policy, Organization and Leadership; President-Elect of the University Council for Workforce and Human Resource Education; and PromoDoc Ambassador for the European Union's Erasmus Mundus Program.

Kimberly S. McDonald is Professor of Organizational Leadership and Supervision and Associate Dean for the College of Engineering, Technology, and Computer Science at Indiana-Purdue University Fort Wayne, USA. Currently, she is also Editor-in-Chief for *Advances in Developing Human Resources*. Prior to joining the faculty at IPFW, she worked in training and development. She has published a variety of book chapters and journal articles, most of which focus on career development.

Rob Poell, PhD, is Professor of Human Resource Development (HRD) in the Department of HR Studies at Tilburg University, the Netherlands. His core field of expertise within HRD is workplace learning. He has worked with many companies, schools and healthcare institutions to professionalize their HRD efforts. He served as Editor-in-Chief for *Human Resource Development International* for three years, and was on the board of directors of the Academy of HRD for three years as well. Rob received his PhD from the University of Nijmegen (the Netherlands) in 1998. Besides workplace learning, he has published on strategies of HRD professionals, continuing professional development, the learning-network theory, managerial coaching, HR policies in schools and on-the-job learning styles, amongst others. He has published more than 30 articles in international peer-reviewed journals and more than 20 chapters in international edited books (plus over 60 articles, book chapters and research reports in Dutch).

Clare Rigg is Head of Department of Business and Hospitality, Culinary and Tourism at the Institute of Technology Tralee, Ireland. Following an early career in economic development and urban regeneration in Birmingham, England, she developed an interest in collaborative working that was further fostered through encountering action learning as an approach to management development in 1990. She has researched and published widely on action learning, critical action learning, learning and organization development, including the co-authored books *Action Learning, Leadership and Organizational Development in Public Services* (Routledge, 2006); *Critical Human Resource Development: Beyond Orthodoxy* (FT Prentice-Hall, 2007) and *Learning and Talent Development* (CIPD, 2011). She is a co-editor of the journal *Action Learning: Research and Practice.*

Tonette S. Rocco is Professor and programme leader of adult education and human resource development at Florida International University, USA, a Houle Scholar, a Kauffman Entrepreneurship Professor, and a former board member American Society for Training and Development, Certification Institute Board of Directors. She is lead editor for *New Horizons in Adult Education and Human Resource Development* published by Wiley On Line.

Darlene Russ-Eft, PhD, is Professor of Adult Education and Higher Education Leadership in the College of Education at Oregon State University, USA. Her most recent books are *Evaluation in Organizations: A Systematic Approach to Enhancing Learning, Performance, and Change* (2009, Basic Books), *Evaluator Competencies: Standards for the Practice of Evaluation in Organizations* (2008, Jossey-Bass), *A Practical Guide to Needs Assessment* (2007, Pfeiffer) and *Building Evaluation Capacity: 72 Activities for Teaching and Training* (2005, Sage). Her recent research has included global studies to identify and validate competencies of evaluators and of instructional designers. She is immediate Past-President for the Academy of Human Resource Development (AHRD) and current director of the International Board of Standards for Training, Performance, and Instruction (ibstpi®). She is a past editor of the *Human Resource Development Quarterly*, and she received the 1996 Editor of the Year Award from *Times Mirror*, Outstanding Scholar Award from the AHRD and Outstanding Research Article Award from ASTD.

Eugene Sadler-Smith is Professor of Organizational Behaviour in the Surrey Business School, University of Surrey, UK. He has a first degree in geography from the University of Leeds, UK. From 1987 until 1994, he worked in the learning and development function of British Gas plc. His PhD (1988–1992, part time) was on the subject of cognitive styles and was supervised by Dr R.J. Riding at the School of Education, University of Birmingham, UK. His current research interests are focused on the role of intuitive cognition in management and organization. His research has been published in peer-reviewed journals such as the *Academy of Management Executive, Academy of Management Learning and Education, British Journal of Psychology, Business Ethics Quarterly, Journal of Occupational & Organizational Psychology, Journal of Organizational Behavior, Management Learning* and *Organisation Studies*. He is the author of a number of books including *Inside Intuition* (Routledge, 2008) and *The Intuitive Mind* (Wiley, 2010).

Jo Thijssen is Emeritus Professor of Strategic Human Resource Management at the Utrecht School of Governance, Utrecht University, The Netherlands. His areas of scholarly interests include HRM- & HRD-strategies, greying workforce, career development and lifelong learning. During the last decade, he published books and articles on employability, the psychological contract and older worker policies.

Denise Thursfield is Senior Lecturer in OB/HRM and programme leader for MSc Human Resource Management at Hull University Business School, UK. Her teaching interests are in human resource management and International HRM. She also teaches philosophical issues in business research to research students. Her personal research interests are in the areas of human resource management and management development. She has previously published in journals such as *Human Resource Development International, Management Learning, Work, Employment and Society* and *Personnel Review*.

Saskia Tjepkema (1970) is a consultant and coach at the international network Kessels & Smit, *The Learning Company*. Originally, she has a background in Educational Science & Technology, specializing in workplace learning, and did her PhD on the topic of learning within self-managing work teams. As a consultant and coach, she supports teams, organizations and individuals in learning and development. She also designs and facilitates leadership programmes. Saskia is also a learning facilitator in several courses from the Dutch/Flemish Foundation for Corporate Education (FCE) and the Foundation's director. The FCE is a platform for professionalization and research into the field of learning & development. She publishes in professional journals and books on a regular basis. Topics that are of great interest to her are: workplace learning, learning organization, knowledge productivity, leadership development, personal entrepreneurship, talent and strength development, Appreciative Inquiry and work teams.

Paul Tosey is a Senior Lecturer at the University of Surrey Business School, UK. His research concerns organizational learning and transformative learning, and he has a special interest in the work of Gregory Bateson, who was a seminal influence on the developers of NLP. His career experience over 30 years includes consultancy, coaching and line management. Paul is an active member of the University Forum for HRD, and currently chairs its Programme and Qualification Activities Committee. He was awarded a National Teaching Fellowship by the Higher Education Academy in 2007. Paul has encouraged and supported a research-minded approach in the field of NLP and convened the first International NLP Research Conference in 2008. Most recently, he has been exploring Clean Language, an innovative coaching practice that is based on metaphor, both as a researcher and as a trained facilitator.

Marianne van Woerkom is Associate Professor at Tilburg University, Department of Human Resource Studies, the Netherlands. She holds a PhD in social and behavioural sciences from Twente University, the Netherlands. Her research interests include learning and development, positive psychology, individual strengths, coaching and teams.

Roland K. Yeo holds a PhD in Human Resource Development from the Leeds Business School in UK and is a Management Learning Researcher and HRD Consultant in Training and Development in Saudi Aramco. He is also associated with the International Graduate School of Business in the University of South Australia as an Adjunct Senior Researcher supervising and contributing in postgraduate research. On a part-time basis, he teaches Organizational Behaviour and Leadership in the EMBA programme at the King Fahd University of Petroleum & Minerals in Saudi Arabia as an Adjunct Associate Professor of Management. Most recently, he co-authored a book with Michael Marquardt, '*Breakthrough Problem Solving with Action Learning: Concepts and Cases*', published by Stanford University Press. His research interests are in organizational learning, knowledge sharing, change management and HRD.

ACKNOWLEDGEMENTS

The authors and publishers would like to thank the following for permission to reproduce copyright material:

Table 1.1 A proposed typology of planned training on the job Source: De Jong, J. A., Thijssen, J. G. L., and Versloot, B. M. (2001) Planned training on the job: A typology, *Advances in Developing Human Resources*, 3(4): 408–414, copyright © 2005 Sage Publications. Reprinted by permission of Sage Publications.

Figure 2.1 Kolb's experiential learning cycle and learning styles. Based on Figure 1. The Experiential learning cycle and basic learning styles. Kayes, A.B., Kayes, D., and Kolb, D.S (2005) Experiential learning in teams, *Simulation and Gaming*, 36 (3): 330–354, Copyright © 2005 by Sage Publications. Reprinted by permission of Sage Publications.

Figure 3.1 Four fields of conversation. Based on Scharmer, C. O. (2000) *Presencing: Learning from the future as it emerges. On the tacit dimension of leading revolutionary change.* Paper presented at the Conference on Knowledge and Innovation. Reprinted by permission of Otto Scharmer.

Figure 4.1 Kolb's experiential learning cycle and learning styles. Adapted from Figure 1. The Experiential learning cycle and basic learning styles. Kayes, A.B., Kayes, D., and Kolb, D.S (2005) Experiential learning in teams, *Simulation and Gaming*, 36 (3): 330–354, copyright © 2005 Sage Publications. Reprinted by permission of Sage Publications.

Figure 4.2 Dual-process model of cognitive styles. From Sadler-Smith, E. (2011) The intuitive style: Relationships with local/global and visual/verbal styles, gender, and superstitious reasoning, Learning and Individual Differences, 21, 263–270. Copyright © 2011 Elsevier. Reprinted by permission of Elsevier.

Box 3.1 Learning from success: Overview of the method. Based on De Haan, E. (2001) *Leren met collega's. Praktijkboek intercollegiale consultatie [Learning with colleagues. Work book intercollegial consultation]*. Assen: Van Gorcum. Reprinted by permission of Eric De Haan.

Box 3.2 Appreciative interview: Overview of the Method. From Cooperrider, D. L., and Whitney, D. K. (2005) *Appreciative Inquiry: A Positive Revolution in Change*. San Francisco, CA: Berret-Koehler. Copyright © (2005) by Scharmer, C. O Berrett-Koehler Publishers, Inc., San Francisco, CA. All rights reserved. www.bkconnection.com. Reprinted with permission of the publisher.

Chapter 3 2*2 questions. Based on De Jong-Van Rooij, M. (2009) *Effectief samenwerken: denken in driehoeken [Effective collaboration: Thinking in triangles]*. Utrecht: Kessels and Smit. Reprinted by permission of Kessels and Smit.

Chapter 6 updated from: Russ-Eft, D. (1997). Behavior modeling. In L. Bassi and D. Russ-Eft (eds), *What Works: Training and Development Practices* (pp. 105–149). Alexandria, VA: American Society for Training and Development. Copyright © 1997 American Society for Training and Development. Reprinted by permission of American Society for Training and Development.

The editors would like acknowledge the help and advice given by Ursula Gavin, Publisher, Business and Management Textbooks, and Ceri Griffiths, Assistant Editor, Business and Finance, at Palgrave. Thanks also to the anonymous reviewers who provided very helpful feedback and suggestions on the book proposal and draft.

ABBREVIATIONS

AC   abstract conceptualization
ACCT   Association for Challenge Course Technology
ADEA   Age Discrimination in Employment Act (1967, US)
AE   active experimentation
AEE   Association for Experiential Education
AEOE   Association for Environmental and Outdoor Education
AI   appreciative inquiry
AL   action learning
ASTD   American Society for Training and Development
BM   behavioural modelling
CAI   computer-assisted-instruction
CAL   critical action learning
CD   career development
CE   concrete experience
CEST   cognitive-experiential self-theory (Epstein)
CHAT   cultural-historical activity theory
CIPD   Chartered Institute of Personnel and Development
CISS   Campbell Interest and Skill Inventory
CPR   cardiopulmonary resuscitation
CSI   Cognitive Style Index
CTC   Chaos Theory of Careers
EE   employee engagement
ELT   experiential learning theory (Kolb)
GE   General Electric
GOT   general occupational themes
HRD   human resource development
JEIT   Journal of European Industrial Training
KCS   Kuder Career Search and Person Match
KELT   Kolb's experiential learning theory

LSI	Leaning Styles Inventory
LSQ	Learning Styles Questionnaire
LTSI	Learning Transfer System Indicator
NHS	National Health Service
NLP	neurolinguistic programming
NSEE	National Society for Experiential Education
OCB	organizational citizenship behaviour
OET	outdoor experiential training
OMD	outdoor management development
OTD	outdoor team development
PDP	personal development plan
PID	Preference for Intuition and Deliberation scale
POS	perceived organizational support
PPE	personal protective equipment
PTS	perceived team support
REI	Rational Experiential Inventory
RO	reflective observation
ROI	return on investment
RPT	reciprocal peer training
SMR	symbolic mental rehearsal
SDS	Self Directed Search
SHRM	Society for Human Resource Management
SII	Strong Interest Inventory
SP	scenario planning
STF	Systems Theory Framework
TCI	team climate indicator
TDI	team development indicator
TMT	top management team
UKCP	United Kingdom Council for Psychotherapies
UWES	Utrecht Work Engagement Scale
WE	work engagement

INTRODUCTION: FRAMING CONTEMPORARY HRD PRACTICE AND THEORY

John Walton and Claire Valentin

INTRODUCTION

This introduction gives details on the rationale and intentions for the book, provides a summary of key themes emerging and outlines the structure and broad format for chapters.

Each chapter provides a critical review of contemporary concepts, practices and orthodoxies in human resource development (HRD). It is intended that these critical reviews will serve as a framework for students and practitioners who are looking to gain a deep insight into concepts that in many instances have become taken for granted. The book will not fit easily within traditional practitioner discourse. The position taken is that if you treat conventional wisdom as being a given then you will not be able to develop expertise, and will be unable to work through ambiguous situations.

Each author worked to the following brief:

How has the term/concept been defined and explained?
Where did the term/construct originate?
What has been its history since?
How has it been popularized and/or applied, to what extent and in what ways?
What claims have been made for it?
What criticisms of it have been made to date?

1

How legitimate are these claims and criticisms?
What alternatives have been suggested?

The way that each author has tackled the brief demonstrates various approaches that can be adopted for conducting an exercise of this nature. Many found it a difficult exercise – the further that you delve into a subject the more perspectives emerge, especially given the range and spread of journals and other sources available, not just as hard copy but also online. Twenty years ago such an exercise would have been far more restricted.

This book provides a critical review of contemporary concepts, practices and orthodoxies in HRD. It focuses on four key areas of HRD thinking and practice: (1) formative concepts; (2) training and development interventions: individual skills development approaches; (3) career development practices; and (4) team development practices. Contributions come from leading scholars across the international HRD and organizational learning academic community.

The contemporary HRD ideas and practices have been chosen from the broad range of popularly adopted approaches in usage, based on contributors' research interests. Many have been around for some time, others are more recent in origin, but most have been subjected to little sustained critique in the HRD literature; quite often significant claims are made that are not necessarily borne out by practice. The approaches that have been identified for inclusion in this book are ready for an examination of both the arguments presented in their favour and the judgements against them.

Through a brief critical review of literature, each chapter identifies the theoretical and empirical starting points of these approaches and outlines the context, history and current utilization. The chapters go on to explore paradigms, identify and examine the taken-for-granted assumptions underpinning practice, and evaluate the claims made for such practices in academic and popular texts. Theoretical critique is enhanced by illustrative cases and, where appropriate, practical examples. Thus, the focus is on a critical analysis of practice, which goes beyond the descriptive or prescriptive focus of much 'popular' or 'practitioner-focused' literature, and the many claims of consultants and specialists. The aim is to create a comprehensive, critical but accessible examination of examples of contemporary HRD practice and theoretical insights, which should appeal to students, faculty and curious practitioners.

The issue of interpretation – words and their varied meanings – has emerged at the outset and throughout the contributions. For example, the original title for the book incorporated the term 'critical reflection', which as Van Woerkom and Tjepkema comment 'is a contested term used in a confusing array of variations' (Chapter 3, p. 59) emanating from different traditions. For example, some people originally interpreted this in the Habermasian emancipatory sense of addressing power inequalities as opposed to an analytical critique of taken-for-granted assumptions in certain areas. Yet we were not looking specifically for issues relating to politics, power and emotionality, although ideological and intuitive interpretations were welcomed if they emerged in the literature; rather our expectation was for a traditional rationalist critique. Even here we were not on firm ground: Van Woerkom and Tjepkema identify alternative approaches that highlight intuitive and emotional aspects.

There are also differences in terms of how contributors perceive a critique as opposed to a review. For example, Russ-Eft (Chapter 6) provides a very informative and thorough review. However, asking people to engage in critical reflection is not unusual: many of the chapters in this book make reference to the occurrence of a proliferation of terms and of associated meanings relating to the topic they are reviewing. Most are not uncomfortable with this issue, and see it as an outcome of the relativism apparent today.

There is a tendency in a number of textbooks to go beyond the level of critique and to make assertions such as 'the evidence proves that' or make normative statements about what ought to be the case, as opposed to 'the evidence to date indicates that'. In this book there is evidence of authors adopting considerable circumspection in making claims about the topic they are considering. Rigg (Chapter 10), taking the pragmatic position of 'warranted assertability' (Dewey, 1938), is circumspect in her evaluation of action learning:

> Theoretically and empirically, we can conjecture that action learning is a powerful method of team building...however any claims made to date require further systematic study to strengthen the evidence base.
>
> (Rigg, p. 250)

Various approaches were taken to conducting the literature review. Rigg, for example, adopted the approach of data searching just for predetermined keywords (in her case action AND learning) in journal abstracts, which gave her in excess of 400 articles from a broad range of journals addressing action learning. Others found a tendency for concepts to be relabelled over time: both of the editors to this volume adopted a snowball technique when looking for origins and history of 'employee engagement' and 'outdoor team development', respectively. This entailed following up alternative terms and references suggested in articles picked up from the original search.

Two broad and linked intellectual issues and influences emerged across the texts. The first relates to definitions, the second to constructivism.

DEFINITIONAL CERTAINTY OR INCOMMENSURABILITY OF PERSPECTIVES

Over the years there has been a division in thinking between HRD researchers on the need for definitional precision, often influenced by perceptions of practitioner requirements. One school of thought is that closure and certainties should be provided wherever possible – nuances of meanings and interpretations are not helpful in terms of providing a yardstick. Harrison and Kessels (2004), for example, bemoan the uncertainty that HRD practitioners experience in the field and their search for clarity in definitions. They propose the following definition:

> HRD as an organisational process comprises the skilful planning and facilitation of a variety of formal and informal learning and knowledge and experience processes, primarily but not exclusively in the workplace, in order that organisational progress and individual potential can be enhanced through the competence, adaptability, collaboration and knowledge-creating activity of all who work in the organisation.
>
> (Harrison and Kessels, 2004, pp. 4–5)

Given the subsequent position taken in their book on the prevailing state of HRD in organizations, this statement reflects what the authors would like HRD to become, more than what it is. With respect to meaning and terminology, Harrison and Kessels make the following comment:

> Academic debate is valuable in stimulating challenge and enquiry. Where, however, the debate becomes protracted and spreads inconclusively into the organisation arena it can be damaging. Ambiguity about HRD's meaning and focus has surrounded the function for many years and has become increasingly unproductive at the practical level.
>
> (Harrison and Kessels, 2004, p. 89)

They quote from a 1999 Chartered Institute of Personnel and Development survey that found training and development practitioners were 'affected by the confusion of meanings and boundaries between such terms as HRM, HRD, training, learning and development' (Darling et al., 1999).

An instance cited in this volume can be found in Valentin's (Chapter 13) discussion of employee engagement, where one source makes a plea for a clear definition, common vocabulary and shared understanding of the concept in order to enable 'practitioners, scholars, and researchers to more readily solve problems and offer solutions' (Shuck and Wollard, 2010 pp. 91–92).

This runs counter to the position of Walton (1999) who commented that many of the concepts underpinning HRD such as learning and development 'are deceptively difficult to capture in concrete words and phrases' (p. 53). He went on to state that: 'When they become attached to other equally complex and abstract constructs the complications and potential connotations seem to multiply exponentially' (Walton, 1999, p. 53).

Many of the contributors to this volume are cautious when they refer to definitions, emphasizing the complex and polysemic nature of the constructs they are dealing with. One source cited by Valentin (Chapter 13) found more than 50 definitions of employee engagement (MacLeod and Clarke, 2009), representing a range of legitimate perspectives. Rigg (Chapter 10) takes the position that *action learning* has eschewed simple definition and has come to take a variety of meanings in practice. She points out that Reg Revans, the originator of the term (p. 231), argued that definition was counterproductive, and that other sources avoided tight definition (e.g. Pedler et al., 2004). Kuchinke (Chapter 9) handles the issue of definition in a slightly different way. He draws on 'the value-neutral' subjective definition of career proposed by Douglas T. Hall, recognizing that it might not satisfy all perspectives. More generally he refers to the futility of current attempts to produce general descriptions relating to concepts such as the nature of work because of their multiple and often incommensurate perspectives leading to a range of meanings and interpretations. Tosey (Chapter 5) offers a 'working description' of neurolinguistic programming (NLP), emphasizing process rather than content. Poell (Chapter 1) restricts himself to giving instances of definitions and perspectives on workplace learning coming from an actor perspective, and indicates their nuances without settling on one definition/perspective.

Van Woerkom and Tjepkema (Chapter 3) refer to different traditions of critical reflection, each of which has its own underpinning theory, leading to paradigm incommensurability if one is seeking an overarching definition. In the HRD field, equally different traditions have emerged over the years, and these are apparent in this volume. For example, Gold and Yeo (Chapter 2) espouse the view that HRD is concerned with the improvement of work performance, and produce a similar but not identical definition to that given by Harrison and Kessels (2004) that reflects this perspective:

> HRD is defined as the facilitation of planned and systematic interventionist activities aimed at unleashing human expertise through a range of learning techniques

and strategies for the purpose of improving work performance as well as changes which emerge informally from actions which are unplanned.

(Gold and Yeo, Chapter 2, p. 33)

At first sight, this seems to adopt a more absolutist approach. On closer reading, they use this definition as a pivotal starting point in their argument, as they recognize in their closing remarks: 'Based on our earlier definition of HRD as being the facilitation of interventionist activities, we view experiential learning as a particular important process on which HRD professionals could capitalise to unleash the human expertise of employees' (p. 53). However, their approach to definition is not seeking universal agreement on their view of HRD. Indeed, as a general point, in order to understand the implications for HRD for a given concept there needs to be some clarity as to what the authors consider HRD to be. Most of the chapters in this volume assume that HRD is operating within an organizational context, and this is entailed when discussing terms such as *employee* engagement.

Differences of opinion on definitions have parallels with how theoretical models and constructs are perceived. There are differences in this volume over how the various contributors treat these issues. Some adopt a perspective in which they try to integrate ideas into a theoretical framework. Gold and Yeo (Chapter 2) present an integrative social constructionist perspective, which they see as their contribution to knowledge. Sadler-Smith (Chapter 4) sees as an important research that aims the harmonization of different constructs. Kuchinke (Chapter 9), on the other hand, in his analysis of careers, suggests a fragmentation perspective as being more appropriate, given the wide variety of contexts – as does Valentin in her exploration of perspectives on employee engagement. Van Woerkom and Tjepkema (Chapter 3) identify additional possibilities around critical reflection without trying to foreclose on one perspective. These contributor differences are not only partly explained by the topics they are considering, but also represent differing world views – as a constructivist would expect.

CONSTRUCTIVISM

A second intellectual influence is constructivism, recognizing that 'there are as many varieties of constructivism as there are researchers' (Ernst, 1995, p. 459) – varieties that are often contradictory (Walton, 2008). Poell (Chapter 1) considers that:

Constructivist approaches have become dominant since the 1990s, certainly in the work and organizational literature on learning. Learning has increasingly been understood as a process of construction, where the learner(s) and the work context influence one another continually. (p. 21)

This echoes the position of Hein (1991) who views constructivism from an HRD perspective as:

The idea that learners construct knowledge for themselves – each learner individually (and socially) constructs meaning – as he or she learns. Constructing meaning is learning; there is no other kind. The dramatic consequences of this view are twofold:

1. We have to focus on the learner in thinking about learning (not on the subject/lesson to be taught).
2. There is no knowledge independent of the meaning attributed to experience (constructed) by the learner, or community of learners.

(Hein, 1991)

Essentially this says that people cannot know 'reality' per se, so inevitably they act according to constructions that they create (Tosey, Chapter 5). By extension, one of the hallmarks of constructivism is that individuals are active agents in the production of their identity, including careers (Hite and McDonald, Chapter 7). Hite and McDonald draw attention to the growth of narrative career counselling in recent years, an approach that emphasizes subjectivity and meaning, as opposed to the constructionism of predetermined career inventories. Kuchinke (Chapter 9) in his discussion on careers points out that the literature he reviewed uses models that incorporate not only constructivism, but also post-structuralism and the postmodern critique of self. Functionalist and modernist conceptions are no longer seen as adequate.

Gold and Yeo (Chapter 2) take the notion of context further in differentiating between social constructivism and social constructionism. Although the two concepts are linked, social constructionism for them is less narrow than constructivism in that the emphasis is on context and how language, talk, physical tools and social interactions can both support and constrain learning efforts.

Thus they see Kolb's experiential learning theory as a process whereby individual experiences can be transformed into a meaningful learning endeavour. As such it is underpinned by constructivist views of interaction and adaptation by learners as individuals. The onus is on the individual learner to generate meaning and understanding from the experiences in which he or she engages. They identify as a problematic assumption of the constructivist perspective 'that learning is independent of context in terms of knowledge storage and transfer' (p. 44). They propose by way of contrast, and in order to fully appreciate experiential learning, an integrated social constructionist perspective that takes into account the language, talk and physical tools that govern the way individuals interact for the creation of knowledge and expertise.

In Van Woerkom and Tjepkema's (Chapter 3) critique of critical reflection, they introduce another variant of constructivism – 'pragmatic constructivism' – a term coined by Brookfield (2000) that builds upon the thinking of John Dewey (1859–1952). Their interest is to criticize it for what they consider to be the overreliance on seeing past experiences as a set of resources that can be objectified and catalogued. They contrast this with the notion of 'mindfulness', which focuses on paying attention to and learning from here and now experiences, including the feelings attached to them.

INTRODUCTION TO CHAPTERS

Part one: Formative concepts

Although all of the chapters in the book address topics that are central to an enhanced understanding of HRD topics, the three that have been included in this Part cover themes that provide a more general context for individual, team or career development.

Rob Poell's (Chapter 1) chapter is a useful starting point, providing a reflective and thought-provoking piece on the whole notion of workplace learning. In differentiating between workplace, work-related and work-based learning, he provides a clear overview of the nuances. He adopts an 'actor' perspective that takes the position that workplace learning can only be undertaken by an employee engaged in situated work activities. He leaves it to the reader to consider the various types of environment in which situated workplace learning could take place. This leaves a tantalizing ambiguity as to what constitutes a workplace. Is it a physical environment? What is the workplace for sales representatives and service engineers? Is your home a workplace? Do you *go to work* or can you be at work wherever you are? Is the notion of the physical workplace – sitting at a desk or by a machine – becoming outdated? Poell makes an interesting reference to the 1980s, which he sees as the period when corporate training – separating learning from working – was at its height. Workplace learning, on the other hand, is evidence of a reversal of that trend.

Jeff Gold and Roland Yeo (Chapter 2) provide an intricately woven analysis of David Kolb's learning cycle and learning styles, incorporating a review of antecedents and a discussion of what some authorities argue are inbuilt limitations to the approach. They move on to consider the concept of experiential learning, from a social constructionist as opposed to a social constructivist perspective, drawing on the insights of the Russian scholars Lev Vygotsky (1896–1934), Mikhail Bakhtin (1895–1975) and Aleksei Leont'ev (1903–1979). That leads them to develop an integrated perspective that gives far greater weighting to the contextual considerations that impact on experiential learning. The subtle distinction between social constructionism and constructivism is essential to understanding this piece of work. It is interesting to compare and contrast their overview of learning styles with the approach taken by Sadler-Smith (Chapter 4) in Part Two.

Marianne van Woerkom and Saskia Tjepkema (Chapter 3) provide a very thoughtful critique of the notion of critical reflection from an individual and group perspective. They emphasize the incorporation of emotion and the unconscious, giving attention to 'mindfulness' as an additional part of the process, which previously has focused on rational cognitive aspects. They then turn their attention to how reflection can be developed in groups. Their starting point is that critical reflection in group settings can be emotionally as well as mentally challenging and that one should always recognize the pivotal role of 'unconscious' processes in learning. To counter the emotional downside, their focus is on accentuating the positive in team building, emphasizing successes achieved and goals to aim for as opposed to problems to be resolved. They provide a number of case study examples of intervention methods. Case study two, on visualizing an ideal finishing point, echoes the scenario planning-case studies discussed by Thursfield (Chapter 11), with the addition of appreciative inquiry methods.

Reflection in groups is more complex than reflection individually. Are their examples instances of reflection 'in action' or 'on action' using the Donald Schön (1991) typology? Reflection on how you are operating in a group can lead to emotional tension, psychological risk and conflict, which is touched upon by Walton (Chapter 12) in his discussion on problems with outdoor learning and T groups, and indeed can emerge in action-learning sets, as mentioned by Rigg (Chapter 10) when she comments upon how they can mirror the emotional fractures that characterize groups, organizations and societies. Van Woerkom and Tjepekema do not specifically address the issue of difference between learning as an individual and learning as a group, or how an individual learns in a group. For example, to what extent do individuals go along with group goals through behaviours such as forbearance, and keep their thoughts and emotions to themselves? This is an interesting arena for further reflection.

Part two: Training and development interventions: Individual skills development

The three chapters that make up this Part discuss specific topics that are focused on individual skill development and learning; each has led to a significant volume of literature over the years.

Eugene Sadler-Smith (Chapter 4) presents a detailed and technical review and critique of learning and cognitive styles, clearly differentiating between them and identifying their foundational theoretical roots as primarily psychological with an emerging contribution from cognitive neuroscience. He comments on the limitations of learning styles, including their emphasis on informed intuition. He makes the point that although learning styles seem to have face validity this is an insufficient criterion on which to make an informed judgement. People might like repertoires such as the user-friendly variant of the David Kolb experiential learning model developed by Honey and Mumford (1992) that has been so popular in the UK over the years, but that does not mean that they are necessarily right. This may present a chasm between practitioners and theorists, with theorists potentially seeing such repertoires as irrelevant if not theoretically well-grounded. Sadler-Smith refers to the importance of having a theoretical base for all aspects of HRD, whilst at the same time not losing sight of the practitioners and the learners. He concludes that one of the challenges for HRD researchers is to develop an overarching framework that integrates the insights from theories of learning styles and cognitive styles that will 'facilitate the achievement of scientifically rigorous and practice-relevant discoveries within the applied domain of HRD research' (Chapter 4, p. 103).

Paul Tosey (Chapter 5), at the outset of his lively, informative and reflective piece, explains that neurolinguistic programming (NLP) has led to polarized positions between strong advocates and confirmed sceptics. His chapter draws on cognitive neurosciences and psycholinguistics in developing a more balanced and nuanced perspective. He offers an interesting historical overview, which charts the context and milestones in the development of thinking on the subject. Whereas other contributors to this book refer to constructivism as a way of explaining the topic they are critiquing, Tosey argues that constructivism is one of the two core constructs of NLP. The other is cybernetics. Useful observations are also provided regarding the evidence base for management thinking generally, and evidence-based research in HRD.

Tosey explains that modelling is the core methodology used in NLP, but it uses it in a more extensive way to how it is understood in behaviour modelling, as presented by Russ-Eft in Chapter 6. 'Modelling' in NLP is the process of adopting the behaviours, language, strategies and beliefs of another person or exemplar in order to 'build a model of what they do ... we know that our modeling has been successful when we can systematically get the same behavioral outcome as the person we have modeled' (Bandler and Grinder, 1979). The 'model' is then reduced to a pattern that can be taught to others.

Tosey mentions that a claim made by practitioners about NLP is simply 'that it works' (Chapter 5, p. 116). He accepts that such a claim is not only highly problematic as a justification from an academic perspective, but also undoubtedly false as a universal rule – no method is going to be successful in all cases. He contends that there may be a wish-fulfilment – sustained by peer pressure – aspect to reporting successes and downplaying failures.

Tosey picks up on another theme relating to language and meaning construction. He takes the principle, generated by the founders of NLP, that communication activates a variety of sense-making processes – and relates it to the perspective of contemporary cognitive linguistics that language does not directly convey meaning; whenever we communicate, we are not simply exchanging information. This, of course, has significance for those who are seeking universally agreed definitions of concepts.

Darlene Russ-Eft (Chapter 6) has conducted a detailed and traditional chronological review of the literature on behavioural modelling (BM). Viewed as no-trial learning, it is contrasted with behaviour modification in which learning is dependent on direct experience and reinforcement. Russ-Eft does not provide a definition of the concept, rather a comprehensive explanation of what it means to her. This is reinforced by the messages she draws from the empirical studies she has discovered. She concludes in a very positive vein about the benefits accruing from BM and registers surprise that it has been used as a training technique less frequently than the research evidence would seem to justify. She finds few examples where it has not been successful and is now looking for ways to enhance performance gains as opposed to merely achieving gains. She contends that no other training technique rests on anything like the research evidence supporting its use. The chapter concludes with a synopsis of studies on BM since 2000.

Part three: Career development approaches

Although there are a number of established career-oriented journals with HRD relevance (e.g. *The Career Development Quarterly*, *Journal of Career*

Assessment and *Career Development International*), the theme of career development, as two of the contributors to this Part comment, has been a neglected theme in the HRD literature, despite its significance for individuals and organizations. Apart from anything else, career development is an important issue for HRD because it is at the boundary of unresolved tensions between individual and organizational perspectives in terms of establishing the prime beneficiary of HRD interventions. For older workers, do HRD interventions cease when they have retired? Hite and McDonald (Chapter 7) suggest that organizations are suddenly becoming more alert to the need to retain talent and that a focus on this topic is timely. They also point out that 'the field of HRD has largely ignored career counselling from both a research and practice perspective' (p. 179).

Linda Hite and Kimberley McDonald (Chapter 7) identify from a detailed literature review a number of limitations in identifying career options through career interest inventories. In particular, they consider that such approaches inappropriately separate work from life choices, and don't take into account the fluidity of today's working environment. In moving on to more recent postmodern approaches, they discuss the difference between constructionist and constructivist approaches, which as we have seen is a theme for a number of chapters in this book. They focus on the narrative mode of thinking about career as a constructivist construct and contrast this with more traditional constructionist use of inventories. Within this narrative mode, they introduce a discussion on life-space mapping, which has its roots in the concept of *life-world*, a mainstream phenomenological term emanating from the work of Edmund Husserl (1859–1938) and Martin Heidegger (1889–1976), and emphasizes the trend towards a constructivist phenomenological orientation of many of the writers in this volume.

Tonette Rocco, Jo Thijssen and Rod Githens (Chapter 8) address the significant theme for HRD of career development and employability for older workers in the Western world within the field of what has been termed gerontology. What constitutes an older worker is a subjective construct and understandings vary between countries. For example, within the US, the 1967 Age Discrimination in Employment Act (ADEA) protects workers who are 40 years of age or older from discrimination based on age. In fact 'industrial gerontology', the study of aging and work, is often seen as applying to middle-aged and older workers (Schulz et al., 2004, p. 580). In some African countries, life expectancy is less than 40 – for example in Swaziland and Mozambique, according to 2005–2010 statistics compiled by the United Nations (UN). In many of the developed Western countries to which Rocco et al. restrict their review, average life expectancy has reached 80 and many forecast it to extend further.

The starting place for Rocco, Thijssen and Githens in viewing the topic is as a phenomenon in the Western world against which judgements have been made, and continue to be made: your initial perceptions of older workers will influence your action for example in giving career advice. Their analysis comes more from a constructionist than constructivist epistemology. They provide a thorough overview of stereotypes about older workers and demonstrate a significant shift in theoretical contributions regarding individual capabilities over the years. They address issues associated with perceptions of older workers and draw upon a substantial body of literature that emphasizes the value of positive thinking in respect of age. They also identify a number of practical HRD suggestions to improve employability both within and outside organizations.

This is a big issue at national level. The baby-boomer generation of the Western world began to turn 65 in 2011, with average life expectancy approaching 80. In the same year, UK legislation at last put restrictions on forcible retirement; there has also been a series of increases in the age at which state pension provisions can be accessed. This trend towards increasing the statutory retirement age has been subject to strikes and disputes across Europe.

Peter Kuchinke (Chapter 9) looks at protean and boundaryless careers, both of which have been presented as alternatives to the traditional career models. He uses these contrasting approaches to emphasize the tensions that exist when one tries to frame the relationship between person and career and how these differ across cultural settings and socio-economic groups. He takes the position that seeking a single career model to account for all contingencies is unlikely to have much theoretical value, even though a unitary, integrated perspective is the basis of most career perspectives. In post-Wittgensteinian mode, he draws attention to fuzzy boundaries between work and non-work aspects of life, and argues that learning how to understand and deal with fragmentation is central to understanding the career diversity. He comments that the study of careers has, surprisingly, been much neglected in the HRD literature. Kuchinke makes the observation that most of us spend the majority of our waking lives engaged with careers. (From a personal perspective, John Walton (Chapter 12) likes this notion in the sense that he has now retired, and argues that he has engaged in a change of career. It also cross-references to Rocco et al. (Chapter 8) and discussions about the older worker.)

Kuchinke discusses integration theory as an important theoretical construct in career thinking. He finds that it is difficult to sustain given the uncertainties, ambiguities and lack of predictability apparent in today's world. He contrasts the unitary integrated world view with a preferred fragmentation perspective, and in so doing provides an interesting focus on the context of work, with challenging assertions about the knowledge economy and the experience of workers.

Part four: Team development

Team development has attracted much attention and investment over the years because of the significance of people working together effectively (and ineffectively) in so many work settings. Valentin (Chapter 13) points to research which indicates that individuals identify more closely with their specific work group than they do with the wider organization. Dysfunctional teams are much more problematic to deal with than difficult individuals, because of the range of relationships entailed. The four chapters in this Part look at different aspects of team development.

Clare Rigg (Chapter 10) provides a comprehensive review of action learning (AL), a popular technique of learning within small group settings. She thoroughly describes the various processes and practices of AL, with supporting examples. Claims made by its proponents and questions raised are examined and considered. An issue with many off-site learning methods is the concern over transfer to the workplace: AL is one approach that seeks to apply learning directly to a work problem. Rigg draws attention to the underdeveloped theoretical underpinning for AL. She cites Marquardt and Waddill (2004) who outline five adult learning schools (behaviourist, cognitivist, humanist, social cognitive and constructivist) that each bears upon AL, but considers that these don't adequately account for the relationship between individual, group and organizational dynamics.

Denise Thursfield (Chapter 11) links to the chapter of van Woerkom and Tjepkema (Chapter 3) in terms of case studies addressing team effectiveness and development through future-oriented approaches. She discusses another instance in which learning can take place in groups: by using scenario planning, and emphasizes scenario planning's role in socially constructed learning. She gives two case examples of scenario planning being used as a learning method and points out that one group did not warm to the method. She draws out some lessons and raises a number of questions for future consideration. Both instances used scenarios, but there was a problem in both cases that the issues were not directly real to the participants. Assumptions around the ability of group members to reflect on and draw upon prior experiences were not manifested. Cross-cultural issues around what are legitimate experiences and relationships between facilitator and group became significant.

John Walton (Chapter 12) looks at another aspect of formal team development – the use of the outdoors as a learning arena for team building. This is a topic that over the years has generated much disagreement as to its merits, with strong advocacy counterbalanced by persistent criticism. The literature review surfaced a wide range of sources and origins as well as significant disagreement and overlap over terminology. More than 30 journals were drawn upon from sources as diverse as *Human Resource Planning, Journal of Adventure Research, Journal of Leisure Research* and *Space and Culture*. Despite the breadth and depth of coverage, and a wealth of informed advice on how to conduct programmes in a variety of outdoor settings, surprisingly few studies were found on pre-existing teams and even fewer demonstrating how learning had been transferred back to the workplace. Much of the literature represented a constructionist position that downplayed the individual tensions and emotions that occur in group settings, and that assumed shared satisfactions would/should result as an outcome of the event and be a measure of improved team effectiveness.

Claire Valentin (Chapter 13) explores the origins and thinking behind the term 'employee engagement', which although it was coined as recently as the early 1990s has become a key driver for many organizations. There is an apparent contradiction in this organizational focus, given the change in the 'psychological contract' in the 1990s from a 'job for life' to a 'job for now' that many commentators such as Hite and McDonald (Chapter 7) have pointed out. Valentin moves the focus from employee engagement with the organization to the work group. Interesting questions emerge on which little research has been conducted. Can work groups contribute to employee engagement? Can a team be engaged? How can HRD interventions such as working with a team contribute to an engaged workforce? From a theoretical perspective, how far does the whole notion of engagement imply a constructionist ideology?

REFERENCES

Bandler, R. and Grinder, J. (1979) *Frogs into Princes: Neuro Linguistic Programming*. Moab, UT: Real People Press.

Brookfield, S. D. (2000) The concept of critically reflective practice. In A.L. Wilson and E.R. Hayes (eds.), *Handbook of Adult and Continuing Education*. San Francisco: Jossey-Bass.

Darling, J., Darling P. and Elliot J. (1999) *The Changing Role of the Trainer*. London: Institute of Personnel and Development.

Dewey, J. (1938) *Logic: The Theory of Inquiry*. New York: Holt, Rinehart and Winston.

Ernst, P. (1995) The one and the many. In L. Steffe and J. Gale (eds), *Constructivism in Education*, 459–486. Hillsdale, NJ: Lawrence Erlbaum.

Harrison, R. and Kessels, J. W. M. (2004) *Human Resource Development in a Knowledge Economy: An Organisational View*. Basingstoke: Palgrave Macmillan.

Hein, G. E. (1991) *Constructivist Learning Theory*. San Francisco, CA: Institute for Learning.

Honey, P. and Mumford, A. (1992) *The Learning Styles Manual*. Maidenhead: Peter Honey Publications.

MacLeod, D. and Clarke, N. (2009) *Engaging for Success: A Report to Government*. London: Department for Business, Innovation and Skills.

Marquardt, M. and Waddill, D. (2004) The power of learning in action learning: A conceptual analysis of how the five schools of adult learning theories are incorporated within the practice of action learning, *Action Learning: Research and Practice*, 1(2): 185–202.

Pedler, M., Burgoyne, T. and Boydell, T. (2004) *A Manager's Guide to Leadership*. London: McGraw-Hill.

Schön, D. A. (1991) *The Reflective Practitioner: How Professionals Think in Action*. London: Ashgate.

Schulz, R., Noelker, L. S., Rockwood, K. and Sprott, R. L. (2004) *The Encyclopaedia of Aging*, 4th edn, vol.1. New York: Springer.

Shuck, B. and Wollard, K. (2010) Employee engagement and HRD: A seminal review of the foundations, *Human Resource Development Review*, 9(1): 89–110.

United Nations, Department of Economic and Social Affairs, Population Division (2010) *World Population Prospects: 2006 Revision*. New York: United Nations Publication.

Walton, J. S. (1999) *Strategic Human Resource Development*. Harlow: Financial Times Prentice Hall.

Walton, J. S. (2008) Scanning beyond the horizon: Exploring the ontological and epistemological basis of future studies, *Advances in Developing Human Resources*, 10(2): 147–165.

part 1
FORMATIVE CONCEPTS

1

WORKPLACE LEARNING THEORIES AND PRACTICES

Rob Poell

INTRODUCTION

The aim of this chapter is to provide a critical evaluation of workplace learning theories and practices. Since the 1990s, workplace learning has become one of the crucial topics in the area of human resource development (HRD). The significant research work done in the 1980s on transfer of training (Baldwin and Ford, 1988; Holton, 1996) did not only show us how corporate training might be made more effective. It also (or even primarily) taught us that no matter how well prepared and executed a formal training course is, the ultimate effect on the workplace is affected much more by the characteristics of the learner (e.g. motivation, intention to apply) and, of course, by the characteristics of the workplace (e.g. supervisor, climate, organization of work) (cf. Holton et al., 2000; Van der Klink et al., 2001). This finding sparked a renewed interest in the concept and practice of workplace learning.

The chapter will first provide an overview of the various concepts associated with workplace learning and their definitions. It will then discuss the historical background of the concept of workplace learning. After an overview of some applications in organizational practice, the chapter will continue with a discussion of the various claims and criticisms associated with workplace learning, as well as an assessment of their legitimacy. It concludes with a brief overview of alternatives that have been proposed for workplace learning.

Throughout the chapter, I will draw on the actor perspective that has informed my writing on the subject in the past 20 years (e.g. Poell and Van der Krogt, 2003a). This means that workplace learning here will be understood as an activity that can only be undertaken by employees; other actors (e.g. managers, HRD practitioners, professional associations, and so forth) can only influence the environment in which employee learning takes place, for example, by offering (and/or making employees go on) formal training courses, by changing the work itself or the work conditions, and by increasing various opportunities for development in the organization (Poell and Van der Krogt, 2003a).

I will argue in this chapter that workplace learning is often, and unrightfully, equated with workplace training or even structured on-the-job training. Changing the emphasis from corporate training to workplace learning obviously has been much more than a play of words, or at least it should have been. While I do not believe that workplace learning can be a tool of management (any more than a potential tool of employees, HRD practitioners, or any other actor), this does not mean that workplace learning is a given, stable reality that can nor will change over time as actors try to impact upon it. All in all, the relatively recent attention to workplace learning is an understandable reaction to the largely unfulfilled expectations of formal training efforts. Workplace learning, however, has always been at the heart of work practices and is not suddenly now the panacea for improved organizational effectiveness. Overformalization of workplace learning could, instead, even diminish its considerable potential.

WORKPLACE LEARNING DEFINED

Stephen Billett, who is a key author on workplace learning, defined it as the learner's participation in situated work activities. He conceived of the workplace as 'a learning environment focusing on the interaction between the affordances and constraints of the social setting, on the one hand, and the agency and biography of the individual participant, on the other' (Billett, 2004, p. 312). Van Woerkom and Poell (2010) likewise described workplace learning as a natural and largely autonomous process derived from the characteristics of the work process and its inherent social interactions; often implicit and sometimes even hard to differentiate from doing the daily work. According to Felstead et al. (2009), learning that goes on in workplaces includes everyday work activity (as well as on-the-job instruction and off-the-job training events).

There are, however, several terms related to workplace learning that one may encounter. Many authors talk about learning *in* the workplace or *at* the workplace, rather than about workplace learning per se. As far as I am concerned, these terms can be used as synonyms to a large extent. A more general concept is work-related learning, which stands for basically any learning activity that takes place in the context of work. However, this term should not be confused with work-based learning, which refers to learning based predominantly in a work setting as part of a formal education programme (often in higher education). I will return to this definitional issue later in the chapter.

Looking at the various definitions of workplace learning and its related concepts, a number of key elements can be discerned. First, learning in work contexts is regarded by many as an activity only the learner can do (cf. Kwakman and Kessels, 2004); the only thing that managers, HRD practitioners, professional associations and so forth can do is to influence the context where employee learning takes place. Learning itself has, of course, been described using many perspectives; a distinction often made in this connection is between behaviourist, cognitivist and constructivist approaches. Constructivist approaches have become dominant since the 1990s, certainly in the work and organizational literature on learning. Learning has increasingly been understood as a process of construction, where the learner(s) and the work context influence one another continually (cf. Billett, 2004; Felstead et al., 2009; Poell and Van der Krogt, 2002). Three types of learning activity are often distinguished (Poell, 2005):

- Learning as a by-product of working; 'incidental learning'.
- Self-initiated learning; often referred to as 'informal learning', which however is not a very useful term if participating in work practices is considered as learning (Billett, 2002). Self-initiated learning is an intentional, conscious pursuit on the part of the learner.
- Learning in formal settings (training courses, seminars and so forth), where other actors than the 'designated' learners have created a programme or curriculum, which the learners 'follow'.

The first two activities have traditionally been associated with workplace learning; the third activity can be part of it but would not by itself be considered workplace learning. Poell and Van der Krogt (2009) have used the term 'learning path' to refer to a particular combination of these three types of learning activity into something that is coherent and meaningful to the learner (see also Poell, 2005).

ORIGIN OF THE TERM

Victoria Marsick is another key author on the topic of workplace learning. As early as 1987 she had published a book entitled *Learning in the Workplace* (Marsick, 1987), soon followed by a collaborative effort with Karen Watkins in the influential *Informal and Incidental Learning in the Workplace* (Marsick and Watkins, 1990). It seems, with hindsight, as if in the late 1980s and early 1990s the world was ready for a (renewed) focus on learning rather than on training and education. Pedler, Burgoyne and Boydell (1991) had coined the term 'learning company' in the United Kingdom, while Peter Senge (1990) had done the same for 'learning organization' in the United States. Lave and Wenger (1991) talked about 'situated learning' on the job to explain how an employee learns the ropes. Learning (in the workplace) was fast becoming the new buzzword in the 1990s, sometimes without thinking through the implications of such a crucial new focus on activities conducted by the employee rather than by the trainer.

Another fertile ground for the concept of workplace learning to gain new prominence was created in the 1980s, when notions around experiential learning and reflective practice became popular among practitioners and academics alike. David Kolb put forward experience as a powerful source of learning and development in the decade when the belief in corporate training (i.e. separating learning from work) was perhaps at the height of its power (Kolb, 1984). No one has since doubted the potential of workplaces to act as powerful contexts of experiential learning – even though that potential is not always capitalized upon or realized (Nijhof and Nieuwenhuis, 2008). Donald Schön showed us how professionals can learn and develop by reflecting both *on* and *in* practice (Schön, 1983), which again contributed greatly to the idea that work can be a rich context for further professional growth. Like experiential learning, the notion of reflection as a crucial activity (or even prerequisite) for learning to occur has never since been challenged much in practice, although it has drawn criticism from academics for its cognitive bias (Jordi, 2011).

HISTORY OF THE CONCEPT

Of course workplace learning as such has always existed. Yet one might say that it was 'rediscovered' in the 1990s. The industrial revolution had created a need for large-scale organizations to have trained employees capable of operating context-independently. In the 19th and 20th centuries, education systems were created to fulfil that need. Learning was deliberately separated from working and the new focus was on schooling and training. In terms of enabling mass production, this was, of course, a great success. However, it also led to the ultimate realization that creating a lot of distance between learning and working caused many problems related to the transfer of training to the workplace. At first, solving these problems was attempted by adding transfer-enhancing measures to training (e.g. Robinson and Robinson, 1989). After a while, however, scholars were starting to question the whole idea of separating learning from working (e.g. Billett, 2002; Wenger, 1998). After Sfard (1998) had distinguished between the acquisition and participation metaphors for learning, adding that both cannot do without each other, constructivism had basically taken over from cognitivism as the leading learning theory, and the world was finally ready to start looking seriously again at workplace learning.

APPLICATION OF THE CONCEPT

First, a disclaimer is in order here. I think of workplace learning as something that is always there in all workplaces at all times. Employees constantly (although usually implicitly) adjust their individual action theories in order to be able to do their job, improve their performance, become or remain a good team member, further their career interests, fulfil their personal development needs and so forth. Most (but certainly not all) workplaces actually provide a conducive environment for employees to be able to do this. Employees can learn, for example, by doing their regular job (assuming it is not too static for too long), by taking on new tasks, by interacting with colleagues preferably with other skill sets, by reflecting on the way they (and others) do things, by looking for already available knowledge and information, by modelling an experienced colleague, by changing work procedures that do not seem adequate to them, by taking lessons learned outside of working life and applying them to the job, by going on a training course that they feel would benefit them, and so forth. My point here is that something that is always there cannot really be 'applied'; it is applied already, all the time, by all involved.

A brief clarification is needed here. One of the problems with the word 'learning' is that it is used both to describe a process and a product, which lends itself to issues of product-process ambiguity in literature. Learning (as a noun, a product) could result from workplace learning (as a verb, describing a process). I normally refer to learning as a verb, a process, rather than a noun, a product.

Having clarified that workplace learning (as a process) is NOT, in my opinion, an intervention, to the extent that actors attempt to treat it like that it will probably not deliver what they hope it will. Workplace learning has its own dynamics, which are shaped by the cultural and historical context in which it takes place as well as by the constant actions undertaken by ALL actors to get it to work for their best interests (Felstead et al., 2009; Poell and Van der Krogt, 2003b). Obviously this does not mean that actors do not try to influence the learning that takes place in the workplace; they do so all the time. However, as soon as other actors than the ones doing the actual learning (i.e. the employees) start consciously influencing that very process (e.g. by setting goals for the employees, by expecting them to develop certain predetermined skills or attitudes, or by simply making them go to a seminar they need to attend), I would argue that they are engaged in training rather than learning in the workplace.

Many of the practices referred to as workplace (or, as per the above, work-based) learning, therefore, are actually workplace training – although the outcomes of such training could be classified as learning gained in the workplace. This terminological confusion is problematic. For example, teacher training institutes (and many other professional bodies) expect their students to learn a lot of their teaching skills on the job, that is, in schools. Hence, they attempt to formalize the learning that should go on in that workplace: by setting learning goals, specifying activities that students should engage in, appointing mentors to guide them through the process and so forth. Naturally, however, the workplace has its own dynamics that cannot be formalized by an outside actor (teacher training institutes). So students gain all kinds of experiences depending on what that particular workplace (and their mentor) can afford them, and depending on what initiatives they themselves take. There is obviously a lot of workplace learning going on as teachers undertake training on-the-job in schools, but not necessarily the learning that the teacher training institute deems the most important. Yet they refer to this activity as workplace learning, part of the formalized curriculum (Timmermans et al., 2011).

Workplace training (e.g. structured on-the-job training; Jacobs, 2003) can actually be a powerful and effective way for employees to develop the necessary knowledge, skills and attitudes. It can be more efficient than classroom training as it takes out part of the 'transfer of training' gap. Employees get to learn and apply the skills they are supposed to develop in the same workplace where they should ultimately use them. Structured on-the-job training, however, presupposes that the work skills to be developed can actually be broken down into neatly structured instructions. This may be true for some types of job but certainly not for all (especially more knowledge-intensive jobs; Poell and Van der Krogt, 2003b).

Table 1.1 A proposed typology of planned training on the job

	Job instruction	Apprenticeship	Inquiry	Self-evaluation
Learning process	Systematic skills training	Socialization/ modelling	Analysis/ problem solving	Feedback plus reflection
Trainee's role	Application/ practice	Participation/ observation	Exploration/ orientation	Goal setting/ evaluation
Trainer's role	Instructor	Master	Tutor	Coach

Source: De Jong et al. (2001, p. 409). Reproduced with permission of Sage Publications.

As long as workplace training is not equated with workplace learning, but rather gets understood as (only) one way to increase the chances that employee learning will actually happen, there is not too much of a problem using both terms in the same sentence. These two terms – training and learning – should not, however, be treated as synonyms as this will only add to the already existing confusion around the term workplace learning. One useful framework that helps to flesh out these differences was presented by De Jong, Thijssen and Versloot (2001). They started from the notion of workplace training, distinguishing between four models, which really form a continuum from workplace training to workplace learning (see Table 1.1). All four forms would be expected to exist in most organizations, although the extent to which one or two of them dominate likely differs across organizations.

CLAIMS ASSOCIATED WITH WORKPLACE LEARNING

A key claim associated with workplace learning is that it is always there, in all workplaces. This was documented empirically by Marsick and Watkins (1990) as well as by Lave and Wenger (1991) and Billett (2001). Amongst others, Poell and Van der Krogt (2003a) have shown, however, that workplace learning differs from one type of work to another (cf. Felstead et al., 2009). An important if much more general claim is that, actually, most learning that employees engage in takes place in the workplace. Marsick and Watkins (1990) asserted that a mere 20 per cent of what employees learn happens through formalized, structured training. A recent Dutch study even found that just 6 per cent of all time that employees spend on work-related learning occurs in training courses and education programmes; the rest is workplace learning (Borghans et al., 2007). Some authors have gone so far as to say that workplace learning is 'more effective' than formal training. While this may actually be more of a testament to the limited effectiveness of formal training, workplace learning is not an intervention, so it is difficult, not to say impossible, to isolate its effects.

Related to the aforementioned (flawed) idea that workplace learning can be equated to workplace training is the claim that workplace learning can be 'used' by managers, HRD practitioners and educators as an effective way of achieving complex goals in employees ('some things are just best learned in practice'). However, workplace learning can never be a tool of management if it is always there anyway. It should be kept in mind that workplace learning is a contested domain, as much as is the organization of work; different actors have different interests and ideas about what and how people should learn on the job (Poell and Van der Krogt, 2003b; Felstead et al., 2009). Still, Poell and Van Woerkom (2011) have managed to show that workplace learning can be supported through mentoring, coaching, facilitation, various team interventions and so forth.

A final claim often heard in relation to workplace learning is that it, especially in its incidental guise, 'cannot be managed or governed'. While this is true to the extent that workplace learning can never be an intervention, one should realize that employees who take (or are brought) to doing new work (especially in a new work environment) will learn new things in new ways (Billett, 2001; Poell and Van der Krogt, 2003b). Nevertheless, it can never be predicted exactly what and how they will learn. By changing the work, the learning that occurs through work changes as well. This is actually one strategy that all actors (not just managers) can use to make things happen in the organization.

WORKPLACE LEARNING CRITICIZED

In view of the above, criticizing workplace learning is like criticizing the earth we walk upon and the air that we breathe. It is just there. So while there is not much point criticizing the practices of workplace learning, there are certainly some misconceptions that have been aired surrounding the term. One such misconception is that workplace learning is always good, positive, to be encouraged. There are many arguments against this claim. A prison is probably one of the best places for self-directed workplace learning, but not necessarily the kind we want as a society. Furthermore, workplace learning can make 'undesirable' practices continue; innovation and double-loop learning do not come easily from workplace learning either. Also, sometimes it is just much quicker and much more effective to send people on a training course.

Finally, sometimes it is necessary to formalize the learning process in a much more structured format, such as when security is an issue (think of pilots) or when employees are after the civil impact of learning (think of diplomas and careers).

Another common misconception around workplace learning is that it is 'not worth looking at because you cannot really manage it'. This is probably why governments and (large) organizations keep emphasizing formal training, even though they may understand that the transfer of training is a big problem. Studies from several countries have shown how much HRD practitioners are struggling with this, aware of the importance of everyday and employee-initiated learning but largely unable to influence it (Chivers et al., 2001; Oostvogel et al., 2011; Poell et al., 2003). On the other hand, the 1990s have seen interesting experiments with employee development schemes and the accreditation of prior (experiential) learning, which have shown organizations the value of encouraging and recognizing workplace learning even though it does not lend itself all that well to functioning as a traditional tool of management.

A final misconception that I should like to highlight here is the idea that, if workplace learning is just there all the time, there is no need to try to improve it. One needs to keep in mind that learning in the workplace is a largely autonomous process often hard to differentiate from daily work – and the fact that this is its strength as much as it is a weakness. On the upside, transfer problems are far less likely to occur in workplace learning than in formal training, fewer investments are needed for training materials and personnel, and employees spend less time being unproductive. Besides these advantages, however, there are a number of potential disadvantages to workplace learning. Some workplaces are badly equipped for learning, both materially (time, space) and socially (coaching, support); creativity and innovation are not necessarily encouraged by forging close links between work and learning; employees may learn the 'wrong' things if there is no careful analysis, delivery and evaluation (Poell and Van Woerkom, 2011). While the lack of creativity and innovation coming from workplace learning is probably difficult to avoid, workplaces can be changed by managers and employees so as to 'invite' more learning – and collaborative reflection can be a powerful means to prevent employees and managers from learning the 'wrong' things (cf. Tjepkema, 2003). To what extent HRD practitioners can play a role in the improvement of workplace learning remains to be seen, as they have relatively little influence on the way in which the work process is organized (Nijhof, 2004).

ALTERNATIVES SUGGESTED FOR WORKPLACE LEARNING

Again, there really is no alternative for workplace learning if it is conceived of as participation in work practices rather than as an intervention. It is just there. As I have mentioned above several times, those actors wanting to change workplace learning will have to change the work process itself. Nevertheless, many people think of workplace learning as another tool of management. Although managers can influence the organization of work, and HRD practitioners can influence the organization of training programmes, ultimately employees are the only ones who can influence what learning takes place. No one else can learn on their behalf or force them to do so (cf. Kwakman and Kessels, 2004). In organizations where managers can actually decide to a very large extent on the organization of work (i.e. not in professional organizations), there is a chance that they get to have an impact on the workplace learning that employees engage in through the way they organize work. In most other organization types, workplace learning is a constantly contested domain that all actors try to influence: employees, managers, HRD practitioners, trade unions and so forth. Whose influence gets to dominate, or whether that can happen at all, will depend on the existing relationships among all actors (Poell and Van der Krogt, 2002; 2003b).

As has already been mentioned, concepts related to workplace learning have been used by managers and HRD practitioners to influence what and how employees learn on the job, especially work-based learning and structured on-the-job training. Crucially, despite what the first term seems to imply, these are both training concepts rather than having anything to do with learning as such. There is definitely always a lot of learning going on in a training setting; however, to what extent this is the learning intended by the training providers is not easily established (Sloman, 2010). Of course, managers can (and often do) ask HRD practitioners to formalize and structure the learning that (in their view) is supposed to go on: by conducting training needs analysis, by setting learning goals for the employees, by offering them training materials in line with those goals, and by evaluating to what extent the employees have 'learned' the intended goals. However, it is easily overlooked that as much as managers are trying to realize their strategies through learning, employees do exactly the same and, compared to managers, they may even hold a much stronger position of power when it comes to learning. Employees acting strategically in the area of learning or professional development have been little researched thus far, but this seems to be a key domain for better understanding the dynamics of workplace learning and HRD at large (Poell and Van der Krogt, 2010).

CONCLUSION

For employees, managers, HRD practitioners and other actors alike, gaining a good understanding of what workplace learning is and what it can do for them is crucial. Research into workplace learning should have the aim of helping each of these actors, especially employees, better understand how they can influence workplace learning for their own interests and purposes. Attempting to have only HRD practitioners to formalize and structure the workplace learning that goes on seems awkward, difficult and, ultimately, ineffective. Employees are strategic actors as much as managers and HRD practitioners (Poell and Van der Krogt, 2010). But how and to what extent do they act strategically? Does this differ from one organizational type of profession to another? And how and to what extent do the various actors operate in learning, work and HRM processes in order to get their ideas and interests realized?

In terms of implications for HRD practice, one might propose that the vision espoused in this chapter suggests that HRD practitioners should have more involvement in structuring workplaces and work practices in order to help create environments conducive to learning (the role of HRD practitioners as learning architects). This, however, is not as unproblematic as it may seem. HRD practitioners still have very little influence on what happens in workplaces, where employees and managers 'rule', and this may not change overnight. I do believe that HRD practitioners can make a very worthwhile contribution here; however, they will first need to gain a foothold in the workplace (and, obviously, out of the training room and into the boardroom; cf. Yorks, 2005). Having said that, HRD practitioners should put more effort into diagnosing what learning is happening in the various workplaces that make up their organization. It would also be worthwhile if they teamed up more with the key stakeholders – the learners themselves – to help the latter develop more understanding of their own learning in the context of the workplace and the organization, which could contribute to their further empowerment. Taylorist (i.e. scientific-management) practices that are still prevalent in many organizations, however, may not be very conducive to this role of HRD practitioners, while at the same time such an HRD role holds the potential of furthering more participative management practices. As ever, it will be up to HRD practitioners to show to managers and to employees what their added value is, not just by presenting strategic policy plans and offering sound learning and development programmes, but also by gaining a more in-depth understanding of the learning processes that occur in the workplace on an everyday basis, so that their plans and programmes will land in fertile ground.

REFERENCES

Baldwin, T. T. and Ford, J. K. (1988) Transfer of training: A review and directions for future research, *Personnel Psychology*, 41(1): 63–105.

Billett, S. (2001) *Learning in the Workplace: Strategies for Effective Practice*. Crows Nest: Allen & Unwin.

Billett, S. (2002) Critiquing workplace learning discourses: Participation and continuity at work, *Studies in the Education of Adults*, 34(1): 56–67.

Billett, S. (2004) Workplace participatory practices: Conceptualising workplaces as learning environments, *Journal of Workplace Learning*, 16(6): 312–324.

Borghans, L., Golsteyn, B. and De Grip, A. (2007) Werkend leren [Learning while working], *Economisch Statistische Berichten*, 92(4509): 260–263.

Chivers, G. E., Poell, R. F. and Chapman, R. (2001) HRD practitioners for changing roles, *Lifelong Learning in Europe*, 6(4): 205–213.

De Jong, J. A., Thijssen, J. G. L. and Versloot, B. M. (2001) Planned training on the job: A typology, *Advances in Developing Human Resources*, 3(4): 408–414.

Felstead, A., Fuller, A., Jewson, N. and Unwin, L. (2009) *Improving Working as Learning*. London: Routledge.

Holton, E. F. (1996). The flawed four-level evaluation model, *Human Resource Development Quarterly*, 7(1): 5–21.

Holton, E. F., Bates, R. A. and Ruona, W. E. A. (2000) Development of a generalized learning transfer system inventory, *Human Resource Development Quarterly*, 11(4): 333–360.

Jacobs, R. L. (2003) *Structured On-the-Job Training: Unleashing Employee Expertise in the Workplace* (2nd ed.). San Francisco: Berrett-Koehler.

Jordi, R. (2011) Reframing the concept of reflection: Consciousness, experiential learning, and reflective learning practices, *Adult Education Quarterly*, 61(2): 181–197.

Kolb, D. A. (1984) *Experiential Learning: Experience as the Source of Learning and Development*. Upper Saddle River, NJ: Prentice-Hall.

Kwakman, C. H. E. and Kessels, J. W. M. (2004) Designing learning in the workplace, *British Journal of Occupational Learning*, 2(1): 17–28.

Lave, J. and Wenger, E. (1991) *Situated Learning: Legitimate, Peripheral Participation*. Cambridge, MA: Cambridge University Press.

Marsick, V. J. (1987) *Learning in the Workplace*. New York: Croon Helm.

Marsick, V. J. and Watkins, K. E. (1990) *Informal and Incidental Learning in the Workplace*. London: Routledge.

Nijhof, W. J. (2004) Is the HRD profession in the Netherlands changing? *Human Resource Development International*, 7(1): 57–72.

Nijhof, W. J. and Nieuwenhuis, L. F. M. (eds) (2008) *The Learning Potential of the Workplace*. Rotterdam: Sense Publishers.

Oostvogel, K., Koornneef, M. and Poell, R. F. (2011) Strategies of HRD practitioners in different organizational types and employment modes: A qualitative study among 18 South Australian HRD practitioners. In R. F. Poell and M. van Woerkom (eds), *Supporting Learning in the Workplace: Towards Evidence Based Practice* (pp. 11–26). Dordrecht: Springer.

Pedler, M., Burgoyne, J. and Boydell, T. (1991) *The Learning Company*. London: McGraw-Hill.

Poell, R. F. (2005) HRD beyond what HRD practitioners do: A framework for furthering multiple learning processes in work organizations. In C. Elliott and S. Turnbull (eds), *Critical Thinking in Human Resource Development* (pp. 85–95). London: Routledge.

Poell, R. F., Pluijmen, R. and Van der Krogt, F. J. (2003) Strategies of HRD professionals in organising learning programmes: A qualitative study among 20 Dutch HRD professionals, *Journal of European Industrial Training*, 27(2/3/4): 125–136.

Poell, R. F. and Van der Krogt, F. J. (2002) Using social networks in organisations to facilitate individual development. In M. Pearn (ed.), *Individual Differences and Development in Organisations* (pp. 285–304). London: Wiley.

Poell, R. F. and Van der Krogt, F. J. (2003a) Learning-program creation in work organizations, *Human Resource Development Review*, 2(3): 252–272.

Poell, R. F. and Van der Krogt, F. J. (2003b) Learning strategies of workers in the knowledge creating company, *Human Resource Development International*, 6(3): 387–403.

Poell, R. F. and Van der Krogt, F. J. (2009) An empirical typology of hospital nurses' individual learning paths. In J. Calvin and S. Carter (eds), *Top Ten Best Papers from the Academy of HRD International Research Conference held in Panama City, FL, USA, 19–22 February* (pp. 46–58). Bowling Green, OH: AHRD.

Poell, R. F. and Van der Krogt, F. J. (2010) Individual learning paths of employees in the context of social networks. In S. Billett (ed.), *Learning Through Practice: Models, Traditions, Orientations and Approaches* (pp. 197–221). Dordrecht: Springer.

Poell, R. F. and Van Woerkom, M. (eds) (2011) *Supporting Learning in the Workplace: Towards Evidence Based Practice*. Dordrecht: Springer.

Robinson, D. G. and Robinson, J. C. (1989) *Training for Impact: How to Link Training to Business Needs and Measure the Results*. San Francisco, CA: Jossey-Bass.

Schön, D. A. (1983) *The Reflective Practitioner: How Professionals Think in Action*. London: Temple Smith.

Senge, P. M. (1990) *The Fifth Discipline: The Art and Practice of the Learning Organization*. New York: Doubleday/Currency.

Sfard, A. (1998) On two metaphors for learning and the dangers of choosing just one, *Educational Researcher*, 27(2): 4–13.

Sloman, M. (2010) *LandD 2020: A Guide for the Next Decade*. Cambridge: Fenman.

Timmermans, M., Poell, R. F., Klarus, R. and Nieuwenhuis, L. F. M. (2011) *Student Teachers' Workplace Learning in Professional Development Schools: About Affordance and Agency*. Paper presented at the annual conference of the American Educational Research Association, held in New Orleans, USA, 8–12 April.

Tjepkema, S. (2003) The Learning Infrastructure of Self-managing Work Teams. PhD dissertation, Twente University, Netherlands.

Van Der Klink, M., Gielen, E. and Nauta, C. (2001) Supervisory support as a major condition to enhance transfer, *International Journal of Training and Development*, 5(1): 52–63.

Wenger, E. (1998) *Communities of Practice: Learning, Meaning, Identity*. Cambridge, MA: Cambridge University Press.

Yorks, L. (2005) *Strategic Human Resource Development*. Mason, OH: Thomson South-Western.

FURTHER READING

Billett, S. (2004) Workplace participatory practices: Conceptualising workplaces as learning environments, *Journal of Workplace Learning*, 16(6): 312–324.

Lave, J. and Wenger, E. (1991) *Situated Learning: Legitimate, Peripheral Participation*. Cambridge, MA: Cambridge University Press.

Marsick, V. J. and Watkins, K. E. (1990) *Informal and Incidental Learning in the Workplace*. London: Routledge.

Poell, R. F. and Van der Krogt, F. J. (2003b) Learning strategies of workers in the knowledge creating company, *Human Resource Development International*, 6(3): 387–403.

Van Woerkom, M. and Poell, R. F. (2010) Implications for research and practice. In M. van Woerkom and R. F. Poell (eds), *Workplace Learning: Concepts, Measurement and Application* (pp. 216-224). London: Routledge.

Wenger, E. (1998) *Communities of Practice: Learning, Meaning, Identity*. Cambridge, MA: Harvard University Press.

2

EXPERIENTIAL LEARNING AND LEARNING CYCLES: TOWARDS AN INTEGRATIVE PERSPECTIVE

Jeff Gold and Roland K. Yeo

INTRODUCTION

Experiential learning theory is a holistic learning model that focuses on the process of how people learn, grow and develop through direct contact and interaction with an experience. It is a model of adult development associated with multi-linearity, where the human learning process is characterized by different levels of cognitive participation and engagement (Kolb, 1981; Ng et al., 2009; Sims, 1983). This multi-level process is facilitated by an internalization of external events, often catalyzed by an experiential context where individuals are involved in reflective and collaborative inquiry, questioning what is going on around them. This theory is relevant to HRD as it is a learning approach that leads to an action-oriented behavioural change operating at an individual and organizational level. HRD is defined as the facilitation of planned and systematic interventionist activities aimed at unleashing human expertise through a range of learning techniques and strategies for the purpose of improving work performance (Megginson et al., 1993; Swanson, 1995; Watkins, 2000) as well as changes that emerge informally from actions that are unplanned (Garrick, 1998).

Experiential learning theory was popularized by David Kolb in the 1970s and 1980s when he introduced the term 'experiential' to an existing body of knowledge on learning from the adult education and psychology literature (Kolb, 1984). When combined, *'experiential learning'* suggests the process of meaning-making and signifying from a context that is bound by a variety of activities, which in turn help an experience take shape. Such a learning experience is aligned to a quote by Aristotle that says: 'For the things we have to learn before we can do them, we learn by doing them' (Bynum and Porter, 2005, p. 9). Drawing a parallel, experiential learning can be said to be learning by doing. This involves an ongoing process of determining the success of each action by reflecting on what went right and wrong with action taking. Through the inevitable process of trial and error, individuals begin to internalize the lessons learned and produce adaptive strategies to take further action. Adaptive strategies are those that have been modified based on changes in an immediate context (Kolb et al., 2000; Miettinen, 2000).

Experiential education versus experiential learning

Kolb (1984) distinguished experiential learning from the concept of experiential education, which focuses primarily on the transactive process between the teacher and the learner mainly facilitated by different learning tools and materials. The transactive nature of learning is derived directly or indirectly from reading or discussion rather than a direct experience that has the greater potential to transform the way the learner thinks, feels and acts. Take horse riding, for example. Experiential education simply allows the learner to go through the material and/or simulation to have an idea of what horse riding is about. Experiential learning takes the learning further when the learner actually goes to the riding ring and has direct contact with a horse. In this context, experiential learning is also conceptually different from cognitive and behavioural learning in that the former is concerned about the way people think rather than how they feel about learning, while the latter does not take into account the subjective or indirect experience that may occur in the learning process (Boot and Reynolds, 1983; Kolb and Kolb, 2009b; Mainemelis et al., 2002). Experiential learning is also different from action learning, which is generally catalyzed by real problems and issues that surround learning and action taking, although there is some overlap between the two learning types. For experiential learning, the trigger to learning is any activity that requires direct or indirect involvement from the learner, which may also be a problem to solve or overcome (Kolb, 1983). It is, therefore, more integrative and dynamic in nature insofar as thinking, doing and acting are concerned encompassing the concepts of a number of learning theories (Kolb, 1981; 1984; Kolb and Kolb, 2005; 2009a).

Against this background, this chapter aims to (1) provide an overview of Kolb's experiential learning, (2) summarize the critiques of Kolb's learning cycle, and (3) propose an integrative perspective of experiential learning with implications for HRD. The contribution of this chapter is therefore three-fold. First, the study extends the theoretical insights of experiential learning and draws on classical theories such as Vygotsky's (1978) socio-cultural theory, Leont'ev's (1981) activity theory and Bakhtin's (1981) philosophy of language to elucidate the interplay of human interaction in social context that characterizes experience. Second, it unravels the conceptual and practical inconsistencies of experiential learning based on several emerging perspectives of learning. Third, it sheds light on how experiential learning, when viewed from a social constructionist perspective, can create optimal learning opportunities for HRD.

THEORETICAL BACKGROUND

The intellectual origins of experiential learning theory are founded on the works of Lewin, Dewey and Piaget. First, Kurt Lewin's (1943, 1951) social psychology theory suggests that behaviour is largely determined by the person himself/herself and the environment. As such, individual behaviour and personalities are both conditioned by the internal (cognitive) state of the individual as well as the experience that he/she encounters directly or indirectly. There is a social dimension to learning that influences the way people feel, think and act, and concepts such as attitude, social cognition, cognitive dissonance and social influence are part of the repertoire of social psychology in which Lewin's work is rooted. This aspect of Lewin's work can be seen in the constructivist perspective of Kolb's experiential learning, which posits that knowledge can be socially constructed through formal and informal interactions. Knowledge is, therefore, stored in the minds of the learners for immediate and future application.

Second, John Dewey's (1958) philosophy of pragmatism emphasizes action and application which, according to functional psychology theory, suggests that what is learned can be adapted to a person's environment. According to Dewey, there is a relation between the mental state of a person and his/her behaviour. A person is, therefore, capable of responding to a mental stimulus by modifying his/her behaviour to solve a certain problem or achieve a particular task. By drawing on past experience, one is able to use tried-and-test methods and explore new ways of adapting to current situations. The new experience in the adaptation process increases the sensory motors of the learner enabling him/her to think, feel and act in more meaningful ways. In other words, experience provides the opportunity for new stimuli, sensations and responses to develop in an ongoing manner when a learner engages in problem solving and action taking.

Third, Jean Piaget's (1969) adaptive model of intellectual development, as part of his theory of cognitive development, played a critical role in helping Kolb formulate his understanding of experiential learning. In particular, Piaget regarded intelligence as constituted of the content of thinking and the process of intellectual activity. These two elements form the basis of mental structures or schemata that enable an individual to adapt to his/her environment through two distinct processes, namely assimilation and accommodation. Assimilation is a mental-framing process through which objects of the environment are viewed as acceptable and agreeable to an individual. Accommodation is a process by which individuals modify their reflex response to transform external objects into a type of reflex action. According to Piaget, the mental frames and action of an individual may not necessarily be in harmony all the time. For instance, a manager may have thought of rewarding or punishing an employee in a certain way. However, consideration of the possible consequences of the manager's action could possibly lead him/her to modify his/her action. Hence, the constant struggle between assimilation (whether to reward or punish an employee) and accommodation (action based on potential consequences rather than what was initially conceptualized) helps promote intellectual growth. This is where learning occurs through the adaptation of the changing environment, which helped Kolb (1984) to understand the importance of conceptualization and experimentation in his learning cycle.

When combined, these three theoretical perspectives from Lewin, Dewey and Piaget helped Kolb (1984) to further conceptualize the dialectical relationships between the four components of his learning cycle, which encompass experiencing, reflecting, thinking and acting in a recursive process. It is worth noting that Kolb is neutral to where the cycle commences.

Assumptions and principles of experiential learning

Extending the nature of learning, Kolb (1984) associates the experiential process with the acquisition of knowledge that transforms experience into a meaningful learning endeavour. It is not merely about drawing out explicit knowledge from tacit knowledge but seeking useful knowledge that allows one to understand and engage in his/her direct experience. In order for genuine knowledge acquisition to occur, there are several fundamental assumptions to be considered, as governed by choice and ability. These are (a) the willingness of the learner to be actively involved in the experience; (b) the ability of the learner to reflect on the experience; (c) the ability of the learner to apply analytical skills in the conceptualization of the experience; and (d) the ability of the learner to utilize decision-making and problem-solving skills in order to transform the new ideas gained through the experience into action (Boyatzis and Kolb, 1997; Chisholm et al., 2009; Fenwick, 2000).

Extending the experience–knowledge–learning interrelation, Kolb conceives of a dialectical relationship between organization and management, both of which are distinct in their approach to learning yet intimately linked. This relationship accounts for the holistic nature of learning, which suggests that it is a major process of human adaptation. Kolb explains that organization is inherently a learning *system* while management is a *process* of learning. Relating this conceptualization to Peter Drucker's (1988) view of leadership and management, which suggests that leadership is doing the *right* things while management is doing things *right*, it can be seen that every learner has the privilege of assuming leadership and control over his/her learning process by choosing what to learn, how to learn, when to learn, who to learn with and why there is a need to learn. The Drucker analogy has helped reinforce Kolb's (1984, p. 41) conceptualization of learning as 'the process whereby knowledge is created through the transformation of experience. Knowledge results from the combination of grasping and transforming experience.' In this context, the 'management' function of learning can be seen as the act of grasping and transforming experience, the choice of which lies in the learner. As a learning system, the 'organization' aspect suggests that learners are active carriers of knowledge and meanings that help interpret their experiences as adaptors of the environment and change (Elsbach et al., 2005; Weick et al., 2005).

Learning processes within a complex system or subsystem should stabilize over time, creating predictable sequences of learning dynamics. The fact that the 'management' of learning is grasping and transforming experience, this suggests a messier process in modes of divergence as compared with the 'organization' of learning, which suggests a more stable process in modes of convergence. This leads to an apparent contradiction, suggesting that as a *process*, learning is dynamic and messy while, as a *system*, it is interdependent and structural based on different experiences (Daft and Weick, 1984; Kirkpatrick and Epstein, 1992). Applying this perspective to Kolb's experiential learning model, it can be seen that learners are involved in generating knowledge and organizing meanings as they make sense of their environment through direct experience. This process is embedded in a system similar to Kolb's learning cycle where learning occurs spontaneously in different stages. As learners go through transitions between the various stages of a learning cycle, they encounter different opportunities to generate and adapt thinking patterns that guide their subsequent actions. For instance, a learner may find that there are previous thinking patterns and habits that obstruct his/her response to solving a particular problem at hand and, as such, is required to unlearn and relearn (Kolb, 1983). In the process, the learner encounters both conflicting and supporting signals from other individuals and the environment to modify his/her mental frames and actions. This is a likely experience in a learning cycle, where learners engage in knowledge exchange helping them to adapt and generate new thinking patterns and learning styles that enable them to optimize their environment for further learning (Kolb and Kolb, 2005; 2009a; 2009b). In view of this, the next section discusses in greater detail Kolb's learning cycle, which incorporates several distinct learning styles.

Kolb's learning cycle/styles

As an extension of his experiential learning theory, Kolb (1984) subsequently developed the Learning Styles Inventory (LSI) aimed at identifying a specific set of learning traits that could persist over time. This is when learning becomes stable whenever a particular style is applied in a context that brings about desirable outcomes. He further associated a learning style as a preference for learning that is not completely rooted in a particular trait but shifts spontaneously from situation to situation while still preserving the long-term stability of a dominant style. Subject to ongoing criticism, this assertion has yet to be established through longitudinal studies. That said, the four dominant learning styles, namely diverging, assimilating, converging and accommodating, are closely related to the learning cycle where each style is located in a distinct quadrant. This is based on Kolb's four-stage experiential learning cycle involving the four adaptive learning modes, namely concrete experience (CE), abstract conceptualization (AC), reflective observation (RO) and active experimentation (AE), as illustrated in Figure 2.1.

Based on this model, the dialectical relationship between the first two modes of learning (CE and AC) suggests the grasping of experience while the relationship between the other two (RO and AE) suggests the transformation of experience. However, there is a creative tension between the four learning modes that triggers unique responses to contextual uncertainties. For instance, the tension between abstraction (part of AC) and concreteness (part of CE) is what Kolb regarded as *comprehension*, which helps the learner to understand the apprehension and interpretation of grasping an experience.

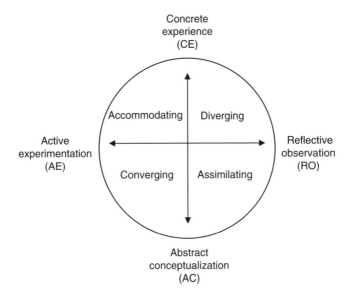

Figure 2.1 Kolb's experiential learning cycle and learning styles
Source: Kayes et al. (2005). Reproduced with permission of Sage Publications.

On the other hand, the active-reflective (part of RO and AE) tension helps the learner to be aware of his/her *intention* to act based on the internal reflection on and external application of transforming an experience (Kolb and Kolb, 2005). The interrelation between Kolb's learning style and learning cycle has provided useful perspectives for education, medical and management training as well as HRD. The following are several practical ways that this interrelation can be brought to practice in a variety of situations:

- *The converging style* falls within the modes of AC and AE, which promote the practical application of ideas through problem solving and decision making. Individuals utilizing this style thrive on objective or technical problems rather than interpersonal problems.
- *The diverging style* engages individuals in CE and RO, bringing out the awareness of their emotional intelligence. This is realized through an in-depth approach to interpreting the values and meanings of their surroundings and the reliance on concrete contexts to generate a variety of perspectives.
- *The assimilating style* relies on AC and RO in a way that increases individuals' cognitive capacity to reason inductively by constructing mental frames that predict future scenarios. Individuals adopting this style enjoy the process of thinking rather than the application of ideas.

- *The accommodating style* allows individuals to thrive on CE and AE by enabling them to make plans to fulfil new experiences. They are also highly adaptive to changing environments as they utilize intuition to solve problems and explore their surroundings through trial and error.

In response to criticism about the concept of learning style as being static, Kolb (1999) argued that experiential learning is a spontaneous and well-rounded learning process as it does not suggest that learners should go through the entire learning cycle to no end. Instead, the learning cycle provides the flexibility for learners to select any stages as deemed appropriate, or merely to focus on one stage that satisfies their immediate needs. Whichever the case, the learning that occurs is wholesome and provides relevance to the learner's immediate context, leading to appropriate actions. In this regard, revisiting Kolb's (1984) developmental model would further reinforce the wholesomeness of his experiential learning theory. This model posits that learning is predominantly related to human development, suggesting that the way individuals learn is directly linked to their personal and professional development. This perspective is supported by three distinct stages, namely (1) *acquisition*, representing the learning process from birth to adolescence; (2) *specialization*, representing formal schooling years to early work through personal experiences of adulthood when social, educational and organizational socializations shape the way learning is perceived and adopted; and (3) *integration*, representing mid-career to later life where less or non-dominant modes of learning are prevalent in work and personal life.

Understanding the three stages of learning from a human development perspective reinforces the interrelation between complexity and relativism in human adaptation. Complexity suggests that humans are capable of generating new ideas and techniques for solving problems that are not particularly predictable, while relativism suggests a capability to modify strategies and actions to satisfy an immediate context even in a state of change. Understanding these two dimensions of human development helps us to appreciate further the dialectical tensions between Kolb's learning modes. For instance, as individuals progress from AC to CE or RO to AE, they undergo an ongoing process of adaptation as they generate and modify their frames of references to produce different types of action for specific purposes. According to Kolb and Kolb (2009a), AC contributes to cognitive complexity, CE to affective complexity, RO to perceptual complexity, and AE to behavioural complexity. The four types of complexity relate to the sensory stimuli of a learner that help him/her make sense of his/her environment in more meaningful ways, as reinforced in Dewey's (1958) functional psychology. In the next section, we discuss several alternative perspectives of Kolb's experiential learning theory (KELT) based on some of the critiques.

CRITIQUES OF KOLB'S EXPERIENTIAL LEARNING THEORY

A number of critics seem to have built on Dewey's (1958) earlier caution about the nature of experience that may truncate the intensity of learning in any given context (e.g. Bowers, 2005; Fenwick, 2001; 2008; Holman et al., 1997; Kayes, 2002). In Dewey's explanation of mis-educative experiences, he cited an example of the subject, Physics, being taught through a lecture format. He suggested that students who might have gone through the direct experience of being in a lecture could possibly end up with two potential responses of that experience: 'I hate Physics' and 'I hate lectures'. Dewey further suggested that experience alone does not necessarily lead to true learning because of the following conditions by which the experiential potential of a distinct context is determined: (1) self-action, where choice, intention and level of initiation subsequently shape action; (2) interaction, where the level of complementariness cannot be assumed to be operating at all times as there are opposing and conflicting forces that keep the dynamics alive; and (3) transaction, where the linearity of the exchange process between learners is undermined by different aspects of human and contextual dynamics that cause different phases of action to occur.

Experiential learning, therefore, needs to be supported by continuity and interaction, taking into consideration the internal and external dynamics that the learner encounters in order to ensure growth and development in the learning process. Given this understanding, KELT, despite its attempt to incorporate these conditions, has been criticized for the lack of depth and integration of self-action, interaction and transaction. The various critiques of KELT have led to several theoretical propositions. First, learning and context are intimately bound such that contextual conditions moderate the way learning takes shape. In turn, the process of learning may actively engage in the various contextual features that produce certain outcomes that could modify these features. Second, the magnified role of reflection leads to emancipatory learning in such a way that reflection releases individuals from the entrapment of assumptions and misconstrued conceptualizations to seek a much more diverse exploration of a phenomenon. Consequently, emancipatory learning gives rise to liberating actions that enhance the richness of experience. Third, the meanings, structures and actions of learning are characterized by critical, institutional and managerial perspectives, suggesting that the multi-linearity of learning is influenced by the shifting conditions under which individuals experience constantly. We now explain below each specific critique of KELT, based on several distinct perspectives of learning.

De-contextualization of learning

Despite the social dynamics of learning, KELT has been criticized for projecting an inward-looking, individual-level learning with a focus on individual learners' cognitive capacity to think and act as independent entities rather than as collaborative agents. To several critics (e.g. Holman et al., 1997; Reynolds and Vince, 2004; Wallace, 1996), this concentration de-contextualizes learning from a psychodynamic perspective, which posits that learning and context are inseparable. Contextual factors such as social status, emotional influence and power relations can affect individuals' response to their learning needs and their interaction dynamics. For instance, openness and trust that enhance the exchange of ideas and perspectives in group settings depend as much on the members' desire to learn as their power of influence on one another.

Internal barriers as potential inhibitors to learning

Extending Dewey's (1938, 1958) caution that experience of itself might not lead to true learning, it is clear that there are barriers to learning that can potentially truncate learning and reduce the meaning of experience. These barriers include an unconscious state of learning in the form of defence mechanism (Kayes, 2002), an emotive state of learning in the form of avoidance and denial (Vince, 1998), and role differentiation that involves power relations (Holman et al., 1997). For instance, learners can be overprotective of themselves if they find their position being threatened in one way or another. Likewise, people may avoid thinking of the brighter side of things if they have been disappointed most of the time due to negative comments or bad news. People may also lose their sense of control under conditions of intimidation and humiliation. These factors are potential inhibitors to learning that are not adequately captured in KELT.

Criticality of reflection

Kolb's proposition of RO in his learning cycle is one that deserves further attention as it is unclear if the roles of reflection and observation are the same.

The point of contention is the ambiguous role of reflection, whether it should take place before or after observation. Equally puzzling is its relationship with observation as it is unclear if reflection can be adequately achieved through observation. Critics (e.g. Bergsteiner et al., 2010; Garner, 2000; Reynolds, 2009; Seaman, 2008) argued that critical reflection is central to all learning activities, particularly from a meta-cognitive perspective. The criticality of reflection adds a much richer dimension to learning than what is assumed in KELT, through an in-depth engagement of underlying issues rather than a surface-level questioning of assumptions (Boud et al., 1985). This is not merely reflecting on issues that are relevant to the immediate context but to the opportunity for subsequent learning and collaboration impacting on a wider community of learning (Lave and Wenger, 1991). Reflection could also take place during the learning process or during a debriefing session after an activity, reinforcing Schön's (1983) distinction between reflection-*in*-action and reflection-*on*-action respectively.

Reflection as an emancipatory process and learning as a reflexive activity

Extending the critical role of reflection, critics such as Boud et al. (1985) and Mezirow (1990) argued that individuals are empowered with the ability to determine the breadth and depth of reflection based on their competence and prior experience. This ability gives rise to emancipatory reflection, where individuals generate assumptions and analyse them in greater depth in order to help them develop response mechanisms either in codified knowledge or concrete action. As such, reflection is not an oversimplified process as projected in Kolb's learning cycle but a self-creation of knowledge and a congruence of ideas based on organizational needs. Reynolds (1997) associated this process with emancipatory learning, suggesting that individuals are given the free will to respond to learning according to their roles in a particular context. From a phenomenological perspective, understanding the roles captures more of the changing dynamics of social relations than the objectivity and relativity as assumed in KELT. Consequently, learning can be said to be a reflexive activity as it is concerned with the role relations and significance rather than the nature in which it occurs. Such reflexivity defines and shapes an experiential context, which forms the boundaries for cognitive participation as learners engage in rigorous mental framing that leads to knowledge exchange (Fenwick, 2003; Hopkins, 1993; Michailova and Wilson, 2008; Michelson, 1999; Reynolds and Vince, 2007; Seaman, 2008).

Constructivist perspective of learning

Although KELT is theoretically underpinned by the constructivist perspective of learning, the underlying assumptions are problematic suggesting that learning is independent of context in terms of knowledge storage and transfer. Some critics went so far as saying that it is not completely accurate to assume that when learners move from one context to another, they bring with them a set of bounded knowledge (meanings) from previous experience and apply it in a new context (Elsbach et al., 2005; Fenwick, 2000). In this example, knowledge has been regarded as a separate substance, which does not take into consideration its potential for social construction through language and cultural practice (Armstrong and Fukami, 2010). The assumption also undermines the dynamics of cognitive participation that enables learners to derive meanings through social interactions in changing contexts. In order to further understand learning as not merely associated with the production of mental concepts, it is important to be aware of the transitory performance of learners, where learning is situated in active participation during which a learner transfers a previously held schema into a concrete experience. It is where knowledge is captured through a momentary action that true learning occurs, suggesting that learning is interdependent of context (Brown et al., 1989).

Institutional perspective of learning

The institutional perspective of learning and change posits that organizational environments are characterized by the proliferation of rules and routines, giving rise to organizational support and legitimacy (Kondra and Hinings, 1998). Institutions are social structures that have been established through a certain degree of resilience, and these take on different forms as individuals construct meanings and enact routines differently through the interpretation of cultures. As such, the interpretive power of individuals can be seen as part of institutional agency where social actions create, reproduce and change institutions (Suddaby and Greenwood, 2005; Zilber, 2002). Based on this perspective, critics (e.g. Hopkins, 1993; Kayes, 2002) believed that KELT is not firmly underpinned by a strong epistemological position to contribute to codified knowledge, thus lacking an institutional orientation. This suggests that KELT does not take into consideration routines, rules, norms and other concrete organizational elements that could account for meanings, structures and actions critical to learning. The critique follows that Kolb's conceptualization of experiential learning is a structural reductionist approach that does not adequately examine the social nature of knowledge construction, particularly the way learners develop their perceptual frameworks in group settings. An institutional perspective can help unravel experience as both a process and an outcome as it takes into consideration the importance of institutional logics, which are deeply held and unchallenged assumptions. These logics in turn create boundaries that govern concrete action by enabling learners to make sense of their environment and determine the right course of action (Suddaby and Greenwood, 2005).

Power and control in the social context

From a critical perspective, scholars such as Boud et al. (1985), Michelson (1999), Vince (1998) and Willmott (1994) argued that the level of spontaneity and predictability of learning in KELT do not take into consideration the legitimacy of power and control in a social context. In any organization, politics and dominant voices are ever-present as power derived from traditions has caused employees not to question authority but accept the way things are. Often, rhetorical strategies can help them to interpret their surroundings based on language and symbolic expressions, also known as hermeneutics. Rhetorical strategies are derived from one's communicative intent evaluated on the basis of persuasiveness and influence. Hence, it is the role of language that gives power to the structuring of social actions (Driscoll and Morris, 2001). From a critical social perspective, language used in the interpretation of surroundings increases self-reflective knowledge and frees individuals from the entrapment of systems and routines. However, the presence of power and control in organizational settings may lead to the manipulation of rhetorical strategies that ultimately truncates and obstructs group learning.

Managerial perspective of learning

From a practical perspective, KELT appears to have produced limiting effects for managers as learning is assumed to take greater effect with a limited range of ideas based on overly specific and narrowly framed problems. This suggests that the transition between learning and action is restrained by the localization of issues in such a way that they can be easily framed to fit into the four stages of the experiential learning cycle (Reynolds, 2009; Willmott, 1994). The narrowness of the problem context may consequently restrict managerial practice as it prevents managers from making sense of the problem based on a much wider context. For instance, managers may not consider the political tensions and conflicts, as well as issues with power relations, that may have a direct influence on the way learning occurs and how problems are solved within the learning cycle (Boot and Reynolds, 1983). According to the sense making perspective, experience cannot be constituted outside of social relations as it requires a much wider and more complex (problem) context from which meaning is constructed and interpreted through dynamic interactions (Daft and Weick, 1984; Weick et al., 2005). To some extent, KELT does not focus much on the richness or 'wickedness' of a problem (Rittel and Webber, 1973), its potential for equivocality or complexity and its surrounding context to promote more effective managerial practice.

Opposing quality of terminologies

Critics such as Bergsteiner, Avery and Neumann (2010) faulted the typology of the experiential learning phases and suggested that there is an oxymoron in the terminologies of all four learning stages: 'abstract conceptualization' (AC), 'reflective observation' (RO), 'concrete experience' (CE) and 'active experimentation' (AE). They labelled each of them as a muddled typology. First, if conceptualization is to seek abstraction, then it negates the epistemological assumption that conceptualization is a process that constructs theoretical assumptions based on clear propositions. The notion of AC further reduces the epistemological possibility of framing emerging issues in identifiable ways. Second, the epistemological contradiction in RO is seen in the opposing cognitive properties of the two notions. For instance, to reflect is to make sense of previous events and activities, while to observe is to be aware of current events and seek forward connection to reality. Third, both CE and AE seem to suggest that there is a less-tangible quality than there really is. As such, by adding the tangible quality of 'concreteness' and 'activeness' to action-oriented activities such as experiencing and experimenting, the tangibility of these activities would appear ambivalent and difficult to comprehend.

Summary of the critiques

The various perspectives discussed reinforce Dewey's (1938, 1958) assumption that experience alone is not the main condition for learning. First, it is apparent that the interrelation of self-action, interaction and transaction requires an understanding of experience as both a conceptual and experimental process. Second, it is the understanding of role identity as a cognitive process that determines the intentionality of learning and action in complex organizational systems. Third, it is the understanding of social relation as a reflexive process that creates the opportunities and challenges for developing meanings, structures and actions in group learning. Integrating the critiques, we argue that the applicability of experiential learning in shifting contexts requires a much more in-depth understanding of the internal and external factors that can turn experience and learning into mutually implicating processes and outcomes. Combining these conditions has helped us to extend the meaning of KELT from a social constructionist perspective, which will be discussed in the next section where we introduce an integrative perspective of experiential learning by drawing on the works of Vygotsky, Bakhtin and Leont'ev.

AN INTEGRATIVE PERSPECTIVE OF EXPERIENTIAL LEARNING

As we have suggested, KELT is underpinned by constructivist views of inter-action and adaptation by learners as individuals, giving little or secondary attention to the complex factors of context that both support but are likely to inhibit learning efforts. We, therefore, propose a social constructionist per-spective of learning. This perspective is linked to social constructivism in some ways but is also different as the emphasis is on context and people's coming together to construct artefacts through social interactions (Bowers, 2005). In order to fully appreciate experiential learning, we propose an integrative perspective which considers language, talk and physical tools that govern the way individuals interact for the creation of knowledge and expertise.

Given our attention to the critiques of KELT, we will attempt to provide some degree of integration drawing from a range of ideas that enable us to move beyond the neatly patterned explanations of experiential learning, with more recognition given to power-laden but ongoing experiential life in which people must work and live. By the term 'neatly patterned explanations', we mean those approaches that attempt, through the completion of diagnostic instruments such as questionnaires, to locate individuals against particular typologies that imply prediction in terms of thinking, feeling behaving and learning. This includes various learning and cognitive-style instruments (such as Honey and Mumford's (1992) Learning Style Questionnaire), many of which have been criticized by Coffield et al. (2004) as lacking independent validation, or by Pashler et al. (2009) as lacking evidence of benefit. For exam-ple, there seems to be a wide range of learning-styles assessment instruments, which have had a significant influence on both education and HRD, all of which in some way or other place learners under particular labels or heading. While appealing, even at an intuitive level, research suggests that many have not been tested or are not considered valid.

Our starting point is the contribution made by the Russian social philosopher and cultural theorist, Mikhail Mikhailovich Bakhtin, and the attention given to life as a continuous series of acts or events that constitute experience. According to Bakhtin (1993), individuals have an unending need to make their lives meaningful and, therefore, at any moment in time, participate in a 'once-occurrent Being-as-event'. A key theme of all Bakhtin's work is that 'the values and meanings that most directly shape our lives emerge from the existential demands of daily living and our *immediate* interpersonal relationships' (Gardiner, 2000, p. 43, *emphasis added*). We experience life 'concretely' through sight, touch, hearing and thought; there is no escaping such experience as we always have a 'non-alibi' within it. That is, as life proceeds in a continuous series of events, what is experienced by us can only be experienced by us; it is unique to us and cannot occur again. As Bakhtin (1993) suggests, 'in all Being, I experience myself – my unique self- as an I . . . .' (pp. 40–41). Thus, rather than a stage of concrete experience in a cycle or a particular preference for learning, we cannot live outside concreteness as life proceeds in a continuous series of events or experience. Further, the sharing of such events with others or an 'otherness' brings to the forefront Bakhtin's notion of dialogism (Holquist, 1990), central to which is the meditational importance of language in providing meaning. As argued by Bakhtin (1986, p. 60), 'All the diverse areas of human activity involve the use of language', where what we say, write or do – our 'utterances' – are fundamentally linked in relation to a response from others, 'otherness' or just ourselves. Utterance and response are crucial to the process of making meaning or sense – or learning – the quality of which is the moment when at least two voices interact. However, there can be no certainty as to the outcome of such interaction. Any 'utterance' by one person has no meaning unless it is responded to by an-other. Meaning is made by the mutual co-ordination of utterance and response, and a failure to find co-ordination is a failure to find meaning:

> If others do not recognisably treat one's utterance as meaningful, if they fail to co-ordinate themselves around such offerings, one is reduced to nonsense.
>
> (Gergen, 1995, p. 37)

The mediation of language and social relations of interaction underpin the work of another Russian psychologist, Lev Vygotsky, who points to the way that higher mental functioning by individuals is based on social relations. This even occurs, he argued, when people are thinking to themselves: 'In their own private sphere, human beings retain the functions of social interaction' (Vygotsky, 1981, p. 164). For Vygotsky, language and other sign systems, derived from social relations and culture, provide some of the tools that enable the completion of action, and this provides the basis of socio-cultural learning theory.

Vygotsky pointed to the role of mediating tools in attempts by humans to complete action. In any action undertaken, a person will have a goal, either explicitly expressed or left implicit, but completion requires the use of mediating tools, which are social and cultural in origin, including psychological tools such as:

> systems for counting; mnemonic techniques; algebraic symbol systems; works of art; writing; schemes, diagrams, maps, and technical drawings; all sorts of conventional signs, and so on.
>
> (Vygotsky, 1982, p. 137)

From this list, language, acquired through interaction with others, is primary. However, Vygotsky also identified physical tools or 'artefacts' made by humans that reflect a particular time, society and culture. For example, the action of writing a book chapter makes use of the tools of a PC and keyboard rather than pen and paper, which were physical tools of book writing in another time and culture. In either case, physical tools are combined with psychological tools in the completion of the action.

Through ongoing interactions with others or 'otherness', we acquire or 'learn' to work with tools to complete actions. Much of this acquisition needs to be considered as informal, non-formal or 'natural' learning (Eraut, 2000) where individuals become socialized into various groupings or communities. In the workplace, such situated learning has been increasingly recognized as the basis for participation in various communities of practice (Brown et al., 1989) where daily interactions with others through conversations and sharing stories allow new entrants to learn what it means to become a practitioner in a particular context through the acquisition of psychological and physical tools.

While tools enable action, they also potentially constrain or set a limit on action. Vygotsky (1978) provided an interesting view of the work of tools in the dynamic interplay between individual mental functioning and social and cultural influences, not only to achieve a goal in action but, through 'reverse action', to shape the subjectivity and identity of individuals. Penuel and Wertsch (1995) argued that the employment of tools provides the means by which individuals come to identify who they are.

Again, much of this is informal learning; however, there are also some clearly recognized occasions when we are learning to join a group such as a profession, a club or an identifiable social grouping such as class. Here, we can point to the organization of tools into what Bakhtin considered as a social language or an accepted way of talking among a group, which shapes what can be said and done or not (Bakhtin, 1981). In terms of experiential learning, there are two considerations on which to focus. First, social languages provide the tools that enable what people can do; therefore, according to Bakhtin (1981), in any event that is unique and once occurrent, language is already present. This multi-voiced connection is referred to as 'ventriloquation':

> The word in language is half someone else's. It becomes 'one's own' only when the speaker populates it with his own intention, his own accent, when he appropriates the word, adapting it to his own semantic expressive intention.
>
> (pp. 293–294)

Second, because we participate in a variety of social and cultural activities, it is likely that we learn to ventriloquate with several social languages. For example, when I am in a crowd at a soccer match, I can quite easily sing or chant with the rest of the crowd, but when I order food in an Indian restaurant I draw on a different social language. It is also possible that some social languages become privileged or even dominating, probably beyond the awareness of the speaker. As Bakhtin (1981) suggested, there is a tendency towards what he refers to as a 'unitary language', the purpose of which is 'to unify and centralise the verbal-ideological world' where unification and centralization are achieved through the power of 'centripetal forces of language', which further produce what is deemed to be 'correct language' and a system of 'norms' that advance official recognition and a particular 'world view' (p. 270). Critical reflection on the voice of social languages can bring to light their potential for domination.

From these perspectives, learning is a process of tool acquisition that occurs in the dialogic dynamic between utterance linked to a response from others, ourselves or otherness – the mere context of our concrete experience. Thus, based on the notion of the ongoing concreteness of being as event, it has to be experiential. Such acquisition can range from the informal and tacit to formally recognized events of learning, but the process is the same – tool acquisition that enables and constrains action in working towards goals. Further, through the organization of tools into social languages, experiential learning provides meanings for what is to be accepted as real and serves a function within a particular historical and cultural context, allowing individuals to join with others in the pursuance of particular practices such as working, playing, fighting wars and so on. However, disturbances and ruptures to what is accepted or normally understood may also be necessary, as part of the dynamics of learning, through critical reflection and reflexivity.

Further, mediated action of individuals always occurs within a context, mostly shared with others, as part of an activity for an agreed purpose, to a greater or lesser extent. All work organizations can be characterized as mediated interdependent actions by individuals as part of a collective activity (Leont'ev, 1981). While learning through the disturbance of tool acquisition can occur for individuals, there are further possibilities for enablement and constraint from the past and the pre-history of the activity, or what Bakhtin (1986) referred to as the 'extraverbal context of realty'. Engeström's (2001) version of cultural-historical activity theory (CHAT) gives prominence to the collective unit of activity system for considering organizational actions and dependencies, which is mediated not only by tools and artefacts but also by rules and social norms, the division of labour into roles and structures and the allowance of communities of practitioners. Each form of mediation is culturally and historically formed and socially applied within actions, and therefore within the activity system as a whole. Uncovering and understanding how such factors bear down on the system is the key to providing the conditions for expanding learning in any context (Sannino et al., 2009).

CONCLUSION AND IMPLICATIONS FOR HRD

In this chapter, we have provided a conceptual overview of experiential learning theory and the consequent development of the learning cycle as developed and popularized by David Kolb in the 1970s/1980s. We highlighted the constructivist nature of KELT that occurs through the interaction and direct contact of a unique individual, often characterized with a preferred learning style, with a specific context as the distinguishing feature of experiential learning. We have shown that while experiential learning and KELT, in particular, have remained popular, there has been a growing and critical literature that points towards the need to move in a new direction.

The contribution of this chapter therefore lies in an integrative perspective realized through a critical understanding and integration of the theoretical critiques of KELT. The social constructionist perspective clarifies and moves beyond Kolb's (1984) narrow interpretation of experiential learning as a constructivist process, as it considers the importance of other contextual factors that influence the social construction of knowledge that accompanies learning. In particular, Bakhtin's philosophy of language, combined with Vygotksy's socio-cultural theory, provides us with the underlying motivation to view learning as a practice that resides in the ambiguity and messiness of internal and external environments.

We believe that our argument has a number of key implications for HRD practitioners and theory. First, Bakhtin's key theme of our participation in a 'once-occurrent Being-as-event' and our continuous 'concrete' existence is surely a reminder that learning events are not just identified as HRD events, whether specified formally or otherwise. It is also an indication that the various diagnostic tools, such as Kolb's LSI, which identify concrete experience as a particular stage in learning, rather miss the possibility of a large variety of moments of concrete existence, from which learning might be derived. In particular, such moments are bound to arise in the context of practice, especially where there are problems or deviations from expectations in practice. As Beckett and Hagar (2002) identified, in moments when practice occurs under pressure, people find new ways of adapting, and adjust to keep going, providing an opportunity for new ways of acting, if such knowledge gained can be shared with others.

Second, in articulating such possibilities for new ways, the 'utterance' of one person can only be made meaningful by the response of another. As we suggest, utterance and response are crucial to the process of meaning making that can be recognized as learning. Whether this occurs through reviews between learners, virtual and electronic boards and so on, such moments provide the basis of knowledge creation and learning. Of course, the response to utterance can remain local, concealed within groups and communities not recognized by HRD practitioners (Collins, 2001), or within individuals, where knowledge is articulated to self but not beyond. It is a task for HRD to support knowledge creation in an organization, wherever it may occur.

Third, bringing people together to share learning supports a Vygotskian view of the development of higher mental functioning. For HRD, tools as mediating devices – whether as language and signs, physical artefacts or, most likely, a combination of both – needs to be reflexively considered within interactions, both as enablers of action and as constraints. In addition, Bakhtin's notion of ventriloquation and the work of social languages point to the need for a closer inspection by HRD of the power of 'the centripetal forces' of language, which can inhibit learning through norms that constrain behaviour and domination of one-way talking that is privileged over another.

Fourth, we have argued that learning is a process of tool acquisition, which always enables new possibilities but can also constrain. In such an acquisition, new tools compete with existing tools, which through 'reverse action' can come to be highly valued by individuals and connect strongly to existing identities. HRD work cannot expect new offerings, as new tools to be easily acquired by learners whether in formal HRD events or elsewhere. There can be no certainty that HRD utterances will be more acceptable than others, and it is only through argument and persuasion that new tools might be accepted (Shotter, 1993).

Finally, understanding that learning is a tool mediated with the potential as a spontaneous process reinforces our proposition that reflexivity is a crucial feature of experiential learning, as learners constantly make sense of what is being learned in practice. Such reflexivity is fundamental to our integrative perspective of experiential learning as underpinned by psychodynamic theories that seek to question 'where we are' (social context) and 'who we are' (identity) in relation to 'what we learn' (action). Taken together, experiential learning can be better understood outside the classroom when it is applied in actual practical contexts through HRD. Based on our earlier definition of HRD as being the facilitation of interventionist activities, we view experiential learning as a particular important process on which HRD professionals could capitalize to unleash the human expertise of employees. Understanding how to build learning into work teams through collaborative inquiry and reflective action-taking is a critically important HRD skill (Sofo et al., 2010). Through the use of appropriate tools and meaningful dialogue, HRD professionals would be able to recognize the opportunities and challenges that reside in work teams in order to help them increase their learning capacity and overcome potential learning ambiguity.

REFERENCES

Armstrong, S. J. and Fukami, C. (2010) Self-assessment of knowledge: A cognitive learning or affective measure? Perspectives from the management learning and education community, *Academy of Management Learning and Education*, 9(1): 335–341.

Bakhtin, M. M. (1981) *The Dialogic Imagination: Four Essays by M. M. Bakhtin*, ed. M. Holquist. Austin: University of Texas Press.

Bakhtin, M. M. (1986) *Speech Genres and Other Late Essays*, ed. C. Emerson and M. Holquist. Austin: University of Texas Press.

Bakhtin, M. M. (1993) *Towards a Philosophy of the Act*, ed. V. Liapunov and M. Holquist. Houston: University of Texas.

Beckett, D. and Hagar, P. (2002) *Life, Work and Learning*. London: Routledge.

Bergsteiner, H., Avery, G. C. and Neumann, R. (2010) Kolb's experiential learning model: Critique from a modeling perspective, *Studies in Continuing Education*, 32(1): 29–46.

Boot, R. L. and Reynolds, M. (eds) (1983) *Learning and Experience in Formal Education*. Manchester: Manchester Monographs.

Boud, D., Keogh, R. and Walker, D. (1985) Promoting reflection in learning: A model, in D. Boud, R. Keogh and D. Walker (eds). *Reflection: Turning Experience into Learning*. New York: Kogan Page.

Bowers, C. A. (2005) *The False Promises of Constructivist Learning Theories: A Global and Ecological Critique*. New York: Peter Lang Publishing.

Boyatzis, R. E. and Kolb, D. A. (1997) Assessing individuality in learning: The learning skills profile, *Educational Psychology*, 11(3/4): 279–295.

Brown, J. S., Collins, A. and Duguid, P. (1989) Situated cognition and the culture of learning, *Educational Researcher*, 18(1): 32–42.

Bynum, W. F. and Porter, R. (eds) (2005) *Oxford Dictionary of Scientific Quotations*. New York: Oxford University Press.

Chisholm, C. U., Harris, M. S. G., Northwood, D. O. and Johrendt, J. L. (2009) The characterization of work-based learning by consideration of the theories of experiential learning, *European Journal of Education*, 44(3): 319–337.

Coffield, F., Moseley, D., Hall, E. and Ecclestone, K. (2004) *Learning Styles and Pedagogy in Post-16 Learning: A Systematic and Critical Review*. London: Learning and Skills Research Centre.

Collins, H. (2001) Tacit knowledge, trust and the Q of sapphire, *Social Studies of Science*, 31(1): 71–85.

Daft, R. L. and Weick, K. E. (1984) Toward a model of organisations as interpretation systems, *Academy of Management Review*, 9(2): 284–295.

Dewey, J. (1938) *Experience and Education*. New York: Macmillan and Co.

Dewey, J. (1958) *Democracy and Education*. New York: Macmillan and Co.

Driscoll, A. and Morris, J. (2001) Stepping out: Rhetorical devices and culture change management in the UK civil service, *Public Administration*, 79(4): 803–824.

Drucker, P. F. (1988) The coming of the new organisation, *Harvard Business Review*, 66(1): 45–53.

Elsbach, K. D., Barr, P. S. and Hargadon, A. B. (2005) Identifying situated cognition in organisations, *Organisation Science*, 16(4): 422–433.

Engeström, Y. (2001) Expansive learning at work: Toward an activity theoretical reconceptualisation, *Journal of Education and Work*, 14(1): 133–156.

Eraut, M. (2000) Non-formal learning, implicit learning and tacit knowledge. In F. Coffield (ed.), *The Necessity of Informal Learning*. Bristol: Policy Press.

Fenwick, T. (2000) Expanding the conceptions of experiential learning: A review of the five contemporary perspectives on cognition, *Adult Education Quarterly*, 50(4): 243–272.

Fenwick, T. (2001) *Experiential Learning: A Theoretical Critique from Five Perspectives*. Ohio State University: ERIC Clearinghouse on Adult, Career, and Vocational Education.

Fenwick, T. (2003) *Learning Through Experience: Through Orthodoxies and Intersecting Questions*. Malabar: Krieger Publishing.

Fenwick, T. (2008) Understanding relations of individual – collective learning in work: A review of research, *Management Learning*, 39(3): 227–243.

Gardiner, M. (2000). *Critiques of Everyday Life*. London: Routledge.

Garner, I. (2000) Problems and inconsistencies with Kolb's learning styles, *Educational Psychology*, 20(3): 341–349.

Garrick, J. (1998) *Informal Learning in the Workplace: Unmasking Human Resource Development*. London: Routledge.

Gergen, K. J. (1995) Relational theory and discourses of power. In D. M. Hosking, H. P. Dachler and K. J. Gergen (eds). *Management and Organization: Relational Alternatives to Individualism*. Aldershot: Avebury.

Holman, D., Pavlica, K. and Thorpe, R. (1997) Rethinking Kolb's theory of experiential learning in management education: The contribution of social constructivism and activity theory, *Management Learning*, 28(2): 135–148.

Holquist, M. (1990) *Dialogism*. London: Routledge.

Honey, P. and Mumford, A. (1992) *The Manual of Learning Styles* (3rd edn). Maidenhead: Peter Honey.

Hopkins, R. (1993) David Kolb's experiential learning machine, *Journal of Phenomenological Psychology*, 24(1): 46–62.

Kayes, A. B., Kayes, D. and Kolb, D.S (2005) Experiential learning in teams, *Simulation and Gaming*, 36(3): 330–354

Kayes, D. C. (2002) Experiential learning and its critics: Preserving the role of experience in management learning and education, *Academy of Management Learning and Education*, 1(2): 137–149.

Kirkpatrick, L. A. and Epstein, S. (1992) Cognitive-experiential self-theory and subjective probability: Further evidence for two conceptual systems, *Journal of Personality and Social Psychology*, 63(4): 534–544.

Kolb, D. A. (1981) Experiential learning theory and the learning style inventory: A reply to Freedman and Stumpf, *Academy of Management Review*, 6(2): 289–296.

Kolb, D. A. (1983). Problem management: Learning from experience. In S. Srivastva and Associates (eds). *The Executive Mind*. San Francisco, CA: Jossey-Bass.

Kolb, D. A. (1984) *Experiential Learning: Experience as the Source of Learning and Development*. New Jersey: Prentice-Hall.

Kolb, D. A. (1999) *The Kolb Learning Style Inventory* (Version 3). Boston, MA: Hay Group.

Kolb, D. A., Boyatzis, R. E. and Mainemelis, C. (2000) Experiential learning theory: Previous research and new directions. In R. J. Sternberg and F. Zhang (eds). *Perspectives on Cognitive, Learning, and Thinking Styles*. Mahwah, NJ: Lawrence Erlbaum.

Kolb, A. Y. and Kolb, D. A. (2005) Learning styles and learning spaces: Enhancing experiential learning in higher education, *Academy of Management Learning and Education*, 4(2): 193–212.

Kolb, A. Y. and Kolb, D. A. (2009a) Experiential learning theory: A dynamic, holistic approach to management learning, education and development. In S. J. Armstrong and C. Fukami (eds), *Handbook of Management Learning, Education and Development*. London: Sage.

Kolb, A. Y. and Kolb, D. A. (2009b) The learning way: Meta-cognitive aspects of experiential learning, *Simulation and Gaming*, 40(3): 297–327.

Kondra, A. Z. and Hinings, C. R. (1998) Organizational diversity and change in institutional theory, *Organization Studies*, 19(5): 743–767.

Lave, J. and Wenger, E. (1991) *Situated Learning: Legitimate Peripheral Participation*. Cambridge: Cambridge University Press.

Leont'ev, A. N. (1981) *Problems of the Development of Mind*. Moscow: Progress.

Lewin, K. (1943) Defining the field at a given time, *Psychological Review*, 50(3): 292–310.

Lewin, K. (1951) *Field Theory in Social Sciences*. New York: Harper and Row.

Mainemelis, C., Boyatzis, R. E. and Kolb, D. A (2002) Learning styles and adaptive flexibility: Testing experiential learning theory, *Management Learning*, 33(1): 5–33.

Megginson, D., Joy-Matthews, J. and Banfield, P. (1993) *Human Resource Development*. London: Kogan Page.

Mezirow, J. (1990) *Fostering Critical Reflection*. San Francisco, CA: Jossey-Bass.

Michailova, S. and Wilson, H. I. M. (2008) Small firm internationalization through experiential learning: The moderating role of socialization tactics, *Journal of World Business*, 43(2): 243–254.

Michelson, E. (1999) Carnival, paranoia, and experiential learning, *Studies in the Education of Adults*, 31(2): 140–154.

Miettinen, R. (2000) The concept of experiential learning and John Dewey's theory of reflective thought and action, *International Journal of Lifelong Education*, 19(1): 54–72.

Ng, K. Y., Van Dyne, L. and Ang, S. (2009) From experience to experiential learning: Cultural intelligence as a learning capability for global leader development, *Academy of Management Learning and Education*, 8(4): 511–526.

Pashler, H., McDaniel, M., Rohrer, D. and Bjork, R. (2009) Learning styles: Concepts and evidence, *Psychological Science in the Public Interest*, 9(3): 105–119.

Penuel, W. R. and Wertsch, J. V. (1995) Vygotsky and identity formation: A socio-cultural approach, *Educational Psychologist*, 30(2): 83–92.

Piaget, J. (1969) *Psychology of Intelligence*. Totowa, NJ: Littlefield, Adams, and Co.

Reynolds, M. (1997) Learning styles: A critique, *Management Learning*, 28(2): 115–134.

Reynolds, M. (2009) Wild frontiers – Reflections on experiential learning, *Management Learning*, 40(4): 387–392.

Reynolds, M. and Vince, R. (2004) Critical management education and action-based learning: Synergies and contradictions, *Academy of Management Learning and Education*, 3(4): 442–456.

Reynolds, M. and Vince, R. (eds) (2007) *The Handbook of Experiential Learning and Management Education*. Oxford: Oxford University Press.

Rittel, H. and Webber, M. M. (1973) Dilemmas in a general theory of planning, *Policy Sciences*, 4(2): 155–169.

Sannino, A., Daniels, H. and Gutiérrez, K. D. (eds) (2009) *Learning and Expanding with Activity Theory*. New York: Cambridge University Press.

Schön, D. A. (1983) *The Reflective Practitioner: How Professionals Think in Action*. London: Temple Smith.

Seaman, J. (2008) Experience, reflect, critique: The end of the 'learning cycles' era, *Journal of Experiential Education*, 31(1): 3–18.

Shotter, J. (1993) *Conversational Realities*. London: Sage.

Sims, S. R. (1983) Kolb's experiential learning theory: A framework for assessing person-job interaction, *Academy of Management Review*, 8(3): 501–508.

Sofo, F., Yeo, R. K. and Villafañe, J. (2010) Optimising the learning in action learning: Reflective questions, levels of learning, and coaching, *Advances in Developing Human Resources*, 12(2): 205–244.

Suddaby, R. and Greenwood, R. (2005) Rhetorical studies of legitimacy, *Administrative Science Quarterly*, 50(1): 35–67.

Swanson, R. A. (1995) Performance is key, *Human Resource Development Quarterly*, 6(2): 207–213.

Vince, R. (1998) Behind and beyond Kolb's learning cycle, *Journal of Management Education*, 22(3): 304–319.

Vygotsky, L. S. (1978) Mind in society: The development of higher psychological processes. In M. Cole, V. John-Steiner, S. Scribner and E. Souberman (eds). *L.S. Vygostky: Mind In Society: The Development of Higher Processes*. Cambridge, MA: Harvard University Press.

Vygotsky, L. S. (1981) The genesis of higher mental functions. In J. V. Wertsch (ed.), *The Concept of Activity in Soviet Psychology*. New York: M. E. Sharpe.

Vygotsky, L. S. (1982) *Collected Works*. Moscow: Pedagogica.

Wallace, M. (1996) When is experiential learning not experiential learning? In G. Claxton (ed.), *Liberating the Learner: Lessons for Professional Development in Education*. New York: Routledge.

Watkins, K. (2000) Aims, roles and structures for human resource development, *Advances in Developing Human Resources*, 2(3): 54–59.

Weick, K. E., Sutcliffe, K. M. and Obstfeld, D. (2005) Organizing and the process of sensemaking, *Organization Science*, 16(4): 409–421.

Willmott, H. (1994) Management education: Provocations to a debate, *Management Learning*, 25(1): 105–136.

Zilber, T. B. (2002) Institutionalisation as the interplay between actions, meanings and actors: The case of a rape crisis centre in Israel, *Academy of Management Journal*, 45(1): 234–254.

FURTHER READING

Argote, L. and Miron-Spektor, E. (2011) Organizational learning: From experience to knowledge, *Organization Science*, 22(5): 1123–1137.

Freedman, R. D. and Stumpf, S. A. (1980) Learning style theory: Less than meets the eye, *Academy of Management Review*, 5(3): 445–447.

Russ-Eft, D. (2000) That old fungible feeling: Defining human resource development, *Advances in Developing Human Resources*, 2(3): 49–53.

Zhao, B. (2011) Learning from errors: The role of context, emotion, and personality, *Journal of Organizational Behavior*, 32(1): 435–463.

Zundel, M. (2012) Walking to learn: Rethinking reflection for management learning, *Management Learning*, doi:10.1177/1350507612440231.

3

POSITIVE AND CRITICAL: ENHANCING CONSTRUCTIVE CRITICAL REFLECTION IN GROUPS

Marianne van Woerkom and Saskia Tjepkema

INTRODUCTION

The concept of critical reflection has gained much popularity in the field of human resource development (HRD). Reflection and critical reflection are generally seen as crucial elements in learning processes of individuals and organizations (Rigano and Edwards, 1998) and as essential practices in developing learning organizations (McCutchan, 1997; Vince, 2001). Reflection recurrently emerges as a suggested way of helping practitioners better understand what they know and do as they develop their knowledge of practice through reconsidering what they learn in practice (Loughran, 2002) and reflective practice is a key component of learning programmes for many practitioners and managers in a wide range of fields (Boud et al., 2006; Swan and Bailey, 2004). Especially for managers, working as a 'reflective practitioner' (Schön, 1983) is regarded as essential. It is believed that by thinking more critically about their assumptions and action, managers can develop more collaborative, responsive and ethical ways of managing (Cunliffe, 2004) and can question and confront the social and political forces that provide the context of their work (Reynolds, 1998).

However, in spite of the widespread use and acclaimed relevance of the term *critical* reflection, it is a contested term used in a confusing array of variations (Finlay and Gough, 2003). This chapter traces the roots of these different approaches to critical reflection or related terms by using Brookfield's (2000) distinction between the traditions of ideology critique, psychotherapy, analytic philosophy and logic, and pragmatist constructivism. An analysis of the definitions of critical reflection from these different traditions reveals that most of these definitions share a common rationalistic bias. We discuss the problems related to this bias and highlight the importance of intuitive and emotional aspects of reflection. Next, we explore some problems that often emerge when engaging a group in critical reflection. We then propose some interventions to foster positive critical reflection in groups, based on the principles of 'appreciative inquiry' (AI) and positive psychology.

CRITICAL REFLECTION: WHAT IS IT?

There is no single theory of critical reflection, and therefore not much consistency in the definitions of the concept (Brooks, 1999; Calderhead, 1989; Finlay and Gough, 2003). Brookfield (2000) identifies four intellectual traditions in which the term critical reflection is used – all with a different meaning: the tradition of ideology critique, the psychotherapeutically inclined tradition, the tradition of analytic philosophy and logic, and the tradition of pragmatist constructivism.

In the tradition of *ideology critique*, critical reflection refers to the process by which people learn to recognize how uncritically accepted and unjust dominant ideologies are embedded in everyday situations and practices (Brookfield, 2000). Although reflection is a mental activity, its aim should be social action (Kemmis, 1985) targeted at revealing and transforming power relations (Alvesson and Willmott, 1996) as providing the basis for a more just society (Reynolds, 1998) and individual autonomy (Mc Carthy, 1978).

In the *psychotherapeutically* inclined tradition, critical reflection focuses on the identification and reassessment of inhibitions acquired in childhood as a result of various traumas (Brookfield, 2000). Through critical reflection, people become conscious of how and why the structure of psycho-cultural assumptions has come to hamper the way they see themselves and their relationships.

In the tradition of *analytic philosophy and logic*, critical reflection refers to recognizing erroneous beliefs, distinguishing between prejudices and facts, opinion and evidence, judgement and valid inference, and being capable of using different forms of reasoning (Brookfield, 2000). To be a critical thinker is to base one's beliefs and actions on reasons and, therefore, critical thinking can be seen as the educational equivalent of rationality (Siegel, 1989).

The tradition of *pragmatist constructivism* emphasizes the role people play in building their own experiences and meanings. In this tradition, critical reflection helps people to understand their experience and to reject universal and generalizable truths (Brookfield, 2000).

Critical reflection as a systematic cognitive process

When we compare the four intellectual traditions and their definitions of critical reflection, we see that all these definitions implicitly typify critical reflection as a systematic cognitive process that is targeted towards a specific ideal and that there is also a large deal of rationality involved in the ideals that critical reflection should serve. Of all traditions, the tradition of analytic philosophy and logic has the strongest focus on rationality, as the principle of this tradition is to stimulate the capability of critically reflecting on itself, instead of any ideal outside of this. Siegel (1997) even sees rationality and critical thinking as completely coextensive because both concepts focus on the significance of reason in believing and acting. In the tradition of ideology critique, we can see a strong focus on the principle of individual autonomy in relation to the influence of societal and political systems. Critical reflection is instrumental in realizing this ideal, as through critical reflection people become aware of the situation that is repressing their autonomy. Also in the psychotherapeutically inclined tradition, critical reflection is understood as a rational way to realize the ideal of individual autonomy and freedom in relation to the restraints of psycho-cultural assumptions. This tradition has a stronger accent on the individual and reflection on the self (Reynolds, 1998; Swan and Bailey, 2004), instead of on trying to transform political realities. The tradition of pragmatist constructivism emphasizes the ideal of individual autonomy by helping people to form their own judgements and to decline generalizable truths. This tradition has strongly influenced the development of a cultural bias favouring reflective discourse and scientific inquiry and, thus, theoretical negligence to the role of affect in learning (Yorks and Kasl, 2002). In this tradition, which is strongly influenced by the work of John Dewey, experience has been conceptualized as a resource that can be catalogued, objectified and reflected on rather than something that is a verb or a felt encounter (Yorks and Kasl, 2002).

Normative aspects of definitions of critical reflection

All conceptualizations of critical reflection are normative, representing 'good thinking' rather than describing observed ways of thinking. This is reflected in the recurrent use of normative expressions such as 'proper reflection on these experiences will result in a form of ideology critique' (Brookfield, 2000, p. 39) and 'although reflection is a mental action its aim should be social action' (Kemmis, 1985). This relates to the preceding points, as theories of rationality are a part of epistemology, which is a normative discipline (Rickert, 1998) resulting in theories of how people ought to think rather than how they actually do think. It might explain the tendency in the literature on critical reflection to focus on debates about what is required in order that critical reflection is right, true and 'really critical'. The psychotherapeutically inclined tradition has been criticized for its strong focus on the individual and reflection on the self (Reynolds, 1998; Swan and Bailey, 2004), thereby distracting attention from political realities. The tradition of analytic philosophy and logic has been criticized for its failure to recognize that assumptions about knowledge play a central role in recognizing a problematic situation (King and Kitchener, 1994); and that steps for approaching a problem, such as formulating and then testing hypotheses, cannot be applied if the individual does not recognize that a problem exists.

Relatively few studies have focused on operationalizing critical reflection (Van Woerkom and Croon, 2008), on the degree to which people are capable of critical reflection or on the extent to which critical reflection actually leads to the realization of particular ideals.

Nevertheless, several studies (Brooks, 1989; Scott, 1991) have shown that critical reflection and rationality are often given too much weight and that intuition, other ways of knowing, emotions and empathy are of equal significance in psychological, convictional or behavioural transformation processes (Taylor, 1997). Furthermore, although in most literature in the field of adult education promoting rationality is seen as a basis for stimulating critical consciousness (Tisdell et al., 2000), the emphasis on rational control and mastery has been criticized as a Eurocentric, masculinist view of knowledge creation (Brookfield, 2000).

THE NEGLECTED ROLE OF THE UNCONSCIOUS IN CRITICAL REFLECTION

Though the more unconscious aspects of experience are often neglected, they may be more important for learning than is generally acknowledged. Implicit learning is the acquisition of knowledge that takes place mostly independent of conscious efforts to learn and largely in the absence of explicit knowledge about what was acquired (Eraut, 2000; Reber, 1993). Laboratory studies show that knowledge of complex patterns may be obtained without intention or awareness and that implicit knowledge surpasses what one can verbalize (Jiang and Chun, 2001; Reber, 1993; Reber et al., 2003). Since implicit knowledge is not available to consciousness, it is also not accessible for critical reflection.

Intuitive practitioners

On the model put forward by Dreyfus and Dreyfus (1986; 2005), experts are intuitive practitioners who base their actions on intuitions that have developed through a long experience in practice, instead of on systematic and laborious problem solving. While rational learning requires agreement about goals, since these require what information should be collected and how it should be analysed, goals are often difficult to formulate or are ambiguous (Sadler-Smith, 2006). Furthermore, rational learning also requires agreement about cause-and-effect relationships since this may inform plans and predictions about future actions and their outcome. However, cause-and-effect relationships may also be ambiguous, effects may be hard to attribute and causes hard to isolate (Sadler-Smith, 2006). Especially in ambiguous situations, facing ill-defined, non-routine problems and when faced with conflicting facts or inadequate information, rational models of learning and problem solving do not perform satisfactorily (Sinclair and Ashkanasy, 2005).

Sometimes people think too much . . .

Cognitive reflection may even impede the learning process in some cases (Taylor, 2001). Instead of critical reflection, sometimes taking a break from the problem or 'sleeping on it' has been shown to be more effective. A study from Dijksterhuis, Bos, Nordgren and Van Baaren (2006), for instance, indicates that where simple choices indeed produce better results after conscious thought, choices in complex matters should be left to unconscious thought. Reflection may not always lead to a realistic self-awareness (Rhee, 2003). In an experiment, students who were given repeated opportunities to reflect about their self-directed change process concerning managerial skills were compared to students who were not given a similar opportunity. Although both groups improved their skills during the programme, the reflective group had a greater awareness of its own change than the comparison group, but overestimated the amount of improvement. Interestingly, despite the greater behavioural change, the comparison group displayed an extremely low level of awareness of change. Moreover, one could question the human capability to engage in critical reflection, since many adults do not operate at the level of cognitive functioning that is needed for this activity (Merriam, 2004). Lakoff and Johnson (1999) even suggest that the metaphor of self-reflection is cognitively unrealistic because it ignores the pervasive and indispensable workings of the cognitive unconscious.

Conscious reflection is not always necessary

Besides the questions whether critical reflection always leads to better outcomes, and whether humans are even capable of critical reflection, there is also evidence that transformative learning does not always develop through conscious reflection. Transformative learning refers to the process of 'constructing and appropriating new and revised interpretations of the meaning of an experience in the world' (Taylor, 2008, p. 5). A review of empirical studies (Taylor, 1997) showed that, in many cases, meaning structures were altered on a non-conscious level outside the awareness of the individual, without deliberate rational examination of assumptions. Ball's (1999) study of transformative experiences among people who had developed a commitment to global sustainability found that they did not recall any period of reflection as part of their transformation: 'Any reflective activities happened inconspicuously perhaps even unconsciously, and in the context of everyday activities' (p. 261). Parks Daloz et al. (1996) found that transformation developed not necessarily through reflection but embedded in encounters with others; over time these increasingly induced a sense of diversity and 'consciousness of connection' (p. 215). Burgoyne and Hodgson (1983) also concluded that transformation seems to occur through a gradual and tacit learning process that gradually erodes one belief and builds another with a gradual accumulation of evidence and experience. Personally relevant learning experiences may offer only subtle messages that only in retrospect may prove to be transformative (Dirkx et al., 2006). Learning does not arise from reflection on experience but from learning in experience – tacit, practical forms of questioning knowledge and exploring constructions of identities and realities (Cunliffe and Easterby-Smith, 2004). For example, in a study on the learning process of intercultural competency, Taylor (1994) found that some participants living in a second culture had seemed to emphasize immediate action more so in response to their intercultural challenges, assuming that thinking about the problem would only slow them down. Several participants experienced a perspective transformation by just trying to accept every situation as it was, in a non-judgemental way, instead of trying to think.

Mindfulness

This way of learning seems to relate to the concept of mindfulness, which can be described as bringing one's complete attention to the present experience and deliberately observing one's internal experiences in an accepting, non-elaborative and non-judgemental way (Baer, 2003). Although the concept of mindfulness seems in a number of aspects quite distinct from the concept of critical reflection (attention to the present instead of reflecting on experience in the past, an accepting and non-judgemental attitude instead of a focus on evaluating and challenging assumptions), several researchers (Baer, 2003; Bond and Hayes, 2002; Langer, 1997) have shown that the practice of mindfulness may lead to changes in thought patterns, or in attitudes about one's thoughts, and to a deeper self-awareness (Healy, 2000).

THE NEGLECTED ROLE OF EMOTIONS IN CRITICAL REFLECTION

A second problem related to the rationalistic bias in most approaches towards critical reflection is that the relation between emotion and reflection has until recently been largely underanalysed and undertheorized in the literature on reflection (Swan and Bailey, 2004). Most theories on critical reflection do not include emotions. When they do, they regard the manifestation of emotions as a need that has to be addressed before actual learning can take place (Dirkx, 2006), emphasizing the importance of controlling or 'de-emotionalizing' emotions (e.g. by treating emotions as facts) (Vince, 2001). Few scholars regard emotion as integral to the meaning-making process and as demonstrative of underlying and unconscious forms of meaning associated with learning (Dirkx, 2006). This reflects a strong cultural bias in Western societies for subordinating feeling and emotion to rational, propositional thought and discourse (Yorks and Kasl, 2002). Within the positivist tradition, emotions are only allowed to play a role of suggesting hypotheses for investigation, but not in testing hypotheses (Jaggar, 1997). However, feminist studies of epistemology have long argued against the stance taken by Western notions of rationality wherein emotions are perceived as the enemy of reason.

Emotion is indispensable to knowledge

Jaggar (1997) argues that although many classic epistemological theories regard emotions as subversive of knowledge, emotion is in fact indispensable to knowledge. Mature human emotions are socially constructed on several levels and are closely related to values. On the one hand, values presuppose emotions; if we had no emotional responses to the world, we should never come to value one state of affairs more highly than another. On the other hand, emotions presuppose values; the object of an emotion is a complex state of affairs that is evaluated by the individual. For instance, one could never feel betrayed without the existence of social norms about fidelity. So, rather than passive or involuntary responses to the world, emotions should be seen as ways in which we actively engage in and even construct the world. The distinction between the cognitive and the affective, or emotional, exists both in psychology as an academic discipline that has been dominant in theory development on learning, and more generally in our culture and language, and can be traced back as far as the ancient Greek distinction between logos and psyche (Illeris, 2002). Learning psychology as a part of cognitive psychology is concerned with knowledge and epistemology, while personality psychology is concerned with the development and structure of the personality, or how we become who we are.

Emotions can spark learning

However, recent research conducted by neurologists and educators shows a strong link between emotion and reason, feelings and thoughts, thereby disproving that emotion is the enemy of reason (Weiss, 2000). Learning does not take place without emotional arousal. Learners need emotions to direct their actions towards particular goals by focusing attention on them and the processes that lead to their realization. Emotion drives attention, which drives learning, memory and problem-solving behaviour. Purely objective reasoning cannot determine what to notice, what to attend to and what to inquire about (Taylor, 2001).

A review of empirical studies revealed that transformative learning is not just rationally driven but also relies strongly on the exploration and resolution of feelings (Taylor, 1997). So, it is very likely that emotions are also needed to start up the process of critical reflection, as has also been shown by Swan and Bailey (2004), who found in their interviews with managers that emotions are often catalysts for reflection. Some managers even saw emotions as more truthful or energizing than the intellect or rationality. By exploring one's feelings, greater self-awareness and change in meaning structures occur (Taylor, 2001). Cope and Watts (2000) found that the critical incidents that led six small business owners to critical reflection were in essence emotional events, representing a period of intense feelings, both at the time and during subsequent reflective interpretation. Although the conflict that one of the business owners experienced with his employees proved very painful and difficult at the time, it resulted both in double-loop learning at an organizational level (Argyris and Schön, 1996) and transformational learning on a personal level.

Emotions may block reflection

On the other hand, emotions may also inhibit critical reflection or make individuals ambivalent towards critical reflection as emotions reflect complex and competing desires – to avoid, to serve, as well as to challenge established expectations, norms and power relations (Reynolds and Vince, 2004). Vince (2002) shows how the anxiety that results from having to say something difficult or challenging, or by the pressures of an unfamiliar task, may either promote or discourage learning. Individuals are faced with a 'strategic moment' (p. 79), where the anxiety can either be held and worked through, towards some form of insight, or it can be ignored and avoided, creating a 'willing ignorance' (p. 79). In that moment of feeling anxious, it is possible to move in either direction, towards learning or away from it. As the experience of critically reflecting on one's own assumptions and actions may provoke even more anxiety than more instrumental forms of learning, this theory seems especially relevant for explaining why critical reflection is so difficult. Only when one is able to hold the uncertainty created by anxiety long enough for risks to be taken, is one capable of critical reflection. This suggests that critical reflection should be conceptualized as an experience linking reason and feeling (Taylor, 2001) instead of an experience of controlling emotions.

ENGAGING GROUPS IN CRITICAL REFLECTION

Interventions aimed at facilitating critical reflection often involve small groups of learners reflecting upon a critical incident that is significant to their professional practice. The purpose of the activity is to examine that incident in order to learn from it. Engaging a group in critical reflection is not always easy.

Engaging in critical reflection can be mentally and emotionally unsettling, and a source of disruption (Reynolds, 1999).

- Although it is often left to the learners to choose either a 'negative' or a 'positive' critical incident, the majority of participants pick a problematic or even traumatic incident but subsequently become distressed discussing – and thus reliving – those experiences (Fook and Askeland, 2007).
- Critical reflection may lead to the questioning of shared understandings and beliefs (theory of action), which may undermine the basis of colleague-ship, promote conflict and cynicism, and may displace individuals to the periphery of their professional group (Brookfield, 2000).
- Also questioning taken-for-granted methods and activities may bring about conflict and render personal or collective decision making more difficult (Reynolds, 1998).

Although many authors writing on organizational learning stress the importance of the role that conflict can play in collective learning (Argyris and Schön, 1996; Senge, 1990; Swieringa and Wierdsma, 1992; Van den Bossche et al., 2006), conflicts about tasks can easily transform into personal conflicts, which may harm informal relationships between workers, and therefore stifle learning rather than promote it (Van Woerkom and Van Engen, 2009). Also, people respond differently when their assumptions are challenged. For some, critical reflection involves replacing one set of certainties with another; for others, the fracturing of firmly held beliefs results in anxiety, feelings of power-lessness and even a (temporary) loss of the sense of identity (Reynolds, 1999).

Another perspective: Appreciative inquiry and related fields

Originally developed in the 1980s, AI (Cooperrider and Whitney, 2005; Barrett, Fry and Whittock, 2011) is now a well-established method for organizational change and a full-fledged alternative to traditional organization development approaches. Instead of focusing reflection on problems or what we do not want, AI is an approach that is based on the idea that it is worthwhile to focus reflection on what we do want (the 'provocative proposition'), and on the glimpses of the desired future that are already existent in the present moment. Surprisingly often, reflection processes such as 'stopping smoking' or 'reducing the amount of customer complaints' get stuck because we do not focus the reflection on what we really want to achieve, but rather on a 'reversed negative'. Both are very different from real positive objectives such as 'living healthy and having plenty of energy' or 'creating happy customers'. And more often than not, reflection focuses on the gap between where a team is 'now' and where it wants to be, rather than on those examples in everyday reality that are already consistent with the desired future (the successes). Proponents of AI (Cooperrider and Srivastva, 1987; Cooperrider et al., 2003; Watkins and Mohr, 2001) argue that traditional problem-focused interventions such as collective group inquiry and critical reflection may be even instrumental in creating the problems that those interventions intend to solve. Teams that focus on discovering organizational problems socially construct an image of deficiency, which may evoke defensiveness, divisiveness and conflict (Cady and Caster, 2000). Representations of deficiency lower team members' self-efficacy and creativity (Fry and Barrett, 2002; Ludema et al., 2001). AI socially constructs an environment of mutual competency and cohesiveness (Bushe, 1998; Cady and Caster, 2000), and teams using AI inquire into organizational successes, best practices and peak experiences (Cooperrider et al., 2003).

Positive psychology

About a decade ago, theorists started to argue that the key to the flourishing of individuals, groups and institutions lay not with repairing negative qualities in life but with building and fostering positive ones (Seligman, 2002; Seligman and Csikszentmihalyi, 2000). Special emphasis was put on the study of strengths and virtues instead of studying weakness and damage (Seligman and Csikszentmihalyi, 2000). This shift in focus, which is referred to as the positive psychology movement, quickly gained popularity amongst organizational researchers and led to several branches of research such as positive organizational scholarship (Cameron and Caza, 2004; Cameron et al., 2003), positive organizational behaviour (Luthans, 2002), strengths coaching (Govindji and Linley, 2007; Linley and Harrington, 2006) and strength-based development (Hodges and Clifton, 2004). Solution-focused change (Cauffman, 2007; Visser, 2009) is another member of this 'family of positive perspectives' (Tjepkema and Verheijen, 2009).

INTERVENTIONS FOR FOSTERING POSITIVE CRITICAL REFLECTION

So far, what we have argued is that critical reflection (a) should not be understood as a totally conscious process; the unconscious and 'things we cannot grasp' are also part of learning; and (b) like all kinds of learning, critical reflection is not devoid of emotion. Or, to put it more sharply: emotion is a strong driver for learning (and may also block it). A positive approach to reflection might be an interesting angle from which to explore interventions for facilitating critical reflection, since this approach is not purely analytical but leaves room for unconscious learning as well, and because it works with positive emotions that fuel behavioural change. In the final part of this chapter, we will therefore explore some of the tools and techniques that can be used for critical reflection in groups.

Reflective dialogue

One important common denominator of all of these interventions is that they are designed to help the group engage in a 'dialogue', not a 'discussion'. Scharmer (2000) has made a clear distinction between different types of conversation. A conversation can be either focused on the 'whole' or on the 'parts' (e.g. one's own interest), and it can be either non-reflective (aimed at affirming existing beliefs) or reflective. A reflective dialogue is characterized by people focusing on parts of the whole, but they do so in an inquisitive way: asking questions, investigating firmly held beliefs in themselves and the other. A generative dialogue is a level of group conversation that goes one step beyond that: the group becomes focused on the whole, and starts thinking of new approaches in order to reach a common goal. In such a conversation – that is almost impossible to get into right from the start – the group is in 'flow': forgetting the time. Also, afterwards, it is hard for the group members to remember how exactly they came to certain conclusions, and which idea came from whom (Scharmer, 2000) (Figure 3.1).

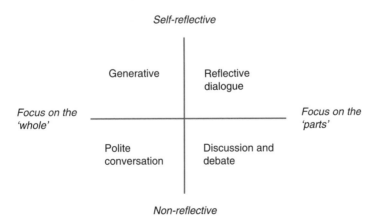

Figure 3.1 Four fields of conversation
Source: Scharmer (2000). Reproduced with permission of Otto Scharmer.

FOCUS ON A POSITIVE GOAL

A second vantage point for effective interventions for critical reflection in groups is that they focus the group's attention towards the desired objective in order to create positive energy for change, whether that is 'solving a problem' or 'building capacity'. Barrett and Fry (2005) describe the 'normative momentum', claiming that in those situations in which the group is faced with conflicts, passive energy and demotivation, the focus should be to get the group back to an acceptable level. Restoration and problem solving will provide energy and a constructive focus for the group reflection. Focusing on the problem itself, or trying to analyse how the problem came about, however, has the potential to 'only make matters worse' partly because they will create thought patterns that help the group explain how they got where they are, but not how to get from there to a better situation. That will create stress and negative emotions that might decrease the group's potential for reflection and learning. In a situation where a group on the whole is not doing too badly, it is even more harmful to focus on the problems – because that will set back the group's self-image – and it is even more powerful to focus energy on 'the dream': where does the group want to go? What is the positive future they want to work towards? This creates positive emotions.

Using tacit knowledge

A third important underlying principle of these interventions is that they leave room for the unconscious, and deliberately try to 'let the unconscious do its work'. Drawing upon Polanyi's (1966) expression 'we know more than we can tell', positive critical reflection techniques deliberately look 'below the surface' and use concepts such as stories and images to also help capture and use that part of our knowledge that is largely implicit and tacit, but best captured in metaphors (Nonaka and Takeuchi, 1995).

The interventions that are described below are:

- positive in outlook and focused on reflection backwards (successes from the past) and inquiry forward (the desired future);
- evoking and using energy for learning and change in a deliberate way;
- mindful of the pivotal role of the 'unconscious' and implicit aspect of learning.

This is not an exhaustive list, but illustrative examples of approaches that have been both documented in professional literature and tried in practice. Three of the interventions (learning from success, learning history and appreciative interview) are rather well documented and tried. The second set (grumpy moments and 2*2 questions, which are explained later in this chapter on p. xxxx) are more experimental in nature and have been tested mainly in the second author's own practice.

INTERVENTION 1: LEARNING FROM SUCCESS

Generally, problems and difficult situations form the starting point for group reflection. One group member puts forward a difficult situation, and others help to find an answer. The technique 'learning from past successes' (De Haan, 2001) takes a radically different vantage point. Instead of a current problem, past successes form the basis for sharing knowledge and learning. These successes may (but don't have to) be linked to current problems. The group then does not dive in at the problem, but rather looks for the 'positive deviance' (Cooperrider and Avital, 2004); those instances in which the problem was not there. For example, a team experiencing problems in their co-operation might look for a situation in which one of them experienced great teamwork. The group can then analyse that successful situation and derive lessons for dealing with the current problem.

Learning from success: Overview of the method

Step 1: Participant introduces success case
One of the participants shares a success story: a positive experience, something that went really well. Others listen and write down what they hear as key factors in the success.

Step 2: Make a list of success factors
Take a flip over and write down the success factors in two columns:

- Left: initiatives, qualities, strengths, activities of the participant who shared the success story;
- Right: context characteristics, support from others ...

The case owner listens and adds to the list.

Step 3: Deepening the understanding
A round of questions and of listening. The group tries to discover the key success factors, or the basic principles, sometimes hidden beneath

---

the ones that were mentioned in the initial flip over. Note these on a second sheet.

Step 4: Evaluation
The group reflects together on the question: what do we learn from this conversation?

Source: De Haan (2001). Reproduced with permission of Eric De Haan.

INTERVENTION 2: APPRECIATIVE INTERVIEW

The process of AI is radically different from the problem-solving approach (Cooperrider and Avital, 2004). Where the problem-solving approach focuses on determining what is not working, analysing the cause of the problems and possible solutions, AI focuses on qualities and what has been accomplished already, the desired future and ambitions for the future. The '4D' process was designed to help groups go through such a process. In an appreciative interview, the first step is to identify the 'positive topic': the objective the group wants to focus the reflection on. Then, the group goes through the following four steps:

- **Discovery:** sharing stories and experiences of instances, or moments, in which the positive topic was already there.
- **Dream**: envisioning a future in which the ideal situation is always there. What would it look like?
- **Design**: determining the point of focus and the ambition. If you want to grow towards the desired future (the dream), what then, in the here and now, do you need to focus on? What do you want to realize in the next months?
- **Destiny**: planning for action.

Overview of the method

Different techniques may be used in designing an AI process, such as storytelling, interviewing, images and movies, dialogue, etc. Here, we focus on the **appreciative interview**, in which team members interview each other in twos or threes, and plenary discuss their findings.

1. Carefully determine the positive topic: what do you want to focus the inquiry upon?
2. Create twosomes, for the interview. These people interview each other with an interview format based on the 4D's. For example:

   (a) Discover: when was the future we want already there? Describe these situations: what did you do? What did others do? What was the effect? What context factors mattered? What qualities did you and other people bring to the situation?

   (b) Dream: imagine a situation in which every day would be like the situation you described in the first step. What would that look like? What would you be doing? And what would others be doing? How would that feel? What would make you proud and happy?

   (c) Design: if you compare your dream to the here and now, what do you need to focus on? What do you need to stop doing? What do you need to start? Where do you want to be in a couple of months from now?

   (d) Destiny: considering your ambition – what will be your first step? Next week... it may be small, but what would be the first practical thing that you can do to work on your objectives?

3. Sharing results from the interviews in a plenary session and deciding on who is going to do what.

Adapted from Cooperrider and Whitney (2005) Reprinted with permission of Berrett-Koehler Publishers

INTERVENTION 3: GRUMPY MOMENTS EXERCISE

Sometimes groups are in a negative frame of mind: complaining or downright angry about a situation. It is very hard to think rationally in such a mindset. A less well-documented reflection exercise that can help to channel that negative energy differently is the 'grumpy moments exercise'. Basically, what this exercise does is help people to understand the cause of their anger, often a value that is threatened or a specific interest that is being ignored. Following Block's (1999) hypothesis that 'someone with resistance is always right' – stick with the resistance for a while and investigate: what sets it off? When people are in touch with their own beliefs and values, they can then focus on ways to do right by them in the current situation.

Overview of the method

1. Formulate groups of two or three participants: small enough for everyone to be actively involved.
2. Groups discuss the following points:

   (a) Remember a grumpy moment: an incident (related to the problem we are discussing) that you were truly angry and grumpy about.

   (b) Describe that grumpy situation like a movie: what happened? Who was involved? What did everyone do? What was the situation? What was the effect?

   (c) What value or particular interest of yours was damaged in that situation? It is obvious that this situation touches a nerve: which one? (You can help the other person by giving some options but be careful to give always more than one option, so as not to steer the person too much).

   (d) Even though you cannot change everything in this situation, what could you do – or what could others do – to meet your interest or your specific value a bit more?

3. Plenary exchange of findings from the interviews with a specific focus on exchanging the answers to question (c) and plenary discussion on question (d): points of action.

INTERVENTION 4: HISTORY LINE

Creating a history line is a way to extract, share and visualize group experiences and group knowledge. It is a very helpful tool for reflection, especially on long-term problems, and if there is a big difference in the amount of time that members have been on the team. Typically, in such situations, reflection becomes more difficult because team members have been going through the same discussion so many times that it becomes harder for them to find a fresh way of thinking that will help them create a breakthrough. And, in the case of 'old' and 'new' team members, sometimes it is hard for the newcomers to fully join in the reflection. They tend to feel that their problems and questions are related to the fact that they are new to the team and, especially when they know that a lot has already been tried to solve a problem, they can feel hesitant to put their ideas to the table. Creating a history line is then a very effective way to get the collective reflection going again. The idea is to create a collective 'map' of the history of an organization, a project, a team or a difficult problem. The group reconstructs and looks backwards, in order to find new ideas on how to go ahead. A history line can be made with a small team or group, but also with an entire organization (Bradbury and Mainemelis, 2001; Bunker and Alban, 1997; Smid et al., 2006).

Overview of the method

There are many variations to making a history line. Here we present a compact exercise that takes about three to four hours with a group of between 8 and 15 persons.

1. Make sure the group is as complete as possible.
2. Decide upon a starting point: where should the history start? (That is a really powerful question to decide with the group. Sometimes people start before the official start of an organization or team).
3. Draw a simple timeline on paper, from start to 'present' – using wallpaper or flip over sheets, taped together to create a long wall of paper.
4. Ask the group to stand in a line, from the start to the present that reflects the moment they joined the organization/team/ project/problem ... Let the group figure it out for themselves: what is the right order? Often seeing the team standing in that order is very interesting and powerful for the team.
5. Make an inventory of important moments with the team. What moments, stories, events should not be left out of the history line of the team? A smart way to do this is to make small groups of people who joined the team at about the same time and ask them to share stories and decide which ones should be on the history line. Have each group write the significant moments on small pieces of paper. After each group has made a stack of papers, the next step is to have a plenary session in which the group tapes all the papers to the wall, one by one. A facilitator is needed here to summarize, and let the story unfold as all the group members put in their input. The focus is

on re-creating the story, getting the facts straight (or at least the way in which they were experienced).

6. The next step is to rate the different experiences: when did you feel you were successful, when not? What is the difference between the two? And the broader question: which patterns emerge?

7. Finally, group participants are asked to think of the next step. If this was the past, what is the next step going to be? What should be the next chapter in the history of this team/organization/project/problem?

Sources: Bradbury (2001): Bunker and Alban (1997); Tjepkema (2011).

2*2 QUESTIONS

Sometimes reflection is not productive, because team members are not really engaged. They think rationally about the problem, but don't involve their drive and emotions. A very simple exercise to tackle this is the 2*2 questions exercise that is also very future-oriented. It consists of two sets of questions.

The first set concerns the objective: where do you want to go? The first question (importance) helps to create focus: what are the reasons for wanting a specific change? What makes it essential? Those reasons can be very diverse: helping a specific client, being able to do your work, fulfilling the strategic agenda, etc. The second question – how will you get there? – then helps to formulate the result that people want to achieve, in a way that people can actually 'see' it happen. So this is not about formulating a performance target or a SMART goal. This is about describing the desired future, like a short film in which people see themselves and their surroundings. For instance, ask them to describe a few critical incidents. Helpful questions: what do you see yourself do? What do others do? What is the effect?

Then comes the second set of questions, which deal with the action: 'How will you get there?' It is not so much reflection on what happens now; it is an exercise to reflect on where you want to go (as an individual or as a team). Question no. 3 – what do you really need? – is asked when you know what is 'the job to be done'. Key here is to get people to think as if they are going on an expedition, with other people. Whom do you need? What resources or tools are necessary? What competencies will these challenges ask of you? These questions help to choose and organize those necessary resources (and/or coaching in order to develop certain skills). The fourth question – what is your first step? – deals with making it concrete, making appointments, setting a target or a date and starting the expedition.

Although this exercise may seem atypical to 'critical reflection', we would argue that it is still useful in this regard. Not all reflection has to be after-the-act. In fact, pro-active critical reflection on topics such as drive and ambition, necessary skills and necessary people may be very helpful. Often, groups tend to start processes without fully thinking through such elements, which may stifle learning and growth along the way (Van Rooij, 2009).

Overview of the method

1. **Importance**: what makes your objective important to you? Why do you want to invest money, time, energy? What meaning does it represent for you?
2. **Result**: what is the result that would make you content? If you picture a movie, or an image of yourself, after you have succeeded … what do you see? What do you see yourself doing, what happened, what do you see others doing? What is no longer there?
3. **Conditions and competences:** whom do you need in order to get to where you want to go? What is necessary to have (in place)? What can't you do without? What competencies will be called upon?
4. **Action:** what will be your first step? What will be the second?

Source: Van Rooij (2009). Based on De Jong-Van Rooij (2009). Reproduced with permission of Kessels and Smit.

CONCLUSION

Common views of critical reflection tend to regard this process as a very rational one. In this chapter, we have argued that emotion and the unconscious factor in learning should also be addressed if we want to facilitate individuals and teams in critical reflection. A significant part of reflection takes place in the unconscious, without us being aware of it, and emotions are an integral part of learning. When critical reflection is approached as a negative process, the ensuing emotions such as fear and anxiety prohibit learning from taking place. The positive organizational approaches to change, such as AI and solution-focused change, provide an interesting vantage point to address these aspects of critical reflection. These approaches link reflection and inquiry to positive experiences and a clear future dream or goal. That makes them very suitable to use for critical reflection. To illustrate that positivity is not the enemy of criticality, we have provided the reader with a number of tools that try to evoke positive emotions, leave room for the unconscious to work as well and enhance constructive critical reflection in groups.

REFERENCES

Alvesson, M. and Willmott, H. (1996) *Making Sense of Management: A Critical Introduction*. London: Sage.

Argyris, C. and Schön, D. A. (1996) *Organizational Learning II: Theory, Method and Practice*. Reading, MA: Addison-Wesley Publishing Company.

Baer, R. A. (2003) Mindfulness training as a clinical intervention: A conceptual and empirical review, *Clinical Psychology: Science and Practice*, 10(2): 125–143.

Ball, G. S. (1999) Building a sustainable future through transformation, *Futures*, 31(3–4): 251–270.

Barrett, F. J. and Fry, R. E. (2005) *Appreciative Inquiry: A Positive Approach to Building Cooperative Capacity*. Chagrin Falls, OH: Taos Institute.

Barrett, F., Fry, R. and Wittockx, H. (2011). *Appreciative Inquiry: het basiswerk*. Houten: Lannoo Scriptum.

Block, P. (1999) *Flawless Consulting: A Guide to Getting Your Expertise Used*. San Francisco, CA: Jossey-Bass/Pfeiffer.

Bond, F. W. and Hayes, S. C. (2002) ACT at work, in F. W. Bond and W. Dryden (eds), *Handbook of Brief Cognitive Behaviour Therapy* (pp. 117–139). Chichester, UK: Wiley.

Boud, D., Cressey, P. and Docherty, P. (eds) (2006) *Productive Reflection at Work*. Oxon: Routledge.

Bradbury, H. and Mainemelis, C. (2001) Learning history and organizational praxis, *Journal of Management Inquiry*, 10(4): 340–357.

Brookfield, S. D. (2000) The concept of critically reflective practice, in A. L. Wilson and E. R. Hayes (eds), *Handbook of Adult and Continuing Education* (pp. 33–49). San Francisco, CA: Jossey-Bass.

Brooks, A. K. (1989) *Critically Reflective Learning Within a Corporate Context*. Unpublished doctoral dissertation. Teacher' s College, Columbia University.

Brooks, A. K. (1999) Critical reflection as a response to organizational disruption, *Advances in Developing Human Resources*, 1(3): 67–97.

Bunker, B. and Alban, B. (1997) *Large Group Interventions: Engaging the Whole System for Rapid Change*. San Francisco, CA: Jossey Bass.

Burgoyne, J. G. and Hodgson, V. E. (1983) Natural learning and managerial action: A phenomenological study in the field setting, *Journal of Management Studies*, 20(3): 387–399.

Bushe, G. R. (1998) Appreciative Inquiry with teams, *Organization Development Journal*, 16 (3) : 41–50.

Cady, S.H. & Caster, M.A. (2000). A diet for action research: An integrated problem and appreciative focused approach to organization development, *Organization Development Journal*, 18(4): 79–93

Calderhead, J. (1989) Reflective teaching and teacher education, *Teaching and Teacher Education*, 5(1): 43–51.

Cameron, K. S. and Caza, A. (2004) Introduction: Contributions to the discipline of positive organizational scholarship, *The American Behavioral Scientist*, 47(6): 731–739.

Cameron, K. S., Dutton, J. E. and Quinn, R. E. (2003) Foundations of positive organizational scholarship, in K. S. Cameron, J. E. Dutton and R. E. Quinn (cds), *Positive Organizational Scholarship* (pp. 3–13). San Francisco, CA: Berret-Koehler.

Cauffman, L. (2007) *Oplossingsgericht management en coaching [Solution Focused Management and Coaching]*. Amsterdam: Boom.

Cooperrider, D. L. and Srivastva, S. (1987). Appreciative Inquiry in organizational life, in W.P.R. Woodman (ed.), *Research in Organization Change and Development* (pp. 129–169). Greenwich, CT: JAI Press.

Cooperrider, D., Whitney, D. and Stavros, J. (2003) *Appreciative Inquiry Handbook*. San Francisco: Berrett-Koehler.

Cooperrider, D. L. and Avital, M. (2004) Introduction, in D. L. Cooperrider and M. Avital (eds), *Constructive Discourse and Human Organization: Advances in Appreciative Inquiry* (Vol. 1, pp. xi–xxxiv). Oxford, UK: Elsevier Science.

Cooperrider, D. L. and Whitney, D. K. (2005) *Appreciative Inquiry: A Positive Revolution in Change*. San Francisco, CA: Berret-Koehler.

Cope, J. and Watts, G. (2000) Learning by doing: An exploration of experience, critical incidents and reflection in entrepreneurial learning, *International Journal of Entrepreneurial Behaviour and Research*, 6(3): 104–124.

Cunliffe, A. L. (2004) On becoming a critically reflexive practitioner, *Journal of Management Education*, 28(4): 407–426.

Cunliffe, A. L. and Easterby-Smith, M. (2004) From reflection to practical reflexivity: Experiental learning as lived experience, in M. Reynolds and R. Vince (eds), *Organizing Reflection* (pp. 30–46). Hampshire: Ashgate.

De Haan, E. (2001) *Leren met collega's. Praktijkboek intercollegiale consultatie [Learning with Colleagues. Work Book Intercollegial Consultation]*. Assen: Van Gorcum.

Dijksterhuis, A., Bos, M. W., Nordgren, L. F. and Van Baaren, R. B. (2006) On making the right choice: The deliberation-without-attention effect, *Science*, 311(5763): 1005–1007.

Dirkx, J. M. (2006) Engaging emotions in adult learning: A Jungian perspective on emotion and transformative learning, *New Directions for Adult and Continuing Education*, 2006(109): 15–26.

Dirkx, J. M., Mezirow, J. and Cranton, P. (2006) Musings and reflections on the meaning, context, and process of transformative learning: A dialogue between John M. Dirkx and Jack Mezirow, *Journal of Transformative Education*, 4(2): 123–139.

Dreyfus, H. L. and Dreyfus, S. E. (1986) *Mind Over Machine: The Power of Intuition and Experience in the Era of the Computer*. Oxford: Blackwell.

Dreyfus, H. L. and Dreyfus, S. E. (2005) Peripheral vision: Expertise in real world contexts, *Organization Studies*, 26(5): 779–792.

Eraut, M. (2000) Non-formal learning and tacit knowledge in professional work, *British Journal of Educational Psychology*, 70(1): 113–136.

Finlay, L. and Gough, B. (2003) *Reflexivity. A Practical Guide for Researchers in Health and Social Sciences*. Oxford: Blackwell Publishing.

Fook, J. and Askeland, G. A. (2007) Challenges of critical reflection: Nothing ventured, nothing gained, *Social Work Education*, 16(2): 520–533.

Fry, R., & Barrett, F. (2002). Conclusion: Rethinking what gives life to positive change, in R. Fry, F. Barrett, J. Seiling, and D. Whitney (eds.), *Appreciative Inquiry and Organizational Transformation: Reports from the Field* (pp. 263–278). Westport, CT: Quorum.

Govindji, R. and Linley, P. A. (2007) Strengths use, self-concordance and well-being: Implications for strengths coaching and coaching psychologists, *International Coaching Psychology Review*, 2(2): 143–153.

Healy, M. (2000) East meets West: Transformational learning and Buddhist meditation. Paper presented at the 41st Annual Adult Education Research Conference (AERC).

Hodges, T. D. and Clifton, D. O. (2004) Strengths-based development in practice, in P. A. Linley and S. Joseph (eds), *Positive Psychology in Practice* (pp. 256–268). Hoboken, NJ: Wiley.

Illeris, K. (2002) *The Three Dimensions of Learning.* Roskilde: Roskilde University Press.

Jaggar, A. M. (1997) Love and knowledge: Emotion in feminist epistemology, in D. T. Meyers (ed.), *Feminist Social Thought: A Reader* (pp. 384–405). New York: Routledge.

Jiang, Y. and Chun, M. M. (2001) Selective attention modulates implicit learning, *The Quarterly Journal of Experimental Psychology*, 54(A): 1105–1124.

Kemmis, S. (1985) Action research and the politics of reflection, in D. Boud, R. Keogh and D. Walker (eds), *Reflection: Turning Experience into Learning* (pp. 139–163). London: Kogan Page.

King, P. and Kitchener, K. (1994) *Developing Reflective Judgment.* San Francisco, CA: Jossey-Bass.

Lakoff, G. and Johnson, M. (1999) *Philosophy in the Flesh: The Embodied Mind and Its Challenge to Western Thought.* New York: Basic Books.

Langer, E. (1997) *The Power of Mindful Learning.* Reading, MA: Addison-Wesley.

Linley, P. A. and Harrington, S. (2006) Strengths coaching: A potential-guided approach to coaching psychology, *International Coaching Psychology Review*, 1(1): 37–46.

Loughran, J. J. (2002) Effective reflective practice: In search of meaning in learning about teaching, *Journal of Teacher Education*, 53(1): 33–43.

Ludema, J. D., Cooperrider, D. L. and Barrett, F. J. (2001). Appreciative inquiry: The power of the unconditional positive question, in P. Reason and H. Bradbury (eds), *Handbook of Action Research*. Thousand Oaks, CA: Sage Publications.

Luthans, F. (2002) The need for and meaning of positive organizational behavior, *Journal of Organizational Behavior*, 23(6), 659–706.

Mc Carthy, T. (1978) *The Critical Theory of Jurgen Habermas.* Cambridge, MA: MIT Press.

McCutchan, S. (1997) *Transformative Learning: Applications for the Development of Learning Organizations.* Paper presented at the Midwest Research-to-Practice Conference in Adult, Continuing and Community Education, Michigan State University.

Merriam, S. B. (2004) The role of cognitive development in Mezirow's transformational learning theory, *Adult Education Quarterly*, 55(1): 60–68.

Nonaka, I. and Takeuchi, H. (1995) *The Knowledge Creating Company. How Japanese Companies Create the Dynamics of Innovation.* New York: Oxford University Press.

Parks Daloz, L. A., Keen, C. H., Keen, J. P. and Daloz Parks, S. D. (1996) *Common Fire: Lives of Commitment in a Complex World.* Boston, MA: Beacon Press.

Polanyi, M. (1966) *The Tacit Dimension.* New York: Doubleday.

Reber, A. S. (1993) *Implicit Learning and Tacit Knowledge. An Essay on the Cognitive Unconscious.* New York: Oxford University Press.

Reber, P. J., Gitelman, D. R., Parrish, T. B. and Mesulam, M. M. (2003) Dissociating explicit and implicit category knowledge with fMRI, *Journal of Cognitive Neuroscience*, 15(4): 574–583.

Reynolds, M. (1998) Reflection and critical reflection in management learning, *Management Learning*, 29(2): 183–200.

Reynolds, M. (1999) Grasping the nettle: Possibilities and pitfalls of a critical management pedagogy, *British Journal of Management*, 10(2):171–184.

Reynolds, M. and Vince, R. (eds) (2004) *Organizing Reflection.* Hampshire: Ashgate.

Rhee, K. S. (2003) Self-directed learning: To be aware or not to be aware, *Journal of Management Education*, 27(5): 568–589.

Rickert, N. W. (1998) Intelligence is not rational: Commentary on Krueger on social-bias, *Psycoloquy*, 9(51). <http://www.cogsci.ecs.soton.ac.uk/cgi/psyc/newpsy?article=9.51&submit=View+Article> (accessed 22 November 2007).

Rigano, D. and Edwards, J. (1998) Incorporating reflection into work practice, *Management Learning*, 29(4): 431–446.

Sadler-Smith, E. (2006) *Learning and Development for Managers*. Oxford: Blackwell Publishing.

Scharmer, C. O. (2000) Presencing: Learning from the future as it emerges. On the tacit dimension of leading revolutionary change. Paper presented at the Conference on Knowledge and Innovation.

Schön, D. A. (1983) *The Reflective Practitioner*. New York: Basic Books.

Scott, S. M. (1991) *Personal Transformation Through Participation in Social Action: A Case Study of the Leaders in the Lincoln Alliance*. Unpublished doctoral dissertation. University of Nebraska.

Seligman, M. E. P. (2002) *Authentic Happiness: Using the New Positive Psychology to Realize your Potential for Lasting Fulfillment*. New York: Free Press.

Seligman, M. E. P. and Csikszentmihalyi, M. (2000) Positive psychology: An introduction, *American Psychologist*, 55(1): 5–14.

Senge, P. M. (1990) *The Fifth Discipline: The Art and Practice of the Learning Organization*. London: Doubleday.

Siegel, H. (1989) The rationality of science, critical thinking and science education, *Synthese*, 80(1): 9–41.

Siegel, H. (1997) *Rationality Redeemed? Further Dialogues on an Educational Ideal*. New York: Routledge.

Sinclair, M. and Ashkanasy, N. M. (2005) Intuition: Myth or a decision-making tool? *Management Learning*, 36(3): 353–370.

Smid, G., Den Boer, G., Busato, V., Halbertsma, L. and Van der Zouwen, T. (2006) *Learning histories in leer- en veranderingstrajecten* [*Learning Histories in Learning and Change Trajectories*], *Mens en Organisatie*, 3–4: 85–97.

Swan, E. and Bailey, A. (2004) Thinking with feeling: The emotions of reflection, in M. Reynolds and R. Vince (eds), *Organizing Reflection*. Hampshire: Ashgate.

Swieringa, J. and Wierdsma, A. F. M. (1992) *Becoming a Learning Organization: Beyond the Learning Curve*. Wokingham, UK: Addison-Wesley.

Taylor, E. W. (1994) Intercultural competency: A transformative learning process, *Adult Education Quarterly*, 44(3): 154–174.

Taylor, E. W. (1997) Building up the theoretical debate: A critical review of the empirical studies of Mezirow's transformative learning theory, *Adult Education Quarterly*, 48(3): 139–156.

Taylor, E. W. (2001) Transformative learning theory: A neurobiological perspective of the role of emotions and unconscious ways of knowing, *International Journal of Lifelong Education*, 20(3): 218–236.

Taylor, E. W. (2008) Transformative learning theory, *New Directions for Adult and Continuing Education*, 2008(119): 5–15.

Tisdell, E. J., Hanley, M. S. and Taylor, E. W. (2000) Different perspectives on teaching for critical consciousness, in A. L. Wilson and E. R. Hayes (eds.), *Handbook of Adult and Continuing Education* (pp. 132–146). San Francisco, CA: Jossey-Bass.

Tjepkema, S. and Verheijen, L. (eds) (2009) *Van kiem tot kracht: een waarderend perspectief voor persoonlijke ontwikkeling en organisatieverandering* [*An Appreciative Perspective on Personal Development and Organizational Change*]. Houten: BSL.

Van den Bossche, P., Gijselaers, W., Segers, M. and Kirschner, P. A. (2006) Social and cognitive factors driving teamwork in collaborative learning environments: Team learning beliefs and behaviors, *Small Group Research*, 37(5): 490–521.

Van Rooij, M. (2009) *Effectief samenwerken: denken in driehoeken* [*Effective Collaboration: Thinking in Triangles*]. Utrecht: Kessels and Smit.

Van Woerkom, M. and Croon, M. (2008) Operationalising critically reflective work behaviour, *Personnel Review*, 37(3): 317–333.

Van Woerkom, M. and Van Engen, M. (2009) Learning from conflicts: The effect of task and relationship conflicts on team learning and team performance, *European Journal of Work and Organizational Psychology*, 18(4): 381–404.

Vince, R. (2001) Power and emotion in organizational learning, *Human Relations*, 54(10): 1325–1351.

Vince, R. (2002) The impact of emotion on organizational learning, *Human Resource Development International*, 5(1): 73–85.

Visser, C. (2009) *Doen wat werkt [Do What Works]*. Culemborg: Van Duuren.

Watkins, J., and Mohr, B.(2001). *Appreciative Inquiry: Change at the Speed of Imagination*. CA: Jossey Bass.

Weiss, R. P. (2000) Emotion and learning, *Training and Development*, 54(11): 44–48.

Yorks, L. and Kasl, E. (2002) Toward a theory and practice for whole-person learning: Reconceptualizing experience and the role of affect, *Adult Education Quarterly*, 52(3): 176–192.

FURTHER READING

Barrett, F. J. and Fry, R. E. (2005) *Appreciative Inquiry: A Positive Approach to Building Cooperative Capacity*. Chagrin Falls, OH: Taos Institute.

Cooperrider, D. L. and Whitney, D. K. (2005) *Appreciative Inquiry: A Positive Revolution in Change*. San Francisco, CA: Berret-Koehler.

Van Woerkom, M. (2010) Critical reflection as a rationalistic ideal, *Adult Education Quarterly*, 60(4): 339–356.

This chapter is substantially revised and updated from Van Woerkom, M. (2010) Critical reflection as a rationalistic ideal, *Adult Education Quarterly*, 60(4): 339–356.

part 2

TRAINING AND DEVELOPMENT INTERVENTIONS: INDIVIDUAL SKILLS DEVELOPMENT

4

LEARNING STYLES AND COGNITIVE STYLES IN HUMAN RESOURCE DEVELOPMENT

Eugene Sadler-Smith

INTRODUCTION

Human resource development (HRD) is an applied field in which theory has an increasingly important role to play (Torraco, 2004). Lynham (2000) described theories in HRD as providing coherent descriptions, explanations and representations of observed or experienced phenomena. Equally importantly, theories also enable causal relationships to be tested and predictions to be made thereby enabling HRD interventions to be designed, implemented and evaluated more effectively. However, Swanson (2001) noted that HRD practice has often been chided for being atheoretical, that is, having no 'thorough scholarly or scientific basis for the ideas and products being promoted' (p. 301). In order to be credible and useful, HRD research and practice must, in the absence of its own theories, draw upon relevant theories from the contributing literatures in its foundational disciplines (e.g. economics, philosophy, sociology, psychology, organizational behaviour).

The above is as true for the topics that are the subject of this chapter, namely learning styles and cognitive styles, as it is for other aspects of HRD scholarship. The foundational disciplines for styles are primarily psychological, with emerging contributions from cognitive neuroscience. In this chapter, I will select and review one model of learning style and one model of cognitive style, which although they are both problematic in a variety of ways and to varying degrees, each satisfies the vital requirement alluded to above: namely, they are founded upon a theoretical base rooted in the traditions of respective base disciplines. My purpose is to explore how, in the context of HRD, learning styles and cognitive styles have been defined and theorized, what their impact on the field of HRD has been and what claims are made for, and critiques offered of, styles in relation to HRD theory and practice.

STYLES IN GENERAL

Learning styles are 'individual differences in learning based on a learner's preference for employing different phases of the learning cycle' (Kolb and Kolb, 2005, pp. 194–195). Cognitive styles are individual differences in preferences for organizing, processing and representing information, which are 'partly fixed, relatively stable and possibly innate' (Peterson et al., 2009, p. 520). Despite the popularity amongst HRD and educational practitioners (Coffield et al., 2004; Zhang and Sternberg, 2009) of learning styles and cognitive styles in general, they have proven to be somewhat problematical. For example, it is claimed that the study of learning styles and cognitive styles would benefit considerably from a unifying model or conceptual framework (Sternberg, 1997, p. 149) underpinned by a coherent body of psychological theory that takes account of the fact that the complex tasks faced in real-world settings (the domain of HRD) make demands on more than one mode of information processing and require different ways of engaging with experiences. Effective learning, problem solving and decision making demands the use of interdependent and integrated aspects of learning, thinking and feeling; hence a vital competence for individuals in modern business environments is the ability to learn and process information in versatile and integrative ways (Coffield et al., 2004; Hodgkinson and Clarke, 2007; Hodgkinson and Sparrow, 2002; Louis and Sutton, 1991), and it is this richness that simple dichotomies (e.g. 'intuition-versus-analysis') or mere process models (e.g. 'the learning cycle') fail to capture. Moreover, the design and use of poorly theorized and psychometrically weak learning and cognitive style instruments is an issue that has been a particularly vexing problem for styles research (Coffield et al., 2004; Hodgkinson and Sadler-Smith, 2003; Kozhevnikov, 2007). However, this is precisely a matter in which theory can help to resolve a number of long-standing questions and debates.

A continued proliferation of poorly theorized style models that fail to reflect both the realities of real-world learning and relevant bodies of knowledge from contributing disciplines, allied to the use of assessment tools of dubious psychometric value, will dilute the concept of styles in general. This may lead ultimately to its demise in all but the most facile and popularist of realms of learning and development, where high-perceived relevance and face validity need not be matched by theoretical, methodological or psychometric rigour. A concomitant risk is that styles may become promoted as a 'quick fix' or 'fad' and hence perceived as being irrelevant to scholarly members of the HRD community. However, it is self-evident to most experienced educators and HRD practitioners that learners do exhibit clear differences in the ways in which they think about problems and decisions, and in how they engage with the learning process. It is important, therefore, that the field of HRD has at its disposal models of styles that are both theoretically robust and practice-relevant. Two selected models (experiential learning styles and intuition-analysis cognitive styles) will be considered as the basis for this review, which aims to be illustrative and representative (rather than systematic and comprehensive) of the potential that a theoretically driven conceptualization of styles has for HRD.

LEARNING STYLES

Although learning styles are conceptualized in a wide variety of ways (as approaches to studying, preferences for different types of instructional methods, etc.; see Riding and Rayner (1998) for a review), the concept of learning styles in HRD is most often associated with experiential learning and the work of David Kolb (b.1939). In the review by Coffield et al. (2004), they highlighted the fact that learning styles in general have tended to be atheoretic or weakly theorized, but that Kolb is a member of a small and select group of learning styles theorists who 'has not only explicitly based his four learning styles in a theory, he has also developed a theory which has been very widely taken-up', for example in education, counselling, and management and business more generally (i.e. HRD) (Coffield et al., 2004, p. 69).

Experiential learning will be the basis for the discussion of learning styles offered in this chapter for two reasons: first, my concern was to root a discussion of styles (both learning styles and cognitive styles) on models that were a priori theorizable; second, the concern of HRD is not with student learning in educational contexts, but is rather the issue of the differences in learning styles in occupational settings. On this basis, models that could be loosely categorized as 'styles' and are theorizable, for example, Entwistle and colleagues' concept of 'approaches to studying' (Entwistle and Ramsden, 1983), were excluded. Moreover, learning style, when conceptualized in experiential terms as expounded by Kolb in his foundational work, is recognized widely within the HRD community as one of the 'tools of the trade', used frequently in coaching and other learning and development interventions and processes (Wilson, 2010).

The origins of experiential learning theory are traceable to the work of William James (1842–1910), C. G. Jung (1875–1961), John Dewey (1859–1952), Kurt Lewin (1880–1947), Jean Piaget (1896–1980), Paulo Freire (1921–1997) and Carl Rogers (1902–1987) (Kolb and Kolb, 2005), with Dewey, Lewin and Piaget perhaps the most influential amongst this group (Kolb, 1984). Kolb's experiential learning theory (ELT) is not only relevant to styles, it is also one of the most influential stand-alone theories of individual learning in HRD (Sadler-Smith, 2006). For example, at the time of Kayes' review in 2002, there had been over 1500 studies, refereed articles, dissertations and papers conducted on ELT. Interest in the model, its theory and its measurement is ongoing, and research papers frequently appear in psychology, management and education journals. A casual search of the EBSCO database conducted in November 2010 revealed 732 peer-reviewed scholarly articles published in the past 25 years that mention explicitly in the text the term 'experiential learning' and the name 'Kolb'; a similarly casual search of Google Scholar without date restriction yielded almost 21,000 hits.

The central axiom of ELT is that learning is a process whereby 'knowledge is created through the transformation of experience' (Kolb, 1984, p. 41). From its roots in Deweyian pragmatism, ELT emphasizes the central role that experience plays in the learning process. Moreover, ELT is also distinguishable from cognitive learning theories, which emphasize cognition over affect, and from behavioural learning theories, which deny any role for subjective experience in the learning process (Mainemelis et al., 2002). ELT is concerned with 'adaptive flexibility' in terms of the extent to which learners 'integrate the dual dialectics of the learning process conceptualizing/experiencing and acting/reflecting' (Mainemelis et al., 2002, p. 8).

The precepts of ELT relevant to our discussions are as follows. Learning is a cyclical process consisting of the four sequential modes of 'concrete experience' (CE), 'reflective observation' (RO), 'abstract conceptualization' (AC) and 'active experimentation' (AE). Alternate pairs of these modes (CE, RO, AC and AE) are the opposite ends (i.e. poles) of two orthogonal dimensions, namely 'grasping' experiences (i.e. CE–AC) (referred to by Wilson (2010) as 'perceiving') and 'transforming' experiences (i.e. RO–AE) ('processing', Wilson, 2010). As a result of 'hereditary equipment', particular life experiences and the demands of the environment, individuals differ in terms of the way in which they prefer to grasp experiences (i.e. by CE *or* AC, but not both) and how they prefer to transform them (i.e. by RO *or* AE, but not both) (Kolb and Kolb, 2005, p. 195), see Figure 4.1. The combinations of the poles of AC–CE and AE–RO are used in the model to generate four learning styles (diverger, assimilator, converger and accommodator), the characteristics of which are summarized by Kolb and Kolb (2005, pp. 196–197), see Table 4.1. The model also has a 'vertical' developmental trajectory comprising three stages, as follows (Kolb, 1984): acquisition: from birth to adolescence in which basic abilities and cognitive structures develop; specialization: from formal schooling to early work and the personal experiences of adulthood in which a specialized learning style develops; integration: from mid-career to later life in which non-dominant modes of learning come to be expressed. Integrated learning involves the creative tension between the four learning modes where the learner 'touches all of the bases' (Mainemelis et al., 2002). Integration comes over time from a resolution of the dialectics inherent in the model. The dialectic and the circular representation resonate, according to Kolb, with the archetype of the mandala (meaning 'circle') that Jung defined

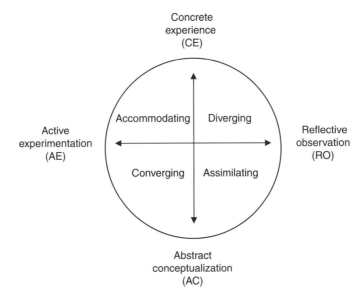

Figure 4.1 Kolb's experiential learning cycle and learning styles
Source: Kayes et al. (2005) reproduced with permission of Sage Publications

Table 4.1 Kolb's learning styles

Accommodators	Divergers
Learn primarily from 'hands-on' experiences, enjoy carrying out plans and being involved in new and challenging experiences, have a tendency to act on 'gut feelings' rather than logical analysis, and prefer to work with others to get things done and test out different approaches.	View concrete situations from different perspectives, perform better in situations that call for the generation of ideas, have broad cultural interests, like to gather information, are interested in people, imaginative and emotional, specialize in the arts, prefer to work in groups, listen with an open mind and like to get personalized feedback.
Convergers	**Assimilators**
Find practical uses for ideas and theories; solve problems and take decisions, are more focused on technical tasks than social and interpersonal issues, prefer to experiment with new ideas, simulations and practical applications.	Can understand a wide array of information and put it into a concise logical form, are less focused on people than on ideas and abstract concepts, privilege 'logical soundness' over 'practical value', and prefer reading, lectures, analysis and having the time to think things over.

Source: Kolb and Kolb (2005; 2009).

as having a quadripartite structure (like a wheel, or flower or cross) wherein poles of light and darkness rotate and resolve.

In the UK, Honey and Mumford (1992) adapted and simplified the concept of experiential learning for use in HRD (and specifically management development) by developing a 'user-friendly' (Woodall and Winstanley, 1998, p. 143) version of the model that consisted of four stages: 'having an experience'; 'reviewing the experience'; 'concluding from the experience'; and 'planning the next step'. The corresponding learning styles are 'activist', 'reflector', 'theorist' and 'pragmatist'. Because Honey and Mumford did not include explicitly the concept of dialectic in their version of experiential learning these do not map 1:1 with Kolb's styles but do correspond with the stages of his cycle. For critical evaluations of the psychometric properties of Honey and Mumford's Learning Styles Questionnaire (LSQ), see Duff (2010) and Sadler-Smith (2001a).

Kolb's Learning Style Inventory (LSI) is a self-report, self-scored instrument in which individuals are required to rank their preferences for each of the four ELT modes (CE, RO, AC and AE) across 12 items (sentence completions corresponding to the four modes, for example, 'I learn best from . . . '), i.e. 48 items in total. By combining CE and AC scores and AE and RO scores, and by interpreting these relative preferences in relation to percentiles, an individual is able to identify their preferred style (i.e. diverger, assimilator, converger or accommodator). Over its 40-year and five-version history, the LSI has undergone a number of modifications and improvements (McCarthy, 2010): in 1985 (LSI-2), 1993 (LSI-2a), 1999 (LSI-3), 2005 (LSI-3.1) and most recently as Kolb LSI-4.0. Kolb himself has gone on record as being resistant to the idea of learning styles becoming stereotypes and the LSI being used to 'pigeonhole' people and their behaviour (Kolb, 1981), presumably because the developmental trajectory is part of the model (but in practice is often overlooked in favour of a simple labelling of individuals).

Kolb and Kolb (2005) acknowledged that much of the debate surrounding ELT centred on the psychometric properties of the LSI, and there has been a long and protracted debate (Coffield et al., 2004) over the LSI's reliability and validity (e.g. Sadler-Smith, 2001b). More recently, Kayes (2002) reported internal consistencies for the LSI-3 of above 0.70 (Cronbach α) for each of the four separate (CE, RO, AC, CE) and combined (AC–CE and AE–RO) scales. Moreover, in a forced-fit two-factor solution (using Principal Components Analysis), Kayes (2005) found that two factors corresponding to the hypothesized AC–CE and AE–RO dimensions accounted for 71 per cent of the variance. Kayes interpreted these findings as corroborating 'prior research supporting the internal reliability of the scales' (2002, p. 249). It should be noted, however, that there is some dispute in the literature regarding analysing forced choice (i.e. ipsatized) scales in this way, and further research using a de-ipsatized form of the instrument might be warranted in order to provide users with further assurances as to its reliability and construct validity.

ELT is a 'well-known' learning theory (Harrison, 2002, p. 8) and has been impactful on the field of HRD. The embracing of ELT may be seen as part of the transition in HRD from an emphasis on training to learning (Woodall and Winstanley, 1998, p. 142), although ELT is 'often presented in a form that arguably distorts Kolb's original [i.e. dialectical] presentation' (Holmes, 2007, p. 225). The ELT and LSI have been used to explore learning and development in a wide variety of fields, for example Kolb and Kolb (2009) reported applications in management, education, information science, psychology, medicine, nursing, accounting and law (see Kayes, 2002). ELT may be operationalized at a number of levels. At its simplest, it may be interpreted as a Lewinian model of a process (akin to other similar problem-solving cycles) with the notion of preferences for the different stages or modes (i.e. styles) bolted on (e.g. in the learning cycle). In this respect, it is highly similar to its derivative, the Honey and Mumford learning cycle and the associated LSQ (see above). Indeed, more recently Kolb and Kolb (2009) have suggested that the four originally identified learning styles (diverger, assimilator, converger and accommodator) may be augmented with four additional styles, each corresponding to the four modes of the cycle (CE, RO, AC, AE). Used in this modified form, it is not easy to see what Kolb's more complex model adds over and above the simpler and more 'manager-friendly' LSQ for HRD applications. At the level of sophistication as originally conceived, ELT is concerned with richer and more complex issues of the tensions between different ways of coming to know the world. The deeper insights that stand to be gained are potentially beneficial to learners in that they may come to understand their own thinking and learning as processes that involve preferences, choices and dialectics, as well as a temporal (whole-life) trajectory. The original formulation of styles (i.e. four of them) is to be preferred over the more recent augmentation (i.e. nine, the eight outlined above plus an additional 'balancing' style; Kolb and Kolb, 2009).

A core idea of Kolb's model is metacognition, i.e. a self-aware and intentional orientation to the processes of learning as well as to their outcomes. Learning style is related to metacognition in several ways: first, metacognition involves 'the active monitoring and consequent regulation and orchestration' of learning processing activities 'in the services of some concrete goal' (Flavell, 1976, p. 232); second, self-awareness of one's habitual and stable preferences for particular aspects of the experiential learning cycle is a necessary precondition for metacognition; third, if HRD practitioners are aware of styles (i.e. their own as well as those of learners), there is an increased likelihood of the effective incorporation of style-related factors into the design of HRD interventions. Eliciting self-perceptions of learning style preferences may 'induce' metacognitive awareness and be especially useful with more difficult learning tasks (Moran, 1991). On the other hand, designing learning materials that suit particular learning styles (i.e. 'matching') might result in learners' increased dependency on a narrow range of habitual information-processing styles, behaviours and strategies, i.e. incorporating styles into HRD might become limiting rather than enhancing (Hayes and Allinson, 1994). Riding and Powell (1993) recommended that the design of learning materials should incorporate a metacognitive dimension, for example, by putting learners into problem-solving situations where they can learn how to become more flexible in their choice and use of strategies, thereby enabling them to become skilled in the development, implementation and modification of learning strategies before any blockages are reached (i.e. metacognition may have an anticipatory rather than remedial function).

As well as critiques of the LSI instrument (see above), ELT itself is not unproblematic. The notion of the 'complete learner' comes under critical scrutiny from Tennant (1988), who argued that the notion of psychological integration inherent in the underlying model is not 'worked out in detail' and in his view is illustrative of a 'Utopian' conception of psychological development (p. 102), which he felt uncomfortable with for several reasons: first, not all situations demand balanced integration of the four stages; second, the LSI is a self-report measure, i.e. preferences for one set of words over another, and not a measure of learning style behaviours per se; third, there is the danger that individuals might be categorized into a more privileged group (i.e. those who can integrate their experiences and construct knowledge) and a less privileged group (i.e. those who are unable to do so) and the words used in the LSI may be confusing and ambiguous to some users. Vince (1998) voiced concerns about the lack of attention in Kolb's model accorded to psychodynamic issues such as power, anxiety, fear and doubt. Reynolds (1997) argued that the individualistic conceptualization is itself limiting; and Holman, Pavlica and Thorpe (1997) contended that the model fails to take into account the significance of social processes. Miettinen (1998) argued that ELT is founded on an idiosyncratic reading of Lewin, Dewey and Piaget. Kayes (2002) responded to these various critiques by arguing that a number of them have 'failed to preserve the fundamental assumptions of ELT', namely the critics appear (paradoxically in some instances) to strip managers of the inherent potential that they have to learn and thereby enable their emancipation (this is axiomatic to ELT), and that this is symptomatic of a critical agenda that 'lacks a developmental pedagogy' (p. 142). Kayes proposed preserving the dialectical nature of ELT whilst simultaneously broadening its theoretical base by accommodating a more complex account of the relationships between worlds of personal experience and social abstraction, for example by embedding experience in a historical, systemic context of language, and the 'multi-paradigmatic' study of learning as 'blurred genre' (p. 143). These latest developments in thinking about ELT, and the associated styles, align with recent developments in critical HRD, for example by viewing learning from a post-structuralist perspective (see Metcalfe and Rees, 2007). Other developments include speculations about the links between ELT and neuroscience and the way that the learning cycle 'arises from the structure of the brain' (Zull, 2002, cited in Kolb and Kolb, 2005, p. 194).

COGNITIVE STYLES

Cognitive ('thinking') styles have been debated in psychology from Galton in the mid-1800s, through James and Jung at the turn of the 19th century, Witkin's seminal work in the middle part of the last century, to the recent contributions of Sternberg and his colleagues (see below). Cognitive styles are consistent individual differences in 'preferred ways of organizing and processing information and experience' (Messick, 1976, p. 4) that are more or less adaptive under different sets of circumstances (Zhang and Sternberg, 2005). There have been numerous descriptive and analytical treatises on the subject (for an up-to-date review see Zhang and Sternberg, 2009), but styles also have been the subject of a number of critical reviews (e.g. Kozhevnikov, 2007); perhaps the most systematic as well as trenchant of these was that of Coffield and his colleagues published in 2004 (research sponsored by the UK government's Learning and Skills Council and Department for Education and Skills and concerned with the question 'Should we [practitioners] be using learning styles?'). Coffield et al. (2004) were essentially pessimistic about the scientific rigour of some styles research and also sceptical about the potential that styles have to improve educational and training practices. That said, their review was not wholly negative: they noted many good points, including the theoretical strengths of Kolb's learning styles model (see above), and the relative strength of Allinson and Hayes' (1996) model of intuition-analysis style in comparison to other available models, theories and measures.

The work of Allinson and Hayes is not only pertinent to our discussions, it is foundational in respect of styles research in management. This is for two reasons: first, the origins of their insightful model may be traced back to a perception of the relevance of styles but a dissatisfaction with Honey and Mumford's learning styles (see above) as an alternative to Kolb (Allinson and Hayes, 1988); second, their systematic analysis focused on the relevance of styles for management practice and organizational behaviour in particular (since much of styles research had been concerned previously with the educational domain, with a number of notable exceptions, for example the work of Kirton, see: Kirton, 2003 for a review and synthesis) in areas such as personnel selection, task design, career guidance and counselling, team building, and training and development (Allinson and Hayes, 1988; Hayes and Allinson, 1994). With respect to the latter, Hayes and Allinson considered the utility both of matching the design of training to the style of the trainee (as Riding and Sadler-Smith (1992) attempted to do) and of mismatching in order that the 'learner develop a wider range of coping behaviours or learning strategies' (Hayes and Allinson, 1994, p. 67). They acknowledged that this gave rise to a difficult dilemma: should HRD 'capitalise on potent cognitive processes ... or improve upon impotent cognitive processes' (1994, p. 67). This is an important matter for HRD practice, but is as yet still largely unresolved.

Hayes and Allinson (1994) were attracted to the notion of the relationship between styles and neurological activity, and the question of whether styles could be classified according to the left-brain/right-brain typology, perhaps thereby pointing to 'important similarities in the wide array of style dimensions reported in the literature' (p. 57). They followed through this line of reasoning in the development of their model of cognitive style by adopting a 'unitary' perspective, i.e. intuition and analysis cognitive styles were conceived as being located at opposite ends of a single dimension of cognitive style, described thus:

> Intuition characteristic of the right brain orientation, refers to immediate judgement based on feeling and the adoption of a global perspective. Analysis, characteristic of the left brain orientation, refers to judgement based on mental reasoning and a focus on detail.
>
> (Allinson and Hayes, 1996, p. 122)

The conceptual basis of this and other work (e.g. Herrmann, 1981) may be traced to the now famous *Harvard Business Review* paper by Mintzberg in 1976 entitled 'Planning on the left side and managing on the right' ('left' and 'right' being the respective hemispheres of the human cerebral cortex). Mintzberg, in drawing attention to his view that management was as much 'art' as 'science', declared that planning was a 'left hemisphere' process (i.e. logical, analytical and verbal) and managing was a 'right hemisphere' process (i.e. creative, intuitive and imagistic). Moreover, he declared that: 'which hemisphere of one's brain is better developed may determine whether a person ought to be a planner or a manager' (1976, p. 49). This idea was gleaned apparently from an interpretation of the psychobiology pioneered by the Nobel Prize Laureate Roger W. Sperry and others, but shaped to fit the management thinking of the time. The scientific basis of the various assertions made by proponents of the left/right brain distinction as applied to the minds of managers (Akinci and Sadler-Smith, 2012) has been called into question from as early as the mid-1980s (e.g. Hines, 1985) but it persists to this day (e.g. Pink, 2005). Recent developments in both cognitive and social psychology, as well as cognitive neuroscience, suggest that a different theoretical position (dual-process theory, or 'two minds model') offers an alternative to the unitary perspective and may provide styles researchers and HRD theory and practice with a more useful lens by which individual differences in the processing of information may be understood and applied.

Conspicuous by its absence from Coffield et al. (2004) is any mention of dual-process formulations of human reasoning (e.g. Chaiken and Trope, 1999; Evans, 2003), notwithstanding the fact that Epstein et al. published their foundational paper entitled 'Individual differences in intuitive-experiential and analytical-rational thinking styles' in the *Journal of Personality and Social*

Psychology in 1996. This is symptomatic of the fact that cognitive styles' researchers themselves have tended to look more broadly and ignore or overlook this potentially important body of theory and research (Akinci and Sadler-Smith, 2012). Stanovich and West (2000), in reviewing the preceding two decades of dual-process theory research, distinguished between two fundamental types of human information processing for which they used the generic terms 'System 1' (contextually dependent, associative, heuristic, tacit, intuitive, implicit/automatic, fast and cognitively undemanding) and 'System 2' (contextually independent, rule-based, analytic and explicit, slow and cognitively demanding). Evans (2003, p. 454) encapsulated this neatly when he described such theories as essentially positing the existence of 'two minds in one brain'.

Dual-process theories provide a simple yet compelling conceptual framework for cognitive style based upon the parallel workings of an intuitive system and an analytical system. These two information-processing modes are qualitatively different in terms of the type of data they draw upon, their operating principles and their outcomes. Moreover, the two systems interact both in their formation and in their operation. For example, in complex tasks under time-pressured conditions, intuitions – referred to by Simon (1987, p. 63) as 'analyses frozen into habit and into the capacity for rapid response through recognition' – enable experts to arrive at involuntary, affectively charged, holistic judgements based on whole-pattern recognition (Dane and Pratt, 2007; Klein, 1998; Salas et al., 2010). Informed intuitive judgement ('intuitive expertise', Kahneman and Klein, 2009) draws upon implicit and explicit knowledge that has become compressed into expertise through appropriate learning, exposure and practice, and feedback (see Hogarth, 2001; 2008). Intuitive expertise is not something that a novice is able to execute effectively (Dreyfus and Dreyfus, 1986), because even though intuition may be fast-to-act it is slow-to-form.

When averaged out over a variety of tasks and the longer term, the majority of individuals have a proclivity to process information using either intuition or analysis, and these predispositions develop as a result of a variety of factors, including age, gender, personality, ability, education and experience, and the nature of the task (Agor, 1989; Allinson and Hayes, 1996; Betsch, 2004; 2008). For example, Betsch (2004) found that people were able to adapt to the requirements of a situation by choosing the appropriate strategy (e.g. opting for intuition when intuitive judgements were appropriate), but preferences led certain individuals to choose intuition more frequently than deliberation (analysis) across all scenarios; that is, certain people tended to opt for their preference (intuition or analysis) in spite of the demands of the task (Betsch, 2008).

As noted above, there is a wide variety of dual-process theories, and on the basis that intuitions are 'affectively charged judgements that arise through rapid, non-conscious and holistic associations' (Dane and Pratt, 2007, p. 40) Epstein's (1994), Cognitive-Experiential Self-Theory (CEST) is considered especially pertinent to a discussion of intuition-analysis because of the importance this theory accords to affect (i.e. 'gut feel', 'hunch' or 'vibes'). The differences between the intuitive and analytical systems in terms of CEST are summarized in Table 4.2 below.

Self-report, in spite of its inherent drawbacks, has been the mainstay of cognitive styles' assessment as a means of eliciting individuals' subjective

Table 4.2 The intuitive and analytical systems

Intuitive system[a]	Analytic system[b]
Operates automatically, preconsciously, nonverbally, rapidly, effortlessly.	Inferential logical system that operates consciously, primarily verbally, slowly and effortfully.
Holistic, associated with affect and operates on the basis of schemas acquired from lived experiences.	Abstract, analytic, and affect-free and evolutionarily the more recent of the two systems.
Mediated by 'vibes' from past events, concrete images, metaphors and narratives;	Its operations are analytic, intentional, effortful, logical and mediated by conscious appraisal of events.
Faster to act but slower to form and more resistant to change than the rational system, and changes with repetitive/intense experience.	Slower, with a more delayed action than the experiential system but changes more rapidly on the basis of strength of argument and new evidence.
Imagistic and non-verbal (encodes reality in concrete images, metaphors and narratives).	Verbal in that it encodes reality in abstract symbols (e.g. words and numbers).
Enables 'holistic problem solving of a different order than that achievable by the rational system alone' (Epstein, 2008, p. 26).	

[a]I have preferred the term 'intuitive' over 'experiential' for three reasons: the term intuition has greater currency in management research (see for example: Dane and Pratt, 2007; Miller and Ireland, 2005); the intuitive system subsumes experientiality; intuition is the operation of the experiential system (Epstein, 2004).
[b]The term 'analytical' is offered as an alternative to 'rational' because there are strong elements of rationality in both systems (Slovic et al., 2004).
Source: Epstein (1994; 2008); Epstein et al. (1996).

perceptions of their preferences for organizing and processing information. From the perspective of dual-process theory, three candidate instruments for styles research in HRD may be considered that are simple, compact and easy-to-use in field settings, namely: the Cognitive Style Index (CSI, Allinson and Hayes, 1996); the Preference for Intuition and Deliberation scale (PID, Betsch, 2004); and the Rational Experiential Inventory (REI, Epstein et al., 1996).

The Cognitive Style Index (CSI) (Allinson and Hayes, 1996) has been used widely and its reliability is claimed to be well established (Coffield et al., 2004). However, the unifactoral structure of the intuition-analysis construct argued for by Allinson and Hayes is problematic in the present context in two respects. First, it is not wholly compatible with a dual-process conceptualization of styles. Second, it fails to stand up to empirical scrutiny in that exploratory and confirmatory factor analytical studies suggest that, contrary to the guidance offered by Allinson and Hayes (1996) and the position adhered to by Hayes, Allinson, Hudson and Keasey (2003), it ought to be scored as two separate intuition and analysis factors (Backhaus and Liff, 2007; Coffield et al., 2004; Hodgkinson and Sadler-Smith, 2003).

More recently, Betsch (2004) developed the 'Preference for Intuition and Deliberation scale' (PID) for the 'reliable, fast and economical' assessment of individual strategy preferences based on the presumption that intuition is not the opposite of deliberation (Betsch, 2008, p. 234). The PID consists of two slightly negatively correlated ($p < -0.20$) nine-item scales, PID-intuition ($0.76 \leq \alpha \leq 0.81$) and PID-deliberation ($0.76 \leq \alpha \leq 0.84$). However, further concurrent and convergent validity studies of this instrument are required, especially in organizational settings using work-based populations. Hence, any assertions regarding its reliability and validity for styles research in HRD must be considered preliminary.

The Rational Experiential Inventory (REI) (Epstein et al., 1996) makes the conceptual presumption of individual differences in preferences for two styles of processing (experiential/intuitive and rational/analytical); the issue of whether these styles are bipolar (i.e. intuitive *or* analytical) or unipolar (i.e. intuitive *and* analytical) was left as an open question by Epstein and his colleagues, to be resolved empirically. Compelling evidence for unipolarity was observed from Epstein et al. in their factor and correlational analyses. Specifically, correlations between scores on the experiential/intuitive ('Faith in Intuition') and rational/analytical ('Need for Cognition') scales of the long (31-item) form of the REI were low and non-significant ($r = -0.07$), thus indicating that 'rational [analytical] and experiential [intuitive] processing are independent' (Epstein et al., 1996, p. 395). A shorter ten-item version of the REI exhibited a similarly low scale inter-correlation ($r = -0.09$) (Epstein et al.,

1996). An experiential (intuitive) thinking style was found to be positively associated with a variety of constructs, including esoteric beliefs, superstitious thinking, openness, positive thinking, naive optimism, favourable interpersonal relationships, extraversion, agreeableness, favourable beliefs about the self and the world, sense of humour, creativity, social popularity, empathy and aesthetic judgement – and negatively associated with categorical thinking (Epstein, 2008, p. 28). More recently, Sadler-Smith (2011) considered the implications of the positive relationship between the intuitive style and predispositions towards superstitious reasoning and its relevance for learning and development (e.g. the potential for intuitive biases accruing as a result of resistance to scientific explanations).

The observation that the rational and intuitive styles are relatively independent, rather than paired opposites, creates the potential for learners to be guided through HRD interventions into making a shift from a 'specialized' (i.e. high/low or low/high) or 'indifferent' (i.e. low/low) orientation to a 'versatile' (i.e. high/high) orientation (see Figure 4.2), thereby enabling them to acknowledge both rationality and intuition as contextually appropriate ways for taking decisions and solving problems (Hodgkinson and Clarke, 2007; Sadler-Smith, 2002). Further evidence for the existence of two independent processing systems (the reflective [C] system and reflexive [X] system) and their underlying neural substrates is offered by Lieberman (2007).

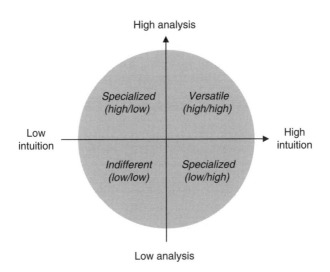

Figure 4.2 Dual-process model of cognitive styles
Source: Sadler-Smith (2001); see: Hodgkinson and Clarke (2007); Louis and Sutton (1991); Sadler-Smith (2002).

More generally, management education and HRD often give priority to the development of learners' rational and analytical reasoning skills (e.g. in strategic analysis, financial or marketing planning, project management). The development of learners' analytical style is not as pressing an issue as the development of their intuitive style; hence my comments pertaining to the application of cognitive styles will focus exclusively on the development of intuition. This is not a new idea; for example, in 1981 Taggart and Robey made a plea for the inclusion of intuition in the management education curriculum. Sadler-Smith and Shefy (2004) argued that little appears to have changed in the intervening decades since Taggart and Robey (1981) in developing this aspect of management education and HRD, and that the rational model prevails because it is safe, familiar, comforting and reassuring, and in many situations (such as those that are computationally complex), it works perfectly well. Intuition, on the other hand, is unfamiliar, disconcerting, paradoxical and ambiguous. They further argued – given that intuition is pervasive, automatic and involuntary – that it cannot be ignored in HRD and that learners have much to gain from acknowledging and understanding their intuitions. Moreover, in certain situations (e.g. time-pressured decisions and creative problem-solving), intuition is important and even necessary, and managers need to be able to harness its potential whilst being aware of its dangers. HRD practitioners can assist managers in developing their intuitive style by attending to several issues, namely: practice, feedback and awareness (Burke and Sadler-Smith, 2006; Emery, 1994; Hogarth, 2001; 2008; Robinson, 2006; Sadler-Smith and Shefy, 2004).

Informed intuition ('intuitive expertise', see Salas et al., 2010) is domain-specific and relies upon pattern matching using complex, domain-relevant schemas (Dane and Pratt, 2007) acquired over time through explicit and implicit learning processes. These complex, expert schemas support fast, non-conscious pattern recognition (Klein, 1998; Simon, 1987). An individual's level of expertise in a domain sets an upper limit on the extent to which he or she can exercise intuitive judgement (a corollary of this is that it is difficult, ill-advised and probably perilous for a novice to engage in intuitive judgement in high-risk situations). In order to become more 'intuitive' in a specific domain, an individual must engage in explicit, focused and deliberate practice. HRD stands well placed to accelerate these processes through mentoring, coaching and role modelling.

Given that the intuitive learning system is operating constantly and without conscious awareness, Hogarth (2001) emphasized the importance of feedback in the learning of intuitions. He drew a distinction between two contrasting types of 'learning structure' for developing intuition: first, those that are favourable, i.e. environments that enhance intuition with timely, accurate, relevant, honest, constructive feedback – these are 'kind' structures for learning intuitions; second, those that are unfavourable and which lead to the development of poor intuitive awareness through little or low-quality feedback – these are 'wicked' structures for learning (Hogarth, 2001). HRD practitioners, but more especially line managers, have an important role in this process since it is they who are likely to be aware of the capabilities of employees, and it is they (i.e. line managers) who are able to set appropriately stretching goals that can enable an individual to venture outside of her or his current zone of competence. Moreover, it is line managers who are likely to be involved in the assessment and monitoring of performance, hence they are uniquely placed to facilitate the acquisition of employees' intuitive expertise and the development of an intuitive style. This applies at all levels of an organization – not only to managers. However, at senior levels strategic intuition has a special role to play, and executive coaching may be used to leverage executive intuition and intuition in top management teams (TMTs) (Mavor et al., 2010; Sadler-Smith and Shefy, 2004). Notwithstanding these suggestions, the acquisition of intuitive expertise is argued to require around ten or more years of learning and practice in order to develop sufficiently complex schemas in a particular domain (Ericsson et al., 2007; Kahneman and Klein, 2009; Salas et al., 2010). The inevitable conclusion is that even though HRD may be able to speed-up the process, there can be no substitute for prolonged periods of intense learning, deep immersion, and sustained effort and practice in order to develop 'intuitive muscle power' (Klein, 2003).

Intuitions, as noted previously, are affectively charged judgements (Dane and Pratt, 2007). Therefore, becoming intuitively aware involves not only treating affect as a form of data, but also being able to distinguish between different forms of affect (e.g. feelings, moods and emotions). The term affect, when used in connection with intuition, refers to a non-emotional feeling (i.e. it does not encompass, for example, happiness or love) (see Sadler-Smith, 2008). Emotions (more intense) and moods (longer lasting) are distinct from the positively or negatively valenced 'affective charge' that accompanies intuitive judgement, the latter was referred to by Epstein (2008, p. 28) as 'vibes', including feelings such as 'disquietude' or 'agitation' (negative valence). As well as not confounding emotions with intuitions, individuals need to be able to distinguish intuitive judgements (i.e. ones that are made on an informed basis and arise rapidly and involuntarily though non-conscious pattern recognition and holistic associations) from biased social judgements made on the basis of individual or cultural prejudices, and from hopes, desires or wishful thinking (Sadler-Smith, 2010). Novel methods such as focusing

(Gendlin, 1981) and mindfulness meditation (Kabat-Zinn, 1990) hold considerable untapped potential for raising learners' awareness of their somatic states and visceral responses, and in enabling individuals to develop a more finely attuned intuitive style (Sadler-Smith and Shefy, 2007).

In sum, intuitive expertise is domain specific and is developed over time through explicit and implicit learning. However, HRD can play a vital role in creating the conditions for and accelerating the acquisition of intuitive expertise.

SUMMARY AND CONCLUSION

In examining the challenges facing HRD, Torraco (2004) noted that theoretical research in HRD takes many forms, including new theories, extensions of existing theories and incorporating new theories into the field; he also questioned whether HRD has reached beyond its theory base. In this chapter, I have argued that as far as styles in HRD is concerned theories are vital, and that there are two viable theories from organizational behaviour (Kolb) and psychology (Epstein) that provide a firm foundation for further research and practical applications. Torraco (2004) also noted that one of the roles of theory in HRD is to define applied problems. In the case of styles, the problem that faces HRD researchers and practitioners is a shared one: how to acknowledge and accommodate individual differences in learning and cognition and to do so in ways that enhance the learning process and its outcomes both for individuals and for the organizations of which they are a part. In so far as an HRD theory of styles is concerned, there isn't one. Therefore, it is necessary to 'borrow' theories from the source fields of psychology and organizational behaviour, and apply these basic research findings to the 'messy' target field of HRD. This is not only 'laudable' (Torraco, 2004, p. 175), in the case of styles it is vital: without drawing upon the requisite theories from source disciplines, any HRD interpretation or application of learning styles and cognitive styles would be untheorized, and could thereby be criticized justifiably – a notable problem with much of styles research and practice for which Coffield et al. (2004) rightly chided styles researchers and practitioners both in management and education. The development and further application of ELT (already well established) and the incorporation of dual-process theory (less well established) into HRD have the potential to create synergies and provide insights for many different aspects of learning, and not merely to the narrow field of styles. One challenge for HRD researchers with an interest in styles and theory is the development of a framework or model that integrates the complementary insights from theories of learning style (e.g. ELT) and cognitive style (e.g. CEST) and which will facilitate the achievement of scientifically rigorous and practice-relevant discoveries within the applied domain of HRD research.

REFERENCES

Agor, W. H. (1989) *Intuition in Organizations: Leading and Managing Productively.* Newbury Park, CA: Sage.

Akinci, C. and Sadler-Smith, E. (2012) Intuition in management research: A historical review, *International Journal of Management Reviews*, 14(1): 104-122.

Allinson, C. W. and Hayes, J. (1988) The Learning Styles Questionnaire: An alternative to Kolb's inventory, *Journal of Management Studies*, 25(3): 269–281.

Allinson, C. W. and Hayes, J. (1996) The Cognitive Style Index: A measure of intuition-analysis for organisational research, *Journal of Management Studies*, 33(1): 119–135.

Backhaus, K. and Liff, J. P. (2007) Cognitive styles and approaches to studying in management education, *Journal of Management Education*, 31(4): 445–466.

Betsch, C. (2004) Preference for intuition and deliberation (PID): An inventory for assessing affect- and cognition-based decision-making, *Zeitschrift für Differentielle und Diagnostiche Psychologie*, 25(2): 179–197.

Betsch, C. (2008) Chronic preferences for intuition and deliberation in decision making: Lessons learned about intuition from an individual differences approach. In H. Plessner, C. Betsch and T. Betsch (eds), *Intuition in Judgement and Decision Making* (pp. 231–248). New York: Lawrence Erlbaum Associates.

Burke, L. A. and Sadler-Smith, E. (2006) Instructor intuition in the educational context, *Academy of Management Learning and Education*, 5(2): 169–181.

Chaiken, S. and Trope, Y. (eds) (1999) *Dual-Process Theories in Social Psychology*. New York: Guildford Press.

Coffield, F., Moseley, D., Hall, E. and Ecclestone, K. (2004) *Learning Styles and Pedagogy in Post-16 Learning: A Systematic and Critical Review*. London: Learning and Skills Research Centre.

Dane, E. and Pratt, M. G. (2007) Exploring intuition and its role in managerial decision making, *Academy of Management Review*, 32(1): 33–54.

Dreyfus, H. L. and Dreyfus, S. E. (1986) *Mind over Machine: The Power of Human Intuitive Expertise in the Era of the Computer*. New York: Free Press.

Duff, A. (2010) A note on the psychometric properties of the Learning Styles Questionnaire (LSQ), *Accounting Education*, 10(2): 185–197.

Emery, M. (1994) *Dr Marcia Emery's Intuition Workbook: An Expert's Guide to Unlocking the Wisdom of your Subconscious Mind*. Englewood Cliffs, NJ: Prentice Hall.

Entwistle, N. J. and Ramsden, P. (1983) *Understanding Student Learning*. London: Croom Helm.

Epstein, S. (1994) Integration of the cognitive and the psychodynamic unconscious, *American Psychologist*, 49(8): 709–724.

Epstein, S. (2008) Intuition from the perspective of cognitive-experiential self-theory. In H. Plessner, C. Betsch and T. Betsch (eds), *Intuition in Judgement and Decision Making* (pp. 23–37). New York: Taylor and Francis Group, LLC.

Epstein, S., Pacini, R., Denes-Raj, V. and Heier, H. (1996) Individual differences in intuitive-experiential and analytical-rational thinking styles, *Journal of Personality and Social Psychology*, 71(2): 390–405.

Ericsson, K. A., Prietula, M. J. and Cokely, E. T. (2007) The making of an expert, *Harvard Business Review*, 85(7/8): 115–121.

Evans, J. St., B.T. (2003) In two minds: Dual-process accounts of reasoning, *Trends in Cognitive Sciences*, 7(10): 454–459.

Flavell, J. H. (1976) Metacognitive aspects of problem solving. In L. Resnick (ed.), *The Nature of Intelligence* (pp. 231–235). Hillsdale, NJ. Lawrence Erlbaum.

Gendlin, E. (1981) *Focusing*. New York: Bantam Books.

Harrison, R. (2002) *Learning and Development*. London: CIPD.

Hayes, J. and Allinson, C. W. (1994) Cognitive style and its relevance for management practice, *British Journal of Management*, 5(1): 53–71.

Hayes, J., Allinson, C. W., Hudson, R. S. and Keasey, K. (2003) Further reflections on the nature of intuition-analysis and the construct validity of the Cognitive Style Index, *Journal of Occupational and Organizational Psychology*, 76(2): 269–278.

Herrmann, N. (1981) The creative brain, *Training and Development Journal*, 35(1): 10–16.

Hines, T. (1985) Left brain/right brain mythology and implications for management training, *Academy of Management Review*, 12(4): 600–606.

Hodgkinson, G. P. and Clarke, I. (2007) Exploring the cognitive significance of organizational strategizing: A dual-process framework and research agenda, *Human Relations*, 60(1): 243–255.

Hodgkinson, G. P. and Sadler-Smith, E. (2003) Complex or unitary? A critique and empirical re-assessment of the Allinson-Hayes Cognitive Style Index, *Journal of Occupational and Organizational Psychology*, 76(2): 243–268.

Hodgkinson, G. P. and Sparrow, P. R. (2002) *The Competent Organization*. Buckingham: Open University Press.

Hogarth, R. M. (2001) *Educating Intuition*. Chicago, IL: The University of Chicago Press.

Hogarth, R. M. (2008) On the learning of intuition. In H. Plessner, C. Betsch and T. Betsch (eds), *Intuition in Judgment and Decision Making* (pp. 91–105). New York: Lawrence Erlbaum Associates.

Holman, D., Pavlica, K. and Thorpe, R. (1997) Rethinking Kolb's theory of experiential learning in management education: The contribution of social constructionism and activity theory, *Management Learning*, 28(2): 135–148.

Holmes, L. (2007) The learning turn in education and training: Liberatory paradigm or oppressive ideology? In C. Rigg, J. Stewart and K. Trehan (eds), *Critical Human Resource Development: Beyond Orthodoxy* (pp. 221–238). Harlow: Pearson.

Honey, P. and Mumford, A. (1992) *The Learning Styles Manual*. Maidenhead: Peter Honey Publications.

Kabat-Zinn, J. (1990) *Full Catastrophe Living: How to Cope with Stress, Pain and Illness using Mindfulness Meditation*. London: Piatkus.

Kahneman, D. and Klein, G. (2009) Conditions for intuitive expertise: A failure to disagree, *The American Psychologist*, 64(6): 515–526.

Kayes, A. B., Kayes, D., and Kolb, D.S (2005) Experiential learning in teams, *Simulation and Gaming*, 36(3): 330–354.

Kayes, D. C. (2002) Experiential learning and its critics: Preserving the role of experience in management learning and education, *Academy of Management Learning and Education*, 1(2): 137–149.

Kayes, D. C. (2005) Internal validity and reliability of Kolb's Learning Style Inventory version 3 (1999), *Journal of Business and Psychology*, 20(2): 249–257.

Kirton, M. J. (2003) *Adaption-innovation in the Context of Diversity and Change*. London: Routledge.

Klein, G. (1998) *Sources of Power: How People Make Decisions*. Cambridge: MIT Press.

Klein, G. (2003) *Intuition at Work*. New York: Doubleday.

Kahneman, D. and Klein, G. (2009). Conditions for intuitive expertise: A failure to disagree. *American Psychologist*, 64(6): 515.

Kolb, A. Y. and Kolb, D. A. (2005) Learning styles and learning spaces: Enhancing experiential learning in higher education, *Academy of Management Learning and Education*, 4(2): 193–212.

Kolb, A. Y. and Kolb, D. A. (2009) The learning way: Metacognitive aspects of experiential learning, *Simulation and Gaming*, 40(3): 297–327.

Kolb, D. A. (1981) Experiential learning theory and the Learning Style Inventory: A reply to Freedman and Stumpf, *Academy of Management Review*, 6(2): 289–296.

Kolb, D. A. (1984) *Experiential Learning: Experience as the Source of Learning and Development*. Upper Saddle River, NJ: Prentice-Hall.

Kozhevnikov, M. (2007) Cognitive styles in the context of modern psychology: Toward an integrated framework, *Psychological Bulletin*, 133(3): 464–481.

Lieberman, M. D. (2007) Social cognitive neuroscience: A review of core processes, *Annual Review of Psychology*, 58: 259–289.

Louis, M. R. and Sutton, R. I. (1991) Switching cognitive gears: From habits of mind to active thinking, *Human Relations*, 44(1): 55–76.

Lynham, S. A. (2000) Theory building in the human resource development profession, *Human Resource Development Quarterly*, 11(2): 159–178.

Mainemelis, C., Boyatzis, R. and Kolb, D. A. (2002) Learning styles and adaptive flexibility: Testing experiential learning theory, *Management Learning*, 33(1): 5–33.

Mavor, P., Sadler-Smith, E. and Gray, D. E. (2010) Teaching and learning intuition: Some implications for HRD and coaching practice, *Journal of European Industrial Training*, 34(8/9): 822–838.

McCarthy, M. (2010) Experiential learning theory: From theory to practice, *Journal of Business and Economics Research*, 8(5): 131–139.

Messick, S. (1976) Personality consistencies in cognition and creativity. In S. Messick (ed.), *Individuality in Learning* (pp. 4–23). San Francisco, CA: Jossey Bass.

Metcalfe, B. D. and Rees, C. J. (2007) Feminism, gender, and HRD. In C. Rigg, J. Stewart and K. Trehan (eds), *Critical Human Resource Development: Beyond Orthodoxy* (pp. 87–105). Harlow: Pearson.

Miettinen, R. (1998) About the legacy of experiential learning, *Lifelong Learning in Europe*, 4(3): 165–171.

Mintzberg, H. (1976) Planning on the left side and managing on the right, *Harvard Business Review*, 54(4): 49–58.

Moran, A. (1991) What can learning styles research learn from cognitive psychology? *Educational Psychology*, 11(3/4): 239–245.

Peterson, E. R., Armstrong, S. J. and Rayner, S. G. (2009) Researching the psychology of cognitive style and learning style: Is there really a future? *Learning and Individual Differences*, 19(4): 518–523.

Pink, D. (2005) *A Whole New Mind: Why Right-Brainers will Rule the Future*. London: Marshall Cavendish International.

Reynolds, M. (1997) Learning styles: A critique, *Management Learning*, 28(2): 115–134.

Riding, R. J. and Powell, S. (1993) Thinking and education. *Educational Psychology*, 13(3/4): 217–227.

Riding, R. J. and Rayner, S. G. (1998) *Cognitive Styles and Learning Strategies*. London: David Fulton.

Riding, R. J. and Sadler-Smith, E. (1992) Type of instructional material, cognitive style and learning performance, *Educational Studies*, 18(3): 323–340.

Robinson, L. A. (2006) *Trust your Gut: How the Power of Intuition can Grow your Business*. Chicago, IL: Kaplan Publishing.

Sadler-Smith, E. (2001a) Three or four learning styles? A reply to Swailes and Senior, *International Journal of Selection and Assessment*, 9(3): 207–214.

Sadler-Smith, E. (2001b) The relationship between learning style and cognitive style, *Personality and Individual Differences*, 30(4): 609–616.

Sadler-Smith, E. (2002) The role of cognitive style in management education, *Academy of Management Proceedings*, C1-C6, Academy of Management Annual Meeting, Denver, Colorado, August.

Sadler-Smith, E. (2006) *Learning and Development for Managers: Perspectives from Research and Practice*. Oxford: Blackwell.

Sadler-Smith, E. (2008) *Inside Intuition*. Abingdon: Routledge.

Sadler-Smith, E. (2010) *The Intuitive Mind*. Chichester: John Wiley and Sons/Jossey-Bass.

Sadler-Smith, E. (2011) The intuitive style: Relationships with local/global and visual/verbal styles, gender, and superstitious reasoning, *Learning and Individual Differences*, 21: 263–270.

Sadler-Smith, E. and Shefy, E. (2004) The intuitive executive: Understanding and applying 'gut feel' in decision-making, *Academy of Management Executive*, 18(4): 76–91.

Sadler-Smith, E. and Shefy, E. (2007) Developing intuitive awareness in management education, *Academy of Management Learning and Education*, 6(2): 186–205.

Salas, E., Rosen, M. A. and DiazGranados, D. (2010) Expertise-based intuition and decision making in organizations, *Journal of Management*, 36(4): 941–973.

Simon, H. A. (1987) Making management decisions: The role of intuition and emotion, *Academy of Management Executive*, 1(1): 57–64.

Stanovich, K. E. and West, R. F. (2000) Individual differences in reasoning: Implications for the rationality debate, *Behavioural and Brain Sciences*, 23(5): 645–726.

Sternberg, R. J. (1997) *Thinking Styles*. Cambridge: Cambridge University Press.

Swanson, R. (2001) Human resource development and its underlying theory, *Human Resource Development International*, 4(3): 299–312.

Taggart, W. and Robey, D. (1981) Minds and managers: On the dual nature of human information processing and management, *Academy of Management Review*, 6(2): 187–195.

Tennant, M. (1988) *Psychology and Adult Learning*. London: Routledge.

Torraco, R. J. (2004) Challenges and choices for theoretical research in human resource development, *Human Resource Development Quarterly*, 15(2): 171–188.

Vince, R. (1998) Behind and beyond Kolb's learning cycle, *Journal of Management Education*, 22(3): 304–319.

Wilson, C. (2010) Tools of the trade, *Training Journal*, January: 65–66.

Woodall, J. and Winstanley, D. (1998) *Management Development: Strategy and Practice*. Oxford: Blackwell.

Zhang, L. F. and Sternberg, R. J. (2005) A threefold model of intellectual styles, *Educational Psychology Review*, 17(1): 1–53.

Zhang, L. F. and Sternberg, R. J. (2009) Preface. In L. F. Zhang and R. J. Sternberg (eds), *Perspectives on the Nature of Intellectual Styles* (pp. xi–xvi). New York: Springer.

FURTHER READING

Akinci, C. and Sadler-Smith, E. (2012) Intuition in management research: A historical review, *International Journal of Management Reviews*, 14(1): 104–122.

Armstrong, S. J., Cools, E. and Sadler-Smith, E. (2012) The role of cognitive styles in management: Reviewing 40 years of research, *International Journal of Management Reviews*, 14(3): 238–262.

Armstrong, S. J. and Fukami, C. (eds) (2009) *The SAGE Handbook of Management Learning, Education and Development*. Los Angeles, CA: Sage.

Sinclair, M. (ed.) (2011) *Handbook of Intuition Research*. Cheltenham: Edward Elgar.

5

NEURO-LINGUISTIC PROGRAMMING (NLP): A CASE OF UNORTHODOX KNOWLEDGE IN HRD?

Paul Tosey

INTRODUCTION

Wilson (2005, p. 3) describes HRD as representing 'the latest evolutionary stage in the long tradition of training, educating and developing people for the purpose of contributing towards the achievement of individual, organizational and societal objectives'. Neuro-Linguistic Programming (NLP), a practice that has become widespread not only in HRD but also in management (Knight, 2002), education (Churches and Terry, 2007), psychotherapy (Wake, 2008), health care (Henwood and Lister, 2007) and more, can be considered part of this stage. In HRD it is used as a method of coaching (Linder-Pelz, 2010), in consulting, and as the subject of management training courses, whether in NLP explicitly or as an approach to subjects such as leadership, communication skills, selling and negotiation.

Tosey and Mathison (2009, p. 24) offer this working description of NLP:

NLP is interested in **how** people communicate, perform skills and create experiences through patterns of thought and behaviour, mediated by language. NLP helps people create more preferable and useful (to them) experiences in the world, typically by attending to and modifying those patterns of thought and behaviour.

This description emphasizes 'how' because NLP is typically interested in the process of communication or behaviour rather than its content. For example, NLP has suggested that the strategy used by people who are good at spelling (see Bandler and Grinder, 1979) involves a process comprising three main steps:

1. visualize the word in your mind's eye;
2. spell it out to yourself (i.e. not out loud);
3. check whether it is correct through feeling (e.g. a gut sense of whether it is right or not).

It is this strategy – the 'how' of spelling – that is of interest in NLP, not the person's knowledge of words themselves. As illustrated by this spelling strategy, NLP can offer innovative ways of thinking and practising that are alternatives to established knowledge. It is probably more fruitful to think of NLP as a system of practical knowledge that offers a range of heuristics (i.e. maps for taking action) than as a rival to academic psychology. By way of analogy, NLP is more like a route map and guide book that offers suggestions or excursions to take by car, than a precise or scientific account of how the car's engine works.

NLP is also a controversial practice, and attitudes towards it are often sharply opposed. The voices of evangelists and diehard critics can drown out a more nuanced spectrum of views and experiences. NLP may therefore represent an interesting case study of unorthodox knowledge in HRD. This chapter will discuss some of the chief criticisms made of NLP.

HOW HAS THE CONCEPT BEEN DEFINED?

One story goes that the founders of NLP, Richard Bandler and John Grinder, created the phrase 'neuro-linguistic programming' with their tongues firmly in their cheeks, and that its quasi-academic obscurity is intentionally mischievous. Yet while NLP is not formally part of any established academic discipline, its constituent terms are neither random nor lacking entirely in connection to academic fields. For example, Grinder spent a year at Rockefeller University where psychologist George A. Miller worked from 1968 until 1979 (Hirst, 1988). Miller, perhaps best known as the originator of the idea that we can hold in mind seven plus or minus two pieces of knowledge at any one time (Miller, 1956), was interested in cognitive neuroscience and psycholinguistics. The term 'neuro-linguistics' was first used by Alfred Korzybski (1941, p. xxxviii), a thinker whose work appears to have been introduced to NLP's founders by the English philosopher Gregory Bateson in the early 1970s.

Dilts et al. (1980, p. 2) offered a reasoned explanation of the terms in the title:

> For us, behaviour is programmed by combining and sequencing neural system representations – sights, sounds, feelings, smells and tastes – whether that behaviour involves making a decision, throwing a football, smiling at a member of the opposite sex, visualizing the spelling of a word or teaching physics. A given input stimulus is processed through a sequence of internal representations, and a specific behavioural outcome is generated.

> 'Neuro' (derived from the Greek neuron for nerve) stands for the fundamental tenet that all behaviour is the result of neurological processes. 'Linguistic' (derived from the Latin lingua for language) indicates that neural processes are represented, ordered and sequenced into models and strategies through language and communication systems. 'Programming' refers to the process of organizing the components of a system (sensory representations in this case) to achieve specific outcomes.

WHERE DID THE TERM ORIGINATE?

Accounts of NLP typically fail to acknowledge its historical, cultural and intellectual antecedents. It is sometimes presented as if it sprang, fully formed, from California in the 1970s, independent of social, cultural and historical contexts and influences. However, a timeline of NLP should probably take us at least as far back as the 1940s. For example, the self-help movement that emerged in the USA in the mid-20th century may have shaped the identity of NLP more than is usually acknowledged. NLP's emphasis on the potential for the person to change themselves and its promises of empowerment and personal success reflect an ethos of self-improvement that can be traced back to Dale Carnegie's *How to Win Friends and Influence People* (first published in 1936) and Norman Vincent Peale's *The Power of Positive Thinking* (1952). Ideas found virtually unchanged in NLP include Carnegie's emphasis on appreciating the other person's point of view and on adjusting one's own response in order to influence other people, and Peale's interest in boosting self-confidence.

Other significant influences include the human potential movement. In the 1960s, California was a hub of countercultural activity – alternative therapies, new lifestyles, experimental rock music, altered states of consciousness and a drug culture whose values were initially formed by the rejection of materialism, coupled with political dissent that was fuelled by revulsion towards the Vietnam War. It became the centre of the growth movement, epitomized by the Esalen Institute that was founded at Big Sur in 1962, in which Virginia Satir and Fritz Perls were both involved. Satir and Perls would become central influences on early NLP.

Tosey and Mathison (2009) argue that NLP's ideas and approach draw from two main intellectual sources. The first is cybernetics (Wiener, 1965), a cross-disciplinary view of how systems are organized based on feedback, which was developed in the 1940s and 1950s; among the key people involved in this development was Gregory Bateson (Montagnini, 2007), who later became a major influence on NLP. Cybernetics is defined as the science of 'control and communication in the animal and the machine' (Capra, 1996, p. 51), the term being derived from the Greek *kybernetes* meaning 'steersman'.

In cybernetics, the concept of *feedback* refers to information through which a system 'knows' whether or not it is on track to achieve its goal. Positive feedback confirms that it is on track; negative feedback informs it that it needs to alter course. In the case of the thermostat, a temperature lower than the threshold at which the thermostat has been set is negative feedback; this activates the switch and turns the heating on. These terms have, unfortunately, become loaded with implications that distort their original cybernetic usage. *Positive* has somehow acquired the sense of meaning 'praise', being something good and desirable, whereas *negative* is thought of as 'criticism', implying the opposite. In the cybernetic sense, both are equally necessary to the effective maintenance of a goal-directed activity. There, positive and negative have no emotional valence, but are simply two types of directives that are only meaningful in the context of the achievement of a goal. Life would be impossible without negative feedback because organisms could not regulate themselves.

This conception of feedback gives rise to the notion of *circular causality*, which is key to understanding not only cybernetics but also the essence of Bateson's thinking and, consequently, NLP itself. Imagine a cat sitting on someone's lap, purring as it is being stroked. Did the cat's purring cause the person to start stroking it? Did the stroking cause the purring? From a cybernetic view, it is not possible to identify a simple, single cause. In the prevailing Newtonian ways of explaining events, however, every event, 'B', has a physical cause, 'A', that is located outside the event itself and prior to it in time – a red ball lands in the pocket of the billiard table because of the angle, velocity and force of the ball that hit it.

The difference between classic mechanical and cybernetic modes of explanation is highly significant. While Bandler and Grinder do not go so far as to state that NLP is a form of cybernetics, they clearly adopt the central principles of cybernetics when they say that 'the basic unit of analysis in face-to-face communication is the feedback loop' (Bandler and Grinder, 1979, p. 2).

The second intellectual influence is constructivism. Essentially this says that people cannot know 'reality' per se, so inevitably they act according to constructions that they create. Constructivism arrives in NLP largely via the work of the Palo Alto Mental Research Institute in the 1960s, in which Bateson again and also Virginia Satir were involved. The Palo Alto researchers were interested in the relevance of logical types and game theory to human interaction. Significantly, they focused on understanding how patterns of behaviour could form, maintain and resolve problems – hence their emphasis on the *pragmatics* of human communication (Watzlawick et al., 1967), which also characterizes NLP.

These social and intellectual influences form the backdrop to the usual, local story of NLP's founding. Fritz Perls, one of the main developers of Gestalt therapy, was an author published by Robert Spitzer. Perls died in 1970, leaving behind him some unfinished work. Spitzer asked Bandler, then aged around 20, to transcribe recordings of Perls at work and edit an uncompleted manuscript, to be published posthumously (i.e. Perls, 1973). Bandler immersed himself in the task, and Spitzer wrote later that Bandler 'came out of it talking and acting like Fritz Perls. I found myself accidentally calling him Fritz on several occasions' (Spitzer, 1992, p. 2). Bandler then met Virginia Satir at a seminar she gave at a property owned by Spitzer, probably in 1972 (Walker, 1996); by this time, Satir had moved on from the Palo Alto institute to become the first director of training at Esalen (Satir, 1978). Spitzer asked Bandler to tape and transcribe a month-long workshop that Satir was due to lead in Canada, intending to turn this material into a book. Bandler was intrigued by Satir's abilities to elicit information from other people, and was fascinated by how she achieved her results. Satir was also impressed with Bandler, describing him as a brilliant young man with a fantastic intellect and a wide-ranging curiosity (Walker, 1996). Towards the end of that workshop, according to O'Connor and Seymour (1990, p. 173):

> Virginia had set up a counselling situation and asked how the participants would deal with it, using the material that she had been teaching them. The participants seemed stuck. Richard [Bandler] came storming down from his room and successfully dealt with the problem . . . Richard found himself in the strange situation of knowing more about Virginia's therapeutic procedures than anyone else, without consciously trying to learn them at all.

These experiences appear to be the origin of the core methodology used in NLP, which is called 'modelling'. This is a kind of reverse engineering applied to human capabilities, 'the mapping of tacit knowledge into explicit knowledge' (Bostic St. Clair and Grinder, 2001, p. 271). Modelling can be carried out unconsciously, effectively by observing an exemplar and absorbing their approach – which is essentially what Bandler did while observing Satir at work – or more consciously and analytically by investigating the language patterns, behaviours, sequences of thought and internal imagery that exponents use – which results typically in an explicated process such as the spelling strategy described above. Through modelling, NLP claims to offer a way to identify the key elements of any human capability, such that another person can reproduce that capability. Regardless of whether modelling is conducted consciously or unconsciously, the test of an effective model is pragmatic; in other words, a person employing the model gains the same results as the exemplar who was the source of the model.

Following these experiences, Bandler went on to study at Kresge College, the sixth college established at the University of Santa Cruz, which is where he met the co-founder of NLP, John Grinder. Grinder, after completing his doctorate at the University of San Diego on 'deletion phenomena' (Grinder, 1971), an aspect of contemporary linguistics, joined the University of California, Santa Cruz as an assistant professor in 1970 (Bostic St. Clair and Grinder, 2001). Kresge was a radical experiment in education (Grant and Riesman, 1978), with its ethos and practices based on T-groups, or sensitivity training – a behavioural-science approach to personal growth and organization development founded by Kurt Lewin. It was intended to be 'an integrated living/learning environment shared (in principle, at any rate) by students, faculty and staff' (Bostic St. Clair and Grinder, 2001, p. 142). Kresge was therefore by no means typical of American college education, nor even of the University of Santa Cruz.

What is most significant in relation to NLP is that Bandler and Grinder, and later Bateson, were involved in the relatively short period during which this experiment in alternative education was at its height. According to Grinder (Bostic St. Clair and Grinder, 2001), he and Bandler met in one of these T-groups. At that time, undergraduates at Kresge could present their own work (i.e. work done outside the curriculum) in order to gain credits. Bandler therefore started a Gestalt group on the campus in the spring of 1972, in which he tried out the interventions and ideas that had emerged from his immersion in Perls' work. Bandler needed to be supervised by a faculty member in order to deliver his course, and had noted that Grinder had interesting ideas about the relationship between the processes of natural language and 'the structure of the human mind' (Bostic St. Clair and Grinder, 2001, p. 143).

The first substantive product of this period, the 'meta-model', appeared in print in a book titled 'The Structure of Magic I' (Bandler and Grinder, 1975b).

Sporting a colourful image of a wizard on the front cover, the book carried a foreword by Gregory Bateson who, with reference to his own previous work on human communication, said: 'Grinder and Bandler have succeeded in making explicit the syntax of how people avoid change and, therefore, how to assist them in changing' (Bateson in Bandler and Grinder, 1975b, p. x).

If modelling is the core methodology of NLP, then the 'meta-model' is its central and fundamental content. As noted above, NLP is typically interested in the process of communication or behaviour rather than its content. The 'meta-model' conceived of grammar and syntax as mirroring cognitive processes, and therefore provides a means by which to understand people's ways of making sense. The model categorizes certain linguistic transformations, or ways in which the 'surface structure' of verbal communication can differ from the 'deep structure', which was assumed to be a fuller description of experience. The model also identifies corresponding questions that are designed to recover the detail of the 'deep structure'. Applications of the model range from psychotherapy, where the practitioner's concern may be to gain deeper understanding of the client's inner world, to business, where the need may be for precision in communication (McMaster and Grinder, 1980).

WHAT HAS BEEN ITS HISTORY SINCE?

We have portrayed NLP as having six 'faces' (Tosey and Mathison, 2009) that reflect its evolving and diverse identities since its founding in the 1970s. The first 'face' is what we have called 'practical magic'. This refers to the naturally occurring patterns of 'excellent communication' that were derived from observing and analysing leading psychotherapists Virginia Satir, Fritz Perls and later hypnotherapist Milton Erickson (Bandler and Grinder, 1975a) in the 1970s. The reference to 'magic' denotes the fact that the results achieved by Satir, Perls and Erickson appeared to many observers to be magical. Bandler and Grinder's contribution was to find a way to account for the difference in effectiveness between these practitioners and others.

The second 'face' is the *methodology* developed through those original NLP studies, which is called 'modelling', as described in the previous section. Emphasis on modelling as the essence of NLP sometimes leads to NLP being described as a form of (applied) 'study', as in 'the study of the structure of subjective experience' (Dilts et al., 1980). For example, Robert Dilts has derived a model of the creative process used by Walt Disney by studying Disney's own accounts of the way he worked (Dilts, 1994). The codified pattern, known as the 'Disney creativity strategy', often appears in the repertoire of NLP techniques, and it has been used with arts students in higher education (Beeden, 2009).

Just from these first two 'faces', one can appreciate that ambiguity arises about the scope and identity of NLP, since it refers both to the *products* of 'modelling' (the first face) and to the *methodology* itself, which can (supposedly) be applied to any human capability. This leads to a situation where the rather confusing claim is sometimes made that any human behaviour that works 'is' NLP.

Our third face of NLP is a philosophy or set of beliefs about the world. In NLP these beliefs are represented typically by a set of what are called 'presuppositions', an example of which is 'the meaning of your communication is the response that you get'. These presuppositions are of interest because they tell us something about the theoretical and intellectual heritage from which NLP is derived, despite a frequent denial from NLP circles that it has any concern with theory. The presupposition cited above is one of several that can be traced back to the science of cybernetics (Tosey and Mathison, 2009).

The fourth identity of NLP is as a technology. Starting in the late 1970s, NLP was made available through training courses as a method to enhance communication and performance. The technology was codified as a 'body of knowledge' comprising the frameworks and techniques described in NLP literature. These have been derived from NLP's insights into effective communication in many fields, including ways in which those insights have been pieced together to create novel techniques. An example is 'six step reframing' (Bandler and Grinder, 1979), a process through which a facilitator enables a person to ask their own unconscious for creative solutions to a problem, which combines the Palo Alto group's work on reframing with Milton Erickson's use of 'hypnotic' language.

The fifth face is as a commercial product, part of the 'self-help' industry, reflected in the many artefacts (e.g. books, audio, video) and events (e.g. seminars, certificated training courses, conferences) available to be consumed. As an indication of the scale of this activity, about 50 training schools operate in the UK alone. It is important to note that NLP training is a highly competitive commercial market and is offered through a number of brands that are often seeking participants' allegiance to certain versions of NLP, with their related views and practices. It includes organizations that act both as training providers and as essentially self-appointed authorities that regulate their own particular brand of NLP certification, both directly and through other affiliated training organizations. There is no overarching body that governs or regulates the entire field.

Table 5.1 The six faces of NLP

Face	Content
'Practical magic'	Patterns of communication derived from early exemplars (Perls, Satir, Erickson).
Methodology	Modelling (the process used to study those exemplars, and which can in principle be applied to any instance of human excellence).
Philosophy	Presuppositions – underlying principles that reflect NLP's world view.
Technology	A multiplicity of techniques and codified practices that may be presented as the 'content' of NLP.
'Self-help' product	Training courses (with levels of certifications), books, media, etc.
Professional modality	A mode of professional help as used in psychotherapy, coaching.

Finally, NLP is available as a mode used by professionals in HRD and other fields, including coaching, consulting, training, psychotherapy and more. It is worth noting that NeuroLinguistic psychotherapy is accredited by the United Kingdom Council for Psychotherapies (UKCP) (Table 5.1).

WHAT CLAIMS HAVE BEEN MADE FOR IT?

Probably three main claims are made for NLP:

1. Through 'modelling', it provides a methodology for studying 'excellence'.
2. It is a method that can be used to bring about personal change for clients (typically by professional helpers).
3. It is a set of techniques that can be used by anyone, in private as well as professional settings, to enhance communication and performance.

With reference to these claims, modelling appears to have exciting potential but lacks the detailed evaluation and documented examples that could make it more convincing to people outside the community of NLP practitioners. Apart from publications based on the work that was undertaken with Milton Erickson (Bandler and Grinder, 1975a; Grinder et al., 1977), which include transcript data, the preferred approach in NLP has been to evidence claims for modelling through behavioural demonstration. In other words, the criterion for success and validity is that the modeller can reproduce the capability that has been studied. From my personal knowledge, perhaps the most extensive modelling project ever undertaken is that through which James Lawley and Penny Tompkins used their NLP training in a project lasting several years to study the therapeutic practice of David Grove, which is known as 'Clean Language' (Lawley and Tompkins, 2000; Sullivan and Rees, 2008). Whereas modelling outputs such as the spelling strategy and the Disney creativity strategy mentioned above are specific capabilities, Lawley and Tompkins have codified an entire approach.

The claims made for NLP as a method of personal change have relied to a great extent on anecdote and live demonstrations on stage. This is not to suggest that anecdotes are without value; see for example Isabel Losada's account (Losada, 2001, pp. 200–201) of someone overcoming their fear of travelling in lifts. The experiences of practitioners constitute a body of evidence, if one that may be difficult to evaluate.

Documented evidence is patchy, however, and has also been hampered by some disdain shown towards formal research since NLP's inception. The body of formal research that does exist is small, inconclusive (Heap, 1988), dated (mostly from the 1980s and the early 1990s) and methodologically narrow, though it is accurate to say that it offers little substantive support for NLP (for a detailed discussion see Tosey and Mathison, 2009). Yet its findings tend to be cited as if they were conclusive and authoritative (e.g. von Bergen et al., 1997), and the additional research that could have developed interim conclusions has not been conducted. NLP has been in something of a catch-22; it is dismissed because it is said that there is no evidence for it, yet there is no evidence for it at least in part because research is not being done.

It must be acknowledged that NLP is by no means alone in HRD in this respect – for example, how often are strategies for managing organizational change offered by consulting organizations thoroughly evidence based? The question of what provides for an evidence-based approach is as complex and contested in HRD as in other fields (McGoldrick et al., 2002; Hamlin, 2007).

Increasingly, NLP practitioners, especially those in the psychotherapy profession, are committed to improving this evidence base. The Association for NLP has supported two international research conferences since 2008, and there is also a welcome trend in recent NLP literature for authors to consider relevant research findings from mainstream psychology and other disciplines (e.g. Bolstad, 2002; Churches and Terry, 2007; Linder-Pelz, 2010; Wake, 2008). This marks a shift of attitude towards research, and usefully counters a tendency for NLP training courses and literature to recycle knowledge that has been in circulation since the 1970s.

On the other hand, a claim often made for NLP by practitioners – which troubles people who are unfamiliar with NLP – is simply that 'it works!'

(e.g. the foreword to Henwood and Lister, 2007). Indeed, Bostic St. Clair and Grinder (2001, p. 3) make the breathtaking claim that the widespread dissemination of NLP 'can be accounted for by a simple observation – the patterning they (i.e. Grinder and Bandler) modeled and coded works. It works across cultures, generations, genders, age groups and fields of application.' This claim is, of course, highly problematic. To suggest that any method is successful in all cases is simply not credible; in the field of health care, the standard of effectiveness is to better the rate of success of the placebo effect. Ironically perhaps, an evidence-based, sceptical approach is typically encouraged in NLP training where trainers exhort participants to test NLP's claims for themselves. Unfortunately, this invitation tends to overlook issues such as that of how rigorous and systematic participants will be in record keeping – for example, will they notice successes but ignore failures? Peer pressure and social conformity also serve to make this kind of testing unreliable.

In an interesting development, it seems that contemporary research findings from academic disciplines such as cognitive linguistics and neuroscience may be offering support to NLP's ideas and practices. For example, the main principle that Bandler and Grinder drew from their practical investigations was that communication activated a variety of sense-making processes, and that these could be identified. Fauconnier (1999, p. 615) reports a very similar perspective from contemporary cognitive linguistics:

> An important general point for cognitive scientists is that language does not directly carry meaning. Rather, it serves as a powerful means of prompting dynamic on-line constructions of meaning that go far beyond anything explicitly provided by the lexical and grammatical forms.

This view is also receiving support in neuroscientific literature. For example, Richardson et al. (2003) have shown that when people listen to certain types of words or phrases, particular neuronal networks in identifiable areas of their brains are activated. Pecher et al. (2004) claim that words activate events in the sensory-motor system of the brain and play a critical role in understanding; Grossman et al. (2006) propose that words represent certain types of categories and activate different parts of the temporal-occipital part of the brain; and Yokoyama and his colleagues (2006) have demonstrated that verbs elicit greater activation of a part of the brain called the left middle temporal gyrus than do nouns. Leynes et al. (2006) claim that inviting people to remember a past experience activates different patterns of neuronal responses to asking them to imagine a future activity. Rizzolatti and his colleagues (2001), and Tettamanti et al. (2005), suggest that we understand an action (and therefore words that represent an action) because the motor representation of that action is activated in our brain by its 'mirror neurons'. Whenever we communicate, we are not simply exchanging information, but directly activating certain neurological processes in ourselves and others.

Whilst such evidence must be used with caution, due to the propensity for promulgating 'neuro-myths' based on partial understanding, the findings cited above appear promising.

WHAT CRITICISMS HAVE BEEN MADE TO DATE?

As well as concerns about the evidence base, as discussed above, the criticisms most commonly made of NLP are that it is a 'pseudoscience', that it lacks theory and that it is manipulative.

The allegation of being a 'pseudoscience' originates from a positivist, falsificationist perspective that by no means singles out NLP. It also challenges a wide range of training, development and organizational change practices found in HRD. If applied strictly, most of these practices would probably have to be regarded as pseudoscientific too. For example, Eisner (2000) critiques not only NLP but also Gestalt therapy, Psychosynthesis and more – in short, any approach to psychotherapy that has not been supported by a dominant form of research, namely clinical trials. Beyerstein (1990, p. 34), similarly, insists that 'double-blind, placebo-controlled evaluations of all medical, psychological, and educational interventions are essential'.

One feature of NLP that leads to scepticism, especially from academics, is the difficulty of identifying its theoretical base. Indeed, practitioners can deny that theory has any relevance to NLP at all. This seems ironic given NLP's reverence for Bateson, who deplored the lack of effective theory in the social sciences, and its roots in cybernetics, as explained above. There is an interesting range of issues behind this stance, some of which raise issues about the nature of knowledge:

1. For the purposes of identifying effective patterns of behaviour, NLP is firmly pragmatist – as noted it is interested in the criterion of 'what works', not with what is 'true'. It is concerned with studying what people actually do, not what they may believe or espouse that they do.
2. In our culture, intellectual, conceptual knowledge is often privileged over practical, experiential knowledge. NLP is interested in holistic and non-conventional forms of knowledge. For example, people are considered

to use two modes of processing, a rational, analytic mode and a more intuitive, holistic mode. The rational mode, which is the mode that can formulate and debate theory, is ineffective for certain purposes, such as that it might not directly enable someone to act effectively.

With regard to the emphasis on the first point – 'what works' – there is clearly potential support from several quarters. I have noted the Palo Alto group's similar emphasis on the *pragmatics* of communication (Watzlawick et al., 1967, p. 13). Dilts and DeLozier (2000) refer to William James' pragmatist philosophy. Bateson, commenting on his view that accepted scientific principles are flawed epistemologically, said 'you and I are able to get along in the world and fly to Hawaii and read papers on psychiatry and find our places around these tables and in general function reasonably like human beings in spite of very deep error. The erroneous premises, in fact, *work*' (Bateson, 2000, pp. 486–487). What remains to be done is to explore NLP's position systematically in relation to, say, Dewey's philosophy of pragmatism.

In relation to the second point, NLP authors have refused to privilege the intellect and have discouraged the temptation to create a belief system out of conceptual knowing. They have also explored 'unorthodox' forms of knowledge from outside Western scientific traditions, especially in DeLozier and Grinder's (1987) reformulation of NLP as 'New Code' in the 1980s. That book, titled *Turtles All The Way Down*, was something of a reaction against the codified, propositional form of early NLP. It was strongly influenced, for example, by Carlos Castaneda's series about (ostensibly) the system of knowledge of a Yaqui Indian sorcerer (e.g. Castaneda, 1970), as well as by experiences of Congolese drumming. Bateson figures again, for example through reference to his anthropological work in Bali, where he developed ideas about art as a form of knowledge (Bateson, 2000).

NLP has developed a reputation for sometimes being practised manipulatively, perhaps through people who are attracted to its discourse of enhancing personal power. The prevalence of concern about the motives of practitioners is worrying. NLP is not *inherently* manipulative, and Hayes (2006, p. 12) suggests that 'the key is to be able to identify those who work well and ethically within NLP – thankfully, they can be found'. Ethical practice is supported actively and unequivocally by codes of conduct such as that produced by the Association for NLP, and the types of ethical reasoning likely to be needed in NLP are discussed by Tosey and Mathison (2009).

Some of the concerns expressed are based on the view that it is inappropriate or unethical to communicate with another person's unconscious without their knowledge and consent. However, it is impossible not to influence other people because that is the nature of communication itself. All who interact with others, professionally and personally, do so at both conscious and unconscious levels, and for good or ill. The debate needs to be not about *whether or not* people exercise influence in the first place, but about *how* someone influences other people through their communication. From this perspective, there is a complex ethical dimension to all human interaction. Given that NLP acknowledges this influence and makes it an explicit part of the practice, it offers the potential advantage that the practitioner can make informed choices. At best, NLP can raise people's awareness of how they may be influencing other people and can encourage them to be more responsible for the effects they have on other people. Arguably, it provides a public service through educating people about such language patterns, and the ability to recognize when others are influencing us.

WHAT ALTERNATIVES HAVE BEEN SUGGESTED?

NLP exists in a marketplace for training, education and development services. As a methodology, there are probably no direct alternatives to NLP's 'modelling'. As a method used by professional helpers, it is most closely related to systemic and solution-focused approaches to coaching and consultancy, and to Clean Language. Many practitioners use NLP as one ingredient in an eclectic approach. As a set of techniques, it competes with many forms of adult education and interpersonal skills training, particularly accelerated learning.

CONCLUSION

NLP represents a long-established if still unorthodox and problematic form of knowledge within HRD, which is used in training, leadership development, coaching and consultancy. It is a complex and contested field, which presents diverse 'faces' to the outside world. This chapter has discussed its definitions, origins and development. Three main claims for NLP as a practice have been identified, and three major criticisms have been explored. There appears to be an obvious need for further research into its claims. This chapter concludes that NLP offers a highly pragmatic and accessible approach to communication and people development that can help with a wide variety of needs for effective performance, change and learning, based on novel and subtle understandings of the relationships between language, inner worlds and behaviour.

REFERENCES

Bandler, R. and Grinder, J. (1975a) *Patterns of the Hypnotic Techniques of Milton H. Erickson, M.D.* vol. 1. Cupertino, CA: Meta Publications.

Bandler, R. and Grinder, J. (1975b) *The Structure of Magic: A Book about Language and Therapy.* Palo Alto, CA: Science and Behavioural Books.

Bandler, R. and Grinder, J. (1979) *Frogs into Princes.* Moab, UT: Real People Press.

Bateson, G. (2000) *Steps to an Ecology of Mind: Collected Essays in Anthropology, Psychiatry, Evolution and Epistemology* (revised edn). Chicago: University of Chicago Press.

Beeden, S. (2009) Applying Dilts' Disney creativity strategy within the higher education arts, design and media environment. In P. Tosey (ed.), *Current Research in NLP* (Volume 1, proceedings of the first international NLP research conference, University of Surrey, 5 July 2008).

Beyerstein, B. L. (1990) Brainscams: Neuromythologies of the new age, *International Journal of Mental Health*, 19(3): 27–36.

Bolstad, R. (2002) *Resolve: A New Model of Therapy.* Carmarthen, Wales: Crown House.

Bostic St. Clair, C. and Grinder, J. (2001) *Whispering in the Wind.* Scotts Valley, CA: J and C Enterprises.

Capra, F. (1996) *The Web of Life: A New Synthesis of Mind and Matter.* London: Harper Collins.

Castaneda, C. (1970) *The Teachings of Don Juan: A Yaqui Way of Knowledge.* Scotts Valley, CA: Penguin Books.

Churches, R. and Terry, R. (2007) *NLP for Teachers.* Carmarthen, Wales: Crown House.

DeLozier, J. and Grinder, J. (1987) *Turtles All the Way Down: Prerequisites to Personal Genius.* Bonny Doon, CA: Grindler, DeLozier and Associates.

Dilts, R. and DeLozier, J. (2000) *Encyclopedia of Systemic NLP and NLP New Codin.* Scotts Valley, CA: NLP University Press.

Dilts, R., Grinder, J., Bandler, R. and DeLozier, J. (1980) *Neuro-Linguistic Programming*, vol. 1: *The Study of the Structure of Subjective Experience.* Capitola, CA: Meta Publications.

Dilts, R. B. (1994) *Strategies of Genius*, vol. 1. Capitola, CA: Meta Publications.

Eisner, D. A. (2000) *The Death of Psychotherapy: From Freud to Alien Abduction.* Westport, CT: Praeger.

Fauconnier, G. (1999) Creativity, simulation and conceptualization, *Behavioral and Brain Sciences*, 22(4): 615.

Grant, G. and Riesman, D. (1978) *The Perpetual Dream: Reform and Experiment in the American College.* Chicago: The University of Chicago Press.

Grinder, J., DeLozier, J. and Bandler, R. (1977) *Patterns of the Hypnotic Techniques of Milton H. Erickson, M.D.*, vol. 2. Cupertino, CA: Meta Publications.

Grinder, J. T. (1971) *On Deletion Phenomena*, Ph.D. San Diego, CA: University of California.

Grossman, M., Koenig, P., Kounios, J., McMillan, C., Work, M. and Moore, P. (2006) Category-specific effects in semantic memory: Category-task interactions suggested by fMRI, *NeuroImage*, 30(3): 1003–1009.

Hamlin, R. G. (2007) An evidence-based perspective on HRD, *Advances in Developing Human Resources*, 9(1): 42–57.

Hayes, P. (2006) *NLP Coaching.* Maidenhead, Berkshire: Open University Press.

Heap, M. (1988) Neurolinguistic programming – an interim verdict. In M. Heap (ed.), *Hypnosis: Current Clinical, Experimental and Forensic Practices* (pp. 268–280). London: Croom Helm.

Henwood, S. and Lister, J. (2007) *NLP and Coaching for Healthcare Professionals.* Chichester: John Wiley and Sons.

Hirst, W. (1988) *The Making of Cognitive Science: Essays in Honour of George A. Miller.* Cambridge: Cambridge University Press.

Knight, S. (2002) *NLP at Work: The Difference that Makes a Difference in Business.* London: Nicholas Brealey Publishing.

Korzybski, A. (1941) *Science and Sanity: An Introduction to Non-Aristotelian Systems and General Semantics* (2nd edn). Englewood, NJ: The International Non-Aristotelian Library Publishing Company, the Institute of General Semantics, Distributors.

Lawley, J. and Tompkins, P. (2000) *Metaphors in Mind: Transformation through Symbolic Modelling.* London: The Developing Company Press.

Leynes, P. A., Grey, J. A. and Crawford, J. T. (2006) Event-related potential (ERP) evidence for sensory-based action memories, *International Journal of Psychophysiology,* 62(1): 193–202.

Linder-Pelz, S. (2010) *NLP Coaching: An Evidence-Based Approach for Coaches, Leaders and Individuals.* London: Kogan Page.

Losada, I. (2001) *The Battersea Park Road to Enlightenment.* London: Bloomsbury.

McGoldrick, J., Stewart, J. and Watson, S. (2002) *Understanding Human Resource Development: A Research-Based Approach.* London: Routledge.

McMaster, M. and Grinder, J. (1980) *Precision: A New Approach to Communication.* Bonny Doon, CA: Precision Models.

Miller, G. A. (1956) The magical number seven, plus or minus two: Some limits on our capacity for processing information, *The Psychological Review,* 63(2): 81–97.

Montagnini, L. (2007) Looking for 'scientific' social science, *Kybernetes,* 36(7/8): 1012–1021.

O'Connor, J. and Seymour, J. (1990) *Introducing Neuro-Linguistic Programming: The New Psychology of Excellence.* London: Mandala.

Pecher, D., Zeelenberg, R. and Barsalou, L. (2004) Sensorimotor simulations underlie conceptual representations: Modality-specific effects of prior activation, *Psychonomic Bulletin and Review,* 11(1): 164–167.

Perls, F. (1973) *The Gestalt Approach and Eyewitness to Therapy.* Palo Alto, CA: Science and Behavior Books.

Richardson, D. C., Spivey, M. J., Barsalou, L. and McRae, K. (2003) Spatial activation during real time comprehension of verbs, *Cognitive Science,* 27(5): 767–780.

Rizzolatti, G., Fogassi, L. and Gallese, V. (2001) Neurophysiological mechanisms underlying the understanding and imitation of action, *Nature Reviews: Neuroscience,* 2: 661–670.

Satir, V. (1978) *Peoplemaking.* London: Souvenir Press.

Spitzer, R. (1992) Virginia Satir and the origins of NLP, *Anchor Point,* 6(7): 19.

Sullivan, W. and Rees, J. (2008) *Clean Language: Revealing Metaphors and Opening Minds.* Carmarthen, Wales: Crown House Publishing House.

Tettamanti, M., Buccino, M., Saccuman, M. C., Gallese, V., Danna, M., Scifo, P., Fazio, F., Rizzolatti, G., Cappa, S. and Perani, D. (2005) Listening to action-related sentences activates fronto-parietal motor circuits, *Journal of Cognitive Neuroscience,* 17(2): 273–281.

Tosey, P. and Mathison, J. (2009) *NLP: A Critical Appreciation for Managers and Developers.* Basingstoke: Palgrave Macmillan.

Von Bergen, C. W., Soper, B., Rosenthal, G. T. and Wilkinson, L. V. (1997) Selected alternative training techniques in HRD, *Human Resource Development Quarterly,* 8(4): 281–294.

Wake, L. (2008) *Neuro-Linguistic Psychotherapy: A Postmodern Perspective.* London: Routledge.

Walker, W. (1996) *Abenteuer Kommunikation: Bateson, Perls, Satir, Erickson und die Anfange des Neurolinguistischen Programmierens (NLP)* (4th edn). Stuttgart: Klett-Cotta.

Watzlawick, P., Beavin, J. H. and Jackson, D. D. (1967) *Pragmatics of Human Communication.* New York: W.W. Norton.

Wiener, N. (1965) *Cybernetics, or Control and Communication in the Animal and the Machine* (2nd edn). Cambridge, MA: MIT Press.

Wilson, J. P. (2005) *Human Resource Development: Learning and Training for Individuals and Organizations* (2nd edn). London: Kogan Page.

Yokoyama, S., Miyamoto, T., Riera, J., Kim, J., Akitsuki, Y., Iwata, K., Yoshimoto, K., Horie, K., Sato, S. and Kawashima, R. (2006) Cortical mechanisms involved in the processing of verbs: An FMRI study, *Journal of Cognitive Neuroscience*, 18(8): 1304–1313.

FURTHER READING

Knight, S. (2002) *NLP at Work: The Difference that makes a Difference in Business*. London: Nicholas Brealey Publishing.

Linder-Pelz, S. (2010) *NLP Coaching: An Evidence-Based Approach for Coaches, Leaders and Individuals*. London: Kogan Page.

Tosey, P. and Mathison, J. (2009) *NLP: A Critical Appreciation for Managers and Developers*. Basingstoke: Palgrave Macmillan.

6
BEHAVIOURAL MODELLING
Darlene Russ-Eft

INTRODUCTION

American industry spends billions of dollars per year on training. With this enormous investment, training professionals and corporate executives should always be looking for ways to get a better payoff from expenditures. This chapter examines the research on behaviour modelling, one of the most popular methods for both interpersonal and technical skills training. The method involves learning some simple rules or key steps of the behaviour and seeing a demonstration of the behaviour to be learned (or the model), which trainees may then imitate or practise. The chapter provides a brief history of behaviour modelling and describes research showing the effects on reactions, knowledge gains claimed, changes in on-the-job performance, and results. This body of research suggests the effectiveness of behaviour modelling in a variety of contexts; however, there are some limitations that are described. The chapter also reviews ways in which to enhance the effectiveness of behaviour modelling. The inclusion and highlighting of learning points can help the learner identify and remember the behaviour. Certain types of behavioural models, such as high status models, can lead to improved performance. Rehearsal, individual feedback, the spacing of training, the use of goal setting and management support of training can have positive impacts on performance.

Research on behaviour modelling began in earnest in the 1960s and has continued through to the present, resulting in the technique being well known and widely discussed. According to Decker and Nathan (1985, p. 1), 'The principles behind behavior modeling are ancient and were possibly best expressed over 2000 years ago by the Chinese philosopher, Confucius, when he wrote:

> I hear and I forget.
> I see and I remember.
> I do and I understand.

...This is what behavior modeling is all about, seeing and remembering, doing and understanding.'

Behaviour modelling training is used in a wide variety of settings, from customer service, clinical interviewing and other interpersonal skills training to cardiopulmonary resuscitation (CPR) training, first-aid training and even hand-combat training. Typically, the training begins with learning a few simple rules or key steps of the behaviour. Then, a demonstration of the behaviour to be learned follows, which is shown in person (or by a live model) or through the use of a video model. After the behavioural model, there may be some imitation or practice of the behaviour, along with feedback from the instructor or from peers.

A unique feature of behaviour modelling is that it can be considered 'no-trial learning' (Bandura, 1965a; 1965b) (see Russ-Eft (1972) for an overview of the theoretical context for Bandura's work). Thus, unlike behaviour modification, learning is not dependent on direct experience and reinforcement. New behaviours can be acquired simply by observing the behaviour of models. However, certain processes facilitate learning using behaviour modelling: attention, retention, motor reproduction and motivation (Bandura, 1977). According to social learning theory, an observer cannot learn unless he or she attends to the behaviour of the model. After having attended to this, the observer must encode and store the behaviour for later retention. Motor reproduction involves actually performing the behaviour. Finally, reinforcement can increase or decrease the motivation for performing the behaviour.

A second unique feature of behaviour modelling is that it attempts to change behaviour directly. Lecture-style training, for example, aims primarily at improving participants' knowledge; the goal is to make people more expert. As a by-product, people may develop changed attitudes and behaviour. Experiential training aims primarily at influencing a participant's attitudes. This may lead to an increased desire for work-related knowledge. Like a lecture, however, experiential training gives no direct help in acting out new knowledge and attitudes. Behaviour modelling, in contrast, comes at behaviour directly. It concentrates on neither knowledge nor attitudes, but on new ways of behaving. A participant's ability and commitment to use the skills are integral to the training (motivation), but, initially at least, how that participant thinks or feels is secondary. (For further elaboration see Goldstein and Sorcher, 1974; Kraut, 1976; Wehrenberg and Kuhnle, 1983; Haston, 2007.)

A final unique feature of behaviour modelling is its widespread use and testing within business and industry. Studies have been conducted that have measured supervisory training (e.g. Byham et al., 1976; Goldstein and Sorcher, 1973; 1974; May and Kahnweiler, 2000; Taylor et al., 2005), appraisal training (e.g. Davis and Mount, 1984), safety training (e.g. Burke et al., 2006; Olson et al., 2009) and computer software training (e.g. Chen et al., 2005; 2006; Chen and Shaw, 2006; Gist et al., 1989). Because of its direct link to behaviour and behaviour change, many people within business and industry find it to be an effective and practical method for delivering training. Organizations do not need employees who merely understand theory; they need employees who use a skill to achieve measurable results.

Measurable results can be described in at least four different ways. These include reactions to training, declarative knowledge, skill and job performance, and results or changes in organizational performance (Taylor et al., 2005). Each of these types of results has been measured in studies of behaviour modelling.

In the aggregate, the research on behaviour modelling is impressive. Because many people are reluctant to read lengthy and detailed research studies, the chapter presents only the conclusions of the major studies, with a table in the Appendix that provides details on all the empirical studies since 2000, as well as citations to all studies and literature mentioned in the chapter. These will allow the reader to investigate further any topic of interest. After a description of the origin and history of behaviour modelling, a summary of the available research evidence is presented, along with some discussion of the criticisms and limitations. The final section focuses on ways to improve effectiveness.

ORIGIN AND HISTORY

Albert Bandura (1965a; 1965b) introduced and tested the concept of behaviour modelling, or observational learning or vicarious learning or no-trial learning. He and his colleagues (e.g. Bandura and McDonald, 1963; Bandura et al., 1961; 1963a; 1963b) demonstrated the effectiveness of this method in affecting learning and performance. Further, Bandura, Ross and Ross (1963a) showed that these effects appeared when using models on film rather than in person.

The first research on behaviour modelling in industry, which was designed at General Electric (GE) and reported by Sorcher and Goldstein (1972) and Goldstein and Sorcher (1973; 1974), studied programmes intended to reduce the turnover among 'hardcore unemployed' employees. Firms needed unskilled labour, but these employees often left their new jobs after only a few weeks.

Goldstein and Sorcher (1974) felt that behaviour modelling would be the ideal solution. Such employees lacked good role models because few of them knew other people who held steady jobs. GE foremen and supervisors also lacked role models who could demonstrate how to deal with new employees. Therefore, parallel but separate programmes were developed for the employees and their supervisors.

Six months after training, the worker turnover rate for those following the usual orientation procedures was almost three times higher than that for employees receiving the behaviour modelling training. Further evaluation showed that, during training, worker productivity was higher and turnover was lower for workers reporting to the supervisors trained in behaviour modelling than for workers reporting to the control group supervisors, who received no training. According to the researchers: '... a one percent overall increase in this plant represented an annual savings of many thousands of dollars per year if it was sustained for that length of time' (Goldstein and Sorcher, 1974, p. 79).

Because of its success, GE expanded this programme to include all first-level supervisors (Burnaska, 1976). Later, other researchers reported on the effects of behaviour modelling programmes that taught communication and interpersonal skill and were developed for first-level supervisors in numerous organizational settings. Behaviour modelling programmes were also used for different levels of staff in a variety of business and industrial settings. For example, Meyer and Raich (1983) described a behaviour modelling programme used to increase sales performance in seven retail stores. The training had a significant positive effect on reducing staff turnover and also on sales performance. The trained group increased their commissions by 7 per cent, but the control group decreased theirs by about 3 per cent.

Byham and Robinson (1976) also reported success with what they labelled 'interaction modelling'. Later, Burke and Day (1986) summarized the results of several different approaches to managerial training, applying the statistical approach of meta-analysis. They reported behaviour modelling to be one of the more effective methods. In addition, a committee of the National Research Council included an examination of techniques for enhancing human performance (Druckman and Swets, 1988; Swets and Bjork, 1990). The committee reported that models of expert performance can serve as an effective foundation for training programmes.

Finally, Russ-Eft (1997) reported on a series of studies of behaviour modelling training programmes undertaken in corporate settings. This chapter provides an update and elaboration of that article and includes not only references to the studies mentioned in the text but also a table (see Appendix) that provides details on studies since 2000.

REVIEW OF AVAILABLE RESEARCH

The table in the Appendix provides an overview to some of the many studies of behaviour modelling, with an emphasis on those undertaken within the workplace. Although much of the earliest work on behaviour modelling tested concepts in laboratory settings – using children, undergraduate or graduate students – later studies that focused on applications within organizations should prove most useful.

The following sections describe some of the major findings from the various studies. These findings are differentiated into (a) reactions, (b) declarative knowledge, (c) job performance and (d) organizational results.

Reactions to training

Behaviour modelling appears to result in positive reactions to training. Russell, Wexley, and Hunter (1984) found that both videotaped and live behavioural models resulted in positive reactions to each part of the training. Similarly, Harrison (1992) found positive reactions to cultural assimilator training and behaviour modelling training as well as to the combination of the two methods. Gist, Schwoerer and Rosen (1989) compared behaviour modelling with computer-aided tutorials for computer software training. The behavioural modelling group reported significantly higher situation ease and overall satisfaction with training than did the tutorial group. Johnson (2000), and Johnson and Marakas (2000), showed that computer self-efficacy improved from pre- to post-training for the behaviour modelling group as compared with control groups. Boatman (2008) found higher levels of self-efficacy and more positive reactions following behaviour modelling training than either instructions review or additional practice (on a computer task simulating an aviation environment).

Positive reactions to training do not necessarily lead to improvements in learning, behaviour and organizational performance. For example, Dixon

(1990) found no significant correlations between tests given after training and participants' ratings of the relevance of the course, their own learning, their enjoyment, or the skill of the instructor. Similarly, Bretz and Thompsett (1992), in a comparison of 'super-learning' methods with a lecture method, found no differences in trainees' learning, even though these trainees expressed more positive reactions to the super-learning methods. As shown by Alliger, Tannenbaum, Bennett, Tracer and Shotland (1997), reaction measures may or may not correlate with transfer of training, depending on how the reaction is defined. Reactions as utility judgements, such as 'I found this training job relevant', showed a positive correlation with transfer of training. In contrast, reactions as affect, such as 'I found this training to be enjoyable', showed little correlation with learning or transfer. Given the mixture of reaction measures used in these studies, we need to look at other measures of training effectiveness.

Declarative knowledge gains

Behaviour modelling tends to produce measurable improvements in participants' knowledge of the subject being trained. These results appear in paper-and-pencil tests as well as assessments conducted using role-playing situations.

Moses and Ritchie (1976) examined the effects of behaviour modelling on learning how to handle employee problems. Trained supervisors received significantly better ratings in an assessment-centre role play than did supervisors who did not receive such training. Latham and Saari (1979), comparing trained and control groups, showed significantly better performance by the trained group in role play and in knowledge tests six months after training. Hogan, Hakel, and Decker (1986) showed that behaviour modelling along with cultural assimilator training for civilian employees of a US military agency yielded significantly improved learning and role-play performance.

A study of the effects of positive and negative models (Russ-Eft and Zucchelli, 1987) included measurement of knowledge gains. Each subject in the testing received both a behavioural and a written test before and after training. Subjects who during training viewed one or more positive models illustrating correct behaviours showed significantly greater knowledge gains in a behavioural role play and in the written test than did those who viewed negative models only.

Harrison (1992) found not only positive reactions but also increased learning with the use of cultural assimilator training and behaviour modelling training, as well as the combination of the two methods. Learning was measured using a multiple-choice test to assess knowledge of general facts regarding conflict avoidance and group orientation. The role play involved an interaction between the trainee and a Japanese employee.

Simon and Werner (1996) examined three different training methods (behaviour modelling, self-paced study and lecturing) for improving computer skills among US Navy personnel. Cognitive learning showed the highest level of improvement among those receiving behaviour modelling training, both immediately after training and four weeks later.

Erlich and Russ-Eft (2013) examined the self-regulated learning strategy levels among community college students involved in academic planning. The academic adviser used cognitive modelling with instructional aids to develop students' academic planning strategies. During the performance phase, students practised this planning strategy and received feedback to improve performance. The pre-post measure of self-regulated learning, determined from a rubric and micro-analytic questions, showed significant improvements from before to after the session.

Taylor, Russ-Eft and Chan (2005) undertook a meta-analysis of 119 behaviour modelling studies. The largest pre-post-training gains appeared for declarative knowledge and procedural knowledge, with effect sizes near 1.0. Similarly, Burke et al. (2006) conducted a meta-analysis of previous studies focused on safety training. This analysis included 95 studies conducted between 1971 and 2003. The researchers found that behaviour modelling showed improved knowledge and skill acquisition as compared with less engaging methods (lecture, videos and preprogrammed instruction).

Together these studies indicate that behaviour modelling training can lead to knowledge gains, particularly in terms of handling interpersonal situations. But the important question is whether such knowledge gains result in changes in behaviours on the job.

Changes in on-the-job performance

Behaviour modelling makes enduring changes in the on-the-job behaviour of participants. Baldwin and Ford (1988) argued that such transfer of training depends on generalization of learning to contexts outside of training as well as motivation and the opportunity to use such skills. All of the studies focusing on job performance attempt to answer the question: 'Do participants in this training improve their on-the-job behaviour?'

The earliest studies of behaviour modelling documented this transfer of training to the work setting (e.g. Burnaska, 1979; Byham et al., 1976; Hards, 1981; McDaniel, 1985; Russ-Eft, 1985; Schoening, 1981; Sevy and Olson,

1982). Latham and Saari (1979) showed significant improvements in job performance for trained supervisors. Superintendents rated supervisors on 35 behavioural observation items developed from a job analysis of effective and ineffective supervisor behaviour. The trained supervisors received significantly higher ratings than the control supervisors one year after training. Similarly, ratings for the two groups were compared using the company's traditional performance appraisal instrument, and significant differences appeared following training.

Porras and Anderson (1981) showed significant improvements in on-the-job behaviour ratings gathered from trained supervisors and their subordinates at a forest products plant. Questionnaires rating the supervisory behaviour were obtained, before and after training, from all supervisors, as well as 30 per cent of the employees reporting to each supervisor. Ratings of the trained supervisors showed significant improvements, as compared with control supervisors.

Davis and Mount (1984) compared the effects of computer-assisted-instruction (CAI) with and without modelling and with no training. The training for middle managers concerned the performance appraisal system and interview. When tested on their knowledge of the appraisal system, those getting behaviour modelling training received significantly better test scores than untrained managers. Of greatest interest here, however, is the fact that the employees of those who received behaviour modelling training showed higher levels of satisfaction with the appraisal discussion than those who received only CAI training or received no training at all.

Sorcher and Spence (1982) examined the use of behaviour modelling to improve race relations between supervisors and employees in South Africa. Six weeks and 20 weeks after training, a positive change in behaviour and attitude appeared for trained supervisors and employees but not for the untrained groups.

Gist, Schwoerer and Rosen (1989) examined the effects of training hospital administrators on a financial software program. One group received behaviour modelling training and the other received a computerized tutorial. The behaviour modelling group showed better post-training performance, more ease with the task and less frustration. Similarly, Simon and Werner (1996) showed improved computer skills for novice US Navy computer users for the behaviour modelling group, as compared with a self-paced study group, a lecturing group and a no-training control group.

Russ-Eft and Zenger (1995) reported on several studies showing significant gains for supervisory training from before to after training in behavioural ratings gathered from trainees, their managers and their subordinates. One analysis used behavioural ratings summarized from 30 different companies; changes in ratings from before to after training were compared for trained supervisors with control-group supervisors. Significant improvements appeared in the ratings for trained supervisors, when gathered from the trainees, their managers and their employees.

Hoover and Russ-Eft (2005) examined the use of behaviour modelling as part of a training regime to examine task-prioritization skills among pilots. Pilots at the same level of training were randomly assigned either to a trained or a control (or no-trained) group. Skills were measured prior to training and showed that the groups were comparable. Following training, significant differences emerged, such that the error scores for the control group were higher than the error scores for the trained group.

The Taylor, Russ-Eft and Chan (2005) meta-analysis of behaviour modelling studies showed skill gains for job behaviours. These gains were much smaller than those for declarative knowledge gains, showing an effect size of about 0.20. The Burke et al. (2006) meta-analysis on various training methods used for safety training showed that the behaviour model led to better results for reducing negative outcomes, such as accidents.

Such behavioural changes provide critical evidence of the effectiveness of training. Nevertheless, many organizations today express concerns with how such behavioural changes relate to organizational performance or bottom-line results.

Bottom-line results

Training in behaviour modelling may result in behaviour changes made on the job, but some decision makers question whether these changes translate into improved organizational performance and productivity. Results of the training do show up in bottom-line or hard measures of organizational performance. Some of these results include higher productivity, reduced worker turnover, fewer labour grievances, reduced scrap rates and lower absenteeism.

Smith (1976) examined the impact of behaviour modelling training on customer satisfaction and sales. He compared the three types of training – a one-day 'traditional' session, a two-day modelling session and a two-day modelling plus team-building session. Managers' communication skills improved from before to after training for the modelling and the modelling plus team-building group but showed no significant changes for the traditional group. No significant differences emerged in level of customer satisfaction at four or ten months after training for any of the groups. Finally, only the modelling plus team-building group showed a significant improvement in sales performance ten months after training.

Porras and Anderson (1981) described a study examining the effects of behaviour modelling supervisory training in a large manufacturing opera-tion of a major forest products company. In addition to measuring changes in supervisory behaviour, they assessed changes in organizational productiv-ity and efficiency on the basis of three main indices of plant performance: total monthly production per direct labour worker hour, average daily plant production and recovery rate (an index reflecting the degree to which a log is effectively converted to an end product). All three measures showed improvement from before to after training.

Meyer and Raich (1983) conducted an evaluation of a behaviour modelling programme used to increase sales performance with sales representatives from 14 retail stores, matched in size, sales and geographic area. Salespersons receiv-ing behaviour modelling training increased their sales by about 7 per cent fol-lowing training, whereas the sales of the control group salespersons decreased by about 3 per cent. In addition, the staff turnover for the sales represen-tatives trained using behaviour modelling was only 7 per cent compared to 22 per cent for the control group.

Russ-Eft, Krishnamurthi and Ravishankar (1994) undertook a cost–benefit analysis on worker training. They measured changes in on-the-job behaviour through self-ratings, supervisor ratings and peer ratings. These behaviour changes were transformed into dollar benefits to the organization by deter-mining the degree of skill change for specific work activities and the amount of work time that trainees spent on these areas. The results indicated that for a sample of 42 trainees out of the total population of 85 trainees, the benefit was approximately US$305,000. In addition, two types of costs were identified – variable costs and fixed costs. Variable costs consisted of the costs for run-ning each training session. Such costs are incurred if and only if a session takes place. The variable costs for this study included trainees' time away from work; trainers' time for preparation and training; and actual materials used during the training. Fixed costs are those that have been or will be incurred even if a specific session never happens. The fixed costs include time for designing the sessions and certification costs. Costs incurred for the entire population of 85 trainees were estimated at approximately US$70,000. If benefits accrued only to the 42 trainees who were assessed and costs were incurred for all 85 trainees, then the net benefit would be $235,000. However, assuming results seen for the 42 trainees were similar for all 85 trainees, total gross benefits of $610,000 would be realized. The net benefits in this case would be $540,000.

Eden and Zuk (1995) compared persuasion and behaviour modelling with the lecture method to overcome the effects of seasickness among naval officer cadets. The cadets used a five-point rating scale to indicate the extent to which they experienced 29 symptoms of seasickness. In addition, performance at sea (in terms of carrying out duties effectively, maintaining social contacts and showing interest in the ship's technical systems) was rated by the shipboard instructors on a seven-point scale. The results showed that the modelling group reported significantly fewer symptoms of seasickness and received significantly better performance ratings from their supervisors than did the control group.

The Taylor, Russ-Eft and Chan (2005) meta-analysis examined organizational results in terms of workgroup productivity and workgroup climate. The assumption in the compiled studies was that supervisors receiving behaviour modelling training would result in changed behaviours leading to changes among their subordinates. Indeed, what was found in the meta-analysis was a positive effect size of about 0.10 for productivity and climate. Although positive, these were much smaller than those for trainee declarative knowledge or job performance, as might be expected.

Results from these various contexts indicate the effectiveness of behaviour modelling in helping organizations achieve results.

Limitations

Current training methods need to take new technologies into consideration. These can include computer-aided instruction, synchronous online instruction, asynchronous online instruction, and simulations. The results of some recent studies suggest that more research is needed to determine the effectiveness of behaviour modelling for these different conditions.

Davis and Mount (1984) compared the use of computer-assisted instruction (CAI) plus behaviour modelling, behaviour modelling only, or no training on an appraisal system. Middle managers who received any type of training had higher test scores than those who received no training. The reactions of employees indicated greater satisfaction with the appraisal system for those whose managers had received behaviour modelling training.

Chen, Olfman and Harris (2005) tested undergraduate students on their knowledge and skills on Microsoft Access. Training was delivered using behaviour modelling in a face-to-face, asynchronous online video, and asynchronous scripted fashion. The face-to-face and video groups showed significantly higher knowledge and skill performance. In a later study, Chen, Ryan and Olfman (2006) compared training in Excel using behaviour modelling in a face-to-face or an asynchronous video delivery. Chen and Shaw (2006) compared behaviour modelling with face-to-face, online synchronous and online asynchronous delivery. Both of these studies found no differences among the training groups.

Murthy et al. (2008) compared behaviour modelling training with simulation training for call-centre trainees. The researchers found that trainees receiving the simulation training showed shorter call durations than the behaviour modelling group; the accuracy levels were no different between the two groups. A second study compared behaviour modelling training with simulation training using either a simple task of a quote-status call or a complex task of a quote-process call. Undergraduate seniors in business were randomly assigned one of the four groups: (a) behaviour modelling with low complexity, (b) behaviour modelling with high complexity, (c) simulation with low complexity and (d) simulation with high complexity. No differences in accuracy appeared for the two training methods for the low-complexity task, but the simulation group showed better accuracy on the high-complexity task.

Conclusions from research

Overall, behaviour modelling has been shown to be an effective training method. It shows positive effects on trainee reactions and self-efficacy, declarative knowledge and job performance. There is also some evidence for organizational results.

The following section describes some of the research related to variations of behaviour modelling designed to lead to further improvements in the training outcomes. Given the previously described limitation, issues with regard to new technologies or the use of simulation training compared with behaviour modelling training may need further investigation.

ALTERNATIVES FOR IMPROVED OUTCOMES

Having assured ourselves that behaviour modelling produces measurable results, we now turn to how we can make those results even better or achieve the same results more economically. The following sections will review ways to enhance the impact of behaviour modelling training.

Type of learning points

A learning point is a written statement accompanying the behavioural model that describes or defines the behaviour. For example, the learning points associated with the task of 'teaching a new job' might include the following learning points: (1) describe the steps of the job; (2) demonstrate the job in short steps; (3) ask the employee to demonstrate the sequence; (4) give feedback showing patience and praise; (5) set a review time. The early work on learning points focused on the effects of providing attentional cues (Eskedal, 1975) or different types of symbolic codes (Bandura and Jeffery, 1973; Bandura et al., 1974).

Mann and Decker (1984) investigated the effect of such learning points on generalization and recall. They hypothesized that the use of learning points would assist the learner in identifying the key behaviours of less distinctive behaviours, such as 'Don't answer leading questions' or 'State your feelings'. Indeed, they found that including such learning points enhanced recall and generalization, particularly with key behaviours that possessed low distinctiveness.

Given that learning points appeared to enhance performance, researchers also attempted to determine which types of learning points prove most effective. As described in a series of studies by Decker (1980; 1982; 1984), three types of learning points have been investigated: (a) summary label, or a brief generalized statement describing the behaviour, (b) rule-oriented or general rules guiding the behaviour and (c) specific descriptions of behaviour. These studies showed that learning points generally enhanced both reproduction and generalization. Reproduction refers to a repetition of the behaviours, whereas generalization refers to adapting the behaviours to some different context. Some differences among the types of learning points emerged: (1) rule-oriented learning points enhanced both reproduction and generalization; (2) behavioural learning points improved reproduction better than any other method but proved inferior to the other learning points in terms of generalization; (3) summary label learning points did not improve reproduction but did enhance generalization. Such results suggest that the type of learning points to be used may depend on the behavioural changes desired.

Learning points may also be generated by trainees or provided by trainers. Trainee-generated learning points come from situations in which trainees observe the behaviour model and then are asked to create some mnemonic to remember the behaviour. In contrast, trainer-provided codes are just that – created by the trainer for use by the trainee. Gerst (1971) studied the effects of symbolic coding processes in behaviour modelling. In this case, subjects were instructed to develop their own codes – summary labelling, imaginable coding or verbal description. All three types of coding led to superior reproduction as compared with a control group. Furthermore, summary labelling performed better than all other conditions in a delayed testing of behavioural reproduction. Hogan, Hakel and Decker (1986) undertook a direct comparison of trainee-generated versus trainer-provided codes. They found that trainee-generated codes resulted in superior performance, even though such codes received lower independent ratings for their quality.

The Taylor, Russ-Eft and Chan (2005) meta-analysis showed that procedural knowledge-skills were enhanced when learning points were presented as compared with no learning points, and when these appeared as rule codes as contrasted with descriptions or summaries of behaviour. However, presenting these learning points during modelling or using them as retention aids appeared to hinder learning and skill development.

Further research is needed about the use of learning points or codes. Of particular importance is an examination of the impact of instructions regarding different types of trainee-generated codes.

Type of behavioural model

Studies have examined various aspects of the behavioural model to determine its impact on improving performance. Baron (1970) reported on previous studies indicating the positive influence on children's imitative behaviour when the model was highly rewarding or highly nurturing. The researcher then examined the impact on imitative behaviour of undergraduate students depending on the degree of similarity to the observer and the level of competence displayed by the model. Similarity had no effect, whereas competence influenced acquisition only during the early trials of the experimental task. The two variables interacted so that a high level of similarity facilitated imitation when the model was successful or competent but interfered with imitation when the model was low in competence.

In contrast, Dowling and Frantz (1975) examined the effect of a facilitative relationship with the model on imitative learning of ethnocentric or non-ethnocentric attitudes. Facilitative models, displaying both empathy and respect, resulted in significantly more imitative learning than either control models or non-facilitative models. Furthermore, these differences remained over a three-week follow-up period. Similarly, Perry (1975) found that high-empathy models, used for counsellor training of clergy, improved empathy in written responses but not in actual interviews. Kloba (1975), and Kloba and Zimpfer (1976), showed the positive effect of high-status models.

In a more recent study, Cellar and Wade (1988) examined the effects of the type of motivation expressed by the model. The intrinsically motivated model expressed interest in the task and engaged in the activity during the free-choice period. The extrinsically motivated model expressed concern about the extra credit points and about doing the experiment right but did not engage in the activity during the free-choice period. This motivational orientation of the model affected the behavioural measures of intrinsic motivation and script-related recognition (where a cognitive script refers to a type of memory trace that can act as a cue).

Some studies have used live enactment of the performance to be modelled, and others have used filmed models. Russell, Wexley and Hunter (1984) compared the use of trainer-led sessions with filmed behavioural models and manager-led sessions with managers modelling the behaviours. These researchers found no differences among the groups. In contrast, Walter (1976) found significant improvements in group problem-solving behaviour with the use of 'acted' as contrasted with 'natural' models.

Most behaviour modelling training done in corporate settings use video models who perform the key behaviours correctly. These are referred to as positive models. Diverse opinions exist on whether or not training programmes should use negative models who perform the key behaviours incorrectly or not at all.

Findings indicated that either positive models only, or a mixture of positive and negative models, result in the highest levels of behaviour change and cognitive gain (Mills, 1985; Newman and Fuqua, 1988; Russ-Eft and Zucchelli, 1987; Trimble et al., 1985, 1991). For a given skill, seeing one negative model along with positive models does not interfere with learning and performance and does lead to higher subjective ratings on personal benefit and on believability. These benefits of a single negative model do not extend to viewing multiple negative models, with no viewing of a positive model. Indeed, those who saw two negative models only within the same training module experienced the least gain and provided the lowest ratings.

Baldwin (1992) examined the effects of positive and negative models on retention and generalization. In this case, the subjects were business students who were being trained in assertive communication. The retention and generalization tests occurred one month after training. After completing a post-study questionnaire and retention measure, each trainee was thanked and permitted to leave. As the trainee left the building, a graduate student, played by an accomplice, tried to sell the trainee some business publications. The price was prohibitively high, but the accomplice indicated that he was trying to raise money for his master's thesis. The interchange was video-taped and later rated by judges who were blind to the trainee's condition. The researcher found that a combination of positive and negative models led to a significant positive effect on generalization to situations outside of training.

Kitsantas, Zimmerman and Cleary (2000) introduced the notion of the 'mastery' model versus the 'coping' model. The mastery model is one who performs flawlessly, while the coping model is one who shows improvement in performance over time. This study trained ninth-grade girls in a physical education class in dart throwing. The researchers found that those who received the coping model had better performance and higher self-efficacy than those who received the mastery model. A later study by Zimmerman and Kitsantas (2002) obtained similar results with college students learning writing revision; that is, the students with the coping model showed significantly improved writing technique compared to those with the mastery model.

The Taylor, Russ-Eft and Chan (2005) meta-analysis indicated that smaller training effects appeared for declarative knowledge with mixed models (both positive and negative) as compared with positive only models. However, greater changes in behaviour resulted with mixed models as compared with positive only models. The picture was unclear in terms of procedural knowledge and skills.

Further research is needed to determine the impact of filmed versus live models, particularly with the increasing use of online synchronous and asynchronous technology. In terms of positive and negative models or of mastery and coping models, research is needed to clarify what conditions lead to better ability to distinguish between positive and negative behaviours and better awareness of the critical behaviours.

One model versus multiple models

Learning and memory researchers agree that repetition leads to better learning and memory, whether done gradually or in an all-or-none fashion (e.g. Guthrie, 1935; 1952; Estes, 1950; 1960; 1964; Hull, 1943; Postman, 1963). Research in behaviour modelling reveals a mixed picture of the use of multiple examples in the training process. Several examples seem to reinforce the skill and emphasize the concepts and substance of the behaviour being taught rather than any specific style (Fehrenbach et al., 1979; Russ-Eft and Zucchelli, 1987; Trimble et al., 1991). However, Baldwin (1992) found negligible effects on learning, reproduction and generalization when comparing the use of one versus two models.

More recently, Olson et al. (2009) examined the effects of the number of behavioural models on the wearing of personal protective equipment (PPE). Participants from a university and from the general public were trained in a simulated baggage-handling task that included background noise. Participants received one of four models: (a) three models with no PPE, (b) three models in which one wore PPE, (c) three models in which two wore PPE and (d) three models in which all three wore PPE. The group viewing the three models wearing PPE displayed a significantly greater use of PPE than did the other groups.

Further research on the issue can help to determine whether the advantage of using multiple models comes from repetition (showing the same model) or from generalization (through the presentation of different models showing the same key behaviours).

Type of rehearsal

Most of the studies on behaviour modelling include a rehearsal or practice component. The type of rehearsal differs from study to study. In some studies, a form of symbolic or covert rehearsal is used, in which trainees rehearse through mental manipulation of symbols representing certain behaviours. Other studies, focusing on behavioural rehearsals, provide structural role-playing exercises, and still others attempt to simulate work experiences.

Bandura and Jeffery (1973) examined the use of symbolic coding and rehearsal in reproducing six complex movements. They found that the combination of coding and rehearsal proved superior to either condition alone. Bandura, Jeffery and Bachicha (1974), and Decker (1980; 1982), showed the effectiveness of symbolic rehearsal in terms of retention and generalization.

Stone and Vance (1976) investigated the impact of behavioural rehearsal, accompanied by feedback on the rehearsed behaviours. Behavioural rehearsal, in contrast to symbolic rehearsal, consists of reproduction of the behaviours to be learned. Such rehearsal, in combination with instruction and modelling, yielded superior performance in a written test and a role play focused on empathetic communication. Decker (1983) showed improved reproduction with behavioural rehearsal, using small groups (of three trainees and a trainer) as compared with large groups (of 12 trainees and a trainer).

Jeffery (1976) compared four different types of rehearsal in learning and performing a construction task: symbolic rehearsal, motor rehearsal, symbolic followed by motor rehearsal, and motor followed by symbolic rehearsal. The accuracy in reproduction immediately after training and one week after training was highest for the symbolic followed by motor performance. Motor followed by symbolic rehearsal and symbolic rehearsal alone also showed relatively high levels of reproduction accuracy.

May and Kahnweiler (2000) examined the effects of what they labelled as 'mastery training' used in conjunction with behaviour modelling in training active listening skills to first-line supervisors and managers. Mastery training involved overlearning, reciprocal teaching and video feedback. The researchers found significant positive effects of mastery training on declarative knowledge retention and skill demonstration. These results did not, however, result in transfer to the job as rated by supervisors, peers and subordinates.

Davis and Yi (2004) undertook two studies examining symbolic mental rehearsal done in conjunction with behaviour modelling. In the first study, students learned Excel, and those using symbolic mental rehearsal showed improved declarative knowledge, but no differences appeared for task performance. In the second study, also using students learning Excel, the researchers found significant effect sizes in immediate and delayed declarative knowledge, as well as immediate and delayed task performance.

The Taylor, Russ-Eft and Chan (2005) meta-analysis examined the effects of various types of rehearsal or practice. Symbolic rehearsal showed positive effects on procedural-knowledge skills, while peer coaching prior to behavioural rehearsal yielded smaller positive effects than did studies that did not mention coaching. Rehearsal that incorporated trainee-generated scenarios showed greater transfer to job behaviour than did trainer-generated scenarios.

Further research is needed to determine which type of rehearsal is most effective for which type of outcome. It may be that symbolic rehearsal or trainee-generated scenarios enhance certain types of outcomes, whereas behavioural rehearsal or trainer-generated scenarios lead to improvements in other outcomes.

Individual feedback

Clearly the purpose of training is to change or improve the behaviours of the participants. Feedback on performance also can lead to improvements in performance (e.g. Ammons, 1956; Ashford and Cummings, 1983; Ilgen et al., 1979; Komaki et al., 1978; Payne and Hauty, 1955). Much of this work showed improvements in production quantity. However, Ilgen and Moore (1987) successfully demonstrated performance improvements along the separate dimensions of quantity *and* quality.

Individual feedback falls within a theoretical framework set forth by Bowers and Franklin (1972). According to these authors, change occurs through the use of: a model of current behaviours; a goal, involving the selection of alternative future behaviours; an activity initiated to attain the goal; and feedback used to compare, confirm, adjust and correct responses.

Fyffe and Oei (1979) examined the effects of modelling and feedback to increase the frequency of reflection of feeling in counselling behaviour of teachers. The combination of modelling with feedback resulted in significant improvements over feedback alone or no modelling and feedback. Similarly, Wallace et al. (1975) found a positive impact of feedback added to lecture and modelling for counsellor training. Also, Decker (1983) showed that the combination of video feedback in addition to verbal feedback led to improved behavioural reproduction of trained behaviours two days after training.

Kitsantas, Zimmerman and Cleary (2000) found that social feedback led to higher performance and self-efficacy. Similarly, Zimmerman and Kitsantas (2002) examined students learning writing-revisions skills. In addition to behaviour modelling, some students received social feedback and others did not. The students receiving social feedback along with modelling showed better performance than those having no feedback.

The use of individual feedback is completely consistent with social learning theory (Bandura and Cervone, 1983). Feedback provides information to the performer that allows a comparison of current and desired behaviours. This comparison motivates the performer to invest further effort to change his or her behaviour or performance standard.

The Taylor, Russ-Eft and Chan (2005) meta-analysis found that studies reporting coaching did not lead to as much gain as those not reporting coaching. On the other hand, a later meta-analysis study on management training programmes by Taylor, Russ-Eft and Taylor (2009) indicated that programmes including practice with feedback resulted in larger effect sizes across multiple reporting sources. Given these differing results, several questions arise. Did the studies include feedback and coaching but simply not report its use? Or, might it be that certain types of feedback and coaching and practice are helpful but only for certain types of skills?

Massed versus spaced training

Research over the past century confirms the general superiority of spacing the training sessions of over time (Dempster, 1988; Ebbinghause, 1985, 1913, 1964; Jost, 1897; Underwood, 1961; Underwood, Kapelak and Malmi, 1976). Although spacing may slow the rate of learning, it may be optimal for post-training effectiveness.

Russ-Eft and Zenger (1995) reported on a study on spacing effects using a programme that trains workers in the interpersonal skills needed to cope with on-the-job problems in a manufacturing setting, comparing sessions held during three full days off-site with sessions held twice a week over five weeks. Trained groups showed significant on-the-job skill gains compared with the control groups in both organizations; those receiving spaced or distributed training showed greater gains than those receiving massed training.

Further research is needed to determine whether there are limits to such spacing effects, particularly with behaviour modelling training. Bahrick et al. (1993) showed improved retention with increasing amounts of spacing. It is important to determine the advantages of spacing, given some of the practical problems that may arise, such as difficulties in scheduling of spaced training.

Participant characteristics

Decker and Nathan (1985) pointed out some characteristics of the observer or participant that can affect the success of behaviour modelling training. Important characteristics mentioned are those relating to attention and reinforcement. These included the individual's workload, capabilities, attention to the materials and expectations for reinforcement.

Porras and Hargis (1982) investigated the effects of personal characteristics on changes in supervisory behaviour as the result of a behaviour modelling training programme. Supervisors in both the trained group and control group received questionnaires before and after a ten-week training programme. Role clarity, control over the job, feelings of competence on the job, self-actualization and self-regard were positively correlated with behavioural change. Role conflict, overload and job-generated stress negatively correlated with change. Demographic variables of education, number of years worked at the company and number of years on the job failed to reach statistical significance.

Russ-Eft and Zenger (1995) described a study comparing supervisors who reported large positive skills gains and those who reported smaller gains from before to after training. Ratings of employees' performance that were related to the bottom line (such as productivity), supervisors' job satisfaction and supervisors' opinions on training were similar for the two groups before training but showed significantly greater gains for supervisors who also reported large positive skill gains.

Johnson (2000), and Johnson and Marakas (2000), examined the effects of computer self-efficacy, anxiety and outcome expectancy paired with behaviour modelling training. College students with little or no experience with Microsoft Excel received behaviour modelling training or a control condition. Those with higher computer self-efficacy and higher outcome expectancy performed better following behaviour modelling training.

More studies are needed that examine trainee characteristics and their effects on the efficacy of behaviour modelling training. For example, it improves self-efficacy and outcome expectancies (Erlich and Russ-Eft, 2013). Might those who begin behaviour modelling training with higher self-efficacy and higher outcome expectancies achieve higher levels of learning and performance?

Greater change over time

One of our most important findings is that positive behaviour change not only lasts but also improves over time. Behaviour modelling, the only kind of training we know that produces such continuing gains, disproves the common assumption that the effects of training must diminish over time.

Porras and Anderson (1981) noted continuing improvement in their study of a supervisory training programme conducted in the manufacturing operation of a forest products company. They found large improvements in supervisory behaviour during the intervention period when comparing the trained with the control group. Also, the trainees maintained or increased behavioural improvements through the six months following training. Similarly, Sorcher and Spence (1982) found increased improvements from 6 to 20 weeks after training.

One reason for typical declines in performance after training is the lack of opportunity to use the newly acquired skills. Schendel and Hagman (1982) showed that refresher training can lead to improved retention. Similarly, Porras and Hargis (1982) found that decay can be reduced as skills are performed and outcomes realized. In this case, skill use became self-rewarding.

The Taylor, Russ-Eft and Chan (2005) meta-analysis examined the issue of the stability of learning and behaviour outcomes over time. Comparison of immediate versus delayed post-tests and regression analysis of post-test effect size on the months between training and post-tests showed that declarative knowledge declined over time. In contrast, regression results indicated *positive* relationships for measures of procedural knowledge-skills and on-the-job behaviour, indicating some increase over time.

Further research on this issue is needed to determine whether this result holds for all procedural knowledge-skills and job behaviours. In addition, research can identify the needed factors affecting such increases, as, for example, opportunities to practise and supervisory support.

Goal setting

Goal setting appears to lead to increased effort and improved performance (Locke and Latham, 1990; Wexley and Latham, 1991; Werner et al., 1994).

Such behavioural improvements occur whether goals are assigned or set participatively (Wexley and Baldwin, 1986). Furthermore, having trainees monitor such goals after training, through the use of check lists, leads to better application of training (Wexley and Nameroff, 1975).

Goal setting can, however, have a negative influence as well. Research by Kanfer and Ackerman (1989) showed that assigning goals in the early stages of learning leads to lower performance when compared with assigning goals at a later time. Difficult, specific goals can impair performance, particularly for novel and complex tasks (Earley et al., 1989). Dweck (1986) contrasted performance goals and learning goals. This researcher argued that performance goals lead to defensive strategies and to interpreting failures or errors as a lack of ability. In contrast, learning goals encourage individuals to increase their efforts when encountering obstacles, leading to improved performance. Klein and Thoms (1995) provided some empirical evidence to support the use of learning goals, but further research is needed to clarify the most effective use of goal setting.

The Taylor, Russ-Eft and Chan (2005) study examined the use of goal setting as part of behaviour modelling. Where goal setting was mentioned, as compared with when no goal setting was mentioned, larger positive effects appeared in terms of job performance.

Again, further research is needed to identify whether such goal-setting effects apply for all behaviour modelling training or only for certain types of training. Also, research can suggest the mechanisms by which the type of goal setting affects later job performance.

Management involvement and support

Much training literature advocates the importance of management involvement and support for any type of training, including behaviour modelling. For example, Baldwin and Ford (1988) included management support as a critical component for transfer of training. Rouillier and Goldstein (1993) confirmed the importance of managerial support and suggested that it might actually lead to greater transfer than various aspects of the training. Based on ratings from training directors, Taylor (1992) found a positive correlation between ratings of immediate supervisors' support for training and training outcomes. Training outcomes included trainee reactions, learning and skill use.

Few studies have actually examined the effects of management support on the results of behaviour modelling training. However, Boyd (1973) compared the effects of two types of counselling supervision – behavioural supervision and recall interrogation – added to behaviour modelling training. Behavioural supervision showed some immediate post-training gains, as compared with recall interrogation, in counselling interviewer behaviour. However, these gains disappeared after 30 days.

Russ-Eft and Zenger (1995) reported on the impact of higher degrees of management support with regard to on-the-job performance. Participants, their managers and their employees reported on participants' skill level before and after behaviour modelling training. In addition, participants reported on their perceived level of management support. Participants reporting high levels of management support were compared with those reporting low levels of management support. Results showed the greatest improvements from before to after training among participants reporting high levels of management support.

Holton et al. (1997), and Holton, Bates and Ruona (2000), developed and validated an instrument measuring transfer climate, or in other words, the work environment facilitating or inhibiting transfer of the training to the job. One of the important factors included in that instrument is that of management support. Furthermore, Russ-Eft (2002) included management support in a typology of factors affecting workplace learning and transfer. The Taylor, Russ-Eft and Chan (2005) meta-analysis of behaviour modelling training compared results where studies mentioned that trainee managers received training along with trainees, compared with those where there was no mention of manager training. Although both groups showed positive on-job behaviour, those that included managers in the training showed larger job-performance gains.

Again, further research on the impact of management support is needed. There may be certain forms of management support that are more effective than others, for certain types of outcomes resulting from behaviour modelling training. In the Taylor, Russ-Eft and Chan (2005) meta-analysis, management support was demonstrated by managers taking part in the training. What other forms of management support can be used to improve training results?

CONCLUSION

The summary effect of all this research has been to provide some validation of and justification for the use of behaviour modelling. Rather than showing behaviour modelling to be a fad, the research has demonstrated both a solid theoretical foundation and significant practical gains in the workplace. Certainly no other training methodology rests on anything approaching the broadly based research evidence that supports behaviour modelling.

In addition, research has shown ways in which to improve the effectiveness of behaviour modelling training. Learning points appear to aid the learner and can lead to improved performance. Behavioural models that emphasize the key behaviours and are of high status yield superior performance gains. In addition, positive models or a mixture of positive and negative models produce greater changes in behaviour than do negative models only. Conditions added to behavioural modelling, such as rehearsal, feedback and goal setting, appear to yield even greater performance improvements. Finally, certain external conditions, such as the spacing of training, participant characteristics, and management involvement and support, can influence the effectiveness of training.

At present, research continues in a few university and industrial settings, but much more needs to be done to fully exploit the power of this methodology and to answer many gnawing questions, among them:

- What is the best way to highlight the key behaviours in video models?
- What is the optimal approach to using behaviour modelling with online and virtual training?
- What is the longevity of participants' changes in behaviour?
- When do declines begin? And, can additional rehearsal or other intervention block such declines?
- When and how should follow-up training be conducted?

Given the effectiveness of behaviour modelling, applications have been surprisingly limited. Most have appeared in supervisory and management training, with some in counselling skills, selling skills and computer-software skills. Future efforts will likely be directed towards expanding the applications of this highly effective approach.

APPENDIX

Overview of the recent studies on behaviour modelling (from 2000)

Author(s) and Date	Purpose	Measures	Design	Sample	Results
Boatman (2008)	Compare effects of two types of behaviour modelling with control groups using on-computer task simulating aviation environment	Ratings of self-efficacy; multiple-choice questions (declarative knowledge); knowledge structure coherence; enjoyment, motivation and utility	Pre-post, with two experimental (coping model or a mastery model) and two control groups with two control conditions (task instructions review or additional unstructured practice)	142 right-handed males enrolled in introductory psychology at University of Oklahoma	Behaviour modelling showed positive effects on learning and transfer, as well as higher levels of self-efficacy and reaction ratings; no difference in results between coping and mastery models
Bolt, Killough and Koh (2001)	Determine effects of behaviour modelling-based computer software training on task complexity and computer self-efficacy	Prior experience, outcome expectations, performance	Randomly assigned students to high-complexity or low-complexity task and to behaviour modelling or lecture method	249 undergraduate students learning linear programming in Excel	Behaviour modelling showed better results in performance and self-efficacy than lecture-based training with high task complexity

Study	Aim	Measures	Method	Sample	Findings
Burke et al. (2006)	Compare effects of least engaging (lecture, videos), moderately engaging (programmed instruction), and most engaging (behaviour modelling) safety training	Safety knowledge, safety performance, safety and health outcomes	Meta-analysis of previous studies	95 studies between 1971 and 2003, with 20,991 participants	Most engaging methods showed better results for knowledge and skill acquisition and for reducing negative outcomes (such as accidents). All three were similar for performance.
Chen, Olfman and Harris (2005)	Compare effects of behaviour modelling with face-to-face delivery and asynchronous online video and scripted conditions	Perceived usefulness and perceived ease of use (satisfaction), multiple-choice knowledge test (knowledge), ability to solve real problem in given time (performance)	Post only on knowledge and performance on Microsoft Access 2002	115 undergraduate students, who had no or limited computer experience, from two different universities learning Microsoft Access 2002	Face-to-face showed higher satisfaction; face-to-face and video showed significantly higher knowledge and performance scores
Chen, Ryan and Olfman (2006)	Compare effects of behaviour modelling with face-to-face delivery and video asynchronous online conditions	Satisfaction, usefulness and perceived ease of use, multiple-choice knowledge test (knowledge), and ability to solve real problem in given time (performance)	Pre-test on Excel and exclusion of those scoring 50 per cent or higher; post only on other measures	83 freshers majoring in management information systems or accounting learning Excel	No significant differences were found between the two conditions on any of the measures

Author(s) and Date	Purpose	Measures	Design	Sample	Results
Chen and Shaw (2006)	Compare effects of behaviour modelling with face-to-face, online synchronous and online asynchronous delivery	Satisfaction, knowledge test (knowledge), and ability to solve real problem (performance)	Measured over six-week period	96 sophomore majoring in management information system learning Microsoft SQL Server 2000	No significant differences were found among the three conditions
Davis and Yi (2004); Experiment 1	Determine effects of symbolic mental rehearsal (SMR) and reciprocal peer training (RPT) in conjunction with behaviour modelling	Post-training questionnaire, declarative knowledge test (5 mins) and a hands-on task performance test (25 mins)	2 by 2 factorial between-subjects design manipulating symbolic mental rehearsal (SMR) and reciprocal peer training (RPT)	192 students in introductory computer course, learning Excel	Significant effect of SMR for declarative knowledge but not task performance; no effect for RPT
Davis and Yi (2004); Experiment 2	Determine effects of SMR on immediate and delayed knowledge, performance and knowledge structure similarity to experts (KSS) in conjunction with behaviour modelling	Immediate and delayed (ten days) knowledge test, performance test; also KSS and reactions	SMR condition and control, no SMR condition	95 students in introductory computer course, learning Excel	Significant effect sizes (Cohen's d) on immediate declarative knowledge (0.60), delayed declarative knowledge (0.54), (delayed declarative knowledge), immediate task performance (0.51), delayed task performance (0.56); no effect on reactions

Study	Purpose	Measures	Design	Sample	Results
Erlich and Russ-Eft (2013)	Examine self-regulated learning in academic planning using social cognitive (and behaviour modelling)	Rubric and micro-analytic questions measuring self-regulated learning in academic planning	Pre-post measures	120 community college students seeking academic planning assistance	Increase in self-regulated learning strategy from before to after counselling session
Hoover and Russ-Eft (2005)	Examine task prioritization skill among pilots	Concurrent task management tests measuring task prioritization errors embedded at 14 locations with flight scenarios	Pre-post measures with control group	27 university flight technology students, with 14 pilots in the trained group and 13 in the control group	Trained and control groups showed no differences prior but significant differences following training, with significantly fewer errors by trained group
Johnson (2000)	Examine effects of computer self-efficacy, anxiety, and outcome expectancy in conjunction with behaviour modelling	Computer self-efficacy questions, measures of anxiety and outcome expectancy, performance task	Pre-post measures with control group (unrelated task), control group (review notes), behaviour modelling group	116 students enrolled in two sections of introductory information systems application course, learning Excel	Behaviour modelling group developed higher computer self-efficacy and better performance scores than control groups
Johnson and Marakas (2000)	Determine effects of behaviour modelling on computer self-efficacy, outcome expectancy, and computer performance	Computer self-efficacy, outcome expectancy, anxiety, performance on Excel	Pre- and post-measures with three groups: (a) control, no training, (b) review notes, and (c) behaviour modelling	116 students enrolled in introductory information systems application course and little or no experience with Excel	Behaviour modelling group showed higher computer self-efficacy and better performance than other groups

Author(s) and Date	Purpose	Measures	Design	Sample	Results
Kitsantas, Zimmerman and Cleary (2000)	Compared effects of behaviour modelling using mastery versus coping model and social feedback with no social feedback	Dart-throwing skill, self-efficacy, reactions	Factoral design: three (no modelling, or mastery modelling, or coping modelling) by two (no social feedback, or social feedback)	60 ninth-grade girls in physical education class, learning dart throwing	Those with coping model showed higher performance and self-efficacy than others. Those receiving feedback showed higher performance and self-efficacy
May and Kahnweiler (2000)	Examined the effects of mastery training (overlearning, reciprocal teaching, video feedback)	Knowledge retention, behavioural skill demonstration, far transfer to the job using 360-degree instrument	Pre- and posttest with behaviour modelling and mastery training versus behaviour modelling and no mastery training	38 first-line supervisors and managers in a consumer product manufacturing plant, learning active listening skills	Significant positive effects of mastery training on knowledge retention and skill demonstration; no effect on far transfer
Murthy et al. (2008), experiment 1	Compare behaviour modelling group with simulation group for call-centre training	Call duration, accuracy	Pre-post, two group (behavioural model versus simulation)	71 call-centre trainees randomly assigned to a group	Call-centre duration significantly shorter for simulation group; no differences between groups in accuracy

Study	Purpose	Measures	Design	Participants	Results
Murthy et al. (2008), experiment 2	Compare behaviour modelling group with simulation group on high versus low task complexity	Accuracy	Post-only with four conditions randomly assigned: 1. Modelling, low complexity 2. Modelling, high complexity 3. Simulation, low complexity 4. Simulation, high complexity	126 primarily undergraduate seniors in business	ANCOVA showed no differences between modelling and simulation on low-complexity task, but on high-complexity task, accuracy was better for simulation group
Nadler, Thompson and Van Boven (2003)	Compare four learning methods (didactic, information revelation, analogical and observational) with control (no learning provided) and two negotiation tasks (job contract and commercial real estate)	Negotiation performance, trade-off score, and learning process check measure on second negotiation	Pre-post with four learning conditions and control (no learning, only experience of first negotiation)	122 undergraduate psychology students, learning negotiation skills	Observation and analogical groups performed significantly better and received better trade-off scores than other groups on second negotiation; analogical and information revelation performed better than control and observational group on articulating learning points

Author(s) and Date	Purpose	Measures	Design	Sample	Results
Olson et al. (2009)	Examine effects of repeated models wearing personal protective equipment (PPE)	Number of time intervals participant wore PPE while performing simulated baggage screening task (with background noise)	Random assignment to one of four conditions: (0) zero of three models wearing PPE, (1) one of three models wearing PPE, (2) two of three models wearing PPE, and (3) three of three models wearing PPE	64 participants recruited from a university with a teaching hospital, and from general population	Group observing three models wearing PPE showed significantly increased use of PPE
Taylor, Russ-Eft and Chan (2005)	Evaluate behaviour modelling for learning, job behaviour and results outcomes	Effect sizes for declarative knowledge, procedural knowledge-skills, attitudes, job behaviours, results for workgroup productivity and results: workgroup climate	Meta-analysis of previous studies	119 independent behaviour modelling studies (published, unpublished, dissertations), with 279 effect sizes	Largest gains for learning, smaller for job behaviour, and even smaller for results outcomes. Declarative knowledge decayed over time, skills and job behaviour remained stable or even increased; greater skill gains with learning points and rule codes. Improved transfer with mixed (negative and positive) models. Practice with trainee-generated scenarios, goal-setting, when trainees' superiors also trained, and rewards and sanctions used on the job

Study	Aim	Method	Sample	Findings
Taylor, Russ-Eft and Taylor (2009)	Examine behaviour modelling outcomes as reported by trainees, their supervisors, their subordinates and their peers	Effect sizes for transfer of managerial training from different rating sources (self, supervisor, peer and subordinate)	Meta-analysis of previous studies	107 independent behaviour modelling studies (published, unpublished, dissertations)	Largest transfer effects for trainees' self-ratings and then from supervisors, with substantially smaller transfer effects for peer and subordinate ratings. Average effect sizes larger and more congruent across sources in training that included opportunities for practice
Truman (2009)	Examine effects of behaviour modelling and group-based learning	Pre-test survey on demographics; training assessment on comprehension level and reaction; evaluation survey collected data on intention to use styles	2 by 3 experimental laboratory design, training context (group-based, individual-based) and training method (behaviour modelling, exploration, and instruction)	84 undergraduate students, learning word-processing skills	Hierarchical regression showed significant effects of behaviour modelling, but no interaction with training context
Yi and Davis (2001)	Compared behaviour modelling with practice only, retention enhancement (symbolic coding and cognitive rehearsal), and retention enhancement with practice	Cognitive learning test, skill-based learning outcome and affective measures (usefulness and ease of use)	3 by 3 Latin square, isolating effects of training time and trainer effects	111 students, training on Microsoft Excel	Retention enhancement plus practice resulted in high cognitive learning tests. No differences appeared in skill-based measures

Author(s) and Date	Purpose	Measures	Design	Sample	Results
Yi and Davis (2003)	Test theoretical model linking modelling-based training to outcomes	Task performance, declarative knowledge, software self-efficacy	Two training conditions: (1) behaviour modelling, and (2) behaviour modelling plus retention enhancement (symbolic encoding and mental rehearsal)	95 freshers business majors recruited from an introductory computer course	Behaviour modelling plus retention enhancement significantly affects outcome measures; also influenced retention processes, but not attention, production or motivation processes of observational learning
Zimmerman and Kitsantas (2002)	Examine effects of behaviour modelling for writing skills	Writing skill, self-efficacy, self-satisfaction	Three (coping model, mastery model and no model) by two (feedback, no feedback) design	72 male and female undergraduates	Those with coping model surpassed those with mastery model who surpassed those with no model. Feedback led to improved skill; but those with mastery model and no feedback surpassed those with no model but feedback

REFERENCES

Alliger, G. M., Tannenbaum, S. L., Bennett, W., Tracer, H. and Shotland, A. (1997) A meta-analysis of the relations among training criteria, *Personnel Psychology*, 50(2): 341–358.

Ammons, R. B. (1956) Effects of knowledge of performance: A survey and tentative theoretical formulation, *Journal of General Psychology*, 54(2): 279–299.

Ashford, S. J. and Cummings, L. L. (1983) Feedback as an individual resource: Personal strategies for creating information, *Organizational Behaviour and Human Performance*, 32(3): 370–398.

Bahrick, H. P., Bahrick, L. E., Bahrick, A. S. and Bahrick, P. E. (1993) Maintenance of foreign language vocabulary and the spacing effect, *Psychological Science*, 4(5): 316–321.

Baldwin, T. T. (1992) Effects of alternative modeling strategies on outcomes of interpersonal skills training, *Journal of Applied Psychology*, 77(2): 147–154.

Baldwin, T. T. and Ford, J. K. (1988) Transfer of training: A review and directions for future research, *Personnel Psychology*, 41(1): 63–105.

Bandura, A. (1965a) Behavior modification through modeling procedures. In L. P. Ullman (ed.) *Research in Behavior Modification* (pp. 310–340). New York: Holt.

Bandura, A. (1965b) Vicarious processes: A case of no-trial learning. In L. Berkowitz (ed.) *Advances in Experimental Social Psychology* (vol. 2, pp. 1–56). New York: Academic Press.

Bandura, A. (1977) *Social Learning Theory*. Englewood Cliffs, NJ: Prentice Hall.

Bandura, A. and Cervone, D. (1983) Self-evaluative and self-efficacy mechanisms governing the motivational effects of goal systems, *Journal of Personality and Social Psychology*, 45(5): 1017–1028.

Bandura, A. and Jeffery, R. W. (1973) Role of symbolic coding and rehearsal processes in observational learning, *Journal of Personality and Social Psychology*, 26(1): 122–130.

Bandura, A., Jeffery, R. W. and Bachicha, D. L. (1974) Analysis of memory codes and cumulative rehearsal in observational learning, *Journal of Research in Personality*, 7(3): 295–305.

Bandura, A. and McDonald, F. J. (1963) Influence of social reinforcement and the behavior of models in shaping children's moral judgment, *Journal of Abnormal and Social Psychology*, 67(3): 274–281.

Bandura, A., Ross, D. and Ross, S. A. (1961) Transmission of aggression through imitation of aggressive models, *Journal of Abnormal and Social Psychology*, 63(3): 575–582.

Bandura, A., Ross, D. and Ross, S. A. (1963a) Imitation of film-mediated aggressive models, *Journal of Abnormal and Social Psychology*, 66(1): 3–11.

Bandura, A., Ross, D. and Ross, S. A. (1963b) Vicarious reinforcement and imitative learning, *Journal of Abnormal and Social Psychology*, 67(6): 601–607.

Baron, R. A. (1970) Attraction toward the model and model's competences as determinants of adult imitative behavior, *Journal of Personality and Social Psychology*, 14(4): 345–351.

Boatman, P. R. (2008) *An Application of Behavior Modeling Training to Complex Skill Acquisition*. Ph.D. dissertation, The University of Oklahoma, United States – Oklahoma Publication No. AAT 3336779.

Bolt, M. A., Killough, L. N. and Koh, H. C. (2001) Testing the interaction effects of task complexity in computer training using the social cognitive model, *Decision Sciences*, 32(1): 1–20.

Bowers, D. G. and Franklin, J. L. (1972) Survey-guided development: Using human resources measurements in organization change, *Journal of Contemporary Business*, 1(1): 43–55.

Boyd, J. D., II. (1973) Microcounseling for a counseling-like verbal response set: Differential effects of two micro models and two methods of counseling supervision, *Journal of Counseling Psychology*, 20(1): 97–98.

Bretz, R. D., Jr. and Thompsett, R. E. (1992) Comparing traditional and integrative learning methods in organizational training programs, *Journal of Applied Psychology*, 77(6): 941–951.

Burke, M. J. and Day, R. R. (1986) A cumulative study of the effectiveness of managerial training, *Journal of Applied Psychology*, 71(2): 232–245.

Burke, M. J., Sarpy, S. A., Smith-Crowe, K., Chan-Serafin, S., Salvador, R. O. and Islam, G. (2006) Relative effectiveness of worker safety and health training methods, *American Journal of Public Health*, 96(2): 315–324.

Burnaska, R. F. (1976) The effects of behavior modeling training upon managers' behaviors and employee perceptions, *Personnel Psychology*, 29(3): 329–335.

Byham, W. C., Adams, D. and Kiggins, A. (1976) Transfer of modeling training to the job, *Personnel Psychology*, 29(3): 345–349.

Byham, W. C. and Robinson, J. (1976) Interaction modeling: A new concept in supervisory training, *Training and Development Journal*, 30(2): 20–33.

Cellar, D. F. and Wade, K. (1988) Effect of behavioral modeling on intrinsic motivation and script-related recognition, *Journal of Applied Psychology*, 73(2): 181–192.

Chen, C., Olfman, L. and Harris, A. (2005) Differential impacts of social presence on the behavior modeling approach, *International Journal of Technology and Human Interaction*, 1(2): 64–84.

Chen, C., Ryan, T. and Olfman, L. (2006) Online behavior modeling: An effective and affordable online software training method, *International Journal of Technology and Human Interaction*, 1(4): 36–53.

Chen, C. and Shaw, R. S. (2006) Asynchronous software training through the behavior modeling approach: A longitudinal field experiment, *International Journal of Distance Education Technologies*, 4(4): 88–102.

Davis, B. L. and Mount, M. K. (1984) Effectiveness of performance appraisal training using computer assisted instruction and behavior modeling, *Personnel Psychology*, 37(3): 439–452.

Davis, F. D. and Yi, M. Y. (2004) Improving computer skill training: Behavior modeling, symbolic mental rehearsal, and the role of knowledge structures, *Journal of Applied Psychology*, 89(3): 509–523.

Decker, P. J. (1980) Effects of symbolic coding and rehearsal in behavior-modeling training, *Journal of Applied Psychology*, 65(6): 627–634.

Decker, P. J. (1982) The enhancement of behavior modeling training of supervisory skills by the inclusion of retention processes, *Personnel Psychology*, 35(2): 323–332.

Decker, P. J. (1983) The effects of rehearsal group size and video feedback in behavior modeling training, *Personnel Psychology*, 36(4): 763–773.

Decker, P. J. (1984) Effects of different symbolic coding stimuli in behavior modeling training, *Personnel Psychology*, 37(4): 711–720.

Decker, P. J. and Nathan, B. R. (1985) *Behavior Modeling Training: Principles and Applications*. New York: Praeger.

Dempster, F. N. (1988) The spacing effect: A case study in the failure to apply the results of psychological research, *American Psychologist*, 43(8): 627–634.

Dixon, N. M. (1990) Organizational learning: A review of the literature with implications for HRD professionals, *Human Resource Development Quarterly*, 3(1): 29–49.

Dowling, T. H. and Frantz, T. T. (1975) The influence of facilitative relationships on initiative learning, *Journal of Counseling Psychology*, 22(4): 259–263.

Druckman, D. and Swets, J. A. (1988) *Enhancing Human Performance: Issues, Theories, and Techniques*. Washington, DC: National Academy Press.

Dweck, C. S. (1986) Motivational processes affecting learning, *American Psychologist*, 41(10): 1040–1048.

Earley, P. C., Connolly, T. and Ekegren, G. (1989) Goals, strategy development and task performance: Some limits on the efficacy of goal setting, *Journal of Applied Psychology*, 74(1): 24–33.

Ebbinghaus, H. (1885). *Über das Gedächtnis: Untersuchungen zur experimentellen Psychologie*. Leipzig, Deutschland: Duncker & Humblot.

Ebbinghaus, H. (1913) *Memory*. H. A. Ruger and C. E. Bussenius (trans.). New York: Teachers College (Original work published 1885).

Ebbinghaus, H. (1964). *Memory*. H. A. Ruger and C. E. Bussenius (trans.). New York: Dover (Original work published 1885).

Eden, D. and Zuk, Y. (1995) Seasickness as a self-fulfilling prophecy: Raising self-efficacy to boost performance at sea, *Journal of Applied Psychology*, 80(5): 628–635.

Erlich, R. and Russ-Eft, D. (2013) Assessing academic advising outcomes using social cognitive theory, *NACADA Journal*, 33(1): 1–18.

Eskedal, G. A. (1975) Symbolic role modeling and cognitive learning in the training of counselors, *Journal of Counseling Psychology*, 22(2): 152–155.

Estes, W. K. (1950) Toward a statistical theory of learning, *Psychological Review*, 57(2): 94–107.

Estes, W. K. (1960) Learning theory and the new mental chemistry, *Psychological Review*, 67(4): 207–223.

Estes, W. K. (1964) All-or-none processes in learning and retention, *American Psychologist*, 19(1): 16–25.

Fehrenbach, P. A., Miller, D. J. and Thelen, M. H. (1979) The importance of consistency of modeling behavior upon imitation: A comparison of single and multiple models, *Journal of Personality and Social Psychology*, 37(8): 1412–1417.

Fyffe, A. E. and Oei, T. P. S. (1979) Influence of modeling and feedback provided by the supervisors in a microskills training program for beginning counselors, *Journal of Clinical Psychology*, 35(4): 651–656.

Gerst, M. S. (1971) Symbolic coding processes in observational learning, *Journal of Personality and Social Psychology*, 19(1): 7–17.

Gist, M. E., Schwoerer, C. and Rosen, B. (1989) Effects of alternative training methods on self-efficacy and performance in computer software training, *Journal of Applied Psychology*, 74(6): 884–891.

Goldstein, A. P. and Sorcher, M. (1973) Changing managerial behavior by applied learning techniques, *Training and Development Journal*, 26(3): 36–39.

Goldstein, A. P. and Sorcher, M. (1974) *Changing Supervisor Behavior*. New York: Pergamon.

Guthrie, E. R. (1935) *The Psychology of Learning*. New York: Harper.

Guthrie, E. R. (1952) *The Psychology of Learning* (revised edn). New York: Harper.

Hards, K. E. (1981) *Supervisory Skill Workshops: Final Report*. Stanford, CA: Stanford University Hospital, Department of Human Resources Development.

Harrison, J. K. (1992) Individual and combined effects of behavior modeling and the cultural assimilator in cross-cultural management raining, *Journal of Applied Psychology*, 77(6): 952–962.

Haston, W. (2007) Teacher modeling as an effective teaching strategy, *Music Educators Journal*, 93(4): 26–30.

Hogan, P. M., Hakel, M. D. and Decker, P. J. (1986) Effects of trainee-generated versus trainer-provided rule codes on generalization in behavior-modeling training, *Journal of Applied Psychology*, 71(3): 469–473.

Holton, E. F., III, Bates, R. and Ruona, W. E. A. (2000) Development of a generalized learning transfer system inventory, *Human Resource Development Quarterly*, 11(4): 333–360.

Holton, E. F., III, Bates, R., Seyler, D. L. and Carvalho, M. B. (1997) Toward a construct validation of a transfer climate instrument, *Human Resource Development Quarterly*, 8(2): 95–113.

Hoover, A. and Russ-Eft, D. (2005) Effect of concurrent task management training on single pilot task prioritization performance, *International Journal of Applied Aviation Studies*, 5: 233–251.

Hull, C. L. (1943) *Principles of Behavior*. New York: Appleton-Century-Crofts.

Ilgen, D. R., Fisher, C. D. and Taylor, M. S. (1979) Consequences of individual feedback on behavior in organizations, *Journal of Applied Psychology*, 64(4): 349–371.

Ilgen, D. R. and Moore, C. F. (1987) Types and choices of performance feedback, *Journal of Applied Psychology*, 72(3): 401–406.

Jeffery, R. W. (1976) The influence of symbolic and motor rehearsal in observational learning, *Journal of Research in Personality*, 10(1): 116–127.

Johnson, R. D. (2000) The role of behavioral modeling in computer skills acquisition – toward refinement of the model, *Information Systems Research*, 11(4): 402–417.

Johnson, R. D. and Marakas, G. M. (2000) The role of behavioral modeling in computer skills acquisition: Toward refinement of the model, *Information Systems Research*, 11(4): 402–417.

Jost, A. (1897) Die assoziationsfestigkeit in ihrer abhängigkeit von der verteilungder wiederholungen, *Zeitschrift für Psychologie und Physiologie der Sinnesorgane*, 14: 436–472.

Kanfer, R. and Ackerman, P. L. (1989) Motivation and cognitive abilities: An integrative/aptitude-treatment interaction approach to skill acquisition, *Journal of Applied Psychology*, 74(4): 657–690.

Kitsantas, A., Zimmerman, B. J., and Cleary, T. (2000) The role of observation and emulation in the development of athletic self-regulation, *Journal of Educational Psychology*, 92(4): 811–817.

Klein, H. J. and Thoms, P. (1995) The setting of goals for skill acquisition. In E. F. Holton III (ed.) *Proceedings from the 1995 Annual Meeting of the Academy of Human Resource Development*. Austin, TX: Academy of Human Resource Development.

Kloba, J. A., Jr. (1975) The effects of model status and participant dependency – independency on adolescent learning of a helping skill using the micro-counseling training paradigm. In *Dissertation Abstracts International* (vol. 36, 2027A). San Francisco, CA: University Microfilms. (No. 797, 75–22).

Kloba, J. A., Jr. and Zimpfer, D. (1976) Status and independence as variables in micro-counseling training of adolescents, *Journal of Counseling Psychology*, 23(5): 458–463.

Komaki, J., Barwick, K. D. and Scott, L. R. (1978) Behavioral approach to occupational safety: Pinpointing and reinforcing safe performance in a food manufacturing plant, *Journal of Applied Psychology*, 63(4): 434–445.

Kraut, A. L. (1976) Developing managerial skills via modeling techniques: Some positive research findings – A symposium, *Personnel Psychology*, 29(3): 325–328.

Latham, G. P. and Saari, L. M. (1979) Application of social-learning theory of training supervisors through behavior modeling, *Journal of Applied Psychology*, 64(3): 239–246.

Locke, E. and Latham, G. P. (1990) *A Theory of Goal Setting and Task Performance*. Englewood Cliffs, NJ: Prentice-Hall.

Mann, R. B. and Decker, P. J. (1984) The effect of key behavior distinctiveness on generalization and recall in behavior modeling training, *The Academy of Management Journal*, 27(4): 900–910.

May, G. L. and Kahnweiler, W. M. (2000) The effect of a mastery practice design on learning and transfer in behavior modeling training, *Personnel Psychology*, 53(2): 353–373.

McDaniel, R. N. (1985) *Effectiveness of a Supervisory Training Program Using Behavior Modeling*. Unpublished master's thesis, Pepperdine University, Malibu, CA.

McGhee, W. and Tullar, W. L. (1978) A note on evaluating behavior modification and behavior modeling as industrial training techniques, *Personnel Psychology*, 31(3): 477–484.

Meyer, H. H. and Raich, M. S. (1983) An objective evaluation of a behavior modeling training program, *Personnel Psychology*, 36(4): 755–761.

Mills, G. (1985) *The Effects of Positive and Negative Models in Learning and Displaying Basic Communication Skills*. Provo, UT: Brigham Young University, Department of Communications.

Moses, J. L. and Ritchie, R. J. (1976) Supervisory relationships training: A behavioral evaluation of a behavior modeling program, *Personnel Psychology*, 29(3): 337–343.

Murthy, N. N., Challagalla, G. N., Vincent, L. H. and Shervani, T. A. (2008) The impact of simulation training on call center agent performance: A field-based investigation, *Management Science*, 54(2): 384–399.

Nadler, J., Thompson, L. and Van Boven, L. (2003) Learning negotiation skills: Four models of knowledge creation and transfer, *Management Science*, 49(4): 529–540.

Newman, J. L. and Fuqua, D. R. (1988) A comparative study of positive and negative modeling in counselor training, *Counselor Education and Supervision*, 28(2): 121–129.

Olson, R., Grosshuesch, A., Schmidt, S., Gray, M. and Wipfli, B. (2009) Observational learning and workplace safety: The effects of viewing the collective behavior of multiple social models on the use of personal protective equipment, *Journal of Safety Research*, 40(5): 383–387.

Payne, R. B. and Hauty, G. T. (1955) The effect of psychological feedback on work decrement, *Journal of Experimental Psychology*, 50(6): 343–351.

Perry, M. A. (1975) Modeling and instructions in training for counselor empathy, *Journal of Counseling Psychology*, 22(3): 173–179.

Porras, J. L. and Anderson, B. (1981) Improving managerial effectiveness through modeling-based training, *Organizational Dynamics*, 9(4): 60–77.

Porras, J. L. and Hargis, K. (1982) Precursors of individual change: Responses to a social learning theory based on organization intervention, *Human Relations*, 35(11): 973–990.

Postman, L. (1963) One-trial learning. In C. N. Cofer and B. S. Musgrave (eds) *Verbal Behavior and Learning* (pp. 295–321). New York: McGraw-Hill.

Rouillier, J. Z. and Goldstein, I. L. (1993) The relationship between organizational transfer climate and positive transfer of training, *Human Resource Development Quarterly*, 4(4): 377–390.

Russ-Eft, D. (1972) A review of learning and behavior theory as it relates to emotional disturbance in children: The behavioral model. In W. C. Rhodes (ed.) *A Study of Child Variance Volume 1: Conceptual Models; Conceptual Project in Emotional Disturbance*. Ann Arbor, MI: The University of Michigan Press.

Russ-Eft, D. (1985) *Preview Client No. 2: Working Training*. Cupertino, CA: Zenger Miller.

Russ-Eft, D. (2002) A typology of training design and work environment factors affecting workplace learning and transfer, *Human Resource Development Review*, 1(1): 45–65.

Russ-Eft, D. F. and Zenger, J. H. (1995) Behavior modeling training in North America: A research summary. In M. Mulder, W. J. Nijhof and R. O. Brinkerhoff (eds) *Corporate Training for Effective Performance* (pp. 89–109). Boston, MA: Kluwer Academic.

Russ-Eft, D., Krishnamurthi, S. and Ravishankar, L. (1994) Getting results with interpersonal skills training. In J. O. Phillips (ed.) *In action: Measuring return on investment* (vol. I, pp. 199–211). Alexandria, VA: American Society for Training and Development.

Russ-Eft, D. and Zucchelli, L. (1987) When wrong is alright, *Training and Development Journal*, 41(11): 78–79.

Russell, J. S., Wexley, K. N. and Hunter, J. E. (1984) Questioning the effectiveness of behavior modeling training in an industrial setting, *Personnel Psychology*, 37(3): 465–481.

Schendel, J. M. and Hagman, J. D. (1982) On sustaining procedural skills over a prolonged retention interval, *Journal of Applied Psychology*, 67(5): 605–610.

Schoening, J. M. (1981) *Effectiveness of a Behavior Modeling Training Program on Management Trainees*. Unpublished master's thesis, Pepperdine University, Malibu, CA.

Sevy, B. A. and Olson, R. D. (1982) *Assessment of Knowledge and Skills Acquired in the Supervision Training Program*. Minneapolis, MN: Personnel Decisions.

Simon, S.J . and Werner, J. M. (1996) Computer training through behavior modeling, self-paced, and instructional approaches: A field experiment, *Journal of Applied Psychology*, 81(6): 648–659.

Smith, P. E. (1976) Management modeling training to improve morale and customer satisfaction, *Personnel Psychology*, 29(3): 351–359.

Smith-Jentsch, K. A., Salas, E. and Baker, D. P. (1996) Training team performance-related assertiveness, *Personnel Psychology*, 49(4): 909–936.

Sorcher, M. and Goldstein, A. P. (1972) A behaviour modelling approach to training. *Personnel Administration*, 35, 35-41.

Sorcher, M. and Spence, R. (1982) The interface project: Behavior modeling as social technology in South Africa, *Personnel Psychology*, 35(3): 557–581.

Stone, G. L. and Vance, A. (1976) Instruction, modelling, and rehearsal: Implications for training, *Journal of Counseling Psychology*, 23(3): 272–279.

Swets, J. A. and Bjork, R. A. (1990) Enhancing human performance: An evaluation of 'New Age' techniques considered by the U.S. Army, *Psychological Science*, 1(1): 85–96.

Taylor, P. J. (1992) Training directors' perceptions about the successful implementation of supervisory training, *Human Resource Development Quarterly*, 3(3): 243–259.

Taylor, P. J., Russ-Eft, D. F. and Chan, D. W. (2005) A meta-analytic review of behaviour modelling training, *Journal of Applied Psychology*, 90(4): 692–709.

Taylor, P. J., Russ-Eft, D. F. and Taylor, H. (2009) The transfer of management training from alternative perspectives, *Journal of Applied Psychology*, 94(1): 104–121.

Trimble, S. K., Decker, P. J. and Nathan, B. R. (1985) *Effect of Positive and Negative Models on Learning: A Report to Zenger-Miller*. St. Louis, MO: University of Missouri-St. Louis, School of Business Administration.

Trimble, S. K., Decker, P. J. and Nathan, B. R. (1991) Effect of positive and negative models on learning: Testing for proactive and retroactive interference, *Journal of Human Behavior and Learning*, 7(2): 1–12.

Truman, G. E. (2009) Behaviour modeling, instruction and exploration training approaches in group and individual contexts, *Behaviour and Information Technology*, 28(6): 493–524.

Underwood, B. J. (1961) Ten years of massed practice on distributed practice, *Psychological Review*, 68(4): 229–247.

Underwood, B. J., Kapelak, S. M. and Malmi, R. A. (1976) The spacing effect: Additions to the theoretical and empirical puzzles, *Memory and Cognition*, 4(4): 391–400.

Wallace, W. G., Horan, J. J., Baker, S. B. and Hudson, G. R. (1975) Incremental effects of modeling and performance feedback in teaching Decision-Making Counseling, *Journal of Counseling Psychology*, 22(6): 570–572.

Walter, G. A. (1976) Changing behavior in task groups through social learning: Modeling alternatives, *Human Relations*, 29(2): 167–178.

Wehrenberg, S. and Kuhnle, R (1983) How training through behavior modeling works. In L. Baird, C. Schneier and D. Laird (eds) *The Training Development Sourcebook* (pp. 133–137). Amherst, MA: Human Resource Development Press.

Werner, J. M., O'Leary-Kelly, A. M., Baldwin, T. T. and Wexley, K. N. (1994) Augmenting behavior-modeling training: Testing the effects of pre-and post-training interventions, *Human Resource Development Quarterly*, 5(2): 169–183.

Wexley, K. N. and Baldwin, T. T. (1986) Post-training strategies for facilitating positive transfer: An empirical exploration, *The Academy of Management Journal*, 29(3): 503–520.

Wexley, K. N. and Latham, G. P. (1991) *Developing and Training Human Resources in Organizations*. New York: HarperCollins.

Wexley, K. N. and Nemeroff, W. F. (1975) Effectiveness of positive reinforcement and goal setting as methods of management development, *Journal of Applied Psychology*, 60(4): 446–450.

Yi, M. Y. and Davis, F. D. (2001) Improving computer training effectiveness for decision technologies: Behavior modeling and retention enhancement, *Decision Sciences*, 32(3): 521–544.

Yi, M. Y. and Davis, F. D. (2003) Developing and validating an observational learning model of computer software training and skill acquisition, *Information Systems Research*, 14(2): 146–169.

Zimmerman, B. J. and Kitsantas, A. (2002) Acquiring writing revision and self-regulatory skill through observation and emulation, *Journal of Educational Psychology*, 94(4): 660–668.

FURTHER READING

Bandura, A. (1965a) Behavior modification through modeling procedures. In L. P. Ullman (ed.) *Research in Behavior Modification* (pp. 310–340). New York: Holt.

Bandura, A. (1965b) Vicarious processes: A case of no-trial learning. In L. Berkowitz (ed.) *Advances in Experimental Social Psychology* (vol. 2, pp. 1–56). New York: Academic Press.

Bandura, A. (1977) *Social Learning Theory*. Englewood Cliffs, NJ: Prentice Hall.

Decker, P. J. and Nathan, B. R. (1985) *Behavior Modeling Training: Principles and Applications*. New York: Praeger.

Goldstein, A. P. and Sorcher, M. (1974) *Changing Supervisor Behavior*. New York: Pergamon.

Latham, G. P. and Saari, L. M. (1979) Application of social-learning theory of training supervisors through behavior modeling, *Journal of Applied Psychology*, 64(3): 239–246.

Russ-Eft, D. (1997) Behavior modeling. In L. Bassi and D. Russ-Eft (eds) *What Works: Training and Development Practices* (pp. 105–149). Alexandria, VA: American Society for Training and Development.

Taylor, P. J., Russ-Eft, D. F. and Chan, D. W. (2005) A meta-analytic review of behavior modeling training, *Journal of Applied Psychology*, 90(4): 692–709.

Taylor, P. J., Russ-Eft, D. F. and Taylor, H. (2009) The transfer of management training from alternative perspectives, *Journal of Applied Psychology*, 94(1): 104–121.

This paper represents a revision and updating of the following work:

Russ-Eft, D. (1997) Behavior modeling. In L. Bassi and D. Russ-Eft (eds) *What Works: Training and Development Practices* (pp. 105–149). Alexandria, VA: American Society for Training and Development.

The adaptation of this previous work has been approved by the American Society for Training and Development (ASTD), but the contents do not represent the opinions of that organization.

part 3

CAREER DEVELOPMENT APPROACHES

7

CAREER INTEREST INVENTORIES IN TIMES OF CHANGE

Linda Hite and Kimberly McDonald

INTRODUCTION

In recent years, career development (CD) has often been overlooked as a viable part of human resource development (HRD). HRD's declining interest in career development appears to coincide with a significant change in the workplace climate. A combination of globalization and advanced technological capabilities prompted some organizations to seek competitive advantage by flattening and downsizing, ignoring the traditional psychological contract that rewarded productivity with promotion and permanence (Savickas et al., 2009). Many employees, particularly those with transferable skills, responded in kind, replacing company loyalty with free agency. Identifying this as 'the new social arrangement of work', Savickas et al. (2009) have observed that this change in the working relationship has had international repercussions. They described current 'occupational prospects' that are 'less definable and predictable' than in the past, 'with job transitions more frequent and difficult', prompting individuals to take more responsibility for their own careers (p. 240). An unintended consequence of these shifts in the employer–employee relationship was that the career development function of HRD seemed to lose its purpose (McDonald and Hite, 2005). This was ironic, since systems attempting to become more effective and efficient depend on a well-trained and high-performing workforce. As the shock of loss begins to wear off and organizations recognize leaner operations as a continuing reality, not just a stage, they are once again beginning to realize the value of career development as a means of attracting and retaining talent. It is timely, then, to explore approaches to CD and to question if the traditional methods adequately meet the realities of the current workplace, either for organizations or for individuals. Since CD appears to be relatively dormant in current HRD preparation and practice, this chapter will explore career planning from the perspective of career counselling theory and application, then offer implications for HRD.

The origins of career development are often linked with the 1909 publication of Parsons' *Choosing a Vocation*, and his idea that individual abilities and the needs of the workplace could, with appropriate planning and guidance, be matched successfully. Parson's plan was the basis for the trait and factor method, matching personal traits with jobs. As this perspective evolved, it became known as the person-environment fit (P-E fit) approach, which carries on the matching tradition to find the best correspondence between person and work environment (Chartrand, 1991; Hansen, 2005; Rottinghaus and van Esbroeck, 2011). Historically, these 'differential' approaches have been considered to be the first of 'four distinct traditions' (p. 100) of career counselling, but it is not just relegated to the history books. Still reviewed and researched, much of the career counselling literature continues to suggest that linking interests and work can result in job satisfaction (Hartung, 2010).

In the ensuing decades, that matching process has often involved completion of standardized instruments designed to assess interests, abilities, or even personality traits that would indicate a propensity towards particular careers. At its worst, the reliance on tests often fostered a 'test and tell' (Sampson, 2009, p. 94) mentality among some practitioners that reduced career guidance to simply reporting the results and trusting the test to provide the right answer. Even when implemented appropriately, standardized career testing in the 21st century has come under scrutiny for potentially being out of touch with current career and workplace realities and yielding data based on 'someone else's construction of reality', instead of the reality of 'each individual on the individual's own terms' (Sampson, 2009, p. 92). At the same time, 'the study of interests remains one of the most researched areas in the field' of career assessment (Patton and McIlveen, 2008, p. 124), and 'vocational interests' are widely accepted as 'powerful predictors of vocational decision-making and behavior' (Sullivan and Hansen, 2004, p. 179). Compared to other types of constructs, interests are considered to be easy to validate and measure reliably (Sullivan and Hansen, 2004). So, although other more holistic approaches (e.g. narrative) to career counselling have risen in prominence and practice in recent years, the idea of matching interests to work persists. It is not surprising, then, that well-known career inventories and models continue to be updated with the intention of better reflecting contemporary interests and constituencies (Donnay et al., 2004; Patton and McIlveen, 2008). This chapter will explore the potential of career interest testing to meet the needs of both individuals and organizations in an era when careers are fluid rather than fixed, and career development processes must be flexible as well as cost effective. Other means of fostering career decision-making and career development will be explored as well, with recommendations to organizations regarding workforce career development.

POPULAR INTEREST INVENTORIES

In their analysis of interest assessment, Dik and Rottinghaus (2013, p. 33) identified four interest inventories as 'the most frequently used': the Strong Interest Inventory, the Self Directed Search, the Campbell Interest and Skill Inventory, and the Kuder Career Search and Person Match. Each will be addressed briefly here as key examples of assessment tools used in career counselling.

While career interest inventories are employed all over the world, many of the instruments have US origins, including the Strong Interest Inventory (SII), arguably one of the best known (Dik and Rottinghaus, 2013; Greenhaus et al., 2010). Originally developed in 1927, the SII was most recently revised in 2012, updating the list of potential occupations to more closely reflect the current job landscape (Herk and Thompson, 2012). The previous 2004 revision was more comprehensive, renewing multiple scales (Herk and Thompson, 2012) and attempting to better reflect a more diverse US workforce (Case and Blackwell, 2008). The men and women in the sample were chosen to represent 'the distribution of racial and ethnic groups in the United States' (Donnay et al., 2004 p. 2). While the updates are commendable, the continued US focus does not address concerns about the accuracy of capturing varied cultural dimensions with this instrument (Case and Blackwell, 2008).

A popular basis for the SII and many other interest-based inventories is Holland's RIASEC hexagon. The hexagon is based on the premise that jobs can be described within six categories (realistic, investigative, artistic, social, enterprising and conventional), and that individual interest patterns can be captured in combinations of these categories to yield potential matches of person to work (Greenhaus et al., 2010; Spokane and Cruza-Guet, 2005). The RIASEC model has endured not just time but also research review. The 'hexagon and

RIASEC typology are ubiquitous and provide the organizational structure for most commercially available interest inventories' (Dik and Rottinghaus, 2013, p. 327). Even as newer approaches have eclipsed the prominence of the interest-matching method for career choice, it continues to be used and cited with frequency. Holland, himself a proponent of the P-E fit approach, used the RIASEC interest sets in developing the Self Directed Search (SDS). Like the SII, it is widely used and attempts to link individual interests to potential occupations (Greenhaus et al., 2010; Spokane and Cruza-Guet, 2005). Unlike some inventories released only to credentialled practitioners, the SDS, first available in the early 1970s, was created for individual use and interpretation (Spokane and Cruza-Guet, 2005). A popular choice because it is so accessible (including an online format), it might prompt career seekers to rely on the results of one instrument as their professional directive, a potential concern among counsellors who advocate for a more holistic approach to career decision-making (Prince et al., 2003).

Two other well-known, often-used and well-validated interest instruments are the Kuder Career Search and Person Match (KCS) and the Campbell Interest and Skill Inventory (CISS). The Kuder is one of the oldest established instruments, originally published in 1939, although revised and updated over the years; while the CISS is among the newest, appearing in 1992 (Greenhaus et al., 2010). Today, both are built on structures similar to Holland's RIASEC, but varied enough to grant them a sense of uniqueness in the field of interest inventory options. For example, six of the seven CISS scales can be paired with the Holland six, showing connections between CISS producing, analysing, creating, helping, influencing and organizing with Holland's realistic, investigative, artistic, social, enterprising and conventional, respectively (Hansen and Leuty, 2007). The seventh for CISS is adventuring, an extension of RAISEC's realistic measure. Like the SDS, the KCS is a self-interpretation instrument, although respondents are encouraged to use it in conjunction with career counselling (Dik and Rottinghaus, 2013).

LIMITATIONS OF INTEREST INVENTORIES

While interest assessment instruments and many others like them continue to be used with frequency in career counselling and development, the literature is also clear that there are limitations to reliance on interest inventories as a main method to address career decision-making and consideration. This has called into question the traditional P-E fit approach. While the P-E fit model has evolved over time so that it often incorporates resources beyond test data, the reliance on standardized measures as a key part of the approach has left it open to criticism in the discourse about contemporary careers. Typical concerns of standardized interest inventories involve applicability regarding gender and cross-cultural differences, ethical use of testing for career development, and questions about effectiveness to adequately address the complexity of current careers. Each will be explored in more detail.

Recent iterations of popular interest inventories have been careful to include gender representation in norming samples in an effort to make the instruments more effective for use with women as well as men. This has not, however, quelled all the concerns about how effectively gender issues are addressed in this type of testing. Fitzgerald and Harmon (2001) cautioned about assuming that just connecting interests to work would make sense when life and work issues were already becoming more intertwined for both men and women, requiring a more nuanced view of how one approaches career choices. They noted too the still prevalent influence of society on women's career preferences (role restrictions, stereotypes) and related issues of equality (pay, promotion, etc.) that add complexity to women's career development and complicate the basic tenants of the traditional P-E fit approach. Whiston and Bouwkamp (2003) extended that concern. They recognized that career practitioners' views regarding gender roles and expectations can pose another hurdle for women seeking career advice. Since the P-E fit approach is more counsellor than client driven, counsellor beliefs and biases are more likely to influence instrument interpretation and outcome, and traditional gender views could inhibit how women clients see their opportunities.

Other researchers have cautioned against the inadequacy of relying only on interests, urging the importance of considering other antecedents that might influence interest inventory responses. Self-efficacy, in particular, has been identified as an important factor to assess along with interest to get a full picture, since women are more likely than men to underestimate their abilities, and that may affect how they portray their preferences regarding career options (Betz and Rottinghaus, 2006; Whiston and Bouwkamp, 2003).

Hansen (2005) also observed concerns regarding interest testing, noting on instruments using the RIASEC (or similar models) that women traditionally score higher in artistic and social fields while men have a stronger showing in realistic and investigative ones. This was reinforced by a study on the 2004 SII. Einarsdottir and Rounds (2009) found that individual items did hold gender bias.

The results indicate that there are different meanings and implications for measured interests between the men and women. Most importantly, women and men with the same level of interest or trait being measured by the GOT's [General Occupational Themes] tend to respond differently to sex-stereotyped items. For example, women are not as likely as men to say they like highly male stereotyped items like auto racer even though they have equally realistic interests. (p. 305)

Whiston and Bouwkamp (2003) identified similar concerns not only with interest tests using RIASEC, but also with inventories based on other types of interest models. This potential skewing of results leads to concerns about the utility of these inventories for women and men with non-traditional career interests (Hansen, 2005). Further, it suggests other potential errors, for example using an instrument normed on a US sample with varied ethnic and racial groups (Einarsdottir and Rounds, 2009). On a larger scale, it might also call into question the continued use of Holland's RIASEC model, since it was created in the 1950s when the workforce as well as the workplace was more homogeneous (Einarsdottir and Rounds, 2009). Since the RIASEC model is widely used and variations proliferate, a review of its continued utility would have major ramifications for interest testing.

Another limitation of interest inventories is their typically Western, and often more specifically, US perspective (Watson, 2006b; Watson et al., 2005). For example, concerns over adapting interest inventories to multicultural use have prompted research focusing on the application of Holland's interest types (Hansen, 2005). Although many studies have suggested validity, they have often been very limited in scope; for example, observing if respondents later entered the field suggested by the test results. This narrow observation dismisses that most interest inventory scales use Anglo-Americans as the sample and that most are prepared for those who speak English fluently (Hansen, 2005). Fouad (2002) has suggested that although studies have not surfaced big differences when interest instruments have been given to multicultural groups, it may be because they are not asking the right things.

> ... researchers may be measuring a set of interests that does not capture the domains on which racial/ethnic groups differ from each other. A review of the items on the SII, for example, indicates no items that could be considered *collectivistic*, such as working toward group goals or being part of a team. Rather, all items are *individualistic*, focusing on individual activities and choices. (p. 288)

Watson (2006b) reinforced the individualistic versus interdependent aspect as a limitation to multicultural use, since the 'collectivist self' (p. 50) is a mainstay of many non-Western cultures and will influence career choices. In this instance, and perhaps in other ways that cultures differ (perceptions of risk-taking, power, etc.), individuals who grow up outside the Anglo-US experience are essentially being measured by instruments developed for a totally different population in a different context. An additional concern is the cultural intelligence of career practitioners. Those with ethnocentric or narrow worldviews not only may misunderstand the needs of multicultural clients but, in that misunderstanding, may verge on unethical practice by inadvertently imposing their own cultural biases and interpretations on the client (Watson, 2006b).

Issues surrounding gender and cross-cultural use of interest inventories are not the only ethical concerns that should be considered. Barak (2001) has questioned the limited theoretical underpinnings of the concept of 'interests', as applied in the matching of interests to careers. He asserted that rather than delving into the complexities of the conceptual nature of 'interests' in humans, interest inventory developers substituted 'likes' and 'dislikes' instead, because it was more expedient (p. 102). This raises doubts about encouraging reliance on objective 'interest' measurements to answer one's career questions.

Another ethical issue related to interest inventories is the proliferation of self-help career assessments. While these types of tests are typically 'less expensive, require less time to complete, and are more readily accessible than tools administrated by a counselor', they also prompt concern on several points (Prince et al., 2003, p. 42). Their unregulated nature means they can vary greatly in quality and theoretical foundations and may be outdated or misleading; they are not designed to address individual differences in skills or insights, and often they are used in place of career counselling, meaning information may be misinterpreted (Prince et al., 2003). Given these limitations, they can result in more harm than benefit.

The limitations of interest inventories are disconcerting. However, perhaps the overarching concern regarding the P-E fit, or the matching approach to career counselling, is the inadequacy to respond to the dynamic nature of the current career landscape. The conventional P-E fit approach is grounded in traditional assumptions about the objective predictable nature of work and linear or at least sequential career paths. Work is considered as separate from other aspects of life, rather than within the context of life choices, and career assessment is viewed as a task to be completed early in life, resulting in a singular career plan. In contrast, 21st-century careers have become increasingly complex, less stable and bounded, decidedly non-linear, individually driven and requiring a lifelong process of exploration and adaptation (Krieshok et al., 2009; Rottinghaus and van Esbroeck, 2011; Savickas et al., 2009). As individuals take more personal responsibility for their careers, it is not surprising that newer, more holistic and more comprehensive approaches appear to be eclipsing the logical positivism of P-E fit. Some researchers clearly suggest that it is too simplistic and needs an overhaul to be of use (Barak, 2001); while others imply that matching interests to work may retain relevance if combined with more progressive and expansive approaches (Rottinghaus and van Esbroeck, 2011; Savickas, 2005). Newer career development models that foster 'adaptability, narratibility, activity, and intentionality' (Savickas et al., 2009, pp. 245–246) prompt individuals to be flexible in how they see their career paths; to use self-reflection to find their work roles; to participate in activities that build career skills; to find their own meaning in work and to determine their own career trajectories. Interest testing may be part of that journey, but it would not be the driving force in the process.

Recognizing the limitations of counselling based on traditional career assessments, scholars increasingly have been developing new methods to assist individuals seeking career counselling. Many of these postmodern approaches focus on qualitative methods as an alternative to traditional, positivistic assessment tools. In the following section, narrative approaches to career counselling will be highlighted as well as some of the theoretical frameworks from which these methods are derived.

NARRATIVE CAREER COUNSELLING

The past 20 years has seen a rise in the use of narrative career counselling. This approach has been embraced and researched internationally, with leading scholars coming from a variety of countries such as Australia (e.g. Patton and McMahon, Pryor and Bright), South Africa (e.g. Watson), Canada (e.g. Bujold) and the United States (e.g. Brott, Savickas). While a lot has been written about narrative approaches (e.g. Brott, 2005; McIlveen and Patton, 2007; Savickas, 2005; Stebleton, 2010), widespread use and discussion of these approaches has yet to appear in the HRD literature, despite some resurgence of a focus on career development in the field (Hite and McDonald, 2008; Park and Rothwell, 2009; Sun and Wang, 2009). It is beyond the scope of this chapter to provide an in-depth exploration of narrative approaches and their underlying theoretical frameworks. However, it is important that HRD scholars and practitioners become knowledgeable regarding how these approaches may address the limitations of more traditional career assessments and better reflect the career development landscape in the 21st century.

Narrative approaches to career counselling rely on the individual's subjective perspective of experiences, interests and beliefs to formulate one's story. Rather than imposing a career view on the client, the data emerge instead from the individual. An advantage of this approach is that the client comes to understand and navigate one's career through the use of his/her own language (Savickas et al., 2009). McIlveen and Patton (2007) explained:

> Narrative career counselling emphasizes subjectivity and meaning. It aims to facilitate self-reflection and elaboration of self-concepts toward an enhanced self-understanding that is subjectively and contextually truthful. It entails a collaborative process in which the client is supported in creating an open ended person story that holistically accounts for his or her life and career, and enables the person to make meaningfully informed career decisions and actions. (p. 228)

Narrative career counselling is grounded in constructivist theoretical frameworks. One of the hallmarks of constructivism is that 'individuals are active agents in the production of their careers' (McMahon and Watson, 2008, p. 280). Patton and McMahon's (2006) Systems Theory Framework (STF), Savickas' (2005) theory of career construction and Pryor and Bright's (2003; 2007b) Chaos Theory of Careers (CTC) are three examples of constructivism theories. All focus on the individual. According to STF, the individual is at the centre of the career development process, taking an active role in constructing and creating one's career (McIlveen and Patton, 2007; Patton and McMahon, 2006). Savickas (2005) indicated three components: vocational personality, career adaptability and life themes are critical in explaining the 'interpretive and interpersonal process through which individuals impose meaning and direction on their vocational behavior' (p. 42). It is through narrative (e.g. stories) that these life themes begin to emerge and help a client to give meaning to one's career (e.g. choices, challenges, changes). CTC, also focusing on the individual level of analysis, views 'each individual from a career development perspective ... as a complex, unique, non-linear, adaptive, chaotic and open system' (Pryor and Bright, 2003, p. 16).

Also critical to all three theories is the importance of viewing individuals as open systems that interact with a variety of influences. While not a major focus of the theory of career construction, Savickas (2005) suggested an open system approach, particularly in his explanation of career adaptability. Recognizing the turbulence of the environments that influence individuals, Savickas (2005) argued that career development is 'driven by adaptation to an environment' (p. 51). The importance of the contextual nature of careers was emphasized again when Savickas et al. (2009) described the life-design counselling framework based on the career construction theory.

Individuals as open systems is a central theme, however, in STF and CTC. STF outlines both content influences and process influences on an individual's career development. Content influences include the individual system (e.g. personality, demographic characteristics, beliefs, skills) and the contextual system, which includes the social system, such as family and peers, and the environmental-societal system (e.g. employment market, globalization and geographical location) (McMahon and Watson, 2008; Patton and McMahon, 2006). Process influences include recursiveness ('the interaction between influences'), change over time and chance (McMahon and Watson, 2008, p. 282).

As observed by Patton and McMahon (2006), the notion of the individual as an open system influenced by multiple systems is a central theme of CTC. In addition, CTC uses principles from chaos theory, originating in mathematics and the physical sciences, and applies them to career development. For example, chaos theorists have identified 'attractors' that are 'general patterns of system behaviors' (Pryor et al., 2008, p. 310). Three of these attractors – point (very goal-driven behaviour), pendulum (indecisive and constant vacillation in terms of thinking and behaviour) and torus (habitual and routine thinking and behaviour) – are indicative of closed-system thinking, which Pryor and Bright (2007b) suggested will not work in 'an open system reality' (p. 384) that is marked by the need for contingency (Pryor and Bright, 2007a). The fourth, the strange attractor, is a complex system that functions 'at the edge of chaos' (Pryor and Bright, 2007b, p. 384), meaning that patterns of functioning (referred to as fractals) are both stable and unstable, and while patterns emerge over time, there are always disruptions in the system (Bright and Pryor, 2011; Pryor and Bright, 2006). According to Pryor and Bright (2007b), this open-system thinking perspective is key to CTC; in other words, the strange attractor is necessary for effective career counselling and development.

Bright, Pryor, Chan and Rijanto (2009), and Patton and McMahon (2006), have recognized the importance of chance events in career development and have incorporated this concept in their theories. Unplanned events can have an enormous impact on an individual's career, yet as Bright et al. (2009) pointed out, this phenomenon has been largely ignored by career scholars. The focus on chance events suggests a dramatic change from the logical positivist view that careers can be carefully planned, controlled and predicted. Bright et al. (2009) highlighted the importance of these events, particularly now:

> Any view of careers which does not also include a vision of chance, uncertainty, the limits of control and the partial nature of our knowledge of outcomes, is ultimately inadequate. This was always the case but it is even more so in the 21st century world of work in which complexity, change, and interconnection are accelerating the rate and potential impact of unplanned and unforeseen events. (p. 22)

Narrative approaches then encourage individuals to create stories that help them understand and develop greater meaning of their careers. Many of these narrative approaches are designed to help individuals explore these concepts outlined in the theories discussed above: what influences have impact on their careers, what life themes emerge from their stories, and how chance events affect their career development. Numerous types of narratives are utilized in career counselling. For example, Peavy (2000) developed a counselling activity called 'life-space mapping' in which a client visually constructs a map of his/her personal world (life-space) enabling one to explore ambiguity, understand one's life situation and ultimately achieve greater clarity regarding the career issue(s) at hand. Interviews are frequently used to better understand influences in a client's career (McIlveen and Patton, 2007) and life themes (Savickas, 2005). Other commonly used techniques include storytelling (Brott, 2001; McMahon, 2006), metaphors (Inkson, 2007) and card sorts (Parker, 2006). It is beyond the scope of this chapter to provide a complete listing and explanation of the various techniques utilized when taking a narrative approach to career counselling. Common elements found in the various methods include the use of both dialogue and writing to develop meaning (McIlveen and Patton, 2007), data emerging from the client rather than imposing a perspective or framework onto the individual, and the counselling relationship as a collaborative process (McIlveen and Patton, 2007) where the role of counsellor changes from 'expert' to 'facilitator' (Watson, 2006a, p. 48). As Bujold (2004) wrote:

> Counselors using narrative approaches in their interventions are facilitators in the meaning making process through which clients... are involved in trying, so to speak, to create, to invent their life in their particular contexts. Those counselors are thus co-creators of the stories their clients tell about themselves, stories that have both fluid and more static aspects. It is not new, of course, to speak of the practice of counseling as both a science and an art, but it is perhaps more appropriate than ever to emphasize this latter aspect when considering the use of narrative in counseling, which requires creative approaches from the practitioners. (p. 478)

Constructivist theories and narrative approaches have emerged due to the criticisms highlighted earlier in this chapter. They have developed in reaction to the logical positivist approach that dominated career counselling through most of the 20th century (e.g. Brott, 2001; Patton and McMahon, 2006; Pryor and Bright, 2003). They also better reflect the complex nature of careers and the world of work in the 21st century (Savickas et al., 2009). In addition, they address one of the criticisms lodged against the traditional P-E fit approach that many of the assessment tools are culturally biased, reflecting the 'cultural beliefs of westernised culture' (Watson, 2006a, p. 49). In other words, narrative techniques have the potential to better meet the needs of *all* potential clients in a diverse world since the client uses one's own language, develops one's own story, and reflects on the contextual influences that impact one's own career (Maree and Molepo, 2006; Savickas, 2011; Stebleton, 2010).

DISCUSSION

It is important to point out that narrative approaches are not a panacea for career counselling. Just as there are limitations to the P-E fit approach, there are potential drawbacks of using narrative approaches in career counselling. Two frequently cited concerns are that narrative approaches are time-consuming and that counsellors need particular skills to effectively utilize these techniques (Bujold, 2004; Stebleton, 2010). Stebleton (2010) provided several recommendations to address these limitations. Regarding the first limitation, he suggested that some techniques may not involve that much time and can be done efficiently and effectively. However, we would contend that an awareness of the complexity of careers should result in a different mindset that recognizes that career development is a lifelong process and that understanding one's career and making decisions about next steps will take time.

Regarding the second concern, Stebleton (2010) pointed out that training programmes exist that help counsellors build the skills necessary to develop what Savickas et al. (2009) referred to as 'narrative competence' (p. 249). Patton and McMahon (2006) emphasized the need for counsellor education to move from its 'positivistic traditions of the past' to more 'holistic approaches' (p. 241) in the future. They outlined ways to improve the counsellor education curriculum that includes broadening the focus of career counselling and the use of innovative learning strategies to better train counsellors.

Up to this point, we have presented a case for alternative approaches to career decision-making rather than the traditional standardized inventories and tests. We do, however, concur with Stebleton (2010) and others who believe that these traditional forms of assessment still have a role in career counselling. Sampson (2009), calling for an integration of both modern and postmodern approaches, provided this rationale:

> Practitioners need to determine which interventions, either modern or postmodern, work best with which individuals and in which settings. Differences in decisiveness, personality, culture, verbal ability, learning styles, language skills,

disability status, and so forth can make a specific career intervention effective for one individual and ineffective for another. (p. 94)

Other examples of this integration include Brott's (2001) storied approach in which both quantitative and qualitative data have been used to help clients construct their stories. Savickas (2005), in illustrating how his theory of career construction, works in a counselling situation, used the RIASEC model as well as qualitative methods to assist a client in making a career choice.

IMPLICATIONS FOR HRD

The field of HRD has largely ignored career counselling from both a research and practice perspective. This is understandable in that career counselling in the past has primarily concentrated on assisting young adults and unemployed individuals in making career decisions (Patton and McMahon, 2006). Traditionally, these targeted groups have not been the focus of HRD efforts, nor has career choice been a major emphasis. For the most part, HRD has been more concerned about helping individuals, once employed, to develop their chosen careers within the context of the needs of the organization (for a more detailed analysis, see Egan et al., 2006).

However, this traditional view of counselling in terms of targeted clients and purpose no longer makes sense, given the changing context of work and careers (Patton and McMahon, 2006; Watts and Fretwell, 2003). Instead a 'lifelong' perspective needs to replace this traditional view so that:

individuals participate in and have access to vocational and career information and guidance, job placement services and job search techniques and training support services throughout their lives (Patton and McMahon, 2006, p.230).

This perspective suggests the need for more integration of career counselling and HRD practices to help individuals with all aspects of their careers. Indeed, Watts and Fretwell (2003) in their report of a study conducted on seven countries' public policies regarding career counselling and guidance argued that, from an economic development perspective, career guidance must be a part of HRD strategy. One of their recommendations was that incentives should be provided to private and voluntary sector organizations to develop career counselling/guidance services.

HRD's lack of involvement in career counselling also might be attributed to the lack of practitioner training in this area. Career counsellors should have special training, and many HRD practitioners do not have the prerequisite skills and knowledge to assume this role. Incorporating more career counselling training in HRD academic programmes might be one approach to addressing this problem. Developing strong partnerships with career counsellors to better assist people in developing and managing their careers could be an option as well, essentially outsourcing for that expertise. Given the reality that individuals throughout their careers may need counselling and guidance, HRD practitioners may need to reconsider how CD is approached to make it both effective and efficient. This might include group counselling approaches and even the judicious use of self-help career assessments (Prince et al., 2003) as more practical ways of meeting this burgeoning need.

CONCLUSION

The traditional matching approach to career counselling has increasingly come under fire in the past 20 years. This chapter highlights some of the major criticisms of this approach and offers narrative-based counselling as an alternative approach. Given the changing nature of careers, HRD as a field needs to reassess its role with regard to career guidance. Becoming knowledgeable about career counselling approaches, and understanding their strengths and limitations, is an early step of this process.

REFERENCES

Barak, A. (2001) A cognitive view of the nature of vocational interest: Implications for career, assessment, counseling and research. In F.T.L. Leong and A. Barak (eds) *Contemporary Models in Vocational Psychology* (pp. 97–131). Mahwah, NJ: Lawrence Erlbaum.

Betz, N. and Rottinghaus, P. (2006) Current research on parallel measures of interests and confidence for basic dimensions of vocational activity, *Journal of Career Assessment*, 14(1): 56–76.

Bright, J. E. H. and Pryor, R. G. L. (2011) The chaos theory of careers, *Journal of Employment Counseling*, 48(4): 163–166.

Bright, J. E. H., Pryor, R. G. L., Chan, E. W. M. and Rijanto, J. (2009) Chance events in career development: Influence, control, and multiplicity, *Journal of Vocational Behavior*, 75(1): 14–25.

Brott, P. E. (2001) A storied approach: A postmodern perspective for career counseling, *The Career Development Quarterly*, 49(4): 304–313.

Brott, P. E. (2005) A constructivist look at life roles, *The Career Development Quarterly*, 54(2): 138–149.

Bujold, C. (2004) Constructing career through narrative, *Journal of Vocational Behavior*, 64(3): 470–484.

Case, J. and Blackwell, T. (2008) Test report: Strong Interest Inventory, *Rehabilitation Counseling Bulletin*, 21(2): 122–126.

Chartrand, J. M. (1991) The evolution of trait-and-factor career counseling: A person x environment fit approach, *Journal of Counseling and Development*, 69: 518–524.

Dik, B. and Rottinghaus, P. (2013) Assessments of interests. In K. F. Geisinger (ed.) *American Psychological Association Handbook of Testing and Assessments* (pp 325–348). Washington DC: American Psychological Association.

Donnay, D., Thompson, R., Morris, M. and Schaubhut, N. (2004) *Technical Brief for the Newly Revised Strong Interest Inventory Assessment: Content, Reliability, and Validity*. Mountain View, CA: CPP. Retrieved May 6, 2013 from <https://www.cpp.com/products/strong/StrongTechnicalBrief.pdf>.

Egan, T. M., Upton, M. G. and Lynham, S. A. (2006) Career development: Load-bearing wall or window dressing? Exploring definitions, theories, and prospects for HRD-related theory building, *Human Resource Development Review*, 5(4): 442–477.

Einarsdottir, S. and Rounds, J. (2009) Gender bias and construct validity in vocational interest measurement: Differential item functioning in the Strong Interest Inventory, *Journal of Vocational Behavior*, 74(3): 295–307.

Fitzgerald, L. and Harmon, L. (2001) Women's career development: A postmodern update. In F. T. L. Leong and A. Barak (eds) *Contemporary Models in Vocational Psychology* (pp. 207–230). Mahwah, NJ: Lawrence Erlbaum.

Fouad, N. (2002) Cross-cultural differences in vocational interests: Between-groups differences on the Strong Interest Inventory, *Journal of Counseling Psychology*, 49(3): 283–289.

Greenhaus, J., Callanan, G. and Godshalk, V. (2010) *Career Management* (4th edn). Thousand Oaks, CA: Sage Publications.

Hansen, J. C. (2005) Assessment of interests. In S. Brown and R. Lent (eds) *Career Development and Counseling: Putting Theory and Research to Work* (pp. 281–304). Hoboken, NJ: Wiley.

Hansen, J. and Leuty, M. (2007) Evidence of validity for the skill scale scores of the Campbell Interest and Skill Survey, *Journal of Vocational Behavior*, 71(1): 23–44.

Hartung, P. (2010) Practice and research in career counseling and development – 2009, *The Career Development Quarterly*, 59(2): 98–142.

Herk, N. A. and Thompson, R. C. (2012) *Strong Interest Inventory Manual Supplement: Occupational Scales Update 2012*. Mountain View, CA: CPP, Inc.

Hite, L. M. and McDonald, K. S. (2008) A new era for career development and HRD, *Advances in Developing Human Resources*, 10(1): 3–7.

Inkson, K. (2007) *Understanding Careers: The Metaphors of Working Lives*. Thousand Oaks, CA: Sage Publications.

Krieshok, T., Black, M. and McKay, R. (2009) Career decision making: The limits of rationality and the abundance of non-conscious processes, *Journal of Vocational Behavior*, 75(3): 275–290.

Maree, K. and Molepo, M. (2006) The use of narratives in cross-cultural career counselling. In M. McMahon and W. Patton (eds) *Career Counselling: Constructivist Approaches* (pp. 69–81). London: Routledge.

McDonald, K. and Hite, L. (2005) Reviving the relevance of career development in human resource development, *Human Resource Development Review*, 4(4): 418–439.

McIlveen, P. and Patton, W. (2007) Narrative career counselling: Theory and exemplars of practice, *Australian Psychologist*, 42(3): 226–235.

McMahon, M. L. (2006) Working with storytellers: A metaphor for career counselling. In M. McMahon and W. Patton (eds) *Career Counselling: Constructivist Approaches* (pp. 16–29). London: Routledge.

McMahon, M. L. and Watson, M. B. (2008) Systemic influences on career development: Assisting clients to tell their career stories, *The Career Development Quarterly*, 56(3): 280–288.

Park, Y. and Rothwell, W. J. (2009) The effects of organizational learning climate, career-enhancing strategy, and work orientation on the protean career, *Human Resource Development International*, 12(4): 387–405.

Parker, P. (2006) Card sorts: Constructivists assessment tools. In M. McMahon and W. Patton (eds) *Career Counselling: Constructivist Approaches* (pp. 176–186). London: Routledge.

Patton, W. and McIlveen, P. (2008) Practice and research in career counseling and development, *The Career Development Quarterly*, 58(2): 118–161.

Patton, W. and McMahon, M. (2006) *Career Development and Systems Theory* (2nd edn). Rotterdam: Sense Publishers.

Peavy, R. V. (2000) A sociodynamic perspective for counseling, *Australian Journal of Career Development*, 9(1): 17–24.

Prince, J., Most, R. and Silver, D. (2003) Self-help career assessment: Ethical and professional issues, *Journal of Career Assessment*, 11(1): 40–58.

Pryor, R. G. L., Amundson, N. E. and Bright, J. E. H. (2008) Probabilities and possibilities: The strategic counseling implications of the chaos theory of careers, *The Career Development Quarterly*, 56(4): 309–318.

Pryor, R. G. L. and Bright, J. E. H. (2003) The chaos theory of careers, *Australian Journal of Career Development*, 12(3): 12–20.

Pryor, R. G. L. and Bright, J. E. H. (2006) Counseling chaos: Techniques for practitioners, *Journal of Employment Counseling*, 43(1): 2–16.

Pryor, R. G. L. and Bright, J. E. H. (2007a) The chaos theory of careers: Development, application, and possibilities, *Career Planning and Adult Development Journal*, 23(1): 49–64.

Pryor, R. G. L. and Bright, J. E. H. (2007b) Applying chaos theory to careers: Attraction and attractors, *Journal of Vocational Behavior*, 71(3): 375–400.

Rottinghaus, P. J. and van Esbroeck, R. (2011) Improving person-environment fit and self-knowledge. In P. J. Hartung and L. M. Subich (eds) *Developing Self in Work and Career* (pp. 35–52). Washington, DC: American Psychological Association.

Sampson, J. (2009) Modern and post-modern career theories: The unnecessary divorce, *The Career Development Quarterly*, 58(1): 91–96.

Savickas, M. (2005) The theory and practice of career construction. In S. Brown and R. Lent (eds) *Career Development and Counseling: Putting Theory and Research to Work* (pp. 42–70). Hoboken, NJ: Wiley.

Savickas, M. (2011) New questions for vocational psychology: Premises, paradigms, and practices, *Journal of Career Assessment*, 19(3): 251–258.

Savickas, M. L., Nota, L., Rossier, J., Dauwalder, J., Duarte, M. E., Guichard, J., Soresi, S., Esbroeck, R. V. and van Vianen, A. E. M. (2009) Life designing: A paradigm for career construction in the 21st century, *Journal of Vocational Behavior*, 75(3): 239–250.

Spokane, A. and Cruza-Guet, M. (2005) Holland's theory of vocational personalities in work environments. In S. Brown and R. Lent (eds) *Career Development and Counseling: Putting Theory and Research to Work* (pp. 24–41). Hoboken, NJ: Wiley.

Stebleton, M. J. (2010) Narrative-based career counseling perspective in times of change: An analysis of strengths and limitations, *Journal of Employment Counseling*, 47(1): 64–78.

Sullivan, B. and Hansen, J. (2004) Evidence of construct validity of the interest scales on the Campbell Interest and Skill Survey, *Journal of Vocational Behavior*, 65(2): 179–202.

Sun, J. Y. and Wang, G. G. (2009) Career transition in the Chinese context: A case study, *Human Resource Development International*, 12(5): 511–528.

Watson, M. B. (2006a) Career counselling theory, culture and constructivism. In M. McMahon and W. Patton (eds) *Career Counselling: Constructivist Approaches* (pp. 45–56). London: Routledge.

Watson, M. B. (2006b) Voices off: Reconstructing career theory and practice for cultural diversity, *Australian Journal of Career Development*, 15(3): 47–53.

Watson, M. B., Duarte, M. E. and Glavin, K. (2005) Cross-cultural perspectives on career assessment, *The Career Development Quarterly*, 54(1): 29–35.

Watts, A. G. and Fretwell, D. H. (2003) *Public Policies for Career Development*. Washington, DC: World Bank. Retrieved May 8, 2013 from <http://www.cedefop.europa.eu/EN/Files/World_Bank_discussion_paper.pdf#>.

Whiston, S. and Bouwkamp, J. (2003) Ethical implications of career assessment with women, *Journal of Career Assessment*, 11(1): 59–75.

FURTHER READING

Gunz, H. P. and Peiperl, M. A. (eds) (2007) *Handbook of Career Studies*. Thousand Oaks, CA: Sage Publications.

Hartung, P. J. and Subick, L. M. (eds) (2011) *Developing Self in Work and Career: Concepts, Cases, and Contexts*. Washington, DC: American Psychological Association.

Inkson, K. and Savickas, M. (eds) (2013) *Career Studies* (Four-volume set). Thousand Oaks, CA: Sage Publications.

Neault, R. A. (2011) Thoughts on theories (Special issue), *Journal of Employment Counseling*, 48(4).

Patton, W. and McMahon, M. (2006) *Career Development and Systems Theory* (2nd edn). Rotterdam: Sense Publishers.

8

THE MYTHS OF AGEING AND DECLINE: CAREER DEVELOPMENT AND EMPLOYABILITY OF OLDER WORKERS

Tonette S. Rocco, Jo G.L. Thijssen and Rod P. Githens

INTRODUCTION

The age at which one becomes an older worker varies by country, as do attitudes about ageing. This chapter focuses on the phenomenon of ageing in developed Western countries. In the US, the law defines an older worker as someone over the age of 40 (Rocco et al., 2003). However, the decision to retire, remain, or return to work occurs between the ages of 55 and 64 (Adler and Hilber, 2009). Demographic changes have created the need to seriously consider career development and employability of this group of workers.

Adult and career development is often represented as an arch: a curved line going up, peaking and then coming down. This arch represents stereotypes of early development stages to the older deteriorating stage. The age represented at the peak of the arch differs historically from 35 to 55 years old. After the peak comes the second half of a life or the second half of a career as human capabilities decline and fall (Thijssen and Rocco, 2010). The message is clear and simple: older people are over the hill. Hendricks and Hendricks (1986) observed that myths about ageing were prevalent and perpetuated by the popular press. Some of these myths concern 'older worker productivity, rigidity, and inability to adjust to new technology' (Rocco et al., 2003, p. 169). Age norms (which maintain that older workers have experience and wisdom while younger workers lack experience and insight) can be just as detrimental as the myths of decreasing capability (Collins et al., 2009). However, recent studies tell us that individual differences within age cohorts are greater than the differences between cohorts, and these individual differences increase during the second half of a career (Thijssen and Rocco, 2010). So, 'differential ageing', by domains of functioning and by subgroups of individuals, during the second half of a career is an important research issue (Baltes and Baltes, 1990; Baltes and Mayer, 1999). Yet, each individual should be evaluated on his or her strengths and weaknesses regardless of age. Therefore, predetermining individual performance based on age norms or myths is counterproductive because of the vast range of individual difference within a cohort.

The large baby boom generation, extended life expectancies and increased quality of life in older adulthood has created the current large numbers of older workers in the developed countries particularly the US, Canada, Australia and Western European countries. This generation has been followed by subsequent smaller generations beginning with Generation X, generally viewed as the generation born between the 1960s and early 1980s. These changes have resulted in current concerns about labour shortages and older worker capabilities. This chapter will provide (a) an overview of research on older worker capabilities, (b) an examination of the assumptions underpinning practice from the popular press and human resources literature, and (c) a discussion of the role of HRD and management in career development for older workers (Thijssen et al., 2008).

PERSPECTIVES ON OLDER WORKER CAPABILITIES

Conventional wisdom holds that getting older is congruent with becoming deficient and incompetent. Butler typifies the underlying assumption as 'ageism as a disease' (Butler, 1989, p. 138). Halfway through the 20th century, Harvey Lehman published the well-known book *Age and Achievement* (Lehman, 1953) in which he explained that there is a significant link between age, performance differences and performance-related capabilities. The book provided scientific support for the long existing *deficiency hypothesis*, the belief that human development can be depicted as a curve showing an increase in mental and physical capabilities during youth and adolescence followed by a gradual decrease from about the age of 35. The notion that a downward spiral in capability follows the upward spiral of the younger years has been regarded as absolute truth for centuries. The biological-psychological parallel regarding the development of all sorts of human capabilities, as described by Lehman, offered an evidential refinement of these prescientific assumptions. Following an intense scientific debate (Lehr and Thomae, 1958; Dennis, 1956), it was found that Lehman's deficiency hypothesis could no longer be upheld. Unfortunately, this did not mean that the corresponding stereotypes were adjusted. Even now, many managers see 'the older workers' as inflexible, less productive and as not employable, while ignoring individual differences among older workers (Collins et al., 2009). Studies examining attitudes of executives, managers and trainers who are given two workers' profiles with identical characteristics, except that one worker is young and the other is old, provide evidence for prevailing ageism (Reio et al., 2000). In this study, when additional training was needed to develop skills in employees, the older worker was denied while the younger worker was afforded the opportunity (Collins et al., 2009). When a workplace infraction was committed, the recommendations include remediation for the younger worker and termination for the older worker. Again the older worker was seen as incapable of growth and development, regardless of characteristics other than age. However, older workers who hold management and executive positions were often seen as valuable enough to rehire after retirement, or so competent and needed that their retirement was not a consideration (Stein et al., 2000).

> Following the rejection of the deficiency-hypothesis, research into development and age continued, partly stimulated by major demographic developments. Development is a process of 'qualitative change in attitudes, values, and understandings that adults experience as a result of ongoing transactions with the social environment, occurring over time but not strictly as a result of time'.
>
> (Taylor et al., 2000, p. 10)

Generally, development is thought of as movement in a positive direction (Smith and Taylor, 2010). This movement is enhanced or driven when one learns. A review of the research on ageing published in *Nature* (Hedden and Gabrieli, 2004) provides insights into ageing and cognition. First, there is little consistent support for age cohort differences in ageing and cognition. This is because two types of data sets exist: those that compared the baby boom (1945–1955) generation to different generations and longitudinal data sets following baby boomers. We do not currently have longitudinal data sets for the generations that came after the baby boomers, so cross generational comparisons are speculative. Second, due to the nature of ageing, sample selection and other factors, it is difficult to ascertain if a decline in function is the result of normal ageing or pathology. Third, processing speed, working memory and information encoding tend to decline across the adult lifespan. Fourth, there is little or no decline in performance, semantic memory or vocabulary until very late in life. More importantly:

> The relative stability of semantic memory and knowledge until late in life indicates that life experience might breed knowledge, and that the combination of these might lead to the wisdom that is often exhibited by older adults.
> (Hedden and Gabrieli, 2004, p. 88)

Current thinking is that older adults use knowledge and experience to shape efficient and effective performance strategies while younger adults rely on processing ability. Fifth, certain cognitive abilities remain stable such as autobiographical memory, emotional processing and automatic memory processes.

Demographic changes have made this discussion a crucial issue at the societal, organizational and individual levels. Specifically, there are not enough skilled replacement younger workers to replace an ageing workforce in Western countries. Societal issues include declining financial support for retirement due to fewer active contributors to retirement funds, and a smaller tax base because of fewer workers, which can impact the provision of public services and facilities. Organizational issues include loss of organizational memory, skilled labour shortages and the need for HR and managers to implement policies and practices designed to retain older workers and confront continued ageism. Personal issues include deciding to remain or to retire, challenges in seeking new jobs and careers and resisting the ageist image of themselves as incompetent with decreasing abilities and skills.

ASSUMPTIONS UNDERPINNING PRACTICE: PERSPECTIVES FROM THE POPULAR PRESS AND PROFESSIONAL LITERATURE

Traditional retirement (i.e. sudden total separation from the workforce) has increasingly become viewed as an outdated concept in the popular, professional and research literature (Rocco et al., 2003). The popular press and professional literature present multiple phenomena regarding this trend (Feinsod, 2009):

- Active older adults who desire to remain engaged in their current career, in a full-time or reduced role, primarily because they want to continue engagement in meaningful work.
- Active older adults who change careers and continue working for personal growth and fulfilment.
- Older adults who have become disengaged with their work, but remain in their current career primarily due to financial reasons.
- Older adults who change careers or work in lower skilled part-time jobs primarily due to financial reasons, but are able to find meaningful and engaging jobs.

Many older adults work for a combination of the above reasons. However, a persistent concern is how HR professionals can increase the engagement of workers who primarily remain employed due to financial reasons. These issues have become more important in the US after millions of older workers lost much of their retirement savings in the recent recession, and governments are working to reduce the retirement benefits of public sector employees. Generally, most of the popular press and professional literature presents older workers from a positive perspective despite ageism in the workplace. This review included the following types of national sources from the UK and the US: the Human Resource Management (HRM) and HRD professional literature, the national business press and nationally known newspapers and news magazines (e.g. *New York Times*). The most significant insights from these sources come in understanding the myths and reality of older workers' challenges, employer attitudes and the specific HR practices utilized. These examples provide insights for future development of policies and practices. Despite the overall positive tone in the literature, many employers are still doing little to retain and recruit among this demographic group.

Perceptions and reality regarding older workers' challenges

Most of the popular and professional literature addressing the challenges faced by older workers discusses conscious and unconscious discrimination from employers (e.g. Fishman, 2010; Luo, 2009; Millar, 2006; Rampell, 2010a; Rich, 2010). As evidence of such behaviour, workforce development programmes exist for older workers to help 'age-proof' their CVs, address questions about being overqualified and tactfully address implicit stereotypes in interview questions (Rich, 2010). In the recent recession, older workers in the US have been less likely to face unemployment than younger workers, but labour statistics show that they seem to have a harder time getting out of unemployment (Rampell, 2010a; Rich, 2010). Rich's (2010) *New York Times* article presents a somewhat ambiguous and slightly negative perspective about the prospects for displaced older workers. He explains that there are not enough new jobs for the population as a whole, 'much less for those in the twilight of their careers' (p. A1). Rich reports that some older workers discover that their technical skills are 'rusty' due to working for the same company for many years.

Rampell (2010a) provides a few possible reasons for the phenomenon of displaced older workers facing difficulty in securing new positions, including that older workers may be more likely to have been employed in industries facing long-term decline. Such industries have been decreasing the size of their workforce for years (e.g. through attrition) and the recession resulted in older employees losing their jobs. Since these industries as a whole have few new openings, older workers face the decision to retrain for a new job or retire. Later, Rampell (2010b) wrote about research reporting that unemployed individuals over 55 years old were more likely to consider taking a job with a cut in pay than were those under 55 years old. They were equally likely to seriously consider changing careers, but less likely to consider relocating for a new job. Despite structural barriers and lack of ability to relocate as reasons for difficulty in finding re-employment, discrimination is an undeniable reality facing older workers. Luo (2009) reports on research of 4000 hypothetical job applicants, showing that older applicants were less likely to get an interview, despite having identical qualifications with younger applicants. Perhaps for a multitude of reasons, some older workers have faced chronic unemployment, resulting in increased entrepreneurial activities or freelance work as the most viable path to re-employment (Rich, 2010). Other displaced older workers choose to participate in job retraining programmes.

In the US, community and technical colleges are portrayed as low-cost, quick sources of retraining for middle-skilled jobs, with those over 60 years old often paying reduced tuition (Leland, 2009; Tyre, 2006). Short-term certificate programmes are particularly appealing to older adults looking for a new career or wanting to enhance existing skill sets (e.g. a computer programmer needing to learn new programming languages). Online workforce development programmes in community colleges are increasingly common and are utilized by older adults seeking career training (Githens, 2007). Despite the popularity of retraining, some experts recommend that those workers forgo retraining in favour of part-time or contract work in their fields of expertise

(Leland, 2009). Despite the risks associated with beginning an entirely new career, many displaced older workers are retraining for new careers because of burnout in their former careers or a desire to take on a new challenge (Leland, 2009).

Employer attitudes

Employer attitudes and practices appear to have shifted in the last ten years, due to the increased enforcement of age discrimination policies and popular assumptions about the need for the knowledge and skills of older workers (see Coy, 2005; Freudenheim, 2005; Weber, 2009). For example, Weber (2009) reported that some employers deliberately avoided offering early retirement programmes during the most recent recession due to bad experiences with knowledge drains after offering such programmes in the past.

Additionally, older workers have come to be seen as having higher levels of 'cognitive pragmatics' (Baltes, 1993; 1997) or 'practical intelligence' (Coy, 2005) in dealing with interpersonal issues and ill-defined problems. Older workers are more likely to be cautiously experimental rather than daringly 'breaking the mold' through radically conceptually different ways of problem solving (Coy, 2005). Despite the limitations of a more incremental approach, Coy explained that older workers contribute ideas generally not considered by younger workers because these new ideas originate from a lifetime of successes and failures. Based on research, older workers are being portrayed as being important contributors to age-heterogeneous work teams, which perform better than age-homogeneous work teams (Miller, 2009). In order to realize such advantages, managers often need training to learn how to address the specific needs of an older workforce and to learn how to fully utilize the talents of older workers.

A traditional motivation for hiring older workers is companies seeking out retirees for part-time careers; increasingly, employers in the retail and service sectors see older workers as a reliable demographic. The senior vice president for the US bookstore chain, Borders, explained that although conventional wisdom was that older workers cost more due to medical problems and sick time, they have found that overall costs are equal across age groups because of decreased training and recruitment costs with older workers (Freudenheim, 2005).

Another motivation for hiring and/or retaining older workers is seen in a *BusinessWeek* cover story, which explains that because of today's rapid rate of knowledge obsolescence, investing in skill development for older workers is a sound practice (Coy, 2005). Because all workers need to be continuously developed, retrained and kept abreast of changes, training is a shorter-term investment than in the past. Therefore, there is less of an advantage in focusing training on younger workers.

Despite progress in portrayals in the popular press and professional literature, Millar (2006) reports on a survey finding that British HR professionals perceive that formal training programmes are received less enthusiastically by older workers. Strebler (2009) reports on research in the UK showing that older workers need individualized developmental support, engagement with their work and a sense of value. While some older workers want access to training and education programmes, others want to be respected for not wanting to participate in such programmes.

HR practices

The review of the literature by Rocco et al. (2003) found few examples discussing older workers being employed at various organizational levels. Specifically, most discussions involved older executives or older adults working in low-skilled jobs. In contrast, examples from the last ten years show gradual changes in which mid-level professionals and those working in middle-skill jobs are being included in such discussions (e.g. Coy, 2005).

Some UK advocacy groups and large employers advocate 'age blind' approaches to training (Bentley, 2007). This view can take the form of treating each employee, irrespective of age, as a person with individual needs. Or, as an HR policy manager of a large UK firm reported, training can be made accessible to all people with no age differentiation. On the other hand, two employment researchers working for policy organizations wrote in professional press articles that some older workers want and need career development and training programmes specifically addressing the needs of older workers (Feinsod, 2009; Strebler, 2009). Despite that perspective, nearly all workplace education programmes targeted specifically at older workers were retirement-planning seminars, rather than skill development programmes or career development programmes specific to the unique needs of older workers (Strebler, 2009).

A 2010 survey by the US-based Society for Human Resource Management (SHRM) and AARP (a US interest group for those over the age of 50) found that US employers are more likely to be preparing for possible future worker shortages through succession planning, knowledge transfer and cross training than through programmes that entice older workers to stay in full-time or part-time positions. Only 24 per cent offer or plan to offer flexible scheduling of workers as a response to this need and only 17 per cent have created or plan to create benefits to entice older workers to stay. In other words, the focus remains on transitioning older adults out of the workforce.

Companies such as Abbott Labs utilize programmes to assist in knowledge transfer to younger workers (McGregor, 2009). Abbott provides older employees with the option of taking four-day working weeks or increasing vacation time to 25 days per year. The employee's salary is reduced based on the reduction in working hours. Yet 401(k) contributions and pension service accruals remain at the level they were at before the reduction in working hours occured. The programme requires a written 'knowledge transfer agreement' to mandate knowledge sharing. Abbott also provides employees with the option of 'emeritus' status, which allows them to return to technical or individual contributor roles, freeing them from management duties and opening up management roles for younger employees with a desire to advance. While valuable and innovative, such programmes seem to approach older workers as transitioning assets rather than as ongoing assets to the employer. These approaches, while being quite innovative, contain the implicit assumption that workers in this life stage want decreased responsibility and mobility.

One proposal for encouraging employers to utilize older workers for longer is to end the traditional connection between pay and seniority (Coy, 2005). Advocates of such an approach contend that pay needs to be connected to productivity in order to encourage companies to utilize older workers more. Feinsod (2009) reports on her research for the AARP, from which she concluded that training programmes needed to be adapted for various age groups, that HRD needs to promote the building of intergenerational teams, and that HR needs to ensure that career path options include part-time and lateral moves for those uninterested in advancement.

Another example of a unique approach is the postal service Guernsey Post Ltd (UK Channel Islands), which has been recognized for innovative approaches in addressing the needs of older workers (AARP, 2010). They provide career development tailored to the needs of older workers, allow for flexible work schedules, offer in-house physical therapy services, and allow postal carriers to transition to indoor positions when physical limitations hamper continued outdoor employment. A unique policy allows carriers to complete routes at their own pace, with some younger workers preferring to quickly complete the route and some older workers preferring to take more time.

These various practices raise questions about how HRD practitioners can implement policies and practices that utilize sound career development theories in considering how to ensure that older workers remain productive, contributing members of organizations and society.

THE ROLE OF HRD AND MANAGEMENT IN CAREER DEVELOPMENT FOR OLDER WORKERS

Younger workers are commonly seen as up-to-date whereas older workers are viewed as obsolete. Growing older is often associated with lagging behind. Younger workers are seen as inexperienced but trainable compared to more experienced but less employable older workers. Although obsolescence has been described and assessed in different ways, many authors have accepted a common core definition of obsolescence: the sum of inadequacies in an individual's portfolio commonly known as 'decreased human capital' and 'depreciation of human capital' (De Grip and Van Loo, 2002; Neuman and Weiss, 1995; Pazy, 2004; Thijssen and Walter, 2006).

In the literature, authors refer to the negative consequences of obsolescence. These consequences are related to (1) diminished work achievement (e.g. restricted labour productivity and income); (2) diminished work motivation (e.g. work satisfaction, effort and the need for premature retirement); (3) diminished career perspective (e.g. lack of employment opportunities in the internal and external labour market) (Jones et al., 2004; Kaufman, 1995; Neuman and Weiss, 1995; Pazy, 2004; Van Loo, 2005). The attention to obsolescence is mainly inspired by two factors: the greying workforce and the organizational need for flexibility in a changing labour market. Being up-to-date and employable at the beginning of a career is not enough if the worker does not continue to update his or her skills. Lifetime employability or career potential needs to be stressed due to its emphasis on acquiring, maintaining and using qualifications aimed at coping with a changing labour market during all career stages (Thijssen et al., 2008).

Studies on ageing show us that the 'arch of deficiency' could be seen as an objectionable metaphor for the development of the average human capabilities (obsolete/up-to-date), and that differences increase between people of the same age as they age (e.g. Lehr, 1987; Thane, 2005; Thijssen and Rocco, 2008). The experience concentration theory describes a process that individuals can use to become more employable (Thijssen, 1992) and has useful practical applications in the HRD field (Thijssen and Van der Heijden, 2003). This theory states that it is experience rather than age that plays a vital role in the development of obsolescence and employability of people. The experience concentration theory begins with a twofold basic premise concerning the connection between age and experience following adolescence: (1) generally, with increasing age there will be a considerable increase in experience *quantity*; (2) generally, with increasing age there will be a considerable decrease in experience *variation*. The two tendencies (increasing quantity and decreasing variation) included in this basic premise will bring about – in respect to ageing – the phenomenon called experience concentration or specialization. Experience concentration is a phenomenon that has a larger impact on development than age. If people are confronted with experience concentration, they will feel increasingly 'at home' in a decreasing domain. This can have positive and negative effects. It is positive in a stable working environment. An example of a negative effect is job fixation, getting stuck in a certain position and refusing or not being offered opportunities to learn outside the home domain. The discrepancy between knowledge, manageability and safety within and outside the domain of experience becomes greater as experience concentration progresses. The willingness and ability to develop new capabilities outside the domain of experience will depend on the degree of experience concentration. The degree of concentration differs among people of the same age. Some workers will show a greater degree of diversity and experience variation, despite their age.

Experience concentration is a structural experience pattern contrasting with experience variation. With younger age groups, one will generally find a pattern involving more experience variation, with older age groups it will generally be a pattern with more experience concentration. Concentration has an effect often found with specialists: experiencing a fairly limited variation of experiences quickly results in a certain expertise and routine allowing for the realization of high labour efficiency within a small range of tasks. Variation has an effect often attributed to generalists. By experiencing a wide range of experiences, you become accustomed to adjusting to changing circumstances while employability opportunities involving new tasks are relatively high. Therefore, someone's experience built up over a certain period may range from relatively restricted (concentration) to relatively broad (variation). However, both the restrictiveness and broadness of these experiences can become quite extreme. We refer to the extreme experience patterns as *experience deprivation* and *experience fragmentation*. It is evident that neither of these two have a positive influence on employability. With age, experience concentration may become evident in three important domains: in a learning strategic domain, occupational domain and socio-cultural domain.

(a) *Learning-strategic domain* (*educational* experience). From a strategic learning point of view, the experience structure at an older age often remains restricted to informal, hands-on learning. The total range of strategies to learn new things may, with age, be reduced to what is sometimes called incidental learning. Where the use of learning activities is concerned, incidental learning adds information to the home domain.

Formal learning activities are generally used less and less as someone ages. A modest educational background is more likely to result in a restriction of formal learning skills and avoidance of future training opportunities. Individuals with advanced educational backgrounds are more likely to pursue learning opportunities. However, entry into new jobs by displaced workers often results in informal and formal learning, which many older workers may not have participated in for many years (Thijssen and Rocco, 2008; Thijssen and Walter, 2006).

(b) *Occupational domain (working* experience). From an occupational point of view, the range of changes often remains restricted to minor task adaptations. Oftentimes, these adaptations result in functional concentration. Older, more experienced workers do not change formal functions regularly, instead these changes are sporadic. For those experiencing some form of occupational concentration, they may continue adapting to simple shifts in tasks brought about gradually and informally. However, more drastic changes in tasks or the working environment are avoided as much as possible. Mobility is avoided (Thijssen, 1992).

(c) *Socio-cultural domain (networking* experience). From a socio-cultural point of view, the experience structure is often restricted to a shift in emphasis from the experience and knowledge one has to the networks one has developed to assist with problem solving. This process results in network concentration. The social environments and cultural group layers within which people move will, with age, often be restricted to a shrinking and rigid network, to a small circle, although the broadening and intensification of networks improves career prospects (Higgins, 2001). The existing network of 'old relations' has, at an older age, the protective function of a convoy (Antonucci, 2001). Usually, network innovations at an older age are an exception (Thijssen and Leisink, 2007).

The earlier this tendency towards experience concentration is recognized, the easier it can be corrected (Thijssen and Van Der Heijden, 2003). Workers and their managers can and must play a role in monitoring and correcting experience concentration. But not every manager is able and ready to provide variation in experience (e.g. cross-training, lateral promotions) to counter concentration. Certain management competencies are needed such as the ability to analyse and use data from evaluations and interviews, to communicate these findings to workers, and to translate the results of the analysis and discussion into appropriate developmental opportunities and/or workforce adaptation. Whether the manager has these competencies or not, the situation is further complicated by older workers who have little faith in their own capabilities and are already anticipating early retirement. Coaching older workers is not always easy. Finally, it is important that line managers are able and willing to pass differentiated judgement on older workers (Collins et al., 2009). This is even more important since the differences with regard to experience concentration/variation among older workers vary considerably and will only increase with age. Recent studies show that line managers make a difference when it comes to older workers continuing to develop their employability. Depending on their coaching abilities, and their willingness to use these abilities, line managers can offer social support to those older workers that they supervise. This willingness is to an extent dependent on the opportunities for action that the organization provides to line managers (Leisink and Knies, 2011). Organizational policies towards older workers have an essential influence on line managers' attitudes and actions. An important role for HRD is to be proactive in encouraging progressive policies and to be active in developing managers to address these career development issues.

Employability refers to a process over the course of a career where employers or an agency provide skill training and progressively challenging jobs (Pearce and Randel, 2004), creating performance-based competencies for employees to fulfil (Berdrow and Evers, 2010). Employability is increasingly used to refer to an organization's need for flexibility. Flexibility includes workers who are able to rotate and do the work that is necessary as free agents rather than as employees (Thijssen et al., 2008). The connotations of the term can be negative when the group has a low degree of career self-management and positive when the group has a high level of career self-management. Those with a high degree of career self-management are positioned to attain 'lifelong employability [which] implies having knowledge, the skills to apply that knowledge in a multidisciplinary, team-oriented, dynamic environment, and engaging in lifelong learning' (Berdrow and Evers, 2010, p. 2).

IMPLICATIONS

The literature provides mixed messages about the future employability of older workers. Studies continue to suggest that older workers are less likely to desire additional training and education, and that organizations are less likely to encourage older workers to participate in additional training and education (Strebler, 2009). Another mixed message is that older workers should retire to make way for younger adults who need work (e.g. Rich, 2010) and that there is a labour shortage because there are too few younger workers (Freudenheim, 2005) available to replace the older workers who retire. Older workers are seen as less adaptable, yet research shows that they use their experience to solve problems and, because of their experience, can come up with innovative ideas (Coy, 2005). Younger workers have difficulty knowing what is a truly new idea for an organization, because they do not possess the organizational history and knowledge base. Another conflicting message is that we need older workers for organizational knowledge, yet we need younger workers because of their capability to learn.

A sound HRD approach includes practices that allow older workers to share their knowledge of the history and practices of the organization with younger workers. Such programmes can be done with full-time older workers approaching retirement, with those who have transitioned to part-time employment, and with returning older workers brought back under contracts. These approaches have the possibility of enhancing productivity of all workers because the younger (newer) workers will have a foundation for their ideas based in knowledge of organizational history. Rarely do we discuss the costs to an organization when younger employees suggest solutions that have been tried and failed previously, but are tried again with a new generation of workers.

The literature is also clear that age does not mean an individual is not capable of learning and growth. Older workers are capable of learning and performing. While they may take longer to process a problem, their solutions are more often correct, decreasing the likelihood that resources will be wasted. Educational programmes for retired adults are growing in the US (Kim and Merriam, 2004), and more retired older adults are learning to use technology (Githens, 2007). HRD practitioners might be wise to debunk the myth that older workers cannot learn and do not want to learn. However, the problem might be that older workers themselves, and their supervisors, continue to accept ageist stereotypes (Collins et al., 2009; Sterns, 2010).

Most importantly, HRD practitioners need to consider ways in which they can foster conditions that will encourage the engagement and contribution of older workers who want to work. As discussed in the previous sections, this can be accomplished through employment policies, management training for those supervising an age-diverse workforce and meaningful professional development for older workers. These approaches need to consider engagement issues for those who desire to stay only for financial reasons. Additionally, those who want to stay for a combination of reasons should be provided with strong mentoring and career development that will enable them to remain as valued employees who continue to develop and contribute to their work groups, organizations and society. HRD can work to create long-term employability strategies that work to strengthen workers' capabilities.

This goal can be accomplished by challenging workers with stimulating positions and worthwhile job training that will keep workers sharp as they age, and help organizations with passing on organizational history as these workers remain engaged.

REFERENCES

AARP (2010) *Guernsey Post Limited: Winner: 2010 AARP International Innovative Employer Award.* Retrieved 2 March 2011, from <http://www.aarp.org/work/employee-benefits/info-11-2010/guernsey_post_limited.html>.

Adler, G. and Hilber, D. (2009) Industry hiring patterns of older workers, *Research on Aging*, 31: 69–88.

Antonucci, T. C. (2001) Social relations. In J. E. Birren and K. W. Schaie (eds), *Handbook of the Psychology of Aging* (pp. 427–453). San Diego, CA: Academic Press.

Baltes, P. B. (1993) The aging mind: Potential and limits, *The Gerontologist*, 33(5): 580–594.

Baltes, P. B. (1997) On the incomplete architecture of human ontogeny, *American Psychologist*, 52(4): 336–380.

Baltes, P. B. and Baltes, M. M. (eds) (1990) *Succesful Aging: Perspectives from the Behavioral Sciences.* Cambridge: Cambridge University Press.

Baltes, P. B. and Mayer, K. U. (eds.) (1999) *The Berlin Aging Study.* Cambridge: Cambridge University Press.

Bentley, R. (2007, September) Grey pride, *Training and Coaching Today*, 10.

Berdrow, I. and Evers, F. (2010) Bases of competence: A framework for facilitating reflective learner-centered educational environments, *Journal of Management Education*. Published online DOI: 10.1177/1052562909358976.

Butler, R. N. (1989) Dispelling ageism: The cross-cutting intervention. In M. W. Riley and J. W. Riley (eds), *The Quality of Aging: Strategies for Intervention.* Newbury Park, CA: Sage Publications.

Collins, M. H., Hair Jr., J. F. and Rocco, T. S. (2009) The older worker–younger supervisor dyad: A test of the reverse Pygmalion effect, *Human Resource Development Quarterly*, 20(1): 21–41.

Coy, P. (2005) Old smart productive, *BusinessWeek*, 78.

De Grip, A. and Van Loo, J. (2002) The economics of skills obsolescence: A review. In A. De Grip, J. Van Loo and K. Mayhew (eds), *Research in Labour Economics* (vol. 21, pp. 1–26). Bingley, UK: Emerald Group Publishing Limited.

Dennis, W. (1956) Age and achievement: A critique, *Journal of Gerontology*, 11(3): 331–337.

Feinsod, R. (2009) How companies are managing 'unretirement' [Electronic Version], *BusinessWeek*, <http://www.businessweek.com/managing/content/nov2009/ca20091116_542782.htm>.

Fishman, T. C. (2010, October 14) As populations age, a chance for younger nations, *New York Times*. <http://www.nytimes.com/2010/10/17/magazine/17Aging-t.html?pagewanted=all&_r=0> (accessed 15 May 2013).

Freudenheim, M. (2005) More help wanted: Older workers please apply, *New York Times* <http://www.nytimes.com/2005/03/23/business/23older.html> (accessed 14 January 2011).

Githens, R. P. (2007) Older adults and e-learning: Opportunities and barriers, *Quarterly Review of Distance Education*, 8(4): 329–338.

Hedden, T. and Gabrieli, J. (2004) Insights into the ageing mind: A view from cognitive neuroscience, *Nature Reviews Neuroscience*, 5(2): 87–96.

Hendricks, J. and Hendricks, C. D. (1986) *Aging in Mass Society* (3rd edn). Boston, MA: Little, Brown and Co.

Higgins, M. C. (2001) Changing careers: The effects of social context, *Journal of Organizational Behavior*, 22: 595–618.

Jones, E., Chonko, L. B. and Roberts, J. A. (2004) Sales force obsolescence, *Industrial Marketing Management*, 33(5): 439–456.

Kaufman, H. G. (1995) Salvaging displaced employees: Job-obsolescence, retraining, and redeployment. In M. London (ed.), *Employees, Careers, and Job Creation* (pp. 105–120). San Francisco, CA: Jossey-Bass.

Kim, A. and Merriam, S. B. (2004) Motivations for learning among older adults in a learning in retirement institute, *Educational Gerontology*, 30(6): 441–455.

Lehman, H. C. (1953) *Age and Achievement*. Princeton, NJ: Princeton University Press.

Lehr, U. (1987) *Psychologie des Alterns* (6th edn). Heidelberg/Wiesbaden: Quelle and Meyer Verlag.

Lehr, U. and Thomae, H. (1958) Eine Längsschnittuntersuchung bei männlichen Angestellten, *Vita Humana*, 1: 100–110.

Leisink, P. L. M. and Knies, E. (2011) Line managers' support for older workers, *International Journal of Human Resource Management*, 22(9): 1902–1917.

Leland, J. (2009, April 1) Skills to learn, to restart earnings, *New York Times*. <http://www.nytimes.com/2009/04/02/business/retirementspecial/02reskill.html?pagewanted=all> (accessed 15 May 2013).

Luo, M. (2009) Longer unemployment for those 45 and older, *New York Times*. <http://www.nytimes.com/2005/03/23/business/23older.html> (accessed 14 January 2011).

McGregor, J. (2009, November 13) How older workers can lighten the load [Electronic Version], *BusinessWeek*. <http://www.businessweek.com/managing/content/nov2009/ca20091111_435788.htm> (accessed 15 May 2013).

Millar, M. (2006, July 28) HR expects most over-50s not to care about training, *Personnel Today*. <http://www.personneltoday.com/articles/28/07/2006/36657/hr-expects-most-over-50s-not-to-care-about-training.htm> (accessed 15 May 2013).

Miller, L. (2009, December 13) The myth of the deficient older employee [Electronic Version], *New York Times*. <http://query.nytimes.com/gst/fullpage.html?res=9407E0DE1E39F930A25751C1A96F9C8B63> (accessed 15 May 2013).

Neuman, S. and Weiss, A. (1995) On the effects of schooling vintage on experience-earnings profiles: Theory and evidence, *European Economic Review*, 39(5): 943–955.

Pazy, A. (2004) Updating as a response to the experience of lacking knowledge, *Applied Psychology*, 53(3): 436–452.

Pearce, J. L. and Randel, A. E. (2004) Expectations of organizational mobility, workplace social inclusion, and employee job performance, *Journal of Organizational Behavior*, 25(1): 81–98.

Rampell, C. (2010a) For older workers, a longer job search, *New York Times*. <http://economix.blogs.nytimes.com/2010/03/05/for-older-workers-a-longer-job-search/> (accessed 15 May 2013).

Rampell, C. (2010b) Older job-seekers more willing to take a pay cut, *New York Times*. <http://ecoomix.blogs.nytimes.com/2010/11/17/older-job-seekers-more-willing-to-take-a-pay-cut/> (accessed 4 February 2011).

Reio, T. G., Sanders-Rejo, J. and Reio, T (2000) Combating workplace ageism, *Adult Learning*, 11(1): 10–13.

Rich, M. (2010, September 19) For the unemployed over 50, fears of never working again, *New York Times*. <http://www.nytimes.com/2010/09/20/business/economy/20older.html?pagewanted=all> (accessed 15 May 2013).

Rocco, T., Stein, D. and Lee, C. (2003) An exploratory examination of the literature on age and HRD policy development, *Human Resource Development Review*, 2(2): 155–180.

Smith, M. C. and Taylor, K. (2010) Adult development. In A. Rose, C. Kasworm and J. Ross-Gordon (eds), *The Handbook of Adult and Continuing Education*. Thousand Oaks, CA: Sage Publications.

Society for Human Resource Management and AARP (2010) *SHRM-AARP Strategic Workforce Planning Poll.* <http://www.shrm.org/Research/SurveyFindings/Articles/Documents/SHRM_AARP_StrategicWorkforcePlanningPoll%20FINAL.PPTX> (accessed 15 May 2013).

Stein, D., Rocco, T. S. and Goldenetz, K. A. (2000) Age and the university workplace: A case study of remaining, retiring, or retaining older workers, *Human Resource Development Quarterly*, 11(1): 61–80.

Sterns, H. L. (2010) New and old thoughts about aging and work in the present and future, *The Gerontologist*, 50(4): 568–571.

Strebler, M. (2009) Training and developing older employees, *Training Journal*, March: 30–33.

Taylor, K., Marienau, C. and Fiddler, M. (2000) *Developing Adult Learners: Strategies for Teachers and Trainers*. San Francisco, CA: Jossey-Bass.

Thane, P. (2005) *The Long History of Old Age*. London: Thames and Hudson.

Thijssen, J. G. L. (1992) A model for adult training in flexible organizations: Towards an experience concentration Theory, *Journal of European Industrial Training*, 16(9): 5–15.

Thijssen, J. G. L. and Leisink, P. L. M. (2007) Ervaringspatroon en beroepsmatige obso-letie van oudere werknemers. In: W. A. M. de Lange and J. G. L. Thijssen (eds), *De waardevolle senior. Personeelsbeleid voor oudere werknemers* (pp. 81–94). Amsterdam: WEMA Uitgeverij BV.

Thijssen, J. G. L. and Rocco, T. S. (2008) *Career and Lifetime Development Revisited*. Paper presented at the workshop on Working at old age: Emerging theories and empirical per-spectives on ageing and work. CEDEFOP, Thessaloniki, Greece, 29–30 September 2008.

Thijssen, J. G. L. and Rocco, T. S. (2010) Development of older workers: Revisiting policies. In CEDEFOP, J. van Loo and S. Bohlinger (eds), *Working and Ageing: Emerging Theories and Empirical Perspectives* (pp. 11–22). Luxembourg: Publications Office of the European Union.

Thijssen, J. G. L. and Van Der Heijden, B. I. J. M. (2003) Evaporated talent? Problems with talent development during the career, *International Journal of Human Resources Development and Management*, 3(2): 154–170.

Thijssen, J. G. L., Van der Heijden, B. I. J. M. and Rocco, T. S. (2008) Towards the employability-link model: Current employment transition to future employment per-spectives, *Human Resource Development Review*, 7: 165–183.

Thijssen, J. G. L. and Walter, E. M. (2006) *Identifying Obsolescence and Related Factors among Elderly Employees*. Tilburg: European AHRD-conference.

Tyre, P. (2006) Community colleges offer older workers an affordable way to reinvent themselves and find their place in a changing economy, *Newsweek*, 147: 53.

Van Loo, J. (2005) *Training, Labor Market Outcomes, and Self-Management*. Maastricht: ROA.

Weber, J. (2009) This time, old hands keep their jobs, *BusinessWeek*, 4118: 50.

FURTHER READING

CEDEFOP, van Loo, J. and Bohlinger, S. (eds) (2010) *Working and Ageing: Emerging Theories and Empirical Perspectives*. Luxembourg: Publications Office of the European Union.

Knies, E. and Thijssen, J. G. L. (2012) *Age, Career Prospects and Employability in the Dutch Police Force*. Paper presented at the EGPA annual conference. Bergen (Noorwegen), September 2012.

Rocco, T. S. and Thijssen, J. G. L. (eds) (2006) *Older Workers, New Directions. Employment and Development in an Aging Labor Market* (p. 186). Miami, FL: Center for Labor Research and Studies, Florida International University.

Thijssen, J. G. L. (1992) A model for adult training in flexible organizations: Towards an experience concentration theory, *Journal of European Industrial Training*, 16(9): 5–15.

Thijssen, J. G. L. and Van der Heijden, B. I. J. M. (2003) Evaporated talent? Problems with talent development during the career, *International Journal of HRDM*, 3(2): 154–170.

9

BOUNDARYLESS AND PROTEAN CAREERS IN A KNOWLEDGE ECONOMY

K. Peter Kuchinke

INTRODUCTION

This chapter provides an overview and discussion of the notion of the protean career, purported to represent an alternative to the traditional career model. The chapter argues against the viability of essentialist and normative notions of work pattern in today's economy. Starting with the observation of the paucity of theorizing of career in the HRD literature, the chapter opens by pointing to the highly diverse aspects of careers across different socioeconomic groups, cultural settings and industries that call into doubt the usefulness of a single career model. This is followed by an account of the historical development of the protean career notion as contrasted to traditional views of career. The chapter closes with an attempt to contrast two approaches to framing the relationship between the person and their career. From a unitary perspective, congruence between the self and one's career is achievable, and this perspective is the foundation of most current career theories. The fragmentation perspective questions the possibility of balance and instead positions the ongoing struggle and fuzzy boundaries between career and non-work aspects of life as a central characteristic of work and life in late modernity. The implications for the theorizing and practising of human resource development (HRD) are discussed.

Few topics have such central importance to the theorizing and practising of HRD as the notion of career, and yet, fundamental discussions about its nature and character and the consequences for individuals, organizations, communities and societies are conspicuously absent in the HRD literature. Although in an early US-based definition (McLagan and Suhadolnik, 1989) career development was included as one of three core dimensions of the field (along with training and organizational development), and although the outcomes of career experiences such as satisfaction and commitment are the staple of HRD empirical research, career theory and research have been neglected for most of the 30-year history of HRD academic publishing. Observers such as Swanson and Holton (2009) attribute the scarcity of career research to the declining role of organization-based career paths and the increased responsibility of individuals for their own career. Organizations, however, continue to rely on stability in staffing of core tasks even while undergoing continuous change (Brousseau et al., 1996), and a voluminous literature has formed in the past 30 years providing detailed analyses of the career landscape (e.g. Gunz and Peiperl, 2007). Although substantial overlap exists, this literature can broadly be divided into the more individually focused tradition of vocational psychology – addressing topics including career choice, career development, career transitions and career counselling – and the more organizationally focused arena of career studies – including career management, career ladders and person-organization fit. Both literatures tend to emphasize the dynamic interplay between the individual and the social, the complex range of choices, tensions, trade-offs and opportunities in today's world of work, and the temporal aspects of working over the span of an individual's life. Both literatures also reflect the need to move beyond functionalist and modernist conceptions to develop models that incorporate constructivism, post-structuralism and the postmodern critique of self. As Collin and Guichard (2011, p. 89) state:

> The core concern of vocational psychology is no longer vocational choice, as it was a century ago, or career development, as it was 50 years ago. In the 21st century [it] has become the continuous construction of self and life design.

The literature on careers is vast and no single book chapter can adequately capture even the major lines of inquiry. Two notions, however, have captured the imagination of researchers and the popular business press over the past 30 years, and will provide the focus for this chapter. Beginning in the mid-1970s, Hall's writing on careers in organizations included the discussion of an emerging form that stood in contrast to the organization-bound form. The protean career is said to be 'characterized by frequent change and self-invention, autonomy, and self-direction – driven by the needs of the person' (Hall, 2002, p. 4) and to require high levels of adaptive competence and motivation. While Hall's early work centred on individual attributes, Arthur and Rousseau developed some 20 years later the notion of the boundaryless career. Contrasting – as does Hall – the bounded (i.e. organization-based) career with a new model, the boundaryless career is said to be an 'interfirm' concept focused on:

> separate but simultaneous treatment of the person and the firm as units of analysis, and the greater appreciation of person-firm interdependencies [such as] networking, learning and enterprise as interwoven with the activities of the firm.
> (Arthur and Rousseau, 1996, p. 12)

With both notions (as well as the broader fields of vocational psychology and career studies) having developed quite independently and separately from scholarship in HRD, the goal of this chapter is to provide an overview and discussion and evaluate their relevance for our field. Both constructs will be treated as closely related for the sake of the argument, setting aside the differences in focus and multiple definitions that have been offered since their inceptions.

Careers are central to the lives of individuals, and most of us spend the majority of our waking hours engaged in them. Careers can be the source of joy and fulfilment, challenge and development, rewards and satisfaction, but also frustration, despair, burnout and failure. In many societies, particularly in the Anglo cluster of cultures (House et al., 2004), but also in many transitioning economies, one's career is closely linked to self-image and identity. Attaining, advancing in, or changing to a different career (or, likewise, failing in a career, selecting the wrong career, being unable to change a career) are central to a person's standing in society and community; the ability to obtain material, social and cultural goods; and the opportunity to learn and prosper in a knowledge-based economy. Careers are not static, they are being played out over time. Given the shortening half-life of knowledge and know-how, careers are said to require periodic or even ongoing effort in the form of professional development, schooling and continuous education, and informal learning in a variety of ways. John Dewey (1930) saw careers as the primary means for individuals to interact with society, to transcend individual and organizational goals, and to offer the chance to contribute to the development of the larger community and society. This perspective is currently central to the efforts of public policymakers in many countries, who point to diminished levels of motivation to enter careers in the skilled trades and in professions, such as engineers, physicians, mathematicians, chemists, physicists and biologists. The shortage of young people preparing for these fields, coupled with the increasing demand for the trades and sciences and the retirement of many individuals in these careers, are said to limit national competitiveness and economic prosperity in many Western countries (see for example: Kantor, 2010).

An ample and often critical body of literature exists in the broader human science literature on the meaning of work and career, with particular emphasis on the effects of the changing social, political, economic and technological landscapes resulting from globalization and the move towards a knowledge and information-based economy in countries around the world. Too little of this literature, however, has flown into the HRD scholarly or practitioner discourse, and thus the purpose of this chapter is to review and discuss the extant career literature and its dominant models, and to encourage deeper thought and application in HRD theorizing and practice. This will be done by first discussing the complex and ambiguous landscape of careers in the early 21st century and by describing contemporary career theories. This is followed by an attempt to distinguish two approaches to framing the relationship between careers and the self, each representative of specific intellectual and research traditions, and each constituting ideal-type models of this complex dynamic. The conclusion will offer ideas about the role of HRD research and practice.

WHAT DO WE MEAN BY *CAREER*?

A reasonable starting point is the attempt to discern the distinctions between and among related terms. Etymologically, the term career is derived from the Latin *carrus*, meaning cart or carriage. In the 16th century, the French usage of *carrière* indicated a racecourse, a gallop at full speed, but also, more generally, a course of action (*American Heritage Dictionary*, 1982, p. 240). The directionality, intensity and temporal dimension of these early uses of the term continue today when we speak about someone's career (e.g. he spent his career in academia), or ask a youngster what career he or she is preparing for or dreaming of. In everyday usage, the term is sometimes used in its weaker form to mean employment in general – US newspapers often contain sections titled 'career opportunities', but the precise notion of career is distinct from and broader than related terms such as work, job, occupation or even profession. One *enters* a career but *takes* a job or *selects* an occupation. A career in advertising, for example, can comprise several jobs, and a career in politics can comprise different occupations and even professions. Careers are built and unfold with dedication and commitment to a variety of personal and social goals, including furthering the public good. While we may say, with regret, that someone became a career criminal, the long-term, dedicated and committed pursuits of, for example, rum running or drug dealing are not considered individually or socially desirable career choices. One of the most prominent career researchers, Douglas Hall, addresses the multiplicity of meanings of the term (Hall, 2002, pp. 8–10), including:

- Career as advancement – emphasizing the notion of upward mobility, promotion in one's organization or field, and general success in an occupation. In this sense, the term is used in judgement: one can succeed in a career or fail to do so.
- Career as profession – here, the term signifies social status with certain occupational endeavours being rated as careers (e.g. a medical career), while others are not (we rarely speak of a career in garbage collecting). The distinguishing characteristic between the two examples lies in the degree of formal education and training, clear pattern of advancement opportunity, and progression from novice to expert with increasing levels of deep subject matter knowledge, regardless of their social value. Modern society would come to a standstill without menial labour – as becomes painfully apparent when municipal employees go on strike and refuse piles up in the city streets – but would, arguably, do fine with fewer cosmetic surgeons performing elective face lifts and tummy tucks.
- Career as a lifelong sequence of jobs – here, the judgemental character contained in the first two meanings is removed. Career denotes the series of positions held over the course of a working life, irrespective of position, level or status. Thus, everyone who works can speak of their career, and this may be described objectively by the number and type of employment and work settings, and also subjectively by the significance and personal meaning assigned to them.

Emphasizing the subjective aspect, Hall (2002, p. 12) proposes a definition of career as the 'individually perceived sequence of attitudes and behaviors associated with work-related experiences and activities over the span of the person's life'. This value-neutral definition points to a sense-making process whereby the individual's cognitive appraisal of their work experiences over time is central to their personal view of career. This subjective definition allows for the individual to assign meaning and value for a particular work episode or aspect of work – for example, the proverbial stone mason working on the grand cathedral of Chartres who views his work not as menial labour but in the service of God. It also allows for the valuation of failure in positions that are held in high esteem by society. A successful investment banker, for example, may assess his or her corporate career as meaningless and turn their skills to serving the needy by becoming a social entrepreneur. The extrinsic aspects of status, reward and advancement opportunities are reduced in favour of the individual construction of the experience. The force of this subjective valuation of career became apparent to the author in a recent interview with an entry-level secretary at a local college who, in a follow-up email, wrote: 'I enjoy what I do and for whom (students, faculty, staff). I must keep smiling and keep the joy, it really helps' (E. Grady, personal communication, 27 January 2011). While the subjective definition of career may be unable to respond to the suggestions of critical theorists of false consciousness or the risks of a colonialization of the self, especially in the corporate context (e.g. Deetz, 1992), it does provide access in the individual experience as constructed, judged and told by the individual; removes the arbitrary distinctions inherent in definitions that differentiate between those with and without career in their working lives; and has formed the basis of most career-focused search programmes in psychology over the past 20 years.

CAREERS IN A CHANGING ECONOMY

While career research emphasizes individual and subjective dimensions, these take place in the context of social, economic, political, demographic and technological trends and developments. Far from presenting a homogeneous picture of work in the current moment, the forces of globalization, communication technology and rising consumer expectations have created a highly complex landscape of work whose characteristics cannot be grasped by catch-all phrases such as global, knowledge or post-industrial. Indeed, a distinguishing characteristic of the current time appears to be the futility to produce general descriptions about the nature of work; instead we are left with attempts to hint at and point to the kaleidoscopic multiplicity and contradictory complexity of work in the early 21st century that offers multiple and often mutually incommensurate perspectives. One prominent perspective is the observation of high levels of dissatisfaction with the institutions in which much of our formal work is done and in which careers are being played out.

Such accounts from the academic side include, among many other sources, the reader edited by Robert Quinn and colleagues (Quinn et al., 2000) with empirical research findings on topics such as corrosive political climates in organizations, overworked and underemployed human resources, chaotic role movements, and the challenges of serving multiple masters in matrix and networked organizational settings. Another example is provided by Harold Leavitt, prominent professor of organizational behaviour at Stanford University, who professes his view that big organizations are unhealthy environments for human beings. He argues that attempts to humanize the workplace, create employee-centred organizations and put into practice the ideal of reaching productivity through people have failed to reach widespread and lasting implementation, despite ardent support by researchers and practitioners since the days of the Hawthorne experiments in the 1920s (Leavitt, 2007). Finally, the *Journal of Managerial Psychology* issued a special issue call for papers on the topic of heavy work investment, such as work alcoholism and very long or dangerous work, but also extreme forms of work drive, fear of failure, need for success, financial needs and employer demand: 'An estimated 22 per cent of the global workforce, or about 614.2 million workers, work more than 48 hours per week... [and] a considerable portion... want to work fewer hours' (Snir and Harpaz, 2011). The attitudinal response to such high work demands and challenging work conditions has been assessed in one country by the nationally representative opinion survey by the Allensbach Institute for Public Opinion Research, whose 2007 survey showed a markedly lower level of commitment to career and work among younger Germans. Only 19 per cent of respondents over the age of 16 declared that they were willing to work hard and put high levels of energy into their work performance. Between 55 and 65 per cent of respondents, of employed and unemployed respondents respectively, were not willing to work longer hours for higher pay, and a majority felt that the central value in their lives centred around their families and friends, not their work (Miegel and Peterson, 2008). Even in the United States – a country rated among the highest in terms of work centrality (Bernstein, 1997) – recent research found that a majority of mid-level managers and professionals would prefer to stop working if the financial necessity to do so was removed. The study further found that commitment to family was regularly rated higher than commitment to work (Kuchinke and Cornachione, 2010).

The popular business press is largely in support of this rather sceptical assessment of the health of work institutions. Apart from the highly publicized reports of accounting scandals, disregard for environmental safeguards, instances of graft and theft, and other acts of corporate malfeasance, the human toll extracted by all types of work organizations is reported on an almost daily basis, be this in public or private firms, for profit or not, corporate, government, religious, or military, domestic or international.

Examples include the rising level of suicides among employees of French corporations during restructuring (Jolly and Saltmarsh, 2009), the widely publicized reports on burnout among senior managers in German multi-national corporations (Marquart, 2011), and the findings of national health studies in Germany of widespread mental and physical suffering as a result of high job demands ('Exhausted Nation', 2011).

The changing nature of work and the characteristics of the knowledge-based economy are, of course, not new topics and have been discussed in various facets in the literature for the past two decades. An early analysis by Robert Reich, Secretary of Labor during the first Clinton administration in the US, predicted a sharp division in the success rate of different education and skill levels, with those individuals benefitting the most who have high levels of education and training, analytical and administrative skills, and the mobility to take advantage of global opportunities (Reich, 1992). This group, labelled symbolic analysts, are viewed as the winners of globalization: as compared to routine production workers and those providing personalized services, their career prospects with current employers are high and their skills in demand and portable to other organizations. Because of the value of their professional contributions, they tend to be well compensated but also often experience high workloads, face intense time pressures and work long hours (Shor, 1991). The 'cognitive elite' has been rewarded with wealth and influence and the inequality among countries, as measured by the Gini index, increased between 1985 and 2005 in economies such as China, the United States, Britain, Japan, Germany, Sweden and India (Rise of the Cognitive Elite, 2011).

The negative conditions of modern work have been described by economists, educators and business ethicists. One might point, for example, to the work of Jeremy Rifkin (1995) whose influential book on the end of work predicted the decline of the global labour force and a structural rise in unemployment in developed and developing countries. With parallel force and insight, Joanne Ciulla (2000) examined the unfulfilled historical promise of technological advancement that would reduce the burden of labour necessary to produce goods and services, create more interesting working conditions, and create a leisure society where the major challenge would be how to spend the increased leisure time creatively.

Work sociology, finally, has produced many detailed reports on knowledge work and the so-called new economy, and there appears to be consensus that the extent to which the current economic landscape is actually new has been overestimated. Two prominent labour sociologists point to the fact that many of the features of the manufacturing-based economy persist today, including mass production, routine work, low skill utilization, low power base of workers, high job insecurity, and discrimination by gender, race and ethnicity.

> The old economy has not been replaced by a new economy; the old economy is operating within the new economy' and 'concerns facing workers today result ... from enduring failures to address the problems of inequality in the old economy'.
>
> (Sweet and Meiksins, 2008, p. xvii)

Alienated labour, dangerous work, greedy institutions, exploitation, harassment and the struggle for control and rewards are said to be as much part of today's world of work as they were in past decades (Volti, 2008). Even though the availability of communication technology and vast amounts of data in the knowledge economy may have altered the range of information available to workers and the process of decision making in flatter organizations, this has been accompanied by increased time pressures, much higher cognitive demands and a rising level of intensity at work (Baldry et al., 2007); 'Employees experiences [in the new workplace] are not radically or qualitatively different' (Holman et al., 2003, p. 6).

At the end of this arguably cursory overview of some aspects of modern work, we return to the premise presented in the opening of this section: the context in which careers are lived out in today's institutions and organizations is complex, dynamic and contradictory. Benefits in the form of challenging assignments, financial and intrinsic rewards, and fulfilling work occur to some individuals some of the time, but this is often accompanied by high levels of stress and personal sacrifices. Living and working on the edge is the norm for some, as was shared with the author in an interview with a regional manager of a global pharmaceutical company in charge of HR for Europe, North Africa and the Middle East:

> When I stand on the shores of the Red Sea at night after a business meeting, I cannot believe the turn my life has taken after growing up in a small village in Germany. It even makes me forget my two divorces and the fact that my children don't want to talk to me any more.
>
> (personal communication, name withheld, 25 September 2007)

For others, work takes the form it always has: poor working conditions, long hours, struggle over benefits and pay, and the risks of getting laid off. Looking globally to factories in developing economies (such as China, India and Vietnam), garment sweatshops (in the US, Mexico or Puerto Rico) and agricultural work, there appears to be little evidence of a widespread adoption of the new economy or use of knowledge and information. Rather, the images of these workplaces would have been all too familiar 100 years to the likes of F. W. Taylor and Henry Ford, or even to textile mill owners in Greater Manchester and the river towns of New England in the 1800s.

TRADITIONAL AND PROTEAN CAREERS

Given the wide range, diversity and complexity of work arrangements, can a single career model or theory capture the plethora of work patterns of any era, let alone the current global moment? The contours of the two dominant models are familiar. The traditional career is said to have been the norm beginning (approximately) with the growth of post-war economies in Australia and New Zealand, North America, Europe and, with two decades' delay, Asia, the Middle East and parts of Africa. It links back to earlier industrial and pre-industrial eras and reflects a primary dominance of the employing organization in charge of career socialization, progression, advancement and separation. At the will (and often the whim) of the employer, there was little room for individual initiative, and career behaviour took place within the rules and bounds of the firm. Advancement was a core value, commitment and loyalty were expected, and rewards were provided for in the form of salary increases and promotions (Hall, 2003). Careers were said to proceed in linear fashion over a lifespan and, for most employees, with a single employer, in a single industry and in a single occupation (Super, 1980). Youngsters purportedly selected a career at an early age and spent their working lives in their chosen fields (Krau, 1997). Dissatisfaction with the lack of expression and the dominance of an organizational value set found expression not only in the arts (examples: Henry Miller's *Death of a Salesman* [1949/1977] and Sloan Wilson's *The Man in the Grey Flannel Suit* [1955/1983]), but also in academic writing (examples: Rosabeth Moss-Kanter's *Men and Women of the Corporation* [1977] and William H. Whyte's *The Organization Man* [1956]). Following the oil embargo and recession of the early 1970s, and the emergence of global competition in advanced manufactured goods and services, North American, European and Asian world economies restructured in the late 1970s and early 1980s. The consequences were increased layoffs, reduction of the role of organized labour, and attempts at finding new ways of gaining employee commitment and high performance, given lower commitments and rewards by employers. Charles Handy's 1989 *Age of Unreason* 'captured this new flexible world of work in his model of the "shamrock organization" with its three clusters of workers (core, part-time, and temporary)' (Hall, 2003, p. 5). Hall's protean career shifted the responsibility for careers from the organization to the individual. Applying a 'free agent' image of the worker as setting his and her work path and contracting at will for interesting or rewarding work, the protean career is characterized by a core commitment to personal and professional growth and freedom, high levels of lateral and vertical mobility, psychological satisfaction as the key reward, and commitment to the work, project, or profession (rather than the organization) as the key attitude (Hall, 1976). The new career model replaces the relational contract between employer and employee – characterized by assumptions of a long-term, committed, full-time and trusting relationship – with a transactional one based on short-term exchanges of benefits and contributions (Rousseau, 1995). Organizations are able to reduce their investment in employee training and development, move to a market-based HR model, and contract with free agents who acquire the requisite skills on their own, selling them to the highest bidder, and who in return take compensation, increase in experience and skill, and a widening professional network. Individuals prospering in the protean career path are said to score high in adaptability (to new situations, projects, demands) and self-awareness (of their skills, preferences, values and so on). They further score high on measures of individuation as measured by the Big Five personality inventory (extroversion, neuroticism, openness to new experiences, agreeableness and conscientiousness), and make career decisions based on a set of personal values. Finally, they are said to possess a 'boundaryless mindset' (Hall, 2003). Hall describes the protean career as a 'path with a heart' and views the construct as closely related to the notion of vocational calling. Invoking core ideals of humanistic psychology, he states: 'The central issue is a life fully worth living . . . The secret is to find your unique genius, your talents that you love to develop and use' (Hall, 2003, p. 9).

Both traditional and protean notions of career should be critiqued for being stereotypical and overly general. While there is little doubt that some individuals in the current era have been able to carve out their own niche and succeeded in remaking their careers in line with their talents, values and desires, there is little evidence to suggest that this model is true for a majority. Rather, as Baldry and colleagues (2007) suggest, many careers continue to follow an organization-driven path. This is particularly so as the rising levels of unemployment in many countries curtail the option to change careers and make a steady career with one employer more desirable. In Greek mythology, Proteus, son of the sea god Poseidon, is characterized by the ability to change his shape at will and thus the term *protean* originally connotes flexibility, adaptability and versatility. Without denying its inspirational value for those who want to better their lot through pluck and hard work, it is hard to envision the protean career as the blueprint for anyone other than an educated elite or a lucky few. According to Hall (2002), the intra-individual challenges to adapt to a turbulent and complex world of work and to develop the metacompetencies required for unbounded careers are substantial. While systematic research is not available, estimates are that less than one-half of adults reach the level of psychological development required for protean career behaviour (Kegan, 1994), and this percentage is certain to decrease if social, economic, political and institutional barriers are considered.

Equally implausible is the wholesale description of the post-war workforce as solely or even primarily traditional: in the 1960s and 1970s, as access to higher education expanded at a rapid rate, as women entered the workforce in large numbers and gained in educational achievement, so did the opportunities for self-directed careers, entrepreneurism and career changes. No systematic evidence was found for a prevalence of either the traditional or protean career model in their respective eras. Both career models seem to represent ideal types that have neither descriptive nor normative value but might, in fact, obscure the stratification of the labour market and the difficulties of many to advance, let alone realize their deeply held goals in their working lives. If, as Hall rightly states, careers are characterized by subjectively held attitudes, meanings and experiences, then individual biography rather than grand theories should be considered. In such an approach, the relationship between identity and career comes to the fore, and thus the next section will examine two patterns for the nexus between self and work.

TWO PERSPECTIVES

To focus the discussion of career theories and their relationship to the individual, Kuchinke (2005) adopted a model developed by Joanne Martin (1992) to describe theories of organizational cultures. These are ideal types but sufficiently differentiated to allow insight into alternative ways of thinking about the relationship between self and work. Integration theories emphasize the unitary, consensual and consistent nature of the individual, its organization around a single theme or purpose and the possibility of congruence and singular focus. Both traditional and protean career theories seem to fall into this category; they presume an overriding sense of direction or purpose without ambiguity, doubt and uncertainty. This unitary perspective might have resulted from a struggle with adversity, often heroic, or a breakthrough in consciousness, the result of a vision or inspiration, often after overcoming difficulties. Historically, the integration view is linked to the notion of 'a calling' and the formulation of the Protestant work ethic. In the North American context, both organization-based and self-directed notions of career are not new ideas. As Braude explains when describing the work ethic of colonial America, the guiding ideology was that:

> no man...need be fettered by caste or class, that achievement in the occupation of one's choice is dependent solely on initiative and ability...[T]he most heinous sin...is the admission of failure to achieve, with the concomitant renunciation of the success orientation altogether.
>
> (Braude, 1983, p. 213)

The myth of rags-to-riches success available to everyone reinforced and popularized this belief to citizen and immigrants to the United States in the 19th century with bestselling books by Horatio Alger, P. T. Barnum and Andrew Carnegie (Wilms, 1986), and appears to have found a reformulation in the protean career.

Where the integration perspective presumes unity among the multiple aspects of individual, the fragmentation perspective removes this assumption focusing instead on flux, multiplicity of meaning, discontinuity, and lack of simplicity and predictability. This category is situated in postmodern thought, with its critique of the modernist agenda of progress, stability and order through grand narratives erected to hide complexity and disguise power relationships. With respect to careers, notions of authenticity, continuity of self and agency are seen as fiction and concealment (Deetz, 1992, p. 291) leading to the fundamental critique of the subject (self) in postmodern philosophy. With the assumption of the ontological unity of the person removed, the self – and the awareness of the self – becomes subject to the push-and-pull of multiple societal forces, adrift in a world of hyper-complexity, paradox, contradiction and inconsistency. Feelings of unity or cohesion, then, are seen as part of a societal script, viewed as fiction produced by dominant discourses and with the aim of maintaining order and stability of power relations. As Martin (1992, p. 156) wrote:

> [A] fragmented self constantly fluctuates among diverse and changing identities, pulled by issues and events...The self is fragmented by a variety of nested, overlapping identities, external influences, and levels of consciousness: The perceiving subject, deluded by imagined notions of its unity and coherence, is in actuality split in such imponderable ways.

Postmodern approaches have been used to address the contradictions, paradoxes and inconsistencies in organizational life (see, for example, Alvesson and Deetz, 1999). At the individual level, the fragmentation perspective has been employed to describe the experience of subordinated groups, such as women and minorities, of middle-class wage earners, and of executives and managers (see Martin, 1992). Individual identity and awareness, in this perspective, are not fixed but arise out of the process of interaction. The individual, thus, is an ongoing puzzle undergoing continual shifts, change and discontinuity, and grand theories of career should be treated with suspicion. Rather, careers should be described akin to biographies, perhaps even novels or poems, that point to the multitude of facets, experiences, meanings, tensions, joys and sorrows inherent in engagement in work throughout a life.

CONCLUSION

This chapter began by pointing to the sparse level of theorizing about careers in the HRD literature, despite the central role of work and career in the field. Among the reasons for this neglect might be an often instrumental stance towards work, given to adopting popular notions without the necessary critical distance or reflection. A large body of research and scholarship has been built in the fields of vocational psychology and career studies that has much promise to inform HRD research and practice and connect the topic to the traditional concerns of the field with individual, organizational and national/global learning and development. A definitional section used Hall's approach to career as the subjective pattern of work experiences over time. This literature is arguably limited as it restricts the notion of career to paid work, leaving out unpaid work, volunteer work, community and civic engagement, and the large area of work done during retirement or periods of unemployment. A sampling of academic and business literatures was presented, showing the complex nature of work organizations in which careers take place. The two dominant career theories were described, and it was argued that neither one was sufficient, on empirical or conceptual grounds, to claim validity beyond a narrow segment of the working population. Despite the implied or explicit presentation as guiding theories in two different social and economic eras, the way in which careers unfold and the way in which individuals describe their careers are ultimately far more differentiated. There is little doubt about the attractiveness of the protean idea, which fits well with an individualistic, liberal notion of the individual as the creator of his or her own fate. Rights, however, are of little use unless there are provisions to exercise them, and here the validity of the protean career as empirical ('how careers unfold') and normative ('how careers should happen') models should be questioned.

Instead, the notion of career as biography was suggested, and the unitary approach to framing the relationship between the individual and his or her career rejected in favour of a fragmented view. The fragmentation perspective lays claim to a more adequate accounting of the actual experience of a career over time and opposes a simplistic, stereotyped or unitary reading. Methodologically, the undertaking will require a focus on phenomenological and other ideographic and in-depth approaches, to focus on self-understanding, language and personal narrative (see Freeman, 1991; Witz et al., 2001).

The importance of renewed theorizing of careers in our own domain of commitment should lie in the exploration of possibilities and alternatives, of helping individuals make sense of their own experience in light of their sets of values, hopes, desires and dreams. This raises the promise of career research that represents not simplistic or abstract notions but reflects the richness and complexity of careers; it includes a focus on the linkages between work and self, of constructing work in the context of the broader notion of the good life. This project is important for the wellbeing of individuals in a turbulent world, but equally for organizations and institutions that can improve through authentic careers. When HRD practice is guided by a narrow view of careers, then advice, intervention and involvement will fail to address deeper and more salient aspects of being at work in this historical moment. As Kuchinke (2005) expressed:

> A fundamental question for HRD practitioners is about the nature of those, whose lives we touch in professional practice, and here practitioners face a choice between actions that diminish the self (personal and other-directed) and those that enhance, explore, and broaden the self (again, both personal and other-directed) in daily practice. This should be seen not only as an ethical question of integrity but an imminently practical one. Relevant professional practice must address fundamental aspects and possibilities of being, and herein might well lay a vast area of potential influence and contribution on part of the HRD profession. (p. 151)

REFERENCES

Alvesson, M. and Deetz, S. (1999) Critical theory and postmodernism: Approaches to organizational studies. In S. Clegg and C. Hardy (eds) *Studying Organizations: Theory and Method*, pp. 185–211. London: Sage.

Houghton Mifflin Company (1982) *American Heritage Dictionary*. Boston: author.

Arthur, M. B. and Rousseau, D. M. (1996) *The Boundaryless Career: A New Employment Model for a New Organizational Era*. Oxford: Oxford University.

Baldry, C., Bain, P., Taylor, P., Hyman, J., Scholarios, D., Marks, Al, Watson, A., Gilbert, K., Gall, G. and Bunzel, D. (2007). *The Meaning of Work in the New Economy*. New York: Palgrave Macmillan.

Bernstein, P. (1997) *American Work Values: Their Origin and Development*. Albany, NY: State University of New York.

Braude, L. (1983) *Work and Workers: A Sociological Analysis*. Malabar, FL: Krieger.

Brousseau, K. R., Driver, M. J., Eneroth, K. and Larsson, R. (1996) Career pandemonium: Realigning organizations and individuals, *Academy of Management Executive*, 10(4): 52–66.

Ciulla, J. B. (2000) *The Working Life: The Promise and Betrayal of Modern Work*. New York: Three Rivers Press.

Collin, A. and Guichard, J. (2011) Constructing self in career theory and counseling interventions. In P. J. Hartung and L. M. Subich (eds) *Developing Self in Work and Career: Concepts, Cases, and Contexts*, pp. 89–106. Washington, DC: American Psychological Association.

Deetz, S. A. (1992) *Democracy in an Age of Corporate Colonialization: Developments in Communication and the Politics of Everyday Life*. Albany, NY: State University of New York.

Dewey, J. (1930) *Human Nature and Conduct: An Introduction to Social Psychology*. New York: The Modern Library.

'Exhausted Nation' [Volk der Erschoepften] (2011) (*Der Spiegel, 4/2011*), 67–75.

Freeman, M. (1991) Self as narrative: The place of life history in studying the lifespan. In T. Brinthaupt and R. Lipka (eds) *The Self: Definitional and Methodological Issues*, pp. 15–43. Albany, NY: State University of New York.

Grady, E. (2011) Personal communication. College of Education University of Illinois at Urbana-Champaign, USA. January 27.

Gunz, H. and Peiperl, M. (eds) (2007) *Handbook of Career Studies*. Thousand Oaks, CA: Sage.

Hall, D. T. (1976) *Careers in Organizations*. Glenview, IL: Scott, Foresman.

Hall, D. T. (2002) *Careers In and Out of Organizations*. Thousand Oaks, CA: Sage.

Hall, D. T. (2003) The protean career: A quarter-century journey, *Journal of Vocational Behavior*, 65: 1–13.

Holman, D., Hall, T. D., Clegg, C. W., Sparrow, P. and Howard, A. (eds) (2003) *The Essentials of the New Workplace: A Guide to the Human Impact of Modern Working Practices*. Hoboken, NJ: Wiley.

House, R. J., Hanges, P. J., Javidan, M., Dorfman, P. W. and Gupta, V. (eds) (2004) *Culture, Leadership, and Organizations: The GLOBE Study of 62 Societies*. Thousand Oaks, CA: Sage.

Jolly, D. and Saltmarsh, M. (2009) Suicides in France put focus on workplace, *International Herald Tribune*, 1(16), 7–8

Kantor, S. (2010) Time of transition: As job markets are affected by technology, another factor is affecting the crafts and trades: Younger generations aren't being taught about them. In *News-Gazette*, pp. A1, A3. Champaign, IL.

Kegan, R. (1994) *In Over Our Heads: The Mental Demands of Modern Life*. Cambridge, MA: Harvard University.

Krau, E. (1997) *The Realization of Life Aspirations Through Vocational Careers*. Westport, CT: Praeger.

Kuchinke, K. P. (2005) The self at work: Theories of persons, meaning of work, and their implications for HRD. In C. Elliott and S. Turnbull (eds) *Critical Thinking in Human Resource Development*, pp. 141–155. Milton Park, UK: Routlege.

Kuchinke, K. P. and Cornachione, Jr., E. B. (2010) The meaning of work and performance-related work outcomes of US and Brazilian managers, *Performance Improvement Quarterly*, 23(3): 57–78.

Leavitt, H. J. (2007) Big organizations are unhealthy environments for human beings, *Academy of Learning and Education*, 6(2): 253–264.

Marquart, M. (2011) Massenleiden Burnout: Wie Firmen Ihre Spitzenkraefte Verbrennen [Burnout epidemic: How companies are burning up their top talent] (*Der Spiegel*).

http: www. Spiegel.de/wirtschaft/service/0,158,druck-74853,00.html. (accessed 24 January 2011).

Martin, J. (1992) *Cultures in Organizations: Three Perspectives.* Oxford: Oxford University.

McLagan, P. A., & Suhadolnik, D. (1989). Models for HRD practice: The research report. Alexandria, VA: American Society for Training and Development.

Miegel, M. and Peterson, T. (2008) *Der Programmierte Stillstand [The Programmed Standstill].* Munich: Olzog.

Miller, H. (1949/1977) *Death of a Salesman.* New York: Penguin.

Moss-Kanter, R. (1977) *Men and Women of the Organization.* New York: Basic Books.

Quinn, R. E., O'Neill, R. M. and St. Clair, L. (2000) *Pressing Problems in Modern Organizations (That Keep Us Up at Night): Transforming Agendas for Research and Practice.* New York: American Management Association.

Reich, R. B. (1992) *The Work of Nations: Preparing Ourselves for 21st Century Capitalism.* New York: Random House.

Rifkin, J. (1995) *The End of Work: The Decline of the Global Labor Force and the Dawn of the Post-Market Era.* New York: J. P. Putnam.

Rise of the Cognitive Elite (2011) A special report on global leaders, *The Economist*: 7–9.

Rousseau, D. M. (1995) *Psychological Contracts in Organizations: Understanding Written and Unwritten Agreements.* Thousand Oaks, CA: Sage.

Shor, J. (1991) *The Overworked American: The Unexpected Decline of Leisure.* New York: Basic Books.

Snir, R. and Harpaz, I. (2011) Special issue call for papers on the topic of types of heavy work investment, *Journal of Managerial Psychology.* <http://www.emeraldinsight.com/products/journals/call_for_papers.htm?id=2997andPHPSESSID=vfhhkp77kr60bdu 3olckk0oeh0> (accessed 27 January 2011).

Super, D. E. (1980) A life span, life space approach to career development, *Journal of Vocational Behavior*, 16: 282–298.

Swanson, R. A. and Holton, III, E. F. (2009) *Foundational of Human Resource Development* (2nd edn). San Francisco, CA: Berrett-Koehler.

Sweet, S. and Meiksins, P. (2008) *Changing Contours of Work: Jobs and Opportunities in the New Economy.* Thousand Oaks, CA: Pine Forge Press.

Volti, R. (2008) *An Introduction to the Sociology of Work and Occupations.* Thousand Oaks, CA: Pine Forge Press.

Whyte, W. S. (1956) *The Organization Man.* Philadelphia, PA: University of Pennsylvania.

Wilms, W. W. (1986) *Captured by the American Dream.* Paper presented at the conference on Vocationalizing Education, University of London, Institute of Education, November 23–25.

Wilson, S. (1955/1983) *The Man in the Grey Flannel Suit.* New York: Four Walls Eight Windows.

Witz, K., Goodwin, D., Hart, R. and Thomas, S. (2001) An essentialist methodology in education-related research using in-depth interviews, *Journal of Curriculum Studies*, 33(2): 195–227.

FURTHER READING

Bernstein, P. (1997) *American Work Values: Their Origin and Development.* Albany, NY: State University of New York.

Capelli, P. (ed.) (2008) *Employer Relationships: New Models of White Collar Work.* New York: Cambridge University Press.

Ciulla, J. B. (2000) *The Working Life: The Promise and Betrayal of Modern Work.* New York: Three Rivers Press.

Cooper, C. L. and Burke, R. J. (eds) (2002) *The New World of Work: Challenges and Opportunities.* Oxford, UK: Blackwell.

Ganz, H. P. and Peiperl, M. A. (2007) *Handbook of Career Studies.* Thousand Oaks, CA: Sage.

Hall, D. T. (2002) *Careers in and Out of Organizations.* Thousand Oaks, CA: Sage.

Holman, D., Hall, T. D., Clegg, C. W., Sparrow, P. and Howard, A. (eds) (2003) *The Essentials of the New Workplace: A Guide to the Human Impact of Modern Working Practices.* Hoboken, NJ: Wiley.

Kuchinke, K. P. (2005) The self at work: Theories of persons, meaning of work, and their implications for HRD. In C. Elliott and S. Turnbull (eds) *Critical Thinking in Human Resource Development*, pp. 141–155. Milton Park, UK: Routlege.

part **4**

TEAM
DEVELOPMENT

10

ACTION LEARNING FOR TEAM AND ORGANIZATION DEVELOPMENT

Clare Rigg

OBJECTIVES

This chapter discusses action learning as an approach to developing teams within and across organizations. It introduces the key principles and practices of action learning, as originally developed, as well as outlining some of the varying interpretations that have evolved over time. A number of practical illustrations are given, before a discussion on the theoretical underpinning of the approach and a critical commentary on some of the major claims made for its efficacy. The chapter concludes by highlighting a research agenda of questions that would benefit from systematic research.

HOW HAS ACTION LEARNING BEEN DEFINED?

Action learning is one of a family of action inquiry approaches to problem solving and learning, which in broad terms means learning from inquiring and taking action on issues that matter to those involved. It is a way of learning with and from others in the course of tackling difficult issues or concerns, typically involving a small group of people (a so-called action learning set) meeting together to question and support one another in experimentation and reflection. Action learning has been employed for a variety of individual and organizational development purposes as well as to address broad systemic and societal problems. It is a mode of inquiry with particular value for situations where people want to change something about their situation, whilst at the same time gaining greater insight into both the issue and their own practice. It is not a simplistic 'learning by doing' as it is sometimes mischaracterized.

Action learning has eschewed simple definition and has come to take a variety of meanings in practice. Revans, the originator of the term, though arguing that definition was counterproductive, nevertheless offered the following elaboration:

> Action learning is a means of development, intellectual, emotional or physical that requires its subjects, through responsible involvement in some real, complex and stressful problem, to achieve intended change to improve their observable behaviour henceforth in the problem field.

> (Revans, 1982, pp. 626–627)

Consistent with avoiding tight definition, Pedler et al. (2004) suggest that action learning is best described as an approach or ethos that has most or all of the following features:

1. **A problem, concern or opportunity:** that needs action taken and is owned by group members. This may be a shared issue, for example, a question of how to change or improve some aspect of organization practice. Alternatively, members may bring their own individual work-related issues to the group. Learning and development are greatest when issues are multi-faceted, with unclear boundaries and several stakeholders, rather than puzzles that have a simple technical right answer. (See later in the chapter for examples).

2. **People – action learners:** a group of people (typically from four to eight, though this can be more or less) who want to see their concern(s) addressed and voluntarily work together in sets of peers. They may or may not have prior experience of working together, but generally come together voluntarily. The set takes responsibility for organizing themselves and to develop their own capacity to solve problems, although, as highlighted below, the use of a set adviser or facilitator is not uncommon. These peers are usually others with comparable issues and in similar organizational hierarchy positions. Members act as critical friends to challenge and support each other's learning.

   Action learning sets meet regularly and allow adequate time within meetings for each member to take the stage, presenting an issue and benefiting from others' questioning insight. Some sets meet fortnightly for two hours over three months until a task is complete. Some meet monthly for half a day over a period of several months, whilst others have been known to exist over years, meeting two or three times a year for 24 hours at a time (see Richards, 2006).

3. **Action as the basis for learning:** problems are ones on which the learners can take action, not merely offer diagnosis. They have scope within their roles and are prepared to try things out experimentally.

4. **Formal instruction is insufficient:** external training, instruction or expertise is not relied upon. Existing codified knowledge, whilst it may be drawn on for a specific problem, may not suit the context of that specific problem.

5. **Questioning:** as the main way to help set members define their tasks/problems and to reflect on their assumptions. The search for fresh questions and questioning insight is seen as more helpful than access to expert knowledge. Learning happens through asking questions, investigation, experimentation and reflection, rather than through reliance on external expertise. Set members are encouraged to ask each other questions, rather than rush to offer solutions. Members learn the value of a good question, received from all peers within the group, for opening up different perspectives. This enables opportunistic learning from action on the problem, to be brought into the action learning set for systematic reflection.

6. **Reflection and feedback:** with the support, questions and challenge of peers within the action learning set, action learners review their experimental attempts to address the task, reflect on their actions, recognize and reframe their assumptions as well as receive feedback.

7. **Profound personal learning and development:** resulting from reflection on action. Action learning helps managers develop meta-skills such as self-insight, wider organization–political understanding and influencing abilities (Revans, 1982; Vince, 2008).

8. **Problems are sponsored and aimed at wider organizational change as well as personal development:** one of Revans' key principles was that action learning can benefit both individuals and organizations, where action learners are drawn from across an organization (Revans, 1982). Sponsorship by a senior manager is important to enable more junior staff to take action and influence change. Having said this, it is also not uncommon for action learning set members to choose their own tasks or problems, rather than have them given to them, and to work on them individually rather than collectively.

9. **Facilitators:** (also termed coach or set adviser) are commonly though not always used. Their role is to model the peer challenge/critical friend behaviours, to help the group establish ground rules and develop

questioning, reflective and inclusive team practices. Good facilitation attends to the process of the group, rather than becoming drawn into the content of discussions or being the expert problem-solver. Facilitators have to be able to tolerate and interpret silence, ambiguity and conflict, as well as to be active listeners who can summarize back to set members.

ACTION LEARNING CYCLE

Action learning is a cyclical process involving iterative steps of action, reflection and review. The original action learning cycle devised by Revans (1982) is known as System Beta, comprising the steps illustrated in Figure 10.1, which are:

1. Survey or observation (ask questions to improve understanding of the situation; collect data for diagnosis).
2. Hypothesis or theory (formulate courses of feasible action).
3. Experiment (test out a course of action).
4. Audit or evaluation (what happened).
5. Review or ratification (comparisons between expectation and experience; draw conclusions and plan another cycle).

More recent evolutions of action learning cycles include the action-planning cycle (O'Neil and Marsick, 2007), which involves the following steps illustrated in a continuous cycle:

Decide
Involve
Implement
Assess results
Feed new cycle
Identify/reframe project
Question assumptions
Determine needs
Gather information
Recommendations

This cycle differentiates from a simple reflective cycle when faced with a challenge of: identify problem – alternative solutions – implement solution – plan next steps. Additional steps are intended to produce double- and triple-loop learning by critically reflecting on the underlying assumptions

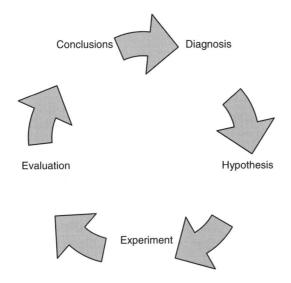

Figure 10.1 Action learning cycle – system beta
Source: Based on Revans, R. (1982) *The ABC of Action Learning*. Bromley: Chartwell-Bratt.

and perspectives on a problem, interpreting the context, reflecting in and on action, assessing unintended consequences and reframing the experience.

THE PROCESS IN PRACTICE

So far the discussion has outlined the traditional principles of action learning, but what might this look like in practice? Box 10.1 provides an initial illustration of action learning in a health-care setting.

Box 10.1 Action learning for nurses

Hull and East Yorkshire NHS Trust and Hull University Business School have collaborated in a development intervention with nurses who have a specific responsibility for 'tissue viability' – prevention of pressure ulcers, with an action learning programme entitled 'Leading Change in Tissue Viability'.

'Sets' of 14 nurses met for a total of six days over a five-month period, primarily using their experience to identify and analyse the current situation, to identify areas for improvement and to develop action plans for implementation. A minimal amount of time was spent on clinical input (half-day) and facilitators introduced a small number of tools to

---

Box 10.1   (Continued)

assist thinking – most notably stakeholder analysis as a framework for the nurses to identify their relationships and influences with other stakeholders involved in tissue viability on the wards.

Participants had the option to present their analysis, action plan and a reflective paper for assessment towards academic credits from the university, and most took up this option. Outcomes from the programme include improved patient benefits such as fewer ulcers, reduced costs (in terms of expenditure on drugs and dressings) and increased confidence and sense of empowerment within the nurses, including a number who have since put themselves forward for promotion. The combination of work on stakeholder relationships, combined with the peer work integral to action learning, was particularly helpful in enabling nurses to address their traditional sense of powerlessness within the medical hierarchy, and to develop their influencing skills within the spaces available to them. At the same time, where blocks to change were identified that resulted from hospital policy or structures, these were taken up either collectively by the nurses or through the facilitators.

As the NHS trust's assistant clinical director said: 'We have paid for investment many times over in the savings we have seen and when I hear a nurse say, "I was on the point of leaving nursing, but this programme has reminded me what the job is about" then I know it was all worthwhile.'

Source: Based on Kellie, Henderson, Milsom and Crawley (2010).

In this context, as in others, a group of people, who may or may not know each other already, agree to embark on action learning for a period of time, so as to tackle a particular problem, to explore an opportunity and/or to develop team working. Typically, the process would be initiated by selected reading and an initial workshop to introduce key ideas of action learning as well as the objectives for its particular use in the context. Meetings thereafter will often follow a format similar to that outlined in Box 10.2.

Box 10.2   Common action learning meeting format

- *Venue is neutral,* quiet and private.
- *Seating is comfortable* with space to move around.
- *Visual resources* such as flipchart and pens are available.

- *Introductions* to begin to build familiarity and trust are encouraged by the facilitator.
- *Ground rules* – the facilitator at the first meeting invites the group to set a small number of ground rules for themselves, to cover issues such as confidentiality, commitment, time, and also to talk through how they might work in practice.
- *Check-in* – a round where each member exchanges immediate distractions and brings their focus to the meeting.
- *Agenda-setting* – the facilitator initiates collaborative agenda setting with the group and agrees timings. Classic agenda items for any meeting include check-in, agreeing agenda, individual time for progress reports, review and check-out.
- *Individual time* – individuals have time to present progress on their issue to the group. Group members listen actively, help the presenter explore and clarify their issue and help them identify actions to take away.
- *Review and check-out* – the group reflect on the effectiveness of the meeting, for example, how useful it was for their learning; what they found difficult; what they would like more or less of.

Typically, one member takes the role of note taker and records decisions.

WHO DECIDES WHAT ISSUES TO WORK ON?

When action learning is commissioned and sponsored by a client, the task to be worked on within an action learning set will frequently be supplied by them. For example, a set might be asked to work on a broad issue such as reducing new product development times or to address a focused problem such as preventing pressure ulcers in a hospital context. Alternatively, when the main purpose of action learning is management/leadership development, it is not uncommon for individuals to create their own questions to work on, for example: 'How do I develop my networking abilities?'; 'How do I address the conflicts in my team?'; 'How do I improve my profile in the company?'

As outlined above, one of the most important roles of peers within action learning is to offer insightful questions to one another. Whether working on a broad issue or a focused problem, a useful set of questions for set members to ask each other is:

- What are we trying to do?
- What is stopping us from doing it?

- What can we do about it?
- Who knows about the problem?
- Who cares about it?
- Who can do anything about it?
- Where can we find out about it?

(For more on questioning, see Pedler et al., 2004). Further research may be required to answer some of these questions, for instance through discussion with the client, other senior managers, or other individuals involved in an issue, as well as collection of documented data such as customer figures and performance metrics. This should help identify a potential action that can be tried out and the resources and allies to assist. After statement and diagnosis of the issue, it is time to test out a possible solution. Individuals bring back the results of their experimentation to the next action learning meeting. Either each individual has time to report back or they are allocated time at intermittent meetings. Peers use questioning to help the presenter reflect on why they got the results they did, what this means and what they have learned in the process. This discussion will often feed into a further cycle.

Box 10.3. presents a further example of what an action learning set dialogue might look like, illustrating how questioning may take place.

Box 10.3   Illustrative action learning set dialogue

Facilitator: Colette will go next. Tell us briefly what your issue is. Everyone else listen without interrupting and make a note of any questions or observations you have.

Colette: My issue is that I feel overloaded, with more and more work given to me, yet I don't seem to be getting recognition for it. A lot of what I am doing really should be my immediate boss's role. You could say he's a brilliant delegator. I know I'm valued by my boss for being able to hold things together. And yet I don't seem to be visible to the managing director. In a way, I suspect it benefits my immediate boss to keep me in my current role. So I'm beginning to feel my development is stagnating. Does that make sense?

Facilitator: Now, we don't want to rush into offering Colette advice or solutions. The value of the group is to help you look at this issue from different angles. Could everyone give Colette as many questions as they can think of. As they throw them out, Colette, don't try to respond, just write them down.

Over the next few minutes, the other eight members of this set generated over 25 questions for Colette. These included:

- Have you spoken with your boss?
- How is he benefiting from the current situation?
- Is your managing director aware of how you feel?
- Does your managing director know you want more development?
- Who else sees this as a problem?
- What have you tried so far?
- What was the result?
- Why do you want to change?
- What do you want to be different?
- What have you got to lose from approaching your managing director?

Facilitator: So, Colette, you have many questions to take away with you, but looking at them now, which two or three stand out for you? Which ones mean most to you?

Colette: This is very helpful. There are several questions here that I haven't asked myself. The one that most leaps out at me is whether my managing director knows I want to progress. I probably haven't made that clear. That definitely gives me some food for thought.

Tony (another group member): So what do you think your options are for approaching him with the issue?

And so the meeting progressed, until Colette's time was up and it was the turn of the next person to present their issue.

ORIGINS OF ACTION LEARNING

Reg Revans is widely accredited as the originator of action learning, starting with his work in the British coal industry in the late 1940s and 1950s, the health sectors in England and Belgium in the 1950s and 1960s and the Belgian Inter-University Programme (Revans, 1982). When pit managers had problems, he encouraged them to meet together in small groups, on-site, and ask one another questions about what they saw, in order to find their own solutions rather than bringing in 'experts' to solve their problems for them. Revans' formative influences included his early training as a physicist at Cambridge University in the late 1920s, where he encountered Nobel prize-winning scientists meeting weekly, not to display their achievements but to learn from one another through 'describing one's very ignorance and, more than that, in trading it with others equally ready to confess their own' (Revans, 1987).

Action learning, as developed by Revans, grew from a mid-20th-century disenchantment with positivism and prevailing cultural beliefs in the dominance of expertise, which fostered the conviction that unless problems can be solved by a purely technical solution, there is more learning to be had through action being taken by those involved with an issue. Revans' key idea was a synergy between learning and action: 'there can be no learning without action and no (sober and deliberate) action without learning'. In other words, learning through activity or work is essential, which makes action learning both an example of experiential learning (Dewey, 1938; Kolb, 1982) as well as of work-based learning (Raelin, 1997).

Revans also had come to the conclusion that learning and improvement were not best helped by relying on external experts or consultants. It is not that there is no role for expertise, but rather that better learning comes from asking questions (Q) of ourselves and our experience as well as from expertise, or what Revans termed, programmed knowledge (P).

Revans summed up the learning to be had from action learning as:

$$L = P \& Q$$

L = learning; P = programmed knowledge, traditional instruction; Q = questioning insight.

INTERCONNECTIONS BETWEEN LEARNING AND ORGANIZATION CHANGE

Individual learning and institutional change were conceived by Revans (1982) as being symbiotic through the interconnection, as illustrated in Figure 10.2 of what he described as three systems:

Alpha – strategic system analysis: a person's context including their value system, external environment and internal resources available. These are the factors most likely to obstruct learning and effective action.

Beta – decision cycle: application of scientific method through steps of survey, trial, action, audit, consolidation, or now more commonly encapsulated in Plan-Do-Review.

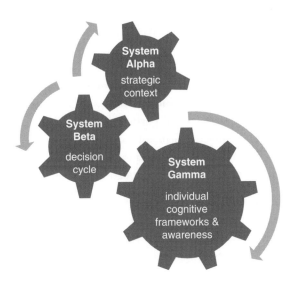

Figure 10.2 Individual learning-organizational change based on Revans'
3 systems model

Gamma – learning system: the person's reflexivity in the sense of their awareness of
their own tacit assumptions, mental frameworks and awareness of others.

WHAT HAS BEEN ITS HISTORY SINCE?

Many of the original applications of action learning were for large system
change, and Revans' original ideas spread internationally, for example through
his 1978 invitation to speak to 100 senior officers of the Indian government's Department of Personnel and Administrative Reform. In more recent
decades, action learning has had considerable application for individual and
team development. Internationally, there are a wealth of examples of the
use of action learning approaches in public as well as private and volun-
tary/community sector development, including Australia (Australian Flexible Learning Framework, 2001); Ireland (Ireland Trainers Network, 2003);
Canada (School of Public Service); America (Global Forum on Executive
Development and Business Driven Action Learning); and the World Bank
Participation and Civic Engagement Group (World Bank, 2005). In Britain,
during the 2000s action learning became established as a core element of
much leadership and management development particularly within individual
public sector organizations.

VARIETIES OF ACTION LEARNING

A variety of interpretations of action learning have now developed across the world, and a study by Pedler, Burgoyne and Brook (2004) found that within the widely employed terminology of action learning the meaning for practitioners and the experience of participants vary considerably. Different varieties share most of the core principles outlined above, but the balance of priority between business objectives and personal learning varies and certain approaches do not even involve a peer group. They include:

- **Critical action learning:** which 'engages participants in a process of drawing from critical perspectives to make connections between their learning and work experiences, to understand and change interpersonal and organizational practices' (Rigg and Trehan, 2004, p. 1).
- **Auto-action learning:** where an individual works alone through cycles of action, reflection and learning systematically and regularly using a consistent set of questions to structure a review.
- **Action mentoring or coaching:** in which one-to-one relations of mentor–mentee or between peers employ learning through cycles of action and reflection.
- **Virtual action learning:** through which questions designed to promote reflection are posed online or through teleconferencing.
- **Self-managed action learning:** in which a group facilitates themselves.
- **Business-driven action learning:** 'a results-focused method and set of principles used by organizations and their teams to address actual business and leadership challenges' (Boshyk, 2010, p. 10).

Attempts to differentiate broad categories of action learning have been provided by Marsick and O'Neil (1999) and more recently by Chenhall and Chermack (2010). Raelin (1999) also made a valuable comparative categorization with not only other action modalities, such as action research, but also participatory research, action science, developmental action inquiry, co-operative inquiry and appreciative inquiry.

Marsick and O'Neil (1999) distinguished four schools of action learning practice, based on how advocates assumed learning takes place:

Tacit School – assumes learning is incidental in the course of participants engaging in working together on a task.

Scientific School – characterized by Revans' original Systems Alpha (situation analysis), Beta (search for a solution) and Gamma (individual as a learning system) (see below for further explanation).

Experiential School – characterized by likening action learning to Kolb's experiential learning cycle with its stages of action, reflection, conceptualization and active experimentation (Kolb, 1982). Learning how to learn is emphasized, as is implementation of solutions, so that action is taken, not merely diagnosis.

Critical Reflection School – calls for deeper and more critical reflection on assumptions, values and unquestioned norms held about organizational and personal practices (Marsick and Watson, 1992; Rigg and Trehan, 2008).

Most features of action learning, as identified in the first part of the chapter, are shared by all schools, but two aspects in particular differ. First is the use of facilitators or coaches, which in the Scientific School have least weight and are advocated only temporarily or not at all. Here, a facilitator may be used to assist a group to form and develop action learning practices and ground rules, but they would withdraw after the initial few meetings. In contrast, exponents of the Critical Reflection School, in particular, place significant weight on strong facilitation to help surface and challenge assumptions (Ram and Trehan, 2010).

A second distinction is the emphasis placed on group process as a source of learning, which in the Scientific School is minimal. In the Experiential School, group process is valued as a source of learning for participants about team dynamics and skills such as chairing, collaboration and decision making. In the Critical Reflection School, group process is central as a source of potential learning about self, others and the organization, because of the way dynamics within a group so often mirror the power relations of the wider organization and society (see, for example, critical action learning, Rigg and Trehan, 2004; Vince, 2006).

The question of what criteria can best differentiate between types of action learning has been approached by others in terms of the purpose and intended outcomes of its use. Pedler et al. (2005) relate this question to Lyotard's (1984) argument that there are three purposes for knowledge:

- Speculative (learning for its own sake).
- Emancipatory (to attain the highest potential and overcome restraint).
- Performative (to resolve problems, to achieve benefits, knowledge to inform action).

Pedler et al. (2005) suggest that action learning is not concerned with speculative knowledge, but sits midway along a spectrum between the other two, emancipatory and performative, or what they term practice. The intent

Table 10.1 Intentions in the uses of action learning

	Individual benefit	Organization benefit
Emancipatory objectives	Individual learning and transformation	Group empowerment/emancipation
Performative objectives	Raise individual performance	Achieve change within a group or organization

underlying use of action learning can also be considered along a second dimension of individual–organizational benefit (Rigg, 2006). Combining these two spectrums, as in Table 10.1, characterizes the intended outcomes of action learning as primarily concerned to prioritize one or other of the following objectives:

- achieve change within a group or organization;
- Raise individual performance;
- Individual learning and transformation;
- Group empowerment/emancipation.

APPLICATIONS

There have been many diverse applications of action learning across the world (Rigg and Richards, 2006; O'Neil and Marsick, 2007). Intended outcomes range from the purely individual to primarily shared and cover a spectrum from performativity (giving priority to achieving business results through problem resolution) through to transformational learning (emphasizing radical personal and/or organizational change). Organizations apply action learning to address discrete problems such as how to reduce wastage, through to more multi-faceted challenges such as stimulating innovation. Public service bodies employ the approach to promote interagency collaboration on persistent social problems. Action learning also finds frequent application in development programmes, both in-company and academic, particularly postgraduate degrees, primarily for individuals who have a level of discretion in their roles.

The next section presents evidence of the extent and reach of action learning's applications. This quantitative illustration is followed by discussion and examples of the ways in which action learning is used for team and organization development in practice.

EXTENT OF ACTION LEARNING APPLICATIONS

A Boolean search of the journal databases Emerald Full-text and Business Source Premier, with the key words action AND learning within journal abstracts, revealed a growing trend in the numbers of articles published on action learning in the period 2000–2010. This is exclusive of specialist journals such as *Action Learning: Research and Practice*, but as Table 10.2 illustrates, it includes a wide range of journals beyond the specialist training, human resource development or management education journals, as well as addressing a diversity of subjects.

In the decade 2001–2010, a total of 422 articles are listed in Emerald Full-text and 282 in Business Source Premier. Because the databases overlap, listing some journals in common, in order to avoid double-counting, the figures have not been collated. Comparative figures for the previous period 1991–2000 were 200 and 155, respectively; 72 and 75 during 1981–1990; 18 and 25 during 1971–1980; and 4 and 2 in 1961–1970. Figure 10.3 illustrates the steady increase in articles per annum during the period 2000–2010, from 17 in 2000 to 51 in 2010. Figure 10.4 tracks the exponential growth in the number of articles published per decade from 1961–1970 up to 2001–2010.

HRD and training journals broadly mirror this growth pattern, although overall they have published few articles on action learning. Of those reviewed (*HRDI, Training and Development, Advances in Developing Human Resources, Journal of Management Education, Journal of European Industrial Training* (*JEIT*) and *Academy of Management Learning and Education*), all except *JEIT* have published fewer than ten articles on action learning in total and of these only five appeared before 2000. *Advances in Developing Human Resources* is illustrative, with a special issue on action learning in April 2010, having previously contained no papers at all on action learning. The pattern in *JEIT* is the exception, having carried an article by Reg Revans in its inaugural edition (Revans, 1977) and 49 others since.

Whilst not an exhaustive scientific study, these figures give insight into the growth of action learning's application. The spread of journals that have carried articles on action learning since 2000, and the range of themes addressed by articles, further illustrates the extent of its application, as shown in Table 10.2. The list reinforces the discussion above on the variety of outcomes for which action learning is used, from individual performative objectives such as management education, and organization performance objectives such as operational improvement, business value, quality management and performance measurement, across to individual and collective learning such as knowledge management and critical organization practice.

Table 10.2 Journals carrying action learning articles 2000–2010

Journal title	Article theme
Academy of Management Learning and Education	Critical management education
Advances in Developing Human Resources	Leadership development
Benchmarking: An International Journal	Benchmarking
British Journal of Management	Multi-disciplinary work
Career Development International	Management education
Development and Learning in Organizations	Teams
Education and Training	Work-based learning/ MBA education/e-learning
Engineering, Construction and Architectural Management	Construction SMEs
European Journal of Marketing	Marketing
Human Resource Management International Digest	Publishing
Industrial and Commercial Training	Adding business value
Integrated Manufacturing Systems	Operational improvement
Interactive Technology and Smart Education	Collaborative learning
International Journal of Contemporary Hospitality Management	Corporate university
International Journal of Educational Management	Leadership for teachers
International Journal of Managing Projects in Business	Project management
International Journal of Public Sector Management	Leading change
Journal of Documentation	Knowledge management
Journal of European Industrial Training	Entrepreneurship
Journal of Facilities Management	Performance measurement
Journal of Intellectual Capital	Learning
Journal of Management Development	Strategic management
Journal of Management Development	Knowledge management
Journal of Organizational Change Management	Critical organization practice
Journal of Systems and Information Technology	Multimedia learning
Journal of Workplace Learning	Construction management
Kybernetes	Conversational pedagogy
Leadership in Health Services	Medical quality management
Learning Organization	Process management innovation
Library Review	Public libraries
On the Horizon	Environmental education
Performance Measurement and Metrics	e-resources
Public Administration Quarterly	South Korean government
Quality Assurance in Education	Tertiary education
Strategic HR Review	Organization performance
Team Performance Management	Project learning

Source: Emerald full-text and Business Source Premier.

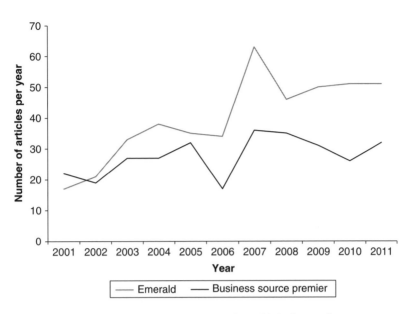

Figure 10.3   Number of action learning articles published annually 2000–2010

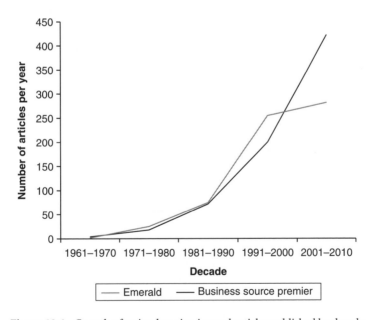

Figure 10.4   Growth of action learning journal articles published by decade

EXAMPLES OF PRACTICE

Table 10.2 provides quantitative insight into the reach of action learning. This section will illustrate in more depth some of the ways and purposes for which action learning has been applied in pursuit of problem resolution, learning and change both to individuals and organizational practice. First, Table 10.3 summarizes how the purpose for using action learning can be differentiated based on the nature of the problem or issue for which action learning is deployed. Distinction can be made between a focus on developing individuals addressing organization issues, stimulating innovation, tackling systemic societal issues and pursuit of policy learning.

EXAMPLES OF TEAM DEVELOPMENT IN PRACTICE

In practice, action learning interventions for team development often combine action learning sets with additional learning interventions, as shown in Figure 10.5. Core will be one or more action learning sets (group or team), with some kind of problem or task to address, which may be a change project or business challenge presented by the sponsor or client (shown as Ti in Figure 10.5). Within an organization, this is likely to be the senior management team or board. When the 'team' to be developed is a multi-agency group, the sponsor is typically a board with composition drawn from across each agency. Individuals may also be encouraged to present their own questions or issues within the sets as well (illustrated as Tii in Table 4). For example, questions of 'how do I manage the conflict in my department'; 'how do I improve my leadership capability'; etc. might be brought to the group for critical challenge.

External expertise (P), whilst certainly not used in all action learning, is often introduced through a variety of methods, including structured workshops and taught modules, masterclasses with high-level speakers or benchmarking visits to other places that have dealt with similar challenges. As discussed above, use of a facilitator or set adviser, even if only temporarily, is also common though not universal. There will often be some form of communication event at the end of the period. This may be a presentation to the board or may be a more elaborate shared-learning event such as a conference.

Figure 10.5 illustrates generic design features. Table 10.4 illustrates a more specific application of action learning designed to develop multi-agency team working. This is an example of the kind of development programme run to strengthen multi-agency working within a locality. Participants are drawn

Table 10.3 Applications and purposes of action learning

Purpose	Key features	Sample action learning issue
Individual professional development	• Focuses on expanding their skills, knowledge + capability • Hope that if they get better at their job the quality of service delivery will also improve	How do I improve my leadership capability? How do I help my team member to improve their ability to think and operate strategically?
Organization performance	• Focuses on addressing issues within one organization • Focus on continuous or radical improvements, reducing waste, cutting costs, increasing customer service • Works to expand the skills, knowledge + capability of many • Hope that if the whole organization improves, the quality of service delivery will also improve	How do we improve productivity? How do we achieve an integrated internal communication system for the planned merger next year? What do we, as the management team, develop ourselves as a high-performing team?
Stimulating innovation	• Focuses on creative exploration of new products, services or ways of doing things	How do we capture customer feedback more effectively? How do we cultivate a corporate innovative culture?
Tackling systemic public service issues	• Works with members from a number of organizations together • Focuses on expanding the skills, knowledge + capability for joint action to improve quality of services delivered • Focuses on building purposeful collaborative relationships and effort • Starts with questions about what impact is wanted for a population/place/community • Building collaborative, interagency working relationships	How can we develop as an effective interprofessional team? Can we identify ways of combining resources to work in this neighbourhood? How can we work together to reduce crime/poverty/ill-health in this community?
Policy learning	• Focus on learning that can inform wider public policy beyond the specific organization and individuals	How do poorly performing organizations turn themselves around? What are the best ways to identify and incubate high growth potential start-up businesses?

Figure 10.5 Common generic elements of an action learning programme

from across the local authority, health, police, fire and rescue services, together with registered social landlords and voluntary bodies. They may have some background of working together, but equally may not, and particularly not as a coherent team. In this context, a core purpose is team building.

Table 10.5 illustrates a model management-development programme based around action learning, designed for the development of a management team within a single organization. In this context, participants are likely to already work together and the purpose is to improve team coherence and performance.

CLAIMS MADE FOR THE TEAM DEVELOPMENT BENEFITS OF ACTION LEARNING

Evaluation data from programmes such as those illustrated above typically report the following benefits for participants (see the journal *Action Learning: Research and Practice* for numerous reports of accounts of practice):

- widening personal horizons;
- increasing job satisfaction;
- building self-confidence;
- improved network ability;

Table 10.4 Action learning designed to develop multi-agency team working in a neighbourhood

Sponsors

Elected councillors, residents and tenants, senior managers from various agencies across the neighbourhood

Delivery team – *internal or external team providing facilitation, running modules*	Change projects (Ti)	Support modules (P)
	Neighbourhood problems that cannot be tackled by one agency alone, e.g.	External expertise brought in, for example through one- or two-day events on themes below to support the work of the action learning sets and support personal development of team members:
	• street safety; • litter and graffiti; • developing comprehensive play provision in the community with the involvement of local people; • improving access to children under four and their families to a range of services; • agreeing a future for a local neighbourhood centre.	• leadership; • project planning & management; • creativity & innovation; • partnership working.
	Action learning sets	**Communication event – programme conference**
	With mixed membership from across different agencies.	An event at which the sets reported achievements, learning and recommendations from the change Projects to the programme sponsors.
	They meet during and between the modules to address one or more change project each.	
	Also a forum for individuals to bring their own individual work issues.	

Programme Partnership Team (PPT)
Senior client members + Seniors from delivery team Work as self-facilitated action learning set

Sponsor
The Chief Executive (CEO)

Table 10.5 Action learning designed to develop management team

Delivery team – *internal or external team providing facilitation, running modules*	Business challenges (Ti)	External expertise (P)
	Business challenges such as: • increased product development rate • improved supplier relations • raising performance	Modules: thematic workshops to support personal development of team members: Visits to other sites to learn from others with more experience Mentors: each individual matched with a mentor to support their personal and career development.
	Action learning sets With membership from across the organization Meeting regularly to address a business challenge and/or individual issues.	**Communication event – presentation to the CEO** An event at which the sets reported solutions, recommendations and learning from the challenge projects to the CEO

- ability to work with others from different professions and organizations;
- positive attitude towards cross-disciplinary working.

Claims for the outcomes of action learning (Revans, 1982; O'Neil and Marsick, 2007; Marquardt and Waddill, 2004 ; Marquardt et al., 2010) can be summarized in three domains:

1. profound personal learning and development;
2. team, organizational and systemic learning;
3. performance/business results.

Underneath these, a further subset of claims can be itemized as meta-skills and improved interpersonal relations. With respect to the first, Watkins and Marsick (1993) suggest that the espoused outcomes of engaging in action learning are multiple, including solutions to day-to-day problems, prevention of recurrence of such problems through double-loop learning, and development of cultural practices of critical reflection. Vince (2008) has argued that through engagement in the combination of action and reflection, participants develop meta-skills such as self-insight, wider organization–political understanding and influencing abilities.

In relation to claims for team relations, Marquardt et al. (2010) argue that action learning enables participants to develop the meta-skills equivalent to the eight key characteristics that the team effectiveness literature highlights as indicative of successful groups, including:

- clear and meaningful goals;
- explicit positive norms;
- strong interpersonal and communication skills;
- competence and commitment around solving problems and performing tasks;
- trust, openness and group cohesiveness;
- ability to manage conflict;
- shared leadership;
- continuous individual and team learning and improvement.

Such relational developments are also seen in interprofessional and inter-agency team working when action learners are drawn from across several organizations, such as a supply chain network or neighbourhood development partnership, and focus on shared challenges, learning and development (Coughlan and Coughlan, 2006; Benington and Hartley, 2009; Rigg, 2011).

Such claims relate to the question of why to choose action learning for team development over alternative methods. Arguments advanced in favour of action learning highlight the facility to do 'team process' work in the course of tackling real issues and therefore its potential to deliver performance gains in conjunction with improved team working.

THEORIZING ACTION LEARNING'S IMPACTS

The potential efficacy of action learning can be explained theoretically with reference to various schools of learning. Practitioners of the scientific approach to action learning base their approach on Revans' (1982) problem-solving model comprising Systems Alpha, Beta and Gamma (as outlined earlier in the chapter). Problems are addressed and learning and change occur through the interaction of the three systems. In System Alpha, participants collect data to analyse the problem context, examining the value system of the person and of the wider organization, the external system affecting decisions on the problem, and the internal system in which the problem-holder operates. In System Beta, the participant tries out a solution, systematically deploying stages of survey, hypothesis, experimentation, audit and review (Revans, 1982). System Gamma is the participant's cognitive framework: their assumptions and prior understanding. Revans (1982) argued that learning occurs when changes to this cognition result from the process of working through the actions of System Beta, asking questions, collecting data and bringing in appropriate 'programmed' knowledge from expertise or literature.

What Marsick and O'Neil (1999) describe as the experiential learning school of action learning is allied to Kolb's cycle of experiential learning (1984). They argue that theoretical roots here include humanistic psychology, with implicit assumptions that learning is a cognitive process deriving from reflection on action. Key to experiential action learning is the review process within the set, which affords individuals the opportunity to reflect on action within the wider organization or system.

The critical reflection approach to action learning is informed by critical theory. Theoretically, the principles are that learning is prompted by deep reflection on underlying assumptions, beliefs and values, which leads to more penetrating insights into the personal and systemic causes of organization problems (Rigg and Trehan, 2004). Mezirow (1991), for example, posits that critical reflection can transform perspectives as people recognize the disjuncture between their previous beliefs and their current experience, and come to radically new understanding (for examples, see Rigg and Trehan, 2004).

Adult learning theory (Boud et al., 1996) also helps explain the potential of action learning, providing explanation of why the search for fresh questions and 'q' (*questioning insight*) might be more helpful than access to expert knowledge or 'p' (in Revans' terms, 1982) on the basis that adults learn from taking action and reflecting on real issues that are of direct concern to them, rather than from lectures or invented case studies that are not related to their experience.

Social learning theory can explain the efficacy of the learning that results from the process of peer interaction and questioning, thereby encouraging double-loop learning (Argyris and Schön, 1974) and action learning overcomes the limitations that individuals, when working alone, can inflict on their own learning by their mental models or unconscious patterns of behaviours. The Tacit School (Marsick and Watkins, 1992) would argue that this happens incidentally, provoked by systematic reflection within the action learning set, whilst the Critical School would advocate for strong facilitation to support the process by which action learning participants become more aware of the values and assumptions that underlie their actions, and learn to take different perspectives. Both would support the claim that participants develop meta-skills such as self-insight, wider organization – political understanding and influencing abilities, as well as skills for learning how to learn and triple loop learning (Bateson, 1972).

LIMITATIONS, FAILURES AND CRITIQUES

The discussion so far has portrayed the positive aspects and claims of action learning. However, this is not to suggest that action learning always works or is immune to critique.

There are many accounts of action learning that did not meet expectations (Yapp, 2006; Lyons and Rigg, 2006; Oliver, 2008; Edmonstone, 2010). Some of the themes raised by these accounts include:

- Tensions between the action learning principle of assumption questioning and a common managerial prerogative for certainty and drive to be seen as in control, which can constrain participants' willingness to expose their assumptions for critique.
- Attitudes to time – perceptions that the reflective cycles of action learning are too time-consuming in a pressurized world.
- Lack of voluntarism in participation – where participants have been compelled to engage in action learning.
- Facilitators that have been too rigid/controlling/dominant.
- Consuming needs of an individual participant dominates the process – where a participant has such significant problems they require one-to-one support or sometimes professional medical attention.
- Unintended consequences – the client brief conflicts with what individual participants want from the process.
- The contracting process is inflexible.
- The contracting process is based on the client having diagnosed a need accurately and commissioning action learning as a predefined solution.
- Senior management support is weak.
- Action learning is strongly countercultural to the dominant organizational norms.
- The client/facilitator is ill-prepared for issues of power and emotion amongst the participants.

A whole chapter could in itself be devoted to exploring these issues, for which there is not space here. Suffice to say that stories of underachievement and failure are as important as those of success in advancing our understanding of action learning as both an internal group process and within its wider organization/ institutional context. Arguably, the existence of such disappointments can be attributed to gaps in our theoretical understanding. The remainder of the chapter will therefore focus on three aspects of action learning that have received critical questioning, in order to highlight the content of those critiques and identify thinking on alternatives or further work:

1. absence of criticality;
2. underdeveloped theoretical underpinning;
3. evidence base for claims.

ABSENCE OF CRITICALITY

Conventional action learning has been criticized for failing to promote critical thinking on the daily realities of participants (Willmott, 1997; Trehan and Rigg, 2007; O'Neil and Marsick, 2007), when reflection is limited simply to an individual's experience of action. The argument is that this neglects that such practice is always undertaken in a context of power and politics, which inevitably gives rise to conflict and tension. Critical action learning is a development of conventional action learning in that it aims to promote a deepening of critical thinking, giving explicit recognition to the role that politics and emotions can play in facilitating or constraining, the scope for learning (Rigg and Trehan, 2004; Vince, 2004; 2008). Key to this process is the emphasis on collective as well as individual reflection, going beyond simple reflection on action (learning from experience), with the reflection of existing organizational, political and emotional dynamics created in action, what Vince (2008) calls learning from organizing.

Critical action learning (CAL) has a number of distinguishing features, including first, a focus on the ways in which power relations, emotions and the unconscious, as brought to the group and played out within it, supports or constrains learning. Action learning has usually viewed the 'action learning set' as the primary vehicle for collaboration, where work-based issues are addressed through questioning and reflection. Critical action learning gives explicit recognition to ways in which action learning sets themselves become arenas for the interplay of emotional, political and social relations, in that they can mirror the range of inequalities, tensions and emotional fractures that characterize groups, organizations and societies. Vince's (2004) concept of 'organizing insight' illuminates the importance of critical collaboration, in other words the opportunity to examine:

the politics that surround and inform organizing . . . to comprehend these politics it is often necessary to question these political choices and decisions, both consciously and unconsciously.

(Vince, 2004, p. 74)

In practice, for example, the facilitator might observe within a group that the pattern of interactions is dominated by some, whilst one or two individuals are barely listened to. The facilitator might simply pose a question as to the significance of this. If the question resonates with group members, it may be used to initiate a discussion on power and status within the group, perhaps extending to parallels within the immediate organization or network. As another example, an individual's presenting of anger on their immediate resource problems at work might be widened through peer or facilitator questioning, to help them locate their own situation in a broader context.

These short examples also illustrate a second distinction of CAL as compared with traditional action learning, which is the implication for a more active facilitation role so as to illuminate the ways in which participants reinforce behaviours or power relations that sustain learning inaction. While traditional facilitation promotes reflection focused on the immediate presenting details of a task or problem, critical facilitation is concerned with promoting a process of critical reflection on the emotional and political processes with the group dynamics and making conscious the social, political, professional, economic and ethical assumptions underlying participants' actions. Supplementing this experiential learning with theoretical learning to form new knowledge, behaviours and insights, facilitation within critical action learning also places importance on supporting transfer of the resultant learning to practise both inside the group and outside within the wider organization (Rigg and Trehan, 2008).

UNDERDEVELOPED THEORETICAL UNDERPINNING

A second area of critique relates to the underdeveloped theorizing of action learning. This applies to our understanding of how and why learning occurs through action learning, but it more acutely applies to our theory of action within action learning. In relation to individuals' learning, Marquardt and Waddill (2004) suggest that learning can be explained through the presence within action learning of five major adult learning schools (behaviourist, cognitivist, humanist, social and constructivist). However, others suggest that the question of learning needs to go further in order to explain the relation between individual, team and organization/systemic learning (Rigg, 2006; Burgoyne, 2009). Understanding the action within action learning is much less developed, with notable exceptions (Fox, 2009; Vince, 2008; Gold et al., 2009).

EVIDENCE BASE FOR CLAIMS

The third area of critique relates to the evidence base for claims regarding the effectiveness of action learning. As highlighted earlier in the chapter, through the growth of practice, there is a burgeoning empirical body of experience within action learning. However, there is a paucity of systematic evaluations and comparative studies of the outcomes from action learning as compared to other methods, or indeed of comparative benefits within differing contexts of the different approaches to action learning, as highlighted earlier in the chapter. For example, there is no systematic experimental evidence to compare the value of action learning for team development with alternative methods. Theoretically and empirically, we can conjecture that action learning is a powerful method of team building because, for example, it simultaneously builds task effectiveness as well as cultivating group process within the working context, whereas alternative team-building methods often take teams outside their context, have less transferability back to a workplace and do not work at so many levels of learning. However, the criticism remains that the claims warrant further systematic study in order to strengthen the evidence base.

CONCLUSION: STRENGTHENING THE EVIDENCE BASE – TOWARDS A RESEARCH AGENDA

This chapter has focused on action learning as an approach to developing teams within and across organizations. It has introduced the origins, interpretations and applications of action learning, which highlights that it is a difficult term to tightly define, as practitioners have evolved varying approaches and designs across the world. Some of the major claims have been highlighted, as well as critiques that are made. The potential of action learning for team development derives from the facility for participants to learn how to work more effectively with others across professional, departmental and organizational boundaries in the process of tackling real issues. In this sense, action learning embodies ideas from adult learning theory, experiential learning and social learning theory, as well as others.

Criticisms relate particularly to the robustness of the theoretical under-pinning, the weak criticality in traditional action learning and the reliance on an empirical – rather than systematically evaluated – evidence base into the contexts, approaches and conditions in which action learning has effect. This chapter concludes by arguing that it is time to develop and implement a research agenda that systematically and systemically investigates and explores a range of questions and issues concerning action learning. These might include, but are certainly not restricted to, the following:

- The problem of action.
- What are the characteristics of participant readiness and organization readiness for action learning?
- What kinds of issues benefit from action learning?
- Who is it not suited for?
- How can it be best combined with other forms of development intervention (e.g. 360, 1–1 coaching)?
- Why is it so powerful?
- How can facilitator independence best be encouraged?
- What are the conditions of effective virtual action learning?
- Comparative effectiveness of different approaches to action learning in different contexts.
- Effectiveness in linking individual, team and organizational learning.
- Comparative effectiveness of action learning for team development com-pared to other approaches.
- Issues in using critical action learning.
- In what contexts are there benefits to combining action learning with other action modalities, such as action research?
- The continuing problem of definition.
- Understanding dysfunction and failure.

REFERENCES

Argyris, M. and Schön, D. (1974) *Theory in Practice: Increasing Professional Effectiveness.* San Francisco, CA: Jossey-Bass.

Bateson, G. (1972) *Steps to an Ecology of Mind: Collected Essays in Anthropology, Psychiatry, Evolution and Epistemology.* New York: Chandler.

Benington, J. and Hartley, J. (2009) *'Whole Systems Go!' Improving Leadership Across the Whole Public Service System: Propositions to Stimulate Discussion and Reform.* London: National School of Government, Sunningdale Institute. <http://www.nationalschool. gov.uk/news_events/newsreleases/items/18-08-2009.asp> (accessed 21 November 2010).

Boshyk, Y. (2010) *What Is Business Driven Action Learning Today?* <4http://www.gel—net. com/download/What_is_BDAL_Today_Yury_Boshyk.pdf > (accessed 5 February 2011).

Boud, D., Cohen, R. and Walker, D. (eds) (1996) *Using Experience for Learning*. Buckingham: Open University Press.

Burgoyne, J. (2009) Issues in action learning: A critical realist approach, *Action Learning: Research and Practice*, 6(2): 149–161.

Coughlan, D. and Coughlan, P. (2006) Action learning in inter-organizational sets. In C. Rigg with S. Richards (eds) *Action Learning, Leadership and Organizational Development in Public Services*, pp. 181–192. London: Routledge.

Dewey, J. (1938) *Logic: The Theory of Inquiry*. New York: Holt, Rinehart and Winston.

Edmonstone, J. (2010) When action learning doesn't 'take': Reflections on the DALEK programme, *Action Learning: Research and Practice*, 7(1): 89–98.

Fox, S. (2009) Following the action in action learning: Towards ethnomethodological studies of (critical) action learning, *Action Learning: Research and Practice*, 6(2): 5–16.

Gold, J., Anderson, L., Clarke, J. and Thorpe, R. (2009) To act and learn: A Bakhtinian exploration of action learning, *Action Learning: Research and Practice*, 6(2): 121–130.

Kellie, J., Henderson, E., Milsom, B. and Crawley, H. (2010) An account of practice: Leading change in tissue viability best practice, an action learning programme for link nurse practitioners, *Action Learning Research and Practice*, 7: 213–219.

Lyons, M. and Rigg, C. (2006) Local authority chief executive action learning sets. In C. Rigg and S. Richards (eds) *Action Learning, Leadership and Organizational Development in Public Services*, pp. 55–65. London: Routledge.

Marquardt, M., Ng, C. S. and Goodson, H. (2010) Team development via action learning, *Advances in Developing Human Resources*, 12(2): 241–259.

Marquardt, M. and Waddill, D. (2004) The power of learning in action learning: A conceptual analysis of how the five schools of adult learning theories are incorporated within the practice of action learning, *Action Learning: Research and Practice*, 1(2): 185–202.

Marsick, V. J. and Watkins, K. E. (1992) *Informal and Incidental Learning in the Workplace*. New York: Routledge.

Marsick, V.J. and O'Neil, J. (1999) The many faces of action learning, *Management Learning*, 30(2): 159–176.

Mezirow, J. (1991) *Transformative Dimensions of Adult Learning*. San Francisco, CA: Jossey-Bass.

Oliver, J. (2008) Reflections on a failed action learning intervention, *Action Learning: Research and Practice*, 5(1): 79–84.

O'Neil, J. and Marsick, V. J. (2007) *Understanding Action Learning*. New York: AMACOM.

Pedler, M. (1997, 2011) *Action Learning in Practice*. London, Gower.

Pedler, M., Burgoyne, T. and Boydell, T. (2004) *A Manager's Guide to Leadership*. London: McGraw-Hill.

Ram, M. and Trehan, K. (2010) Critical action learning, policy learning and small firms: An inquiry, *Management Learning*, 41(4): 415–428.

Revans, R. W. (1977) An action learning trust, *Journal of European Industrial Training*, 1(1): 2–5.

Revans, R. W. (1982) *The ABC of Action Learning*. Bromley: Chartwell-Bratt.

Revans, R.W. (1987) *Opening Speech*. Revans action learning workshop, IMCA Buckingham, 18 December. Cited in Levy, M. and Delahoussaye, M. (2000) *Reg Revans: A Man of Action Training Journal Abstract*.

Richards, S. (2006) Learning and leading: action learning for chief probation officers. In C. Rigg with S. Richards (eds) *Action Learning, Leadership and Organizational Development in Public Services*, pp. 66–78. London: Routledge.

Rigg, C. (2006) Understanding the organisational potential for action learning. In C. Rigg with S. Richards (eds) *Action Learning, Leadership and Organizational Development in Public Services*, pp. 41–51. London: Routledge.

Rigg, C. (2011) Systemic action and learning in public services, *Action Learning; Research and Practice*, 8(1): 15–26.

Rigg, C. and Trehan, K. (2004) Reflections on working with critical action learning, *Action Learning, Research and Practice*, 1 (2). 149–165.

Rigg, C. with Richards, S. (2006) *Action Learning, Leadership and Organizational Development in Public Services*. London: Routledge.

Rigg, C. and Trehan, K., (2008) Critical reflection in the workplace: is it just too difficult?, *Journal of European Industrial Training*, 35 (5): 374–384.

Trehan, K. and Rigg, C. (2007) Working with experiential learning: A critical perspective In practice. In M. Reynolds and Vince R. (eds) *The Handbook of Experiential and Management Education*. Oxford: Oxford University Press

Vince, R. (2004). Action learning and organizational learning: Power, politics, and emotion in organizations, *Action Learning: Research and Practice*, 1(1): 63–78.

Vince, R. (2008) 'Learning-in-action' and 'learning inaction': Advancing the theory and practice of critical action learning, *Action Learning: Research and Practice*, 5(2): 93–104.

Watkins, K.E. and Marsick, V.J. (1993) *Sculpting the Learning Organization: Lessons in the Art and Science of Systemic Change*. San Francisco, CA: Jossey-Bass.

Willmott, H. (1997) Critical management learning. In J. Burgoyne and M. Reynolds (eds) *Management Learning*, pp. 161–176. London: Sage.

Yapp, C. (2006) Levels of action learning, and holding groups to the experience. In C. Rigg and S. Richards (eds) *Action Learning, Leadership and Organizational Development in Public Services*, pp. 103–116. London: Routledge.

Zuber-Skerritt, O. (2009) *Action Learning and Action Research – Songlines through Interviews*. Rotterdam, NY: Sense Publishers.

FURTHER READING

The journal *Action Learning: Research and Practice* – international journal dedicated to the advancement of knowledge and practice through action learning. <http://www.tandfonline.com/loi/calr20>.

Pedler, M. (ed.) (2012) *Action Learning in Practice*. London, Gower.

Revans, R. (1982) *The ABC of Action Learning*. Bromley: Chartwell-Bratt.

Rigg, C. and Richards, S. (2006) *Action Learning, Leadership and Organizational Development in Public Services*. London: Routledge.

11

FACILITATING GROUP LEARNING THROUGH SCENARIO PLANNING

Denise Thursfield

INTRODUCTION

A scenario is defined as a 'story about the future that is plausible and internally consistent' (Galer and van der Heijden, 2001, p. 850). Scenario planning 'is a way to learn about these futures through seeking, in an informed and disciplined way, to map out the many different ways in which they could evolve' (ibid). The roots of scenario planning are linked to futurism studies and strategizing. From its futurist roots, scenario planning is a tool for analysing, debating and communicating big issues. In the context of its strategizing roots, scenario planning is not so much about what might happen as what should be done if events conspire to produce particular scenarios (Lindgren and Bandhold, 2009). Scenario planning is well established as a decision-making and strategizing tool for business and organizations. Its origins can be traced back to the 1950s and the work of Hermann Kahn for the RAND corporation (Chermack and Walton, 2006). Scenario planning developed further during the 1970s through the seminal work of Wack at Royal Dutch/Shell (Selin, 2007; Wack, 1985).

A second and more recent, branch of scenario planning is related to the tradition of organizational learning, and it has been argued that there is a case for scenario planning to be 'recognized as a core strategic learning tool in

254

HRD' (Chermack and Swanson, 2008, p. 130). From this perspective, scenario planning is concerned with the construction of shared visions and world views and collective development of strategy through scenarios. Scenario planning as an organizational learning tool is comparable with Senge's (1990) notions of shared mental models and team learning. This is because the construction of scenarios requires the co-operation and communication associated with team learning and the construction of shared cognitive models of the future.

A third less well-researched branch of scenario planning relates to its use as a pedagogical tool to support learning in the classroom. Classroom learning is defined here as formal learning associated with learning programmes such as management development, MBA and MSc courses and usually involves learners from disparate organizations or full-time students. In the two former examples, the focus is on strategizing and HRD within organizations. This chapter sets out to explore the theoretical underpinning of scenario planning and to develop the method from its roots as a business strategy and organizational learning tool to one that can promote learning in a classroom context. Specifically, the aim is to explore and evaluate the extent to which scenario planning can be used to engender group and collective learning within the formal classroom setting. The rationale for this aim is threefold. First, it relates to an observed need (by the author of this chapter) to develop pedagogical tools to engender classroom participation by students who do not, for cultural and other reasons, engage in classroom dialogue. Second, to develop a classroom exercise that is rooted in a social learning rather than a solely individual cognitive paradigm. Third, to begin to address a gap in the literature: the use of scenario planning as a pedagogical tool for facilitating formal classroom learning. Although there is a wide literature on scenario planning, there is no work exploring its appropriateness in the classroom environment.

To achieve its aims, the chapter will draw out the pertinent characteristics and principles of scenario planning and present analysis of their applicability to the classroom teaching and learning experience. It will be argued that both the process of constructing scenarios and the use of scenarios as a planning and strategy tool are pertinent to scenario planning as a classroom-based learning tool. In this context, the objectives of the chapter are to critically review the literature on scenario planning, to describe the use of scenario planning to date and to evaluate two examples of classroom-based scenario planning. Evaluation of the data is based on the observations and subjective reflections of the author.

The chapter begins with a literature review that incorporates definitions, history and methods of scenario planning. It also explores the claims made for the technique and the criticisms that have been put forward. This is followed by a consideration of how scenario planning might be used as a classroom-based HRD tool. Next is a description and discussion of two examples of classroom-based scenario planning. Both examples are taken from the teaching experience of the author. Finally, the chapter presents a general analysis of the usefulness of scenario planning in classroom-based HRD.

LITERATURE REVIEW

It is argued that in an unstable and uncertain environment rational, technical and predictive strategizing is futile. Organizations require learning, not prediction, if they are to deal with uncertainty (Mintzberg et al., 1998). Scenario planning (SP) sets out to explore the ambiguities and instability of the environment and to engender multiple narratives to explain the world (Burt et al., 2006). Through SP, organizations are able to prepare for uncertainty by imagining various futures and creating possible responses that develop understanding beyond existing ideas (Chermack and Lynham, 2002; Walton, 2008).

SP functions at the individual and organizational level. It is a tool for ordering individual perceptions through the creation of mental maps and cognitive models (Wilson, 1998). It encourages members of the organization to challenge their assumptions and preconceptions through exploration of the future involving stories and possible outcomes (Chermack, 2004). People are core to SP, as insights gained through individual exploration can be linked to an organization's strategy (Burt and Chermack, 2008). For Wack, obsolete assumptions on the part of managers cause strategic failures in organizations (Wack, 1985). He argued that the key aim of SP is to identify managers' fixed views and to help them reperceive reality in order to realign their mental models with environmental uncertainty. SP has been linked to experiential learning, reflection, theory building and action (Galer and van der Heijden, 2001).

In terms of historical use, SP has been applied at the societal, industrial and organizational levels. Kahane (2002), for example, describes how it was used to understand the future during South Africa's transition from apartheid to democracy. It has also been used to explore the future of rural areas in England and Wales (Foa and Howard, 2006). At the level of industries, Davies et al. (2005) investigated the role of SP in knowledge-based strategic decision making in the European airline industry, whilst Yeoman and McMahon-Beattie (2005) describe the use of SP by the Scottish tourism organization VisitScotland. At the organizational level, SP has been used by organizations ranging from large supra-national organizations to individual companies. Bertrand et al. (2000), for example, explored possible futures of the European Union. Provo et al. (1998) argued that organizations can use SP on three levels: at the macro-level to explore whole industries, at the competitive level and at the level of product development. Finally, Pollard and Hotho (2006) explore the combination of SP and crisis management to give organizations a view on achieving strategic plans. At the level of the organization, Moyer explores the use of SP in the interpretation of external events at British Airways in the 1990s (Moyer, 1996). Ramirez and van der Heijden (2007) investigate the role of SP in identifying strategic options in four case-study companies. Borjeson et al. (2006) also identified three forms of SP: predictive, explorative and normative. Predictive scenarios are concerned with outcomes in the context of specific conditions, explorative with possibilities over a long-term time horizon and normative with the likelihood of achieving desired objectives. Predictive scenarios relate to outcomes whilst exploratory scenarios emphasize process. These themes are taken up by Burt and Chermack (2008) who propose two main SP dimensions. The first has general process aims whilst the second is concerned with organizational exploration or decision making. Scenarios can also be divided into positive or negative futures (Masini, 1993).

In terms of underlying ontology and epistemology, SP can be argued to have roots in both objective realist and hermeneutic paradigms. Walton (2008) draws upon previous studies to argue that it can be categorized into three paradigms. First, predictive empirical studies aim to know a predetermined future and the process of SP is to identify trends. From a cultural interpretivist tradition, the aim is to gain an insight into differing perspectives on the future and involves comparison between multiple scenarios. From the post-structural and critical paradigms, scenarios are used to challenge problematic assumptions and power relations.

The predictive empirical studies identified by Walton are rooted in a positivist, realist ontology. From this perspective, there is a reality that can be identified and quantified. The very act of identifying issues, problems and environmental conditions associated with SP is, it can be suggested, premised on the assumption of some form of objective reality. Moreover, the positivist approach is linked to the rationalist notion of predictability and planning, which emphasizes the outcomes of the method rather than the process (Chermack and Swanson, 2008). From the interpretive, post-structuralist and critical paradigms, the construction of scenarios through dialogue is the basis of reality. Reality is not fixed, it is imagined and negotiated. As Walton argues: 'in choosing between options and acting on them, we are in effect influencing the future and shaping, even if only in a small way, how it will map out'

(Walton, 2008, p. 156). The negotiated nature of SP and the absence of fixed reality suggest a strong social constructionist underpinning. Even where there is an identification of 'real' issues and problems, the story of how these issues and problems might unfold in the future is entirely socially constructed.

With respect to learning, SP is linked to both cognitive models and social learning theory. The cognitive approach is apparent in the idea that SP, at the level of the individual, is about the reframing of individuals' mental models and a realignment of individual managers' inner models with the uncertainty of the environment (Wack, 1985). From this perspective, SP is about changing the ways in which people view things. It is not concerned with the collective construction of meaning; learning is an individual endeavour rather than collective and intersubjectively created. Thus, according to Selin (2007), 'an individual's view of the world is formulated within his or her unique perceptual system, which serves to filter experience and information into awareness, conceptualization, or an image of reality' (Selin, 2007, p. 34). On the other hand, from a social learning perspective, it is taken for granted that learning is necessarily social. This is because individual subjectivity is inseparable from the group or society. Individual subjectivities are forged in the context of people's participation in the social world, in particular through dialogue with others. From this perspective, learning is never a solely individual endeavour.

Despite the variation in approaches to SP described above, there are many similarities between methods of construction. According to Borjeson et al. (2006), SP necessarily begins with the generation of ideas through workshops and/or brainstorming. This phase is particularly important to the construction of explorative scenarios. The next phase is the integration stage where, if a social constructionist approach is adopted, integration will occur through dialogue and conversation. The process of SP usually takes place in structured workshops. The topic of interest is identified and a number of scenarios are developed. Each scenario includes identification of organizational and environmental forces for change, the relationship between these forces and future uncertainties (Provo et al., 1998).

In socially constructed scenarios, meaning is created as scenarios are built through the medium of collective narrative. The use of narrative is not, moreover, simply about the construction of meaning. It also relates to the process of construction and the learning that takes place as people reflect together to create new perspectives. Such learning is connected to both content and process of learning. Content concerns what we understand about the possible future under discussion, whilst process is about learning within groups through intersubjective dialogue.

A number of claims have been made for SP. The benefits of the technique are argued to occur at both the individual and organizational levels, and there is an assumption that individual benefits can be captured by the organization. Bood and Postma (1997) argue that SP can overcome the tendency of organizational members to think within existing rules, norms and assumptions. It can also overcome disagreement caused by conflict and the tendency towards group-think. The process of SP enables an exploration of personal understanding and the construction of shared memories of the future. It can reframe the mental models that exist in people's heads (Kahane, 2002). This process occurs when people articulate their model and share it with others with different experiences and perspectives. SP also engenders greater commitment to change, which is developed through dialogue. Moreover, where organizations adopt holistic, creative and future thinking processes, the result will be a culture of learning and change (Yeoman and McMahon-Beattie, 2005).

Provo et al. (1998) distinguish between the types of benefit to flow from SP. At the level of strategic planning, it can be used to help an organization prepare for change, foster both entrepreneurialism and protectionism, cope with the complexity of change, foster individual and organizational learning and enhance organizational decision making. At the level of the individual, SP is linked to various paradigms of learning. From the cognitive perspective, it helps an individual improve their perceptual ability and their understanding of the forces within their organization. From the humanist perspective, it emphasizes the importance of human emotions in relation to change. Finally, at the level of behaviourism and human behaviour, SP improves the quality of individual strategic thinking and personal decision making.

SCENARIO PLANNING AND HRD

SP is linked to organizational learning through its emphasis on the development of a shared understanding of possible futures. It also helps develop organizational members' understandings of organizational structures and facilitates identification of possible future discontinuities. It aims to enable organizations to prepare for new realities and to make sense of them when they arrive (Galer and van der Heijden, 2001). Rothwell and Kazanas (1989) suggest that as part of a futuring approach HRD practitioners may also contribute to strategic formulation by designing structured exercises that can aid decision making. They give scenario formulation as an example of such exercises.

As a tool for organizational and group learning, SP is significant because it facilitates strategic dialogue between a wide variety of organizational members holding different perspectives (Chermack and Swanson, 2008). It seeks to align the mental models of numerous individuals and provides a ready-made language through which to discuss strategy. Chermack et al. (2007) describe this process as 'strategic learning through conversation' (Chermack et al., 2007, p. 380). Strategic conversation requires a common language and understanding and a willingness to engage in rational argumentation, including a willingness to critique ideas and have one's own ideas critiqued (van der Heijden, 1997).

The adoption of SP can also provide HRD professionals with a voice in the strategy process. Moreover, HRD is a crucial bridge between the ideas to emerge from SP and their implementation. Finally, SP is closely associated with organizational change and can be developed as a methodology for HRD (Provo et al., 1998). The remaining sections of this chapter will explore the extent to which SP can be developed as a method for classroom-based HRD. It will consider how principles relating to the development of shared understandings, collective sense-making, strategic dialogue and learning through conversation, and the ability to critique and be critiqued can facilitate group learning within the classroom. The aims are to develop a learning strategy that encourages students to engage in dialogue and participate in socially constructed learning, to assist students in their understanding of the forces that shape their discipline and to help them think through ideas and project these forward into the future.

SCENARIO PLANNING AND CLASSROOM-BASED GROUP LEARNING

The development of SP as a classroom-based HRD tool requires construction of a set of clear aims that are linked to the characteristics of scenario planning described above. It is suggested here that these aims can be categorized as outcome aims, process aims and ontological concerns. In terms of outcomes, aims are to:

1. Engender an understanding of a particular topic, practice or discipline.
2. To engender an understanding of the complexities within the topic, practice or discipline. Such understanding is developed as individuals and groups grapple with the interrelationships between organizational and environmental variables. It is also developed through consideration of alternative futures. This aim is consistent with both the predictive and exploratory frameworks described earlier. Exploration relates to an

evolution of understanding pertaining to developments within a topic or practice and the relations between the two. Prediction is concerned with the possible outcomes of interaction between organizational and environmental variables.

Process aims relate to intersubjective interactions within the group and are to:

1. Promote learning and group work through the sharing of experience and knowledge.
2. Support learning and group work through the promotion of dialogue.
3. Encourage the social construction of meaning through narrative.
4. Encourage a questioning of existing perspectives and mental maps at both the individual and collective level in order to open up a space for new possibilities and ideas.

Ontological concerns are to:

1. Position classroom-based SP within the interpretivist ontology and epistemology. Although the identification of variables has been linked to a realist, rational, positivist ontology, learning in SP is firmly linked to the collective construction of meaning through narrative.

The methods of classroom-based SP also follow the steps described earlier by Borjeson et al. (2006) and Provo et al. (1998). The activity begins with an idea generation session followed by a narrowing of scenario parameters. This might involve the generation of questions or negative and positive statements. The next step is to construct a collective mental 'map' of consequences, which draws links between variables and states of affairs. Following this, students are tasked with the construction of a narrative around the map, which describes the scenario in more detail. Through these steps, SP encourages students to engage in a variety of learning exercises. For example: independent thinking through the generation of ideas and selection of relevant variables; the linking of concepts in order to construct mental maps; and the social construction of meaning through narrative creation.

CRITICISMS

Despite the growing popularity of SP, there are a number of criticisms to be found in the literature. Some of these criticisms are relevant to SP as a classroom-based learning tool and thus require consideration. Others criticisms are less relevant. At the level of ontology, SP that is rooted in the technical-predictive-empirical paradigm is criticized because it cannot 'capture the mindset of managers' (Chermack et al., 2007, p. 384). Effective SP is, according to Chermack et al., dependent upon conversation and dialogue. Foa and Howard (2006), on the other hand, point to a lack of methodological specificity within SP and an overreliance on subjective analysis. They suggest that whilst a strength of SP is its avoidance of determinism, it can be formulaic and dependent on preconceived visions. It can also lead to a lack of precise forecasts. These criticisms might be relevant to organizations, but not to classroom-based HRD. Whereas the aim of SP in organizations is concerned with outcomes, the aims of classroom SP are to promote understanding of a topic and facilitate intersubjective learning. Its use as an HRD tool is premised on intersubjective learning through conversation. Subjectivity and intersubjectivity are therefore strengths rather than problems.

A second critique is the absence of a means of identifying the processes within SP that lead to success and the lack of empirical evidence of its ability to enhance performance (Keough and Shanahan, 2008; Verity, 2003). Although these criticisms are concerned with issues such as individual managers' willingness to admit a lack of knowledge of the future and the impact of organizational factors such as culture and leadership, the critique is relevant to classroom-based HRD. Specifically, analyses of the processes within SP that engender intersubjective group learning.

Further criticisms of SP concern the participants. The first suggests that SP may be constrained by bounded rationality. Participants may lack the ability to consider all possible choices and consequences of choices. This critique is less relevant to SP as a pedagogical tool because, again, emphasis is given to the process rather than the outcome. Moreover, it is further argued that SP overcomes bounded rationality as participants learn from one another and exchange information (Keough and Shanahan, 2008). It is suggested, moreover, that in order for SP to be successful, significant decision makers within the organization must want to find a better way to reach a decision. They must be prepared to engage in new ways of thinking and adequate time must be given to the process. For example, to do homework, absorb ideas and think together. In classroom-based SP, the issue is whether students can be encouraged to participate and view the process as a useful learning experience.

In terms of the practice, Selin (2007) argues that the abbreviated forms of SP that occur within rushed contexts are a corrosion of Wack's work and asks whether SP can be relevant under these conditions. However, she also says that there are some advantages to short cursory methods. Such methods may be necessary, less expensive and quicker, offer inspirational thinking and unleash creative potential. Atomized methods can also serve to articulate existing knowledge and expectations which, even if superficial, can be a good starting point. This is particularly pertinent to the classroom setting where time is constrained by timetabling.

Burt and Chermack (2008) in their critique of SP identify key issues that require further research. These include an integrative focus on the learning that occurs through scenario planning. A common problem is, they argue, the tendency to come back to the official future. There is, however, no 'official' future in the classroom setting, and any scenarios must be constructed from the beginning. A further critique is that the lack of a unifying best practice model is a drawback of the method, although it is suggested by these authors that such a model may emerge over time. The notion that one best practice model can be established and applied to a multiplicity of situations is challenged here. Case study evidence suggests that in the situated classroom setting different circumstances influence the process and thus modify the way in which SP is conducted. Research is also needed into the cognitive barriers that can impact on learning in SP and the willingness of leaders to take scenarios seriously. This chapter explores and attempts to theorize some of these barriers to learning. It also considers the extent to which student-participants view the tool as useful and relevant and, therefore, their willingness to participate.

Case Study 1: Managers of lifelong learning in Estonia

An SP exercise was used during a three-day management development course for managers of lifelong learning in Estonia. The aims of the exercise were to develop an understanding of the substantive issues and social, economic and political context of lifelong learning and to develop an understanding of SP as a tool for learning. Specifically, the objectives were:

1. To facilitate an understanding of lifelong learning in relation to social, economic and political factors. Such understanding is necessary in the context of the uncertain environment in which lifelong learning is practised, particularly in relation to developments within the European Union.
2. To encourage students to share their own experiential knowledge and to learn from one another's experience.
3. To develop an understanding of the social paradigm of learning amongst participants.
4. To furnish participants with knowledge of SP in order that the tool be used in their own organizations.

The class consisted of around 20 managers from around the Tallinn area of Estonia. Participants had not met before the commencement of the course and were employed in a variety of organizations ranging from a religious college to training managers in commercial organizations and managers of further education institutions. None of the managers had met prior to commencement of the course.

The SP exercise attempted to follow the steps described below:

1. Identification of organizational and societal issues or problems relating to lifelong learning. Issues identified included course development, recruitment and the viability of training.
2. Identification of political, economic and social contextual factors.
3. Articulation of identified issues and problems into two questions. For example, 'how well will tertiary colleges recruit in the next decade?' and 'how can training in sector X remain relevant in the context of a changing environment?'
4. Construction of a shared mental map, and the development of a positive and negative set of possible consequences for both questions referred to in 3 above in which developed consequences are linked to the environmental factors identified in step-2.
5. Write up the sequence of consequences and links as a narrative in order to construct shared meaning and to identify possible futures for lifelong learning in Estonia.

This exercise most closely resembles the framework model of SP. It attempts to link macro-factors with micro-organization issues to develop a general understanding of issues and processes. The exercise is, moreover, exploratory in that it begins with no parameters. Students were not given guidance on the types of issue or what contextual factors might be relevant. In short, they were not provided with terms of reference. Finally, the exercise was of a short-term duration in that it took place over a one-day period.

In terms of the effectiveness of the exercise, the outcome was largely negative. Students found it difficult to grasp what was expected of them despite clear and repeated instructions. More direction was requested and students asked for detailed guidance over what types of issues, problems and environmental variables they should identify. This group of students found it difficult to identify issues from their own experience. A second obstacle to emerge related to an absence of intersubjective dialogue and even basic knowledge sharing. Students were placed in four groups of five and were asked to share ideas and identify generic issues relating to steps 1 and 2. However, despite requests to enter into conversation, participants tended to work individually and keep their thoughts to themselves. Few ideas concerning issues and problems were identified. Similarly, few questions were generated during stage 3 of the process.

Stages 4 and 5 of this exercise required intersubjective dialogue in order to collectively create a narrative around a possible or imagined future. However, participants spent little time on this task and, despite requests to do so, were unwilling to continue for longer than 45 minutes. Few possible consequences and links to environmental factors were identified. Moreover, the narrative was short, perfunctory and in all groups was written and constructed by one individual.

The outcome of this exercise in the context of the original aims was less than successful. In terms of the first aim, each group was unable to identify more than three issues and some identified only one or two. This was despite being asked to produce a list of at least ten. There was little understanding of connections between the problems faced by different organizations or between organizations and environmental factors.

With regard to the second objective, the relative absence of conversation made such knowledge sharing impossible. Moreover, the absence of in-depth interaction between participants prevented an understanding of the social and intersubjective dimension to learning. Indeed, during feedback on the exercise, students expressed a view that learning about the problems and issues faced by organizations other than their own was of little interest to them. What they wanted was to be informed of the issues by an 'expert'. They appeared to subscribe to an individualistic cognitive information-processing form of learning in which they are given accurate information to absorb rather than co-create understanding. The essence of scenario planning, both as a business tool for thinking about possible futures and as a tool to engender group learning, was rejected by this group of managers.

Case Study 2: Multinational MSc HRM students in the UK

An SP exercise was used during an induction session for a multinational group of MSc HRM students in the UK. Students were from various countries in Europe, the Far East, the Middle East, Africa and the Indian subcontinent. Thirty students were present for the induction session and had met only briefly prior to this session. The aims of the SP exercise were as follows:

1. To introduce students to the complexities of HRM, for example in terms of competing theories around HRM, cross-cultural issues and the potential

problems that might arise in transferring HRM theory and practice between cultures.

2. To introduce students to group-learning methods and the social intersubjective paradigm of learning.
3. To give students the opportunity to get to know one another.

The exercise took place over one afternoon. Students were placed in five groups of six. Care was taken to ensure a mix of nationalities within each group. The exercise differed slightly from the first case study in that students were given parameters at the start. This was because many were new to the discipline of HRM and needed a degree of guidance. The students were given a short company case study to read prior to the session. They were then asked to identify ten HR issues or problems from the case study. The remaining stages followed those described in the first case study.

Although of a shorter duration, this exercise was more successful than that described in the first case study. After introducing themselves to one another, stages one and two involved brainstorming. Participation was good in all five groups. With a few exceptions, individuals appeared keen to contribute to the discussion. Four groups were able to identify ten issues and the fifth identified eight. Stages three to five ran smoothly in that questions were generated and mental maps developed. Narratives were constructed and reported to the rest of the class. A good degree of participation was observed and in three of the groups a 'chairperson' was seen to be ensuring that everyone in the group had an opportunity to express their view.

General observations showed that conversations with groups were intense and groups often needed to be moved on to the next stage. Eventually, the exercise ran out of time and overran past its scheduled finish time. In terms of feedback, students said they enjoyed the exercise and that it was different to previous learning experiences. The group appeared to have embraced the idea of social and collective learning.[1] Moreover, the exercise generated a number of questions about the substantive HRM issues identified and discussed.

DISCUSSION

The aims of SP as a classroom-based learning tool have been categorized into outcome aims, process aims and ontological concerns. Further concerns to emerge from the literature are to identify the processes that lead to successful SP and group learning, to identify whether students view SP as useful, if a shortened or 'atomized' version can be useful and whether it is possible to identify best practice in classroom-based SP.

In terms of outcome aims, businesses and organizations use SP to engender understanding of the world, to imagine the future and to enhance decision making (Burt et al., 2006; Chermack and Lynham, 2002; Walton, 2008). In the classroom, this translates into an understanding of a subject area and its complexities. The case study evidence suggests that SP had mixed results in terms of this aim. It was assumed prior to the activity that the participants in the first case study would, as suggested by Galer and van der Heijden (2001), bring and reflect upon experiential knowledge of lifelong learning, because all participants were practising managers in the area. It appeared, however, that participants did not consider their personal experience to be valid knowledge and wished to be 'taught' about lifelong learning despite their wealth of experience. The absence of clear parameters may also have been problematic for this group. Their experience contrasts with the second case study, and it can be suggested that, in a classroom setting, participants need to be provided with an initial framework. This is because unlike SP in organizations, participants do not have a shared memory or understanding on which they can draw. Subject-specific scenarios require subject-specific guidance.

With regard to process aims, it is unclear why knowledge sharing and intersubjective dialogue and conversation did not develop in the first case study but did in the second. One explanation might be the absence of guidance at the outset. On the other hand, if the argument of this chapter is accepted – as in that all learning is social and intersubjective and that meaning is forged in relation to the group or society – the explanation for the difference must be understood in terms of the particular conversational event. Thus, in the first case study both verbal and non-verbal interaction is rooted in an individualistic understanding of learning. Intersubjectivity resulted in the social construction of an understanding that SP was not useful, either as a means of extending knowledge or as a means of learning. Indeed, participants commented after the exercise that they 'could not see the point of discussing opinions'. In this instance, there was no challenge to the cognitive assumptions of participants or to individual and collective cognitive maps. The second case study, on the other hand, embraced the opportunity to converse and explore ideas. They intersubjectively constructed an enthusiasm that appeared to be infectious and their cognitive assumptions about the nature of learning were challenged and, for many, appeared to be reframed. The difference between the two groups cannot be explained by individual prior knowledge, as the second group had less than the group in the first case study. The explanation seems to relate to the nature of the intersubjective reaction. It can also be argued that the quality of group learning is dependent on the course that intersubjective understanding takes.

This case study evidence suggests that willingness to participate, as identified by Burt and Chermack (2008), is crucial to both organizational SP and classroom-based activities. Explanation of why one group rejects SP whilst another accepts it may depend on circumstances. Learning is necessarily situated and thus influenced by situational dynamics. The dynamics of the first case study differed from the second. Participants were practising managers with a prior understanding of learning that was at odds with the pedagogical method of the classroom activity. Their prior experience influenced their intersubjective construction of meaning and their willingness to engage with the process. The second case study, on the other hand, entered the situated learning activity with no prior understanding, and participants were more willing to embrace the method. There were also issues of power relevant to each situation. In the first case study, participants were consumers in the sense that they were autonomous, practising managers attending a three-day course out of choice. The second case study relates to postgraduate students attending an induction event with their course leader. They were, as such, a 'captive audience' and their willingness to participate may relate to their keenness to do well on the course.

The development of a best-practice model as called for by Burt and Chermack (2008) also ignores the situated nature of learning. A number of steps relating to the generation of ideas, formulation of scenario parameters and construction of futures have been identified (Borjeson et al., 2006; Provo et al., 1998), but it can be argued that these need to be adapted to the specific learning environment. It can also be argued, however, that classroom-based SP requires clear guidelines at the outset in order to move the process forward. There is, moreover, no conclusion to be drawn from these two case studies in relation to the duration of SP. Both examples correspond to Selin's (2007) description of abbreviated SP. In the first case study, the length of time spent on the exercise was irrelevant to the outcome. In the second case study, the process did unleash what Selin terms creative-thinking potential, despite being a short cursory exercise.

As a method of engendering group learning, the ontological underpinning of SP is the most pertinent issue. Learning through SP is linked to groups because learning is intersubjective and socially constructed. The perceptions of individuals within the group are forged through interaction and conversation. Knowledge sharing and the exchange of ideas are important elements in this process. The construction of meaning through intersubjective dialogue is crucial to group learning. The direction of intersubjective dialogue is, nevertheless, situated, evolving and organic and cannot be controlled. It can, as in the example of the first case study, evolve in opposition to group learning rather than facilitate the process.

CONCLUSION

This chapter has explored the extent to which SP can be adapted from its origins as a business and organizational strategic tool into a tool for classroom-based HRD. In particular, it has addressed the value of SP as a method of engendering group learning and an intersubjective, dialogical understanding of learning amongst students. The chapter began by outlining the meaning, historical use, methods and criticisms of SP. It has also considered the use of SP as an organizational tool for HRD and as a pedagogical tool for use in the classroom. The chapter then presented a description of two examples of classroom-based SP in practice. Finally, a discussion of the issue to arise from the use of SP in the classroom was made and a number of conclusions reached. First, in a classroom environment, students need to be given clear guidelines at the outset of the activity. Second, SP can be affected by willingness to participate, and that participation is determined by prior experience and understandings. Most importantly, however, willingness to participate is influenced by situated variables. Third, there is no best-practice model because learning is situated, and each learning event is unique. Finally, SP is rooted in intersubjective ontology and is linked to group learning through dialogue and conversation. It is also linked to group learning in that individual cognition is rooted in social interaction. It is, however, impossible to control the direction of the construction of meaning, and this is sometimes detrimental to group learning. Despite these criticisms, it can nevertheless be argued that scenario planning, with its emphasis on knowledge sharing, the exchange of information and collective construction of meaning, is ideally suited to classroom-based HRD.

Note

1. This observation is supported to some extent by students' general participation during class discussions and activities.

REFERENCES

Bertrand, G., Michalski, A. and Pench, L. R. (2000) *European Futures: Five Possible Scenarios for 2010*. Cheltenham: Edward Elgar.

Bood, R. and Postma. T. (1997) Strategic learning with scenarios, *European Management Journal*, 15(6): 633–647.

Borjeson, L., Hojer, M., Dreborg, K. H., Ekvall, T. and Finnveden, G. (2006) Scenario types and techniques: Towards a users guide, *Futures*, 38(7): 723–739.

Burt, G. and Chermack, T. J. (2008) Learning with scenarios: Summary and critical issues, *Advances in Developing Human Resources*, 10(2): 285–295.

Burt, G., Wright, G., Bradfield, R., Cairns, G. and van der Heijden, K. (2006) Limitations of PEST and its derivatives to understanding the environment: The role of scenario thinking in identifying environmental discontinuities and managing the future, *International Studies of Management and Organizations*, 36(3): 78–97.

Chermack, T. J. (2004) The opportunities for HRD in scenario planning, *Human Resource Development International*, 7(1): 117–121.

Chermack, T. J. and Lynham, S. A. (2002) Definitions and outcome variables of scenario planning, *Human Resource Development Review*, 1(3): 366–383.

Chermack, T. J. and Swanson, R. A. (2008) Scenario planning: Human resource development's strategic learning tool, *Advances in Developing Human Resources*, 10(2): 129–146.

Chermack, T. J., van der Merwe, L. and Lynham, S. A. (2007) Exploring the relationship between scenario planning and strategic conversation quality, *Technological Forecasting and Social Change*, 74(3): 379–390.

Chermack, T. J. and Walton, J. S. (2006) Scenario planning as development and change intervention, *International Journal of Agile Systems and Management*, 1(1): 46–59.

Davies, F., Moutinho, L. and Hutcheson, G. (2005) Constructing a knowledge-based system to aid scenario-based strategic planning: An application to the European airline industry, *Intelligent Systems in Accounting, Finance and Management*, 13(2): 61–79.

Foa, R. and Howard, M. (2006) Use of Monte Carlo simulation for the public sector: An evidence-based approach to scenario planning, *International Journal of Market Research*, 48(1): 27–48.

Galer, G. S. and van der Heijden, K. (2001) Scenarios and their contribution to organizational learning: From practice to theory. In Dierkes, M., Berthoinantal, A., Child, J. and Nonaka, I. (eds) *Handbook of Organizational Learning and Knowledge* (pp. 849–864) Oxford: Oxford University Press.

Kahane, A. (2002) Civic scenarios as a tool for societal change, *Strategy and Leadership*, 30(1): 32–37.

Keough, S. M. and Shanahan, K. J. (2008) Scenario planning: Toward a more complete model for practice, *Advances in Developing Human Resources*, 10(2): 166–178.

Lindgren, M. and Bandhold, H. (2009) *Scenario Planning: The Link between Future and Strategy.* Basingstoke: Palgrave Macmillan.

Masini, E. B. (1993) *Why Futures Studies?* London: Grey Seal Books.

Mintzberg, H., Ahlstrand, B., and Lampel, J. (1998) *Strategy Safari: A Guided Tour through the Wilds of Strategic Management.* New York: Free Press.

Moyer, K. (1996) Scenario planning at British Airways: A case study, *Long Range Planning*, 29(2): 172–181.

Pollard, D. and Hotho, S. (2006) Crises, scenarios and the strategic management process, *Management Decision*, 44(6): 721–736.

Provo, J., Ruona, W. E., Lynham, S. A. and Miller, R. F. (1998) Scenario building: An integral methodology for learning, decision-making and human resource development, *Human Resource Development International*, 1(3): 327–340.

Ramirez, R. and Van der Heijden, K. (2007) Scenarios to develop srategic options: A new interactive role for scenarios in strategy. In Sharpe, B. and van der Heijden, K. (eds) *Scenarios for Success: Turning Insights into Action* (pp. 89–120) Chichester: Wiley.

Rothwell, W. J. and Kazanas, H. C. (1989) *Strategic Human Resource Development.* London: Prentice Hall.

Selin, C. (2007) Professional dreamers. In Sharpe, B. and van der Heijden, K. (eds) *Scenarios for Success: Turning Insights into Action* (pp. 27–51). Chichester: Wiley.

Senge, P. (1990) *The Fifth Discipline: The Art and Practice of the Learning Organization.* London: Century.

Van der Heijden, K. (1997) *Scenarios, Strategies and the Strategy Process.* Breukelen: Nijenrode University Press.

Verity, J. (2003) Scenario planning as a strategy technique, *European Business Journal,* 15(4): 185–195.

Wack, P. (1985) Scenarios: Shooting the rapids, *Harvard Business Review,* 63(6): 139–150.

Walton, J. (2008) Scanning beyond the horizon: Exploring the ontological and epistemological basis for scenario planning, *Advances in Developing Human Resources,* 10: 147–165.

Wilson, I. (1998) Mental maps of the future: An intuitive logistics approach to scenarios. In Fahey, L. and Randall, R. M. (eds) *Learning from the Future: Competitive Foresight Scenarios* (pp. 81–108). New York: John Wiley.

Yeoman, I. and McMahon-Beattie, U. (2005) Developing a scenario planning process using a blank piece of paper, *Tourism and Hospitality Research,* 5(3): 273–285.

FURTHER READING

Burt, G. and Chermack, T. J. (2008) Learning with scenarios: Summary and critical issues, *Advances in Developing Human Resources,* 10(2): 285–295.

Chermack, T. J. and Swanson, R. A. (2008) Scenario planning: Human resource development's strategic learning tool, *Advances in Developing Human Resources,* 10(2): 129–146.

Sharpe, B. and van der Heijden, K. (eds) (2007) *Scenarios for Success: Turning Insights into Action.* Chichester: Wiley.

Walton, J. (2008) Scanning beyond the horizon: Exploring the ontological and epistemological basis for scenario planning, *Advances in Developing Human Resources,* 10: 147–165.

12

A CRITIQUE OF OUTDOOR TEAM DEVELOPMENT

John Walton

INTRODUCTION

Team building has become a mantra in human resource development (HRD) literature, with much written and recommended in terms of how people could function better in work groups. Within the HRD field, there have been many approaches that emphasize the importance of providing learning experiences away from the workplace for existing teams, which would generate behavioural changes that could be transferred back to the day-to-day work environment. In broad terms, the approaches can be divided into those that take place at indoor locations and those that focus on the outdoors; and those that are activity-based and those that are non-activity oriented. This chapter, in concentrating on activity-based outdoor team development (OTD) for existing teams, also contrasts the approach with other types of experiential team learning, including sensitivity training that was particularly fashionable in the 1960s and 1970s.

The Chartered Institute of Personnel and Development (CIPD and Cannell, 2008) comments that outdoor development is a multi-million-pound international industry that constitutes a sizeable sector of the training market. Simpson (2009) further points out that it is a high-value sector. Although (unlike executive coaching) (Maher and Pomerantz, 2003) the author has not been able to trace any articles discussing from a marketing perspective what stage on the product life cycle the industry has reached, like executive coaching, it is also very competitive. Simpson (2009) concludes that generally the

UK training market is oversupplied with providers, 'many of whom may be operating below the margins of sustainable viability' (p. 5). It is therefore not surprising that many claims have been made in practitioner brochures for the benefits arising out of outdoor development, including for existing teams. They typically take the following form: carefully developed in close partnership with clients and audited by independent experts our outdoor development programmes are a proven, cost effective way to improve communication, performance and success of individuals and work teams. Claims for benefits can be very broad ranging: one US organization suggests on its website that as a result of engaging in its outdoor activities and team initiatives based on experiential learning principles, group energy will be so focused as to enhance communication skills, relationship building, leadership skills, trust, decision making, delegation, collaborative problem-solving, resource utilization, change management and much more. Supporting affidavits are provided by grateful clients.

Yet in the corporate world the approach has long had its critics, being seen by many as no more than an excuse to take whole management teams out of the workplace to risk life and limb with no tangible benefits (Zemke, 1978). This perspective is still present in some quarters. On the 14 July 2011 edition of BBC Radio 4's business conversation programme *The Bottom Line*, two of the three CEOs present voiced strong criticisms of outdoor team-building exercises. One stated that he would never work for a company that would have him dangling on a rope, another claiming that whereas good bonding developed at the workplace was natural, taking people on adventure activities was 'wrong'. The proponent from Carlson Wagonlit Travel strongly took the other point of view. He referred to a recent top management team-building event that involved his top team going 200 miles north of the Arctic Circle and engaging in activities such as riding on sledges pulled by dogs and reindeers. He cited benefits such as learning how to rely upon each other when facing challenges, enhanced team cohesiveness and sharing of a common experience.

Wagner et al. in their 1991 article also challenge the perspective that outdoor development is more than just an expensive fad and claim that when all the evidence is in it will *probably* be ranked as an effective HRD strategy, particularly for enhancing team development for work groups (p. 147). One thrust of this chapter is to ascertain whether, in the intervening 20 years, this claim has been substantiated.

After discussing terminology and scope, the chapter summarizes the typical features and design principles of OTD and reviews the origins of these activities. In tracing its intellectual and practice roots, it looks at traditions of healthy mind and healthy body, Hébertism and the evolution of ropes (challenge) courses, the origins of the Outward Bound movement and the significance of the wilderness. It identifies from the academic literature benefits claimed, together with supporting arguments, as well as critiques such as problems of evaluating transfer of learning from an outdoor setting to the workplace. It makes a comparison with other experiential team-learning perspectives, including sensitivity training/T-groups; these were particularly popular in the 1960s and 1970s as an approach to engineering attitude change within work groups. These also operated in a location distant from the workplace, termed (at the time) a 'cultural island', cut off from the distractions of the day-to-day. It ends with providing a synthesis of claims made and the evidence on which they are based. In the final analysis, what differentiates outdoor team-building activities in terms of learning outcomes from those based on the indoors? What is the evidence of an isomorphic connection in which learning obtained from experiences in one setting is transferred to another?

TERMINOLOGY AND SCOPE

Outdoor team development (OTD) can be seen as a subset of a broader field of outdoor experiential training (OET) that emphasizes the significance of the outdoors as a learning and developmental arena, meeting objectives 'through direct experience in the environment using its resources as learning materials' (Hunt, 1989, p. 17). Outdoor team development (OTD) should be differentiated from outdoor management development (OMD) in that although operating as a more effective team leader is usually considered a desirable outcome, the focus is not on existing teams. The 'environment' and how it is used is subject to various interpretations. Cousineau (1976) referring to Hébertism talks about 'an opportunity to discover one's own potential and limitations in moving about in the natural environment using a network of natural and manmade obstacles placed in a forested area' (p. 8). Other sources emphasize the 'wilderness' aspects of the environment. Others, as we shall see, treat the environment as a general source of learning opportunities wherever suitable spaces can be found, and include outdoor activities provided in urban locations. The outdoors has also been treated in the UK as a means-to-an-end as opposed to an end in itself: the skills developed are not designed to be used in outdoor settings but to increase the effectiveness of participants' work behaviour (Jones, 1996).

As many commentators have pointed out, there is a bewildering array of labels associated with this area. Jones and Oswick (2007) identified more than 50 in their overview of OMD alone. Key words used to search for journal sources on programmes relevant to this chapter included (in addition to outdoor) adventure, encounter, wilderness, ropes (high and low), Hébertism, outward bound, urban, challenge and expedition, in combination with training, development, education, learning, experience, courses and so on. Each one of these elicited useful data but had to be carefully interpreted because of their polysemic nature. *Challenge* at one level is a generic term to highlight one of the features of outdoor learning – in that activities should be challenging for participants. But it also has a narrower connotation. References to *challenge courses* are often a synonym for *ropes courses*, an approach first used in the early 1960s in the United States and which have become increasingly popular. For example, Attarian (2001) estimated that over 15,000 challenge courses existed in the US at the beginning of this century as opposed to 700–1000 in the early 1980s. Attarian and Holden (2001) suggest that the reason for the increase is due to the growth of experientially based training and development programmes designed as a method to motivate employees and produce high-performing teams. OMD provides another illustration of the variety of connotations associated with a term: it 'can be used to describe anything from an afternoon of activities on a hotel lawn to a month of outdoor adventure training in the Scottish wilderness' (Jones and Oswick, 2007, p. 327).

There are a number of organizational types that commission OTD. In addition to corporate clients, for many years some universities have been using the outdoors as a component for leadership development and team building within professional postgraduate management programmes such as MBAs. Some of these involve activities that are at the high physical end of OTD. Since 1998, students on the University of Pennsylvania Wharton School Executive MBA have done a leadership trek in the Himalayas, ascending from Kathmandu to the base camp of Mt Everest (Kass and Grandzol, 2011).

The growth in providers, courses and clients has been paralleled by a trend towards increased professionalization. A number of universities are offering degrees in the field of Adventure Training and Education, often with a focus on developing provider facilitation and awareness skills. For example, in the UK, the University of Worcester offers a BSc in Outdoor Adventure Leadership and Management. Areas covered include safety management, environmental awareness, coaching analysis and business management. The broad spread of electives for the Outdoor Education degree programme at the University of South Australia include: Wilderness and Adventure Education, Outdoor Leadership and Philosophical Issues, and Environmental Interpretation. The Texas A&M University master's programme in Outdoor Education includes units on Ropes Course and Group Processes, Outdoor Experiential Education and Leadership in Outdoor Education.

Professional associations abound, with various orientations and membership bases. In the UK there is an Institute for Outdoor Learning, which in addition to a magazine aimed at supporting the professional development of outdoor practitioners has a professional accreditation scheme. The European Institute for Experiential Learning and Outdoor Adventure was founded in 1996 as the first European-wide grouping of educators concerned with the learning potential of challenging natural environments (Becker and Schirp, 2008). Organizations in the US that fully or partially espouse the outdoors as a learning arena include the California Association for Environmental and Outdoor Education (AEOE), the National Society for Experiential Education (NSEE), the Association for Experiential Education (AEE) and the Association for Challenge Course Technology (ACCT).

According to the AEOE's website, it was founded in 1954 as the Association of Outdoor Education, and was the first such grouping of outdoor educators in the US; 'environmental' was added to its name in 1971. It 'supports and inspires educators in their quest for the knowledge, skills, and attitudes essential to help all learners understand, appreciate and care for their environment'. As an integral part of achieving its mission, it encourages direct experience outdoors. The NSEE, founded in 1971, is a non-profit membership association of educators, businesses and community leaders serving as a national resource centre for the development and improvement of experiential education programmes nationwide. It is not exclusively or even primarily focused on the outdoors but has developed a useful set of good practice principles for all experientially based programmes, wherever they are conducted. These emphasize that the activities that constitute the overall experience must have, in order to make them authentic, a real-world context and/or be useful and meaningful in reference to applied situations typically faced by participants. In order to increase the likelihood of this occurring, there should be appropriate advance preparation involving all the parties; awareness by the facilitators of the real-world context in which participants operate; and a flexible plan with continuous monitoring. Also highlighted is the importance of reflection, defined as the element that transforms simple experience into a learning experience. This should be supported by acknowledgement of progress and accomplishments during and at the end of the programme, in order to provide sustainability of learning.

The AEE is a non-profit, professional membership association dedicated to experiential education and the students, educators and practitioners who utilize its philosophy. Members include ropes course operators; school, college and university staff and faculty; therapists; outdoor education practitioners; organizational development specialists; experience-based professionals working in non-profit, private and academic spaces; and members of many other areas of experiential education. Members do team-building and corporate events relevant to this chapter. The organization also accredits programmes and sponsors a journal. The ACCT, a professional trade organization that began in 1993, writes standards for constructing and managing challenge courses (ACCT, 2004).

TYPICAL DESIGN PRINCIPLES OF OTD

OTD is a variant of 'outdoor education', a generic term that encompasses a range of organized activities that take place in predominantly outdoor settings to achieve a variety of aims, dependent on the participants. Outdoor education 'involves having a group navigate a course of mental and physical challenge activities to improve its team relationships, group dynamics, cooperation and communication' (DuFrene et al., 1999, p. 24). OTD is also a variant of experiential education, a term that has been further subdivided by Karen Warren (1998; 2005; Warren and Loeffler, 2000) into 'outdoor experiential education'. The outdoor settings – with specific pre-planned goals and supporting problem-oriented activities, presence of trained leaders/facilitators and co-operative small group living – are designed to act as mechanisms of change at individual and group levels (Baldwin et al., 2004). Jones and Oswick (2007) contrast the wilderness-based 'macro-dynamic' outdoor pursuit activities emanating from the outward-bound tradition (this chapter refers to these as type A programmes) with the shorter in duration problem-solving challenge courses that tend to be more group-oriented and that take place in centre-based locations with specially constructed facilities (type B programmes). The programmes can range from those entailing pursuits such as canoeing, rock climbing or even mountain climbing – that is, with a high physical challenge (type A) – compared to those that involve 'metaphoric problem solving exercises' (Ibbetson and Newell, 1998, p. 240) where the landscape is gentler and the activities of a type that have traditionally been done indoors (type B). Wagner et al. (1991) refer to type A courses as wilderness training programmes, often termed survival courses, where the participants live and eat outdoors and engage in strenuous activities such as white-water rafting. They contrast these with type B outdoor-centred programmes where the activities take place using specially designed facilities – but eating, sleeping and debriefing take place indoors. 'Semi-wilderness' is used by the Outdoor Education Group, an Australian non-profit outdoor provider, to reflect the environment in which many such type B courses are conducted.

The elements and constituents of OTD are relatively consistent. The ideal-typical components are five to seven days of retreat in a residential setting in which all the activities involve outdoor physical challenges or 'adventures' incorporating group problem solving and resolution. The participants usually number 16–18 maximum. Typical physical activities for type B programmes include high/low rope challenges and team obstacle courses. High-rope challenge courses focus on individual development, as compared to low challenge courses that tend to focus primarily on group problem solving activities ranging from sitting on the ground to operating at a height of up to 12–13 feet (Rohnke et al., 2007) and are more likely to incorporate games, icebreakers and group trust activities (Martin et al., 2006). Most are used for a variety of recreational, educational, developmental or therapeutic purposes – as in adventure therapy – (Priest and Gass, 2005) in settings as diverse as camps, hospitals and corporate training centres (Rohnke et al., 2007; Gillis and Speelman, 2008). Delegates range from schoolchildren engaged in adventure activities, disturbed adolescents on recovery programmes to business executives. There is often an element of competition between groups, although this has been removed by some providers following negative participant feedback (Ibbetson and Newell, 1999).

A number of studies have tried to establish a set of core characteristics for outdoor training. They build on what Broderick and Pearce (2001) refer to as the 'experiential/adventure paradigm' (p. 241) highlighting from Flor (1991) 'experiential learning processes, challenge and reflection, a co-operative group environment, consensual decision making, a novel setting, dissonance, unique problem-solving situations, uncertainty and risk-taking and the use of metaphors'. Although most studies relate experiential learning to the learning cycle of Kolb (1984), Broderick and Pearce (2001) follow Richards (1992) in seeing a distinctive adventure-based experiential learning model that with its four phases of separation, encounter, return and reincorporation has its roots in the adventures of Ulysses in ancient Greek mythology.

One of the most comprehensive lists is that produced by Jones and Oswick (2007, p. 328) who, from their content analysis of 180 articles, identified the following features that constitute a 'non-abstract, generalizable ideal type' of OMD (their framework assumes that it is preferable to deal with a pre-existent work group but this is by no means always the case):

1. Be underpinned by experiential learning theory.
2. Aim to improve participants' understanding and management of self and others.

3. Be collaboratively designed by provider and sponsor to improve the performance of an existing work group, team or department, as part of a broader management and/or organization development process.
4. Consist of a five to seven days programme, in a residential, wilderness setting, with all activities taking place outdoors.
5. Involve physically challenging and progressively more complex problem-solving tasks that permit high discretion about the methods used.
6. Task completion requires co-operative and integrated team effort and the exercise of management skills.
7. Half of the training time be spent on structured facilitated reviews that focus on process issues arising, not technical aspects of the task.

The review process involving a facilitator varies in practice – typically the higher the level of physicality, the less extensive is the review, since the exercises are designed to 'speak for themselves' (Ibbetson and Newell, 1998).

OTD is usually associated with leadership development and personal development. The assumption is that the outdoor activities and design principles in tackling one area also cover the others. The leadership issue is addressed because it is assumed that for each team there will be a leadership role. Hattie et al. (1997) in their review of the effects of adventure education programmes identified group 'support' and 'challenge' as two major ingredients of the positive effects, along with 'difficult goals' and 'feedback'.

CLAIMS

From the practitioner and academic literature, the following claims can be identified for OTD for corporate programmes/delegates:

1. It accelerates learning.
2. It enhances the leadership, teamwork and problem-solving skills – and levels of interpersonal trust, communication and team cohesiveness – required for organization success (Williams et al., 2003).
3. It leads to an improvement in conflict-handling skills (Burke and Collins, 2004a).
4. These skills and levels of awareness can be transferred back to the actual workplace and become relatively permanent (for groups such as MBA, the purpose is to improve team-working within a programme with the intention that this will enhance the team-working skills of participants in settings outside the course).

5. It develops risk tolerance and capability.
6. It can be fun as well as challenging (Wagner et al., 1991; Williams et al., 2003).

Each of these claims will be considered during the course of the chapter.

ORIGINS AND HISTORY

Expeditionary learning, adventure training and the notion of *challenge* have been ascribed to Kurt Hahn (1886–1974) who was the pioneering educator behind Gordonstoun School for boys (co-educational from 1972), which he originally joined as a consultant in 1934, and the Outward Bound movement that he co-founded in 1941. He is identified with an educational philosophy of self-development for young people through overcoming adversity in challenging outdoor situations (Jones and Oswick, 2007). He recommended that training for all through the sea or the mountains be seen as 'character building activities good for the future worker, soldier, clerk, scholar, business man, lawyer or doctor' (Hahn, 1947). Adventure training, as experienced on Outward Bound courses, was intended to develop such personal qualities through psychologically and physically taxing individual and group encounters with unfamiliar situations (Hoberman and Mailick, 1992; Broderick and Pearce, 2001).

Hahn (1965) rejected as misleading the concept of *mens sana in corpore sano* – 'healthy body healthy mind', reputed to originate from the pre-Socratic philosopher Thales and popularized in Satire X of the Roman poet Juvenal who died early in the 2nd century CE. His view is that 'a youngster with a sensitive mind needs to build up physique as part of developing powers of endurance to handle the strains of responsible citizenship' (Hahn, 1965). He emphasizes that the reverse is not the case – there are too many examples from history of a strong physique not resulting in a sensitive mind.

Of themselves these precepts are gender neutral, although Hahn in his works most frequently refers to boys and there is little evidence that OMD or OTD until recent years was for mixed groups. Neill (1997) makes the point that articles in the 1960s and 1970s tended to be written by men and there was no indication of any female participation. Taking Australia as an example, even though by the late 1970s advertising and publicity for Outward Bound courses emphasized that they were open to both men and women, men outnumbered women by six to one (Richards, 1977).

Jones and Oswick (2007) identify the British tradition as emanating from the officer-selection outdoor command courses developed for the military during the Second World War, although they could have gone back much further in time. For example, in 1729 the Royal Naval Academy, subsequently renamed the Royal Naval College, was founded in Portsmouth for training would-be officers aged between 13 and 16; the five-year programme included two years at sea (Lewis, 1939). In the 20th century, particularly after the Second World War, the benefits of the outdoors as a training arena were extended to indoor occupations, initially for young adults on industrial apprenticeship schemes (Richards, 1991).

Other sources include Georges Hébert (1875–1957) who, although his focus was on individual health and wellbeing as opposed to team building, was specifically influential in the evolution of ropes courses. Influenced by the ideas of the 18th-century philosopher Jean-Jacques Rousseau as expressed in *Émile: or On Education* and the notion of 'l'education dans la nature', Hébert saw the outdoors as a source of moral values and virile character (Cousineau, p. 3). He developed his method when responsible for physical education in the French navy between the two world wars. Hébertisme was introduced to North America (Canada) in 1949 by two French officers in the Canadian army who became familiar with the approach when serving in France during the Second World War. Cousineau (1976) argues that the Hébertism site – otherwise termed the outdoor education centre – should be easily accessible yet remote enough to create an atmosphere of fantasy: for adults the opportunity to enjoy again those things that they did when children.

Artificial climbing walls, which are a feature of many outdoor centres, date back to the first part of the 20th century when one was developed in Milan, Italy, using iron rungs for hand and footholds (Attarian, 2001).

THE NATURE OF THE ENVIRONMENT

Outdoors training is normally associated with an environment far away from human habitation, the 'great outdoors' – a wilderness or semi-wilderness location. But this is not a universal rule. Snow (1997) considers that it is possible to reap at a fraction of the cost many of the benefits associated with the 'great outdoors' for low ropes challenge courses by utilizing resources close to the workplace such as fields and parking lots. A number of organizations now run outdoor corporate training events for clients in urban settings, quite apart from the outdoor team activities popularized through television programmes such as *The Apprentice*, which have scarcely been an advertisement for team building. One UK provider, Cumulus, specifically differentiates between the corporate team-building events they run in 'the great outdoors' with those that make use of urban outdoor areas such as parks, canals, zoos and streets for the challenges and activities: 'City locations are ideal for clients that require an immediate and local event that is easy to travel to and close to other facilities and transport links.' Another refers to the popularity of urban adventure challenges that involve teams navigating around a city with a map and compass and en route resolving a series of conundrums, challenges and problems.

What differentiates wilderness or semi-wilderness settings from urban locations is the natural aspect of the environment and its symbolic significance as an open space arena in which to engage in challenges. This perspective emanates from a long tradition. In the US the term 'wilderness' is often used to describe the setting in order to emphasize that the activities take place in environments that are relatively unaffected by human development – recognizing that wilderness is a subjective construct, something that can be experienced as good and to be preserved and enjoyed, or bad and needing to be tamed or avoided (Nash, 1982, first published 1967). Wilderness has a particular nuance in the US: 'Wilderness was the basic ingredient of American culture. From the raw materials of the physical wilderness, Americans built a civilization. With the idea of wilderness, they sought to give their civilization identity and meaning' (Nash, 2001, p. xi). It also has a legal status, defined as 'an area where the earth and its community of life are untrammelled by man' (Wilderness Act, 1964).

Henry David Thoreau (1817–1862) and John Muir (1838–1914) both wrote in the 19th century about the benefits of spending time in the American wilderness. Muir's lobbying of the US Congress led to the establishment in 1890 of the first national parks, those of Yosemite and Sequoia: 'Muir has profoundly shaped the very categories through which Americans understand and envision their relationships with the natural world' (Holmes, 1999, p. 178).

Open spaces are not always seen as a source of challenge: 'we consider open spaces to be places that *enable* a "psychological escape" or an opportunity to think in a less pressured way, about the circumstances of daily life, whether or not we do so in a solitary or companioned way' (Rubinstein, 1997). They provide scope for reflection, and learning greater self and other awareness (Russell et al., 1998).

Overall, there is an ongoing tension about the environment that is reflected in a number of practitioner brochures. On the one hand, it can be seen as providing an opportunity where fun can be had, where groups can enjoy stunning settings. On the other hand, as one outdoor provider expressed it, you could be exhilarated and challenged by 'jumping into the sky to catch a trapeze'.

ISSUES IDENTIFIED IN THE LITERATURE

Physical risk and psychological safety

Risk is defined by Collinson et al. (2007) as 'exposure to the possibility of some loss, including physical or emotional trauma' (p. 50). Essentially, it is the increased likelihood of undesirable consequences occurring. Perceived risk is a skewed and subjective view of the potential for loss. It can, but not always will be, distinctly different from real risk (Davis-Berman and Berman, 2002). OTD includes an environment in which there are likely to be issues around physical safety and where psychological risk is encouraged (challenge). The physical risk can be addressed in terms of the 'dynamics of accident equation' (Hale, 1984) in which human hazards (physical condition, experience, skills, communication) plus environmental hazards (weather, terrain, equipment) = accident potential. Human dangers are treated as subjective in the sense that the less experience that a course member has of a particular terrain, or activity within such a terrain, the higher the danger. The onus of responsibility to reduce the potential for accidents falls on the outdoor leader, through detailed preparation (Martin et al., 2006).

Psychological safety is always an issue with learning if we accept the Argyris and Schön (1978) definition of single-loop learning as a process of detecting and correcting errors. It is seen by some as an essential feature of experiential learning in general and outdoor training in particular: 'Participants should be encouraged to take psychological but not actual risks through experiential learning methods' (Irvine and Wilson, 1994, p. 31). Learning in teams is always more fraught because of issues of losing face in the presence of others. In OTD anxiety levels are heightened by the novelty and uncertainty surrounding the tasks but are supposed to be leavened by the intention to develop mutual trust and co-operation. Implicit in adventure training is an untested assumption that people need to learn how to deal with risks, that it is typically beneficial for people to take such risks, and that the benefits of dealing with risk and challenge in the outdoors can be transferred to other settings (Wolfe and Samdahl, 2005). But in a prescient vein, Wolfe and Samdahl go on to ask whether risk taking is a universally desirable trait for corporate executives responsible for large sums of other people's money. They also make the point that transfer is normally evaluated in terms of benefits such as increased trust in team settings. But what if an actual outcome is increased mistrust? Are we sure that only positive outcomes are being transferred into future situations?

There is little discussion on such 'relationship risk' in the literature. Burke and Collins (2004b), for example, report that a high percentage of managers responding to their questionnaire emphasized the development of conflict-handling skills within teams as a result of OMD. Unfortunately, they give no information about how many were reporting back on courses organized for work groups; nor of any ongoing relationship issues that had occurred and been resolved.

Workplace transfer

One of the distinctive features of OTD is the construction of unique challenges designed to foster creative thought and tolerance of change but that are not directly related to the participants' day-to-day job responsibilities (Smith and Vaughan, 1997; Williams et al., 2003). This has implications for how the learning is seen to be relevant and transferable back to the workplace.

The key to the effective use of the outdoors is to design a course strong in isomorphs (similarities between behaviours at work and outdoors) and then enable participants to discover the relevance and transfer of their learning back to the workplace (Jones, 1996). Irvine and Wilson (1994) address the issue of the relevance of the outdoors to the workplace and comment on the apparent paradox: 'On the one hand the advantage of the outdoors is that it is both unique and novel and breaks down the workplace barriers. On the other hand, what is advocated [in the HRD literature] is replication of the workplace environment' (p. 32). They state that this principle was one in which Kurt Hahn believed when he tried to emulate – in a 26-day course on marine skills and survival training – the environment in which young British merchant seamen operated during the Second World War. They recognize that unless one is dealing with groups for whom the outdoors is a key part of their role, such as sailors, this is not feasible – and suggest that a core component of OTD is that 'the programme of activities should ideally reflect the workplace environment' (p. 33).

Burke and Collins (2004a) take a different perspective. They substitute 'fidelity' for isomorphism as the received term for the extent to which the tasks in the learning arena are congruent with those faced in real life. Following Bransford et al. (1979), they suggest that low-fidelity experiences of the sort confronted on OMD courses can lead to higher levels of transfer for managers than high-fidelity experiences because of the cognitive problem-solving skills called upon, which are important for handling the unprogrammed decision-making aspects of their role.

Drawing upon Bacon and Kimball (1989), Priest and Gass (2005) refer to the use of direct isomorphic links in which there is a direct connection between the activities undertaken and those experienced in day-to-day settings; and indirect metaphorical approaches that in some way or another can create a spontaneous (the activity speaks for itself) or analogous (the facilitator helps to provide the link) connection. They refer to the value of 'structured metaphoric transfer' planning in which, in advance of the event, activities that are most likely to result in spontaneous or analogous connections for the client are decided upon. They give as an example of an analogous metaphor the relationship between a ropes course and the challenges of life. This is not totally convincing and could be construed as more akin to a 'here and now' transfer (aha moment) in the mind of an individual as opposed to something that necessarily causes subsequent behavioural change.

There is also, of course, a difference between the challenges of life that an individual faces and those challenges faced by teams at work. The likelihood of generating collective understanding that results in workplace change being transmitted by this means is significantly more complex, as has often been pointed out. Woodman and Sherwood (1980), although not dealing with OTD, conclude that the research evidence available to them in 1980 indicated that team building might result in attitudinal change but not in behavioural change. They saw no evidence that convincingly linked team building to performance improvements of work groups. Irvine and Wilson (1994), discussing OMD, comment that the concept – that in a one-week course individuals will be fundamentally affected in their behaviour towards others – appears rather optimistic. It is expecting too much for teams to realistically work through the Kurt Lewin (1947) unfreeze – change – freeze process over such a short time. In other words, strong reservations are being expressed over a crucial aspect of the claim relating to accelerated learning associated with outdoor learning.

Reported studies of OTD and their approach to evaluation

A number of studies have commented on the problems of obtaining realistic evaluations of the benefits of team-building interventions, whatever their nature. Jones and Oswick (1993) commented that although over 200 benefits have been attributed: 'Supporting evidence is most commonly in the form of the personal testimony of those providing the training, or selective, positive accounts from participants' (p. 10). Most evaluations of team-building interventions are conducted by the facilitators themselves, which creates doubts about their objectivity (De Meuse and Liebowitz, 1981; Rushmer, 1997). Rushmer comments from the perspective of an external provider on the generic problem of access and non-availability of data as well as on the changing circumstances confronting organizations that make realistic evaluations of benefits problematic.

In terms of existing work teams undergoing OTD, studies are very limited. The Gillis and Speelman (2008) study – in their US-based meta-analysis of quantitative-based studies published between 1986 and 2006 – specifically focused on challenge (ropes) courses and activity outcomes from these: 'Studies in which participants were involved in *any* other activity (e.g. swimming, backpacking) during the period of study were excluded' (p. 115). Only six of the 44 sources they identified dealt with developmental activities for adults, and their article gives no indication that any of these included existing work teams. Their broad conclusion is that the quantitative data obtained corroborated the positive impact on group relationships that are claimed for challenge courses from qualitative sources. They also state that most of the studies they drew upon relied upon self-report data.

A number deal with students undertaking OTD as part of obtaining an academic qualification. For example, Mazany et al. (1995) and Kass and Grandzol (2011) discuss its use for team development on an MBA programme. Shivers-Blackwell (2004) reported on a one-day programme for MBA students in which the casual outdoor environment was supposed to provide a relaxed, fun and challenging atmosphere. However, many respondents didn't find this to be the case. This is not a surprising finding. There is no reason to assume that all participants will share the same sense of fun and positive anticipation of a challenging atmosphere. In any case, the one-day programme didn't give enough time to engage in the 'place'.

Sometimes these represented a group from the same organization but not from the same team. For example, the Jones and Oswick (2007) study reported on 19 team leaders from the same organization attending a seven-day outdoor residential programme as part of a postgraduate certificate course. The programme would have been excluded from the Gillis and Speelman (2008) meta-analysis referred to above in that it incorporated a series of wilderness expedition-type activities as well as those exercises located in the centre grounds. The evaluation process focused on various approaches to obtaining participants' perceptions, including interviews and learning logs that each completed. Particularly revealing were the comments, some hostile, made about the unremitting and uncomfortable pressure to be part of a team. These were mitigated to some extent by greater awareness of team processes and how these could be linked to theoretical perspectives introduced in earlier classroom sessions. But the overall conclusion was that such programmes 'are not a panacea for change but may ironically result in participants' existing attitudes becoming increasingly entrenched and more difficult to modify' (p. 339). Additionally, it was argued that contrary to what might be predicted from many authors' and providers' claims, if their study was typical of a wider population, the learning acquired from activities held indoors or on hotel lawns was at least as significant for developing work-related skills and understanding as that obtained on wilderness expeditions.

Ng (2001) reports on a single organization study from Singapore where 345 participants worked as 15 teams over a two-day challenge course incorporating typical ropes activities. The pre-course test followed by a post-test evaluation method showed three positive teamwork attitudinal changes, social support, task participation and team spirit, recognizing that the teams used on the course were not pre-existing. There was no indication as to how durable the changes were or whether they were reinforced back at the workplace.

Ibbetson and Newell (1998) describe two methods based on delegate self-report that they used with managers from two client programmes in order to evaluate perceptions of team effectiveness and climate. Only one of these groups operated as a team, meeting once a month to discuss strategy. The team development indicator (TDI) developed by Bronson (1990) was used *during* each programme to gain a global measure of how effectively individuals think that their team is working together. It was not used outside of the programme. The team climate indicator (TCI) designed by West (1994) contains five sub-scales: (1) participative safety, concerning participation in decision making, sharing information and feeling secure when making proposals; (2) support for innovation, concerning support for creative ideas and commitment to the development of innovation; (3) vision, concerning whether goals are clear, shared and attainable; (4) task orientation, concerning commitment to achieving excellence; and (5) social desirability. It was completed by team members at the induction day, one month prior to the programme's commencement and subsequently administered at the follow-up session back in the workplace, approximately four months after each programme. Ibbetson and Newell (1999) report that team member's perceptions of support for innovation and productivity increased across the course of the study, but overall there was a difficulty in quantifying any bottom-line benefits.

They can offer no evidence that transfer of learning to the workplace actually occurs, arguing only that transfer is a difficult concept to measure and applies to all forms of training. They restrict their requirements of core concepts underpinning OTD to: reviewing the processes used to achieve the desired outcomes in tasks and making links and connections to the workplace, which are essential if transfer of learning is to be achieved (p. 35).

Return on investment (ROI)

There is remarkably little evidence regarding ROI resulting from outdoors training in general. Williams et al. (2003) commented that 'while it is easy to demonstrate [outdoor training's] popularity for leadership development and team building, it is much more difficult to demonstrate that [it] is a prudent investment' (p. 45). They were not able to trace a single published study of ROI in the field and only one (McEvoy et al., 1997) dealing with level-4 organization results outcomes. Williams et al. (2003) in their analysis went no further than showing how, on return from an outdoor programme, if factors such as labour turnover and absenteeism declined the ROI could be calculated: they were not able to provide any specific empirical evidence of direct improvements resulting from the programme. They make the same point as Pine and Tingley (1993) that this situation is endemic of the evaluation of 'soft skills' training in general.

Not only has very little has been written in the literature on the investment attractiveness of the outdoors in terms of ROI, but there is also very little written on what governs the purchasing decision. Clements et al. (1995), in their guidance to in-house trainers responsible for purchasing, suggest that programmes are to be preferred when participants attend voluntarily, and consider that they are of particular value in helping newly formed teams to gain a sense of working together. Burke and Collins (2004a; 2004b) in their two articles did not look at OMD from the perspective of sponsor/commissioner, only from the points of view of the providers and participants. As a result, the question wasn't asked why outdoor activities were chosen in the first place and what made them attractive as an investment. McEvoy and Buller (1990) drew attention to ritualistic and symbolic overtones, such as being selected to attend such a course as being indicative of the organization's confidence in the participants. They also stated that the selection choice of the outdoors by one of their clients was a deliberate attempt, on return to the workplace, to encourage greater risk taking and going beyond normally experienced comfort zones. But, as we have seen, since their article was written, there has been increasing evidence that it is difficult to provide hard evidence of the benefits of the outdoors over the indoors. One conjectural answer that governs choice of the outdoors, building on the symbolic overtones that McEvoy and Buller (1990) refer to, is that instead of it being a commercial consideration it reflects a zeitgeist, an unconscious spirit of the age that generically treats the 'outdoors' as a 'good' place that people will want to engage with; a temporary escape from the urban environments where so many live. Taking the US as an example, it is reported that two-thirds of Americans aged 16 and over participate in outdoor activities at least once a year in search of a 'solution to the pressing problems of obesity and inaction' in the cities that 80 per cent of them inhabit (Outdoor Industry Association, 2006). It would be interesting to establish how many of those making the training decision themselves have previously attended an outdoor programme and have enjoyed it; or, if not, have positive perceptions about the outdoors as a place to be.

Evaluation of space and place

The language of space and how its use is interpreted is the subject of proxemics (Walton, 1999). Proxemics deals with the nature and effect of the special separation that individuals naturally maintain. Broderick and Pearce (2001) comment that outdoor activities that require participants to touch each other can raise concerns and cause emotional distress, especially for multicultural groups. The same could be said equally for multigender groups. Proxemics, however, doesn't extend beyond the interpersonal study of space and doesn't deal with how one constructs one's place in the world (Munn, 1996) or interprets a given place. Spaces are not just in the landscape but equally in peoples' minds, customs and preconceptions (Rockefeller, 2001 cited in Low, 2003). In the UK literature on outdoor learning, there is little indication of a concern with 'place-responsiveness' (Harrison, 2010). Justifications for going to an area away from one's normal locale rarely include developing a greater understanding of place. The setting is seen as a source of challenge from which learning experiences can be gained, a culturally constructed worthwhile space in which to engage in a set of pre-arranged activities and perhaps to have fun. The assumption is made that any cultural and symbolic associations attached to the location will either be shared or not significant. Stokes (2008) picks up in the following quotation an implicit assumption that underlies the question: why am I here in this place?

> One of the most endearing qualities of the British is their eccentric tendency to row boats across oceans, climb impossible mountains, and so on . . . It is not surprising, therefore, that a small but thriving industry has grown up around the development of executives through confrontation with nature.
>
> (Mant, 1981, p. 83, cited in Stokes, 2008, p. 26)

Wattchow (2008) draws attention to the importance of recognizing cross-cultural differences in how individuals experience space and place when formulating experiential encounters within the environment. Is place experienced as culturally constructed space? Or as a site imbued with intrinsic meaning? Such issues, if unrecognized, could have significant influence on team-building activities. The notion of challenge is also not an automatic association with wilderness environments. Loeffler (2004) in a North American review of college-based adventure programmes found that many participants considered the outdoors to be a place where stillness, calm and peace could be found.

A sense of place emerged in the study by Pohl et al. (2000), which considered whether there are gender connotations associated with the outdoors. They developed the following set of core themes identified by women as part of a wilderness recreation experience:

1. Escape (from norms, everyday demands, and distractions).
2. Challenge and survival (physical and mental).
3. New opportunities (learning new skills).
4. Natural awe and beauty (connection to nature).
5. Solitude (isolation, time to focus, mental revitalization). (p. 422)

These themes were further developed into a set of transferable outcomes seen by the women as relevant to their everyday life: self-sufficiency (including increased confidence and assertiveness); change in perspective (including reprioritizing and new world view); connection to others (including strengthening relations and seeing others in a new light); and mental clarity (including increased sense of purpose, problem-solving skills and self-reflection). It is not to be expected that 'connection to nature' is going to feature prominently in corporate training programmes concerned with instrumental skills enhancement at the workplace, but the study reinforces the claim that how one views 'place' can significantly affect motivation of participants.

Cultural specificity

Most studies in this field emanate from the English-speaking world; it has been suggested that OMD and OTD emanate from an Anglo-Saxon tradition and that the concept has limited potential to be transferred across cultures. Stokes (2008) pursues this in his Anglo-French comparative study, where he contends that OMD is significantly less utilized in France. He sees the explanation for this as rooted in a French education tradition that emphasizes classroom-based lecture-oriented activities, and a thought process that focuses on logic and philosophically grounded reasoning as opposed to pragmatic decision making. He concludes that the particular Anglo-Saxon ethnocentric legacies, cultural representations and underlying assumptions raise doubts about the validity of OMD and OTD if transferred to other contexts. Stokes' view is that the origins of outdoor training in the UK incorporate taken-for-granted assumptions around leadership, character and team building, through challenge, struggle and working together in wilderness adventures – as exemplified by Dr David Livingstone in 19th-century Africa, Scott and the ill-fated Antarctic expedition, and heroic military exploits in situations of adversity throughout the history of the British Empire. Although not specifically addressed, this clearly has implications for applying OTD to multicultural, mixed gender teams in global companies. Varying cultural norms is one of the reasons given by Clements et al. (1995) for making attendance voluntary.

IS THERE ADDED VALUE OVER INDOOR EXPERIENTIAL TRAINING?

A particular challenge to outdoor training is in identifying the added value it has as compared to conducting activities in indoor residential settings. There are a number of studies that feel this has not been demonstrated. Clements et al. (1995) noted that outdoor experiential training produced no greater behavioural change than indoor experiential training, although they did comment positively on the high level of emotion resulting from engaging in real challenges. Broderick and Pearce (2001), building on the detailed comparison of outdoor and indoor experiential learning events produced by Clements et al. (1995), comment that 'experiential learning in novel settings' (p. 244), one of the key benefits claimed by proponents of the outdoor, can occur equally effectively in indoor settings and at a relatively lower cost. They continue to argue that: (1) The development of team-building, interpersonal and problem-solving skills through innovative approaches to experiential learning is a common feature of indoor training. (2) Age, gender and other biases associated with outdoors activities such as emotional discomfort and safety concerns over their physical nature are avoided. Only psychological safety is not guaranteed; all learning involves some risk and challenge. (3) Everyone can participate in indoor exercises and the range of these is not constrained by weather. (4) Learning transfer is more readily effected because the experiences undergone are likely to be closer to those engaged in at the workplace. Snow (1997) makes a further comment that exercises need only simple props such as rubber balls, rope and blindfolds. Assuming the above to be valid conclusions, what is distinctive to OTD is the sense of adventure, physical challenge, the high level of emotion likely to arise out of real experiences confronted, and setting. Choice then becomes a matter of judgement based on the characteristics of the group and assumptions about the culture of the organization, mixed in with any preconceptions and symbolic associations held by the commissioning agent about the environment.

Indoor team building away from the workplace, which draws upon the principles of experiential learning, has long been practised. There are various approaches to this, two of which are highlighted and reviewed below and compared with OTD. Sensitivity training has been chosen for a number of reasons. In the 1960s and 1970s, it became very popular as an approach to corporate team building, since when it has virtually disappeared. The literature on sensitivity training also emphasized the problems of transfer back to the workplace and creating a sense of psychological safety, neither of which were fully resolved. This leads to the following analysis in terms of whether the issues that led to the decline of T-groups have messages for providers of outdoor team development. The Coverdale approach emanating from the UK has been chosen because its origins are well documented and distinctive and the company is still in existence, affording opportunities for a longitudinal comparison over nearly 50 years.

TEAM BUILDING, SENSITIVITY TRAINING AND T-GROUPS

Highhouse (2002) draws attention to the popularity of T-groups and sensitivity training in the 1960s and 1970s that today have virtually disappeared from the literature; and that as Gilley (1987) observed from a marketing perspective had gone beyond the product life-cycle saturation stage and were in the final stages of decline in the late 1980s. Highhouse (2002) uses the term 'T-group' (short for 'basic skill training group') to encapsulate all management-related sensitivity or encounter-group experiential training concerned with interpersonal dynamics. Sensitivity or T-group training, or 'laboratory education' as it has also been called (Argyris, 1964), was initially designed as a method for developing more effective group practices and focused on immediate here-and-now feedback on experiences observed within the group (Argyris, 1964; Campbell and Dunnette, 1968). The term 'sensitivity training' and the concept of basic skill training were developed in the US shortly after the end of the Second World War by the group consisting of Kurt Lewin and colleagues Ronald Lippitt, Leland Bradford and Kenneth Benne, who went on to form the National Training Laboratories in Bethel, Maine, in 1947 as a centre for their practice. The shortened term T-group was in common use by 1949.

French et al. (1978) noted a four-stage historical progression in T-group membership, from 'stranger' groups that had no prior connection to 'cousin' groups consisting of people from the same organization but different departments to 'family' groups consisting of existing work units to 'team development'. In 1956, the first homogeneous groups for executives were conducted (Highhouse, 2002, p. 281) albeit not from the same company; prior to then, delegates had come from a variety of occupational groups. In 1958, T-groups for managers from the same company were inaugurated by Robert Blake (of Managerial Grid fame) and subsequently run both off-site and on-site. This was not always successful; Chrysler used such groups in the early 1970s but found it a disastrous experience (Highhouse, 2002, p. 281).

Campbell and Dunnette (1968) summarize the key aims of T-groups as: increased self-awareness and awareness of the behaviour of others in a social context; increased awareness of factors inhibiting group processes together with diagnostic skills in identifying them; increased action skill; and 'learning how to learn' facility. A foundational idea was that participants would attend a venue cut off from day-to-day contingencies, a so-called 'cultural island' where they could focus on the training process without the normal day-to-day distractions (Bradford, 1967; Campbell and Dunnette, 1968). The original expectation was that the training period would be over a two-to-three-week period in order to cement or freeze any behavioural change. Today, this might seem a long period but, as Argyris (1964) pointed out, this is far less than is required for therapy. As we have seen, securing long-term behavioural change has been an issue for OTD, where course duration rarely exceeds a week and in many cases is less.

A number of issues specific to the development of existing work teams presented themselves soon after the introduction of family groups, as it became recognized that the effectiveness of the unstructured T-group approach with its orientation towards interpersonal behavioural issues was undermined by problems arising within a group that has a past and a future (Woodman and Sherwood, 1980). These included psychological barriers to team learning; and how to transfer what is learned in the T-group situation to the organizational setting (Schein and Bennis, 1965; Campbell and Dunnette, 1968). These were partly resolved by a shift in methodology towards 'a more focused, defined process of training a group of interdependent people in collaborative work and problem solving procedures' (Dyer, 1977, p. 23). Interventions were introduced that focused directly on the task, with interpersonal issues being important only in so far as they interfered with task accomplishment (French et al., 1978). But the underlying cause of the psychological barriers remained: 'According to its practitioners, a crucial aspect of the T group is the creation of anxiety and the open expression of feelings in an atmosphere of psychological safety' (Campbell and Dunnette, 1968, p. 79). They also commented that the difficulty of achieving psychological safety for existing groups could not be overemphasized. Interpersonal problems persisted. One of Highhouse's sources in a personal communication went so far as to state that internal groups from the same organization were the most destructive he had ever experienced (Highhouse, 2002, p. 284).

The T-group was originally designed for heterogeneous individuals meeting in an isolated setting who probably would never come together again; as such the disclosures and open expression of feelings encouraged do not constitute the same sort of threat to each individual's psychological safety as is the case with work groups who subsequently have to face each other in the world back home (Schein and Bennis, 1965). Schein and Bennis went on to suggest that non-work-group participants could reduce the level of anxiety felt by treating the whole exercise as akin to a game that has no long-term implications back in the real world. The closer one got to real work groups, the more the need to concentrate on actual organizational problems if one was to achieve a probability of transfer – but, in doing so, one reduced the likelihood of achieving the aims of a T-group as originally understood. As we have seen, this issue of psychological safety is a key concern to OTD as well – the anxieties may be different but they still exist and are intrinsic to the notion of the outdoors as a source of 'challenge' – and are often encouraged as an essential component of experiential learning.

EVALUATION OF SENSITIVITY TRAINING/T-GROUPS

In a comprehensive evaluation of T-groups, Campbell and Dunnette (1968) differentiate between internal and external criteria, following Martin (1957). 'Internal criteria' are measures linked directly to the operation of the training programme such as opinions of delegates concerning what they considered they had learned. 'External criteria' are concerned with subsequent job behaviour: 'The relationship between internal and external criteria is the essence of the problem of transfer to the organizational setting' (Campbell and Dunnette, 1968, p. 81).

Campbell and Dunnette refer to studies that used a 'perceived change' (1968, p. 81) measure as the basic external criterion. This takes the form of an open-ended question asking a superior, subordinate or peer to report any changes in delegates' behaviour in the job situation at some point after they have returned to work. A typical question is as follows: over a period of time, people may change in the ways they work with others. Do you believe that the person you are describing has changed his/her behaviour in working with people over the last year as compared with the previous year in any specific ways? If yes, please describe (p. 87). Questions such as these can equally be applied for evaluating the benefits of OTD. However, as Rushmer (1997) has pointed out, the conduct of such a critical incident type method depends on gaining organizational access; and the evidence indicates that this is not often forthcoming.

Campbell and Dunnette (1968) concluded that researchers must (1) Specify more clearly the expected behavioural outcomes of T-group training including the kinds of situations where particular behaviours will be appropriate or inappropriate. (2) Give more attention to the relationship between individual differences and particular training effects. (3) Address the impact on training outcomes and effects of factors such as organizational characteristics, leadership climates, organizational goals. (4) Compare the behavioural benefits of T-group training with those emanating from other training methods and learning experiences in order to establish cost-effectiveness. (5) Establish the impact of trainer demeanour such as approach to feedback and general encouragement on inducing new behaviours and feelings of psychological safety. (6) Consider how training transfer is supported.

This interesting set of criteria from 1968 could equally well be applied to OTD today. They add as a concluding rider to their critique that positivistic evaluation studies have limitations in that they fail to capture the spirit of T-group interventions and the positive/negative energy levels generated by participants at the time.

This overview of T-groups is very informative both in terms of anxiety levels experienced by some participants and problems of measuring and sustaining transfer of learning back at the workplace. Argyris (1964) claimed that there was at best a six-month heightening, and that this was followed by a fall-off. There are other areas of parallel with OTD. Highhouse (2002) draws attention to the influence that the T-group has had in terms of use of the cultural-island concept, although it could be argued that the sense of isolation is nowadays reduced with the development of mobile phones and Internet access in even the most remote of locations. And as Clements et al. (1995) point out, a key lesson to remember from the sensitivity-training days was that when people got back to work the old patterns were still in place. Previous problems could be aggravated given the evidence of the entrenching of attitudes within teams that Jones and Oswick (2007) refer to as a possible unintended outcome.

COVERDALE

An early example of experiential team building from the UK is the Coverdale approach to training and learning initiated in the 1960s. The Coverdale model, as explained by Roche and Waterston (1972), was that skills could not be taught like knowledge, through lectures, but rather were learnt empirically from experience. However, the learning was not accidental. The founder, Ralph Coverdale, also emphasized 'learning how to learn' as a foundational construct. This means adopting a systematic approach to building on experiences: 'Doing something, seeing what happens, incorporating this new knowledge in planning a new run at the task, trying it again and continuously improving is the basis of learning' (Roche and Waterston, 1972, p. 45). Coverdale training was presented as essentially a system of self-development of individual managers, contributing to effective teams and flexible and adaptive company organizations. The training took place in a residential setting away from the workplace in a '*safe* atmosphere' – an echo of what Schein and Bennis (1965) referred to as a climate of 'psychological safety' – where new approaches could be tested drawing upon a mixture of indoor problem-solving exercises. A typical programme at the time lasted for a week and consisted of 20 managers operating in groups of six to seven. Examples of case studies given were of family groups, i.e. from the same organization – as are more recent examples/testimonials from the Coverdale website.

Coverdale is still in existence. As part of the research for this chapter, I spoke in 2011 with the CEO, Dave Heddle, in order to establish whether there had been any changes in approach in the intervening years. There is still a focus on experiential learning, and some of the old exercises such as 'tower building' are also used today. Nowadays, some outdoor activities have been introduced such as 'build a structure'. Training for stranger groups no longer takes place – participants are from cousin or family groups only. The time scale has been reduced from a week, sometimes 'squeezed' (as Dave put it) into two days and without the residential element, with training taking place closer to the work premises. As he explained, where this 'squeeze' is specified by clients, a lot of the learning benefits are lost, such as talking with others in the evening and instead being able to escape into a new environment. Essentially, like all providers, Coverdale is trying to balance time, cost and quality. The notion of psychological safety is still there but less is made of it. However, if an individual seems bruised, they are given special support. The focus, explained at the outset of each course, is on learning about others and learning about self, with regular reviews provided for individuals. The review process incorporates observations on 'could do more of/could do less of'. In terms of physical safety, only one task has a physical safety element. A key differentiator claimed with outdoors specialists is the emphasis on a 'very robust review mechanism', although outdoor providers might challenge this. Every task has a review built in, drawing upon the concept of hierarchy of purpose that incorporates consideration of overall purpose, daily purpose and task purpose. Each task is reviewed based on a three-stage schemata: Preparation – do – review. Also emphasized in the reviews is the process of transition from course to workplace.

The Coverdale review is included here because of the opportunity to look at a specific provider approach to indoors experiential team learning based on a published article dating from the early 1970s – and to note changes 40 years later. Key points emerging are the shift towards a limited involvement in OTD, the focus on company-specific programmes and the pragmatic decision to move away from the one-week cultural-island concept if required by clients. No specific published research evidence was available of improved team performance in the workplace as a result of attending Coverdale programmes.

CONCLUSION

Much has been written on outdoor learning from a range of perspectives, and this chapter provides an overview of a number of these. The nature of the environment has been pursued and the particular significance of open spaces in a wilderness or semi-wilderness setting has been discussed. Although team building has long been emphasized as a benefit arising out of OMD, relatively little has been written from an academic perspective on OTD specifically and even less on its utilization within existing work teams. From a comparative research perspective, this situation was compounded by the absence of a clear classification system that differentiates between categories of work teams. For example, the team issues confronting a group of senior managers located in different locations who only meet once a month are likely to be different to those faced by a unit whose members work together in the same room on a day-to-day basis. Key points arising out of the review are:

1. Although many participants in the studies reviewed gave highly positive feedback, a significant minority reported serious misgivings about some part – or all – of the programme they had attended. One issue was a felt expectation that in order to demonstrate team loyalty and bonding it was necessary to constantly be in the company of other team members. For some, the resulting intensity was perceived as 'emotional labour' creating

tensions that could not be satisfactorily unpacked within the timescale of the programme.
2. This issue is not unique to outdoor events – it was a problem with T-groups as highlighted by Highhouse (2002) – although the existence of a physical element can aggravate the situation, the more prolonged the physical activity, the more likely it is for tensions to occur.
3. Taken together with comments about the importance of all members of a work group attending a team-building event, it would seem that OTD has the potential to be damaging unless the group is relatively homogeneous; the greater the degree of challenge, the greater the risk of accentuating short-term and creating longer-term relationship problems. Relationship risk is, accordingly, an additional ingredient to be added to psychological and physical risk when evaluating OTD.
4. There is also no evidence from the literature that such outdoor events resolve existing group problems and should not be treated as a way of dealing with them.
5. Stranger or cousin groups seem less likely to face psychological safety issues such as loss of face.
6. Despite the symbolic associations with the natural environment being a place of learning, this chapter has not established that these are influential in the choices made by those responsible for commissioning team-building activities. Indeed, no studies have been discovered that look specifically at commissioning motives.
7. Ideally, members of an existing team should be given the opportunity to contribute to the decision-making process over the appropriateness of an OTD programme in advance of the decision being taken. Additionally there is no guarantee that just because one group has had a successful experience this will also apply to subsequent groups. This of course applies to any team-building event. There were no studies discovered that reported that this took place.

The concluding remarks focus on the three questions asked in the introduction:

1. What differentiates outdoor team-building activities from those based on the indoors in terms of learning outcomes?

This chapter reaches the same conclusion as Clements et al. (1995): there is not enough evidence available to reach a final judgement. As with all team building, there is no guarantee of a satisfactory outcome. Some studies have found little difference and claim that all of the benefits claimed for the outdoor can equally be obtained from indoor learning activities. Others suggest that there is no significant additional benefit from activities operating at the higher physical end of the spectrum. Others have argued strongly in favour of the environment as a source of specific challenge that cannot be replicated indoors; others have found some unanticipated negative outcomes arising out of the intensity of the process – akin to those that led to the declining popularity of T-groups since the 1970s.

2. What is the evidence of an isomorphic connection in which learning obtained from experiences in one setting is transferred to another?

The literature emphasizes indirect and metaphorical links, with some evidence that the closer to the shorter problem-solving activities associated with residential challenge courses, the more apparent the connection is to participants. Some sources suggest that learning about team behaviours discussed theoretically beforehand in classroom situations are reinforced through outdoor activities. Long-term performance benefits for existing teams have never been demonstrated, although there is anecdotal evidence of greater confidence by individuals over risk taking and engaging in joint problem solving. There are insufficient studies to draw any firm conclusions.

3. Has the claim made by Wagner et al. (1991) that outdoor development will be ranked as an effective HRD strategy, particularly for enhancing team development for work groups, been substantiated?

The jury is still out. There is insufficient evidence of evaluation of work groups to make a firm judgement. There is a possibility that complete work groups will become less favoured compared to cousin or stranger groups, because of the additional psychological and relational stress imposed. In other words, learning about team working will be more effective with those you are not involved with on a day-to-day basis; a central message from sensitivity training relevant for the outdoors. However, this seems to be less of an issue for providers of indoor experiential learning; taking Coverdale as an example, some now only focus on groups coming from the same organization. But there is a trend towards a greater range of choices being offered by providers as opposed to relying on conventional outdoor programmes; these include urban outdoor training events.

My experience of groups is that if they have a 'history' of conflict then neither outdoor nor indoor team-building events are going to resolve the problem. If they get on well and the programme is well organized, then they will have fun, engage in the activities and benefit from the setting and time spent together, wherever it is located.

There are a number broader unanswered issues relating to this whole area:

1. Given the indirect and metaphoric isomorphic aspects of OTD, how do we handle the learner readiness item on the Holton (2000) Learning Transfer System Indicator (LTSI) scale, defined as the prior understanding of how the training will contribute to job-related development? What is the relationship between individual learning and team development needs?
2. Should attendance on such team-building activities be voluntary? Baldwin et al. (2000) consider that in organizational contexts the motivational value of voluntary attendance has not been demonstrated and that attendance should be required for any significant training initiative. Clements et al. (1995) take a different view emphasizing the importance of attendance being voluntary for this type of event, because of the physical safety element entailed and varying cultural norms. Clearly, a team-building event in which members of the team were absent would lose much of its value.
3. Much is made of collective sharing of exciting and fun outdoor experiences, and its particular value for newly formed teams has been mentioned – but how then does one integrate future team members who have not shared such experiences?
4. Reference has been made to participants valuing the fact that money has been spent on them. But is that sufficient to counter experiences that members find overly and unnecessarily challenging?

REFERENCES

ACCT (2004) *Challenge Course Standards* (6th edn). MI: Association for Challenge Course Technology.

Argyris C. and Schön, D. (1978) *Organizational Learning: A Theory of Action Perspective*. Reading, MA: Addison-Wesley.

Argyris, C. (1964) T-groups for organizational effectiveness, *Harvard Business Review*, 42(2): 60–74.

Attarian, A. (2001) Trends in outdoor adventure education, *Journal of Experiential Education*, 24(3): 141–149.

Attarian, A. and Holden, G. T. (2001) *The Literature and Research on Challenge Courses: An Annotated Bibliography*. Raleigh, NC: North Carolina State University.

Bacon, S. B. and Kimball, R. O. (1989) The wilderness challenge model. In R. D. Lyman (ed.) *Residential and Inpatient Treatment of Children and Adolescents* (pp. 115–144). New York: Plenum Press.

Baldwin, C., Persing, J. and Magnuson, D. (2004) Role of theory, research, and evaluation in adventure education, *Journal of Experiential Education*, 26(3): 167–183.

Baldwin, T. T., Ford, K. J. and Naquin, S. S. (2000) Managing transfer before learning begins: Enhancing the motivation to improve work through learning. In E. F. Holton III, T. T. Baldwin, and S. S. Naquin (eds) Managing and Changing Learning Transfer Systems, *Advances in Developing Human Resources*, 2(4): 23–35.

Becker, P. and Schirp, J. (eds) (2008) *Other Ways of Learning: The European Institute for Experiential Learning and Outdoor Adventure 1998–2006*. Marburg: BSJ.

Bradford, L. P. (1967) Biography of an institution, *Journal of Applied Behavioural Science*, 3(2): 127–143.

Bransford, J. D., Franks , J. J., Morris, C. D. and Stein B. S. (1979), Some general constraints on learning and memory research. In L. S. Cermack and F. I. M. Craik (eds) *Levels of Processing in Human Memory* (pp. 331–354). Hillsdale, NJ: Lawrence Erlbaum Associates.

Broderick, A. and Pearce, G. (2001) Indoor adventure training: A dramaturgical approach to management development, *Journal of Organizational Change Management*, 14(3): 239–252.

Bronson, J. (1990) *Team Development Indicator*. Mountain View, CA: Performance Dynamics Group.

Burke, V. and Collins, D. (2004a) Optimising skills transfer via outdoor management development: Part I: The provider's perspective, *Journal of Management Development*, 23(7): 678–696.

Burke, V. and Collins, D. (2004b) Optimising skills transfer via outdoor management development: Part II: The client's perspective, *Journal of Management Development*, 23(8): 715–728.

Campbell, J. P. and Dunnette, M. D. (1968) Effectiveness of T-group experiences in managerial training and development, *Psychological Bulletin*, 70(2): 73–104.

CIPD and Cannell, M. (2008) *Outdoor Development*. Wimbledon: CIPD Factsheet.

Clements, C., Wagner, R. J. and Roland, C. (1995) The ins and outs of experiential training, *Training and Development*, 49(2): 52–56.

Collinson, R., Panicucci, J. and Prouty, D. (2007) *Adventure Education: Theory and Applications*. Champaign, IL: Human Kinetics.

Cousineau, C. (1976) *Hébertisme*. Toronto, ON: Ontario Ministry of Culture.

Davis-Berman, J. and Berman, D. (2002) Risk and anxiety in adventure programming, *Journal of Experiential Education*, 25(2): 305–310.

De Meuse, K. and Liebowitz, S. (1981) An empirical analysis of teambuilding research, *Group and Organization Studies*, 6(3): 375–378.

DuFrene, D. D., Sharbough, W., Clipson, M. and McCall, M. (1999) Bringing outdoor challenge education inside the business communication classroom, *Business Communication Quarterly*, 62(3): 24–36.

Dyer, W. G. (1977) *Team Building: Issues and Alternatives*. Reading, MA: Addison-Wesley.

Flor, R. (1991) Building bridges between organisational development and experiential/adventure education, *Journal of Experiential Education*, 14(3): 27–34.

French, W. L., Bell, C. H. and Zawacki, R. A. (1978) *Organization Development: Theory, Practice and Research*. Dallas, TX: Business Publications.

Gilley, J. W. (1987) Lifelong learning: An omnibus for research and practice, American Society for adult and continuing education, reproduced in J. W. Gilley and S. A. Eggland (1989) *Principles of Human Resource Development*. Reading, MA: Addison:Wesley.

Gillis, H. L. and Speelman, E. (2008) Are challenge (ropes) courses an effective tool?: A meta-analysis, *Journal of Experiential Education*, 31(2): 111–135.

Hahn, K. (1947) *Training for and Through the Sea: Notes for Address given to the Honourable Mariners' Company in Glasgow on 20 February*. <http://www.kurthahn.org/writings/train.pdf> (accessed 20 May 2013).

Hahn, K. (1965) *Harrogate Address on Outward Bound: Address given at Harrogate Conference on 9 May*. <http://www.kurthahn.org/writings/gate.pdf> (accessed 20 May 2013).

Hale, A. R. (1984) Is safety training worthwhile? *Journal of Occupational Accidents*, 6(1): 17–33.

Harrison, S. (2010) Why are we here? Taking place into account in UK outdoor environmental education, *Journal of Adventure Training and Outdoor Learning*, 10(1): 3–18.

Hattie, J., Marsh, H. W., Neill, J. T. and Richards, G. E. (1997) Adventure training and outward bound: Out of class experiences that make a lasting difference, *Review of Educational Research*, 67(1): 43–87.

Highhouse, S. (2002) A history of the T-group and its early applications in management development, *Group Dynamics: Theory, Research, and Practice*, 6(4): 277–290.

Hoberman, S. and Mailick, S. (1992) *Experiential Management Development*. New York: Quorum Books.

Holmes, S. (1999) *The Young John Muir: An Environmental Biography*. Madison, WI: University of Wisconsin Press.

Holton, E. F. III (2000) What's *really* wrong: Diagnosis for learning transfer system change. In E. F. Holton III T. T. Baldwin, and S. S. Naquin (eds) Managing and Changing Learning Transfer Systems, *Advances in Developing Human Resources*, 2(4): 7–22.

Hunt, J. (ed.) (1989) *In Search of Adventure*. Guildford: Talbot Adair Press.

Ibbetson, A. and Newell, S. (1998) Outdoor management development: The mediating effect of the client organization, *International Journal of Training and Development*, 2(4): 239–258.

Ibbetson, A. and Newell, S. (1999) A comparison of a competitive and non-competitive outdoor management development programme, *Personnel Review*, 28(1/2): 58–76.

Irvine, D. and Wilson, J. P. (1994) Outdoor management development: Reality or illusion, *Journal of Management Development*, 13(5): 25–37.

Jones, P. J. (1996) Outdoor management development: A journey to the centre of the metaphor. In C. Oswick and D. Grant (eds) *Organization Development: Metaphorical Explorations* (pp. 209–205). London: Pitman.

Jones, P. J. and Oswick, C. (1993) Outcomes of outdoor management development: Articles of faith? *Journal of European Industrial Training*, 17(3): 10–18.

Jones, P. J. and Oswick, C. (2007) Inputs and outcomes of outdoor management development: Of design, dogma and dissonance, *British Journal of Management*, 18(4): 327–341.

Kass, D. and Grandzol, C. (2011) Learning to lead at 5,267 feet: An empirical study of outdoor management training and MBA students' leadership development, *Journal of Leadership Education*, 10(1): 41–62.

Kolb, D. A. (1984) *Experiential Learning: Experience as the Source of Learning and Development*. New Jersey: Prentice-Hall.

Lewin, K. (1947) Frontiers in group dynamics: Concept, method and reality in social science; social equilibria and social change, *Human Relations*, 1(1): 5–41.

Lewis, M. (1939) *England's Sea-Officers*. London: George Allen and Unwin.

Loeffler, T. A. (2004) A Photo elicitation study of the meanings of outdoor adventure experiences, *Journal of Leisure Research*, 36(4): 536–556.

Low, S. M. (2003) Embodied spaces: Anthropological theories of body, space and culture, *Space and Culture*, 6(9): 9–18.

Maher, S. and Pomerantz, S. (2003) The future of executive coaching: Analysis from a market lifecycle approach, *International Journal of Coaching in Organizations*, 1(2): 3–11.

Mant, A. (1981) Developing effective managers for the future: Learning through experience. In C. L. Cooper (ed.) *Developing Managers for the 1980s*, Chapter 5. Basingstoke: Macmillan.

Martin, B., Cashel, C., Wagstaff, M. and Breunig, M. (2006) *Outdoor Leadership: Theory and Practice*. Champaign, IL: Human Kinetics.

Martin, H.A. (1957) The assessment of training, *Personnel Management*, 39(2): 88–93.

Mazany, P., Francis, S. and Sumich, P. (1995) Evaluating the effectiveness of an outdoor workshop for team building in an MBA programme, *Journal of Management Development*, 14(3): 50–68.

McEvoy, G. M. and Buller, P. F. (1990) Five uneasy pieces in the training evaluation puzzle, *Training and Development Journal*, 44(8): 39–42.

McEvoy, G. M., Cragun, J. R. and Appleby, M. (1997) Using outdoor training to develop and accomplish organizational vision, *Human Resource Planning*, 20(3): 20–28.

Munn, N. D. (1996) Excluded spaces: The figure in the Australian aboriginal landscape, *Critical Inquiry*, 22(3): 446–465.

Nash, R. F. (1982) *Wilderness and the American Mind* (3rd edn). New Haven, CT: Yale University Press.

Nash, R. F. (2001) *Wilderness and the American Mind* (4th edn). New Haven and London: Yale Nota Bene.

Neill, J. T. (1997) Gender: How does it affect the outdoor education experience? In *Catalysts for Change: Proceedings of the 10th National Outdoor Education Conference*. Sydney: The Outdoor Professionals, pp. 183–192.

Ng, H. A. (2001) Adventure learning: Influence of collectivism on team and organizational attitudinal changes, *Journal of Management Development*, 20(5): 424-40.

Outdoor Industry Association (2006) *State of the Industry Report*. <http://www.outdoorindustry.org/research.market.php?action=detailandresearch_id=29> (accessed 12 November 2011).

Pine, J. and Tingley, J. C. (1993) ROI of soft-skills training, *Training*, 30(2): 55–60.

Pohl, S., Borrie, W. and Patterson, M. (2000) Women, wilderness, and everyday life: A documentation of the connection between wilderness recreation and women's everyday lives, *Journal of Adventure Research*, 32(4): 415–434.

Priest, S. and Gass, M. A. (2005) *Effective Leadership in Adventure Programming* (2nd edn). Champaign, IL: Human Kinetics.

Richards, A. (1991). The genesis of Outward Bound. In M. Zelinski (ed.) *Outward Bound: The Inward Odyssey* (pp. 8–11). Boulder, CO: From the Heart.

Richards, A. (1992) Adventure based experiential learning. In J. Mulligan and C. Griffin (eds) *Empowerment through Experiential Learning* (pp. 155–162). London Kogan Page.

Richards, G. E. (1977) *Some Educational Implications and Contributions of Outward Bound*. Sydney, NSW: Australian Outward Bound Foundation.

Roche, S. G. and Waterston, J. (1972) Coverdale training: Building on ability, *Training and Development Journal*, 26(2): 44–48.

Rockefeller, S. A. (2001) *Where are you Going? Work, Power and Movement in the Bolivian Andes*, Doctoral dissertation, Department of Anthropology, University of Chicago.

Rohnke, K., Rogers, D., Tait, C. M. and Wall, J. B. (2007) *The Complete Ropes Course Manual*. Dubuque, IA: Kendall/Hunt.

Rubinstein, N. J. (1997) The psychological value of open space. In L. W. Hamilton (ed.) *The Benefits of Open Space*, Chapter 4. New Jersey: The Great Swamp Watershed Association. <http://www.greatswamp.org/Education/rubinstein.htm> (accessed 20 May 2013).

Rushmer, R. K. (1997) How do we measure the effectiveness of team building? Is it good enough? Team Management Systems – A case study, *Team Performance Management*, 3(4): 244–260.

Russell, K. C., Hendee, J. C. and Cooke, S. (1998) Potential social and economic contributions of wilderness discovery as an adjunct to the Federal Job Corps Program, *International Journal of Wilderness*, 4(3): 32–38.

Schein, E. H. and Bennis, W. G. (1965) *Personal and Organizational Changes through Group Methods: The Laboratory Approach*. New York: Wiley.

Shivers-Blackwell, S. L. (2004) Reactions to outdoor teambuilding initiatives in MBA education, *Journal of Management Development*, 23(7): 614–630.

Simpson, L. (2009) *The Private Training Market in the UK, IFLL Sector Paper 2*. Leicester: NIACE.

Smith, D. and Vaughan, S. (1997) The outdoors as an environment for learning and change management, *Industrial and Commercial Training*, 29(1): 26–30.

Snow, H. (1997) *Indoor/Outdoor Team Building Games for Trainers: Powerful Activities from the World of Adventure based Team Building and Ropes Courses*. New York: McGraw-Hill.

Stokes, P. (2008) Outdoor management development as organizational transformation: A study of Anglo-French paradoxical experience in the application of alternative human resource development approaches, *International Journal of Cross Cultural Management*, 8(1): 23–39.

Wagner, R.J., Baldwin, T. T. and Roland, C. C. (1991) Outdoor training: Revolution or fad, *Training and Development Journal*, 45(3): 51–56.

Walton, J. S. (1999) *Strategic Human Resource Development*. Harlow, UK: Financial Times Prentice Hall.

Warren, K. (1998) A call for race, gender, and class sensitive facilitation in outdoor experiential education, *Journal of Experiential Education*, 21(1): 21–25.

Warren, K. (2005) A path worth taking: The development of social justice in outdoor experiential education, *Equity and Excellence in Education*, 38(1): 89–99.

Warren, K. and Loeffler, T. A. (2000) Setting a place at the table: Social justice research in outdoor experiential education, *Journal of Experiential Education*, 23(2): 85–89.

Wattchow, B. (2008) Moving on an effortless journey: Paddling, river-places and outdoor education, *Australian Journal of Outdoor Education*, 12(2): 12–23.

West, M. (1994) *Effective Teamwork*. Leicester: BPS Books.

Wilderness Act (1964) U.S. Code Vol. 16, sec.1132(c).

Williams, S. D., Graham, T. S. and Baker, B. (2003) Evaluating outdoor experiential training for leadership and team building, *Journal of Management Development*, 22(1): 45–59.

Wolfe, B. and Samdahl, D. (2005) Challenging assumptions: Examining fundamental beliefs that shape challenge course programming and research, *Journal of Experiential Education*, 28(1): 25–43.

Woodman, R. W. and Sherwood, J. J. (1980) The role of team development in organizational effectiveness: A critical review, *Psychological Bulletin*, 88(1): 166–186.

Zemke, R. (1978) Personal growth training. *Training*, May.

FURTHER READING

Broderick, A. and Pearce, G. (2001) Indoor adventure training: A dramaturgical approach to management development, *Journal of Organizational Change Management*, 14(3): 239–252.

Campbell, J. P. and Dunnette, M. D. (1968) Effectiveness of T-group experiences in managerial training and development, *Psychological Bulletin*, 70(2): 73–104.

Ibbetson, A. and Newell, S. (1999) A comparison of a competitive and non-competitive outdoor management development programme, *Personnel Review*, 28(1/2): 58–76.

Jones, P. J. and Oswick, C. (2007) Inputs and outcomes of outdoor management development: Of design, dogma and dissonance, *British Journal of Management*, 18(4): 327–341.

Stokes, P. (2008) Outdoor management development as organizational transformation: A study of Anglo-French paradoxical experience in the application of alternative human resource development approaches, *International Journal of Cross Cultural Management*, 8(1): 23–39.

Wolfe, B. and Samdahl, D. (2005) Challenging assumptions: Examining fundamental beliefs that shape challenge course programming and research, *Journal of Experiential Education*, 28(1): 25–43.

13

EMPLOYEE ENGAGEMENT INTERVENTIONS: HRD, GROUPS AND TEAMS

Claire Valentin

INTRODUCTION

In the 20 or so years since the term employee engagement (EE) was first introduced (Kahn, 1990), there has been a burgeoning interest in the concept. EE is commonly described as a combination of commitment to the organization and its values, a willingness to help out colleagues, motivation, job satisfaction and discretionary effort by employees (CIPD, 2008). There is still considerable debate around EE; for example, is it a vital new concept for the future of business, or simply a reworking of familiar concepts such as commitment and motivation? One school of thought suggests that it is poorly conceptualized and has gained popularity with little empirical evidence of its validity. Despite its popular adoption, human resource development (HRD) theorists have been slow to mount the EE bandwagon (Shuck and Wollard, 2010); however, there is now an emerging interest in EE from an HRD perspective.

This chapter will critically explore the rise of the concept in management thinking, and discuss its significance for HRD, and for working with groups and teams. Most writing on EE focuses on the experience of the individual employee and their relationship with the organization. There has been little research to date that specifically focuses on the significance of EE in the context of work groups and teams, and the role of co-workers and work groups/teams in facilitating engagement, although this does feature implicitly in much EE thinking. Recent work (CIPD, 2011) suggests that there can be a variety of 'loci' for engagement, including the task, work colleagues and the organization. Given the significance of team working in organizations, HRD's experience of team learning and development may provide a useful focus for its contribution to this emerging area of practice and research.

The chapter will draw on emerging literature on EE, and unlike some earlier work from an HRD perspective, for example Shuck and Wollard (2010), will draw on research into 'work engagement' and on related aspects such as motivation, commitment, leadership and team development. The chapter first looks at how engagement is described and the arguments as to its significance for organizations, and examines common practices that claim to facilitate engagement, drawing out a number of controversies from research in business, management and psychology. The chapter goes on to discuss EE and HRD, arguing that HRD may be an inherent 'driver' of engagement. It then examines some of the antecedent concepts such as motivation and commitment, suggesting that there is much in research, in these areas that has not been surpassed by more recent claims for EE. The chapter goes on to discuss work on the 'locus of engagement', examining evidence that people may be more engaged with their work group than with the organization as a whole, and the implications particularly for HRD.

The chapter concludes that EE is a construct that should not be adopted uncritically by the HRD field. There is much of interest in research, but there are also considerable areas of debate. Commonly used engagement measures are often used without consideration of context or their limitations. Measures may focus on a general level and say little about the different experiences of individuals, and the nuances of factors that impact upon engagement may be ignored. The final section examines a range of debates and draws a number of conclusions concerning EE and HRD.

ORIGINS AND DEFINITIONS OF AND CLAIMS FOR THE EMPLOYEE ENGAGEMENT CONSTRUCT

The term EE was coined by William Kahn in 1990 in a paper in the *Academy of Management Journal* entitled 'Conditions of personal engagement and disengagement at work'. Kahn took an ethnographic approach in his studies of summer camp counsellors and staff in an architecture firm. His specific concern was in exploring the experience of the individual at work; what it means for a person to be 'psychologically present' during 'work role performances', and how they can be 'disengaged'.

> I define personal engagement as the harnessing of organization members' selves to their work roles; in engagement, people employ and express themselves physically, cognitively, and emotionally during role performances. I define personal disengagement as the uncoupling of selves from work roles; in disengagement they will withdraw and defend themselves physically, cognitively, or emotionally during role performances.
>
> (Kahn, 1990, p. 694)

Other writers explore the idea of engagement and consider how organizations might be able to enhance EE towards achievement of organizational goals. As well as drawing on Kahn, work has drawn on research into related concepts such as motivation, burnout, commitment, empowerment and organizational citizenship behaviour (OCB), which includes discretionary or 'extra-role' behaviour. Studies have sought to demonstrate that EE is measurable; that it can be correlated with performance; that it varies between individuals; and that employers can impact on people's level of engagement, the latter being of particular relevance to HRD interventions (Allen and Meyer, 1990; Macleod and Clarke, 2009).

In common with many such constructs, there is no one agreed definition of EE; during the course of a major review for the UK government, MacLeod and Clarke (2009) came across more than 50 definitions. Definitions of EE encompass attitudes, behaviours and outcomes; as in Kahn's work, elements of the experience of engagement can be emotional, cognitive and physical. Shuck and Wollard (2010) carried out a literature review to identify the seminal foundations of EE from the perspective of HRD. Their definition focuses on the individual employee and on the organizational interest: 'an individual employee's cognitive, emotional, and behavioural state directed towards desired organizational outcomes' (2010, p. 103). Others mention motivation and willing contribution of effort (often cited as a willingness to 'go the extra mile' for the employer), positive emotions such as job satisfaction and feelings of empowerment, feelings of connection towards colleagues and to the organization, with a resulting positive impact upon performance (CIPD, 2008; Gatenby et al., 2009).

There is often an emphasis on the role of the organization in fostering engagement and specifying the desired outcome of engagement, suggesting a two-way relationship between employer and employee (Robinson et al., 2004). Engaged employees are said to feel commitment to organizational values and to be motivated to contribute to the success of the organization, whilst experiencing a sense of wellbeing. Macleod and Clarke (2009) talk of a 'virtuous circle', where the preconditions trigger engagement and the results reinforce it:

> Engaged organizations have strong and authentic values, with clear evidence of trust and fairness based on mutual respect, where two-way promises and commitments – between employers and staff – are understood and are fulfilled.
>
> (MacLeod and Clarke, 2009, p. 8)

In the psychological literature, it is common to refer to 'work engagement' (WE), a more in-depth exploration of the individual experience than in some of the management literature, as might be expected. Three dimensions of the experience of WE have gained much attention. High levels of energy and mental resilience are referred to as *vigour*. A strong involvement in one's work coupled with a sense of significance and pride is termed *dedication. Absorption* describes the experience of full concentration and being engrossed in work (Fairlie, 2011, p. 509). WE seeks to capture that workers should experience their work:

> as stimulating and energetic and something to which they really want to devote time and effort (the *vigour* component); as a significant and meaningful pursuit (*dedication*); and as engrossing and something on which they are fully concentrated (*absorption*).
>
> (Bakker et al., 2011a, p. 5)

Although there are common elements to the definitions of EE (Brewster et al., 2007), and those of WE, they carry different emphases, underpinning assumptions and purposes, and tend to be largely from a normative perspective. Many are very broad, presenting overarching concepts and vision statements rather than being strictly definitions (Dicke, 2007).

Higher levels of EE have been associated with better financial performance in the private sector, better outcomes in the public sector and innovation. Engagement has been correlated with reduced sickness absence, reduced turnover, enhanced customer focus and advocacy for the organization. Brewster et al. (2007) conducted an extensive literature search and face-to-face interviews, looking at what outcomes organizations were seeking from engagement. Findings included a desire to increase customer satisfaction and promote customer loyalty, improve customer service, facilitate change management, sustain growth and reduce turnover, to attract, retain and motivate staff.

Differences have been found in levels of engagement between types of work and workplaces, and differences in respect to levels of engagement. 4-Consulting (2007) found that the most engaged employees tend to be those in the youngest and oldest age groups, and that managers and professionals have greater levels of engagement than their colleagues in supporting roles. Robinson et al. (2007) also found that managers have higher levels of engagement than staff in operational, professional or support roles. Those in operational roles were found to have higher engagement levels than support staff. Perhaps surprisingly, professionals were found, overall, to have the lowest organizational engagement levels of all groups, in contrast to the findings by 4-Consulting.

Attridge (2009) identified a general pattern of distribution of engagement amongst employees, which fell into three basic groups. The top 20 per cent are highly engaged: such employees 'work with passion and feel a profound connection to their company' (Attridge, 2009, p. 387). Sixty per cent are moderately engaged. However, there is concern over the 20 per cent of employees who were found to be actively disengaged. It is claimed that these employees are not just unhappy in their work, but they undermine more engaged co-workers. Overall indicative figures suggest that levels of engagement in the UK are lower than they could be. Gallup suggests that in 2008 the cost of disengagement to the economy was between £59.4 billion and £64.7 billion (Robinson et al., 2007).

EE has become big business with large and small consultancies offering to enhance engagement. Governments have commissioned major studies and put significant resources into the issue. For example, a UK government website launched in 2010 to help leaders and senior managers across the public, private and third sectors 'reap the benefits of EE' claims that: 'In an era of constrained resources, where nearly every organization is seeking "more for less", there are few industries that can afford to ignore EE' (Macleod, 2010 online). Others argue that to compete effectively, companies must enable employees to apply their full capabilities to their work.

> Contemporary organizations need employees who are psychologically connected to their work; who are willing and able to invest themselves fully in their roles; who are proactive and committed to high performance standards.
>
> (Bakker et al., 2011a, pp. 4–5)

Despite the widespread popularity of EE, there are competing interpretations in how it is defined and perceived, and there is still limited academic research to back up many claims made as to its worth. How engagement develops, how it is measured, and whether there are different types of engagement are all subject to debate. Some sources refer in general terms to engagement and its 'presumed positive consequences' (Macey and Schneider, 2008, pp. 3–4), whereas others identify different types of engagement, for example cognitive engagement, emotional engagement and behavioural engagement (Shuck and Wollard, 2010). Studies cover different sectors and use different methodologies, use a variety of definitions of engagement, focus on different elements of engagement, look at different performance outcomes, and at the contextual nature of engagement (Macleod and Clarke, 2009). Studies have been carried out by academics, consultancies and policymakers, each having potentially different interests and expectations. This clearly presents problems when reviewing findings.

Practitioner models of engagement (Zigarmi et al., 2009) tend to focus on the practicalities such as how to use the construct, and on outcomes. Research methodologies have been accused of being based in some cases 'on anecdotal experience and good marketing' (Shuck, 2011, p. 17). Engagement as a 'folk' term has been used to refer to a psychological state, a 'performance constructed disposition', or a combination of the two (Macey and Schneider, 2008). As a psychological construct, it has been used to refer to both role performance and an affective state, including mood states and more temporary emotional states. It is also referred to as a disposition or trait, or the tendency to experience events, circumstances and situations more positively (Macey and Schneider, 2008, p. 11). Macey and Schneider (2008) present a useful conceptual framework, which distinguishes between trait engagement, state engagement and behavioural engagement. They suggest that engagement as 'state' has received more attention, either implicitly or explicitly, than other perspectives.

PRACTICES TO BUILD AN ENGAGED WORKFORCE

Having introduced the concept of EE, this section looks at some of the common practices that organizations employ to attempt to increase engagement. As a starting point, engagement is typically measured by an employee attitude survey to assess how employees feel about issues in their work such as pay and benefits, communications, learning and development, line management and work-life balance (CIPD, 2008). There are a number of such surveys available. For example, one widely used measure of engagement is the Gallup Workplace Audit (Harter et al., 2002). This consists of 12 questions around the experience of work, including such things as being clear around expectations, having resources to complete work requirements, support and recognition from managers, opportunities for development, and social relationships. The ratings from all 12 of these questions are then combined into an index – being engaged, not engaged or disengaged.

The EE index developed by Robinson et al. (2004) also has 12 attitudinal statements. These are listed under the following categories: commitment to the organization and identification with its values; belief that the organization enables the individual to perform well; being a good organizational citizen, i.e. having a willingness to help others and be a good team player, to 'go the extra mile' and understand the wider context of the business. The indicator gives a score from one (highly disengaged) to five (highly engaged), with three as the neutral midpoint (Robinson et al., 2007, p. 3). Towers Perrin (2008) developed a four-category scale with questions under the categories of: think, feel, act – extra effort, act – stay.

The Utrecht Work Engagement Scale (UWES) (Schaufeli and Bakker, 2003) has 17 questions, and unusually is available freely online in over 20 languages (results contribute to ongoing research). It focuses on the individual's feelings and experience, including such statements as 'At my work, I feel bursting with energy', and 'I feel happy when I am working intensely', which provides a focus more on the psychological experience of the employee. It measures three different forms of behaviour (proficiency, adaptivity and proactivity) and three levels at which role behaviours can contribute to effectiveness (individual, team, organization), giving rise to a matrix of nine subdimensions of performance (Parker and Griffin, 2011, p. 65).

There is not space here for an in-depth analysis and comparison of engagement surveys, other than to note that they exhibit some similar features but also some possibly quite significant differences, and that some have been subject to more research than others. Latham (2007), discussing work motivation, suggests that attitude surveys are a useful way to assess the current thinking and the 'affect' of employees. Others are critical of such surveys when applied to EE, especially those developed out of practice rather than for research. Measures of engagement are accused of being 'composed of a potpourri of items representing one or more of the four different categories: job satisfaction, organizational commitment, psychological empowerment, and job involvement' (Macey and Schneider, 2008, pp. 6–7). For example, the distinction between 'engagement' and 'satisfaction' is poorly conceptually clarified, and often there is simply a relabelling of measures used to assess job satisfaction (or climate or culture) as 'engagement'. Measures of 'conditions of engagement' are labelled as measures of engagement itself (Macey and Schneider, 2008). There is neither any assessment of the *state* of engagement nor any indication of affect, energy or passion. As Macey and Schneider (2008, p. 8) note, this has conceptual limitations:

> Although there may be room for satisfaction within the engagement construct, engagement connotes activation, where satisfaction connotes satiation... 'Satisfaction' surveys might ask employees to describe their work conditions, and this may be relevant in assessing the conditions that *provide for* engagement (state and/or behavioural), they do not directly tap engagement. Such measures require an inferential leap to engagement rather than assessing engagement itself.

Generic measures of engagement do not highlight differences between groups of people: cultural, generational or related to the nature of the job. Definitions may therefore need to be more relevant to the organizational context (Brewster et al., 2007). Surveys that are tailor-made for the organization may be more useful, developed on the basis of interviews with samples of employees or focus groups (Latham, 2007). The efficacy and limitations of assessments that intend to measure EE needs to be further explored (Flesher, 2009). This echoes some concerns over the construct validity of organization commitment questionnaires (Ashman, 2007).

Measuring engagement is usually a precursor to interventions to promote engagement, followed by a 'package' of measures aimed both at the level of the individual employee and the wider organizational level (Attridge, 2009). Factors that have been found to impact on engagement include leadership and management style; open, two-way communication; issues such as pay and benefits; fair and equal treatment; employing the 'right' workforce; career development and training; working hours; and health and safety (4-Consulting, 2007, p. 1). 'Drivers' of engagement are identified in 'clusters' – for example, the organization, management and leadership, and 'working life' (McBain, 2007). Robinson et al. (2007) distinguish between main drivers and subdrivers, arguing also that there is variability between and within organizations, and also individual differences. Bakker et al. (2011a) suggest that 'job resources' such as autonomy, social support from colleagues and skill variety can play both an intrinsic and extrinsic motivational role for the individual worker: 'Results show that increases in social support, autonomy, opportunities to learn and to develop, and performance feedback were positive predictors of ... work engagement' (p. 6).

The role of managers, and in particular the line manager, has emerged as a key factor in enabling and building engagement. Alimo-Metcalfe et al. (2008) carried out a three-year longitudinal study of 46 mental health teams working in the UK National Health Service (NHS). The study identified three dimensions to the leadership culture that supported engagement: engaging with others, visionary leadership and leadership capabilities. Employee engagement requires clear systems, processes and guidelines; a culture of engaging with staff, the antithesis of the 'blame culture'; and support for adaptability, experimentation, learning and innovation (Alimo-Metcalfe et al., 2008). The notion of 'engaging leadership' includes involving staff in developing a shared vision, being loyal to them, supporting them through coaching and mentoring, to help develop positive attitudes to work and a sense of well-being. Others argue that 'engaging managers' should facilitate and empower rather than control or restrict their staff; they should listen, provide feedback, and offer support and recognition for effort (Macleod and Clarke, 2009).

HRD AND EMPLOYEE ENGAGEMENT

Despite the burgeoning popularity of EE, most of the research and writing has emanated from the HR or wider business literature. Shuck and Wollard (2010) and Shuck (2011) produced some of the first papers to consider EE from a purely HRD perspective. However, HRD is embedded in EE practices and theorizing. HRD processes and practices are inherent within most discussions on EE, and form a key part of practices claimed to facilitate engagement. There are references to training and development, learning processes, and specific interventions such as coaching and mentoring. There may be a general statement, along the lines that 'training and development opportunities' have been shown to contribute to engagement, or a more specific reference to a range of training and development interventions.

Robinson et al. (2007), for example, developed an EE diagnostic tool, which includes training, employee development and career development, arguing that these are key factors in helping employees feel valued and involved, and are seen to be major drivers of engagement. Questions in their engagement survey specifically focusing on training, employee development and career development included:

> I am encouraged to learn new skills.
> My line manager takes employees' development seriously.
> I am able to take time off work for training.
> I have many opportunities for training.

I am given adequate training to do my current job.
My training needs are regularly discussed.
I feel I have equal access to training and development opportunities.
This organization actively supports my continuing professional development.

They note that: 'In general, receiving training during the previous 12 months had a positive impact on engagement levels' (Robinson et al., 2007, p. x). Engagement scores were higher for those who had received one or two days' training, rising for those with three to five days, and six to ten days. Interestingly, those with over ten days' training showed a drop in engagement scores. They speculate that high levels of training might indicate for some respondents a performance problem that needs to be tackled.

They also ask about less formal development opportunities, such as secondments, coaching, multidisciplinary working and special projects. They found a direct relationship between respondents' views of development opportunities and their engagement levels: '40 per cent of those who thought that their development opportunities were good or excellent were highly engaged. Only 2 per cent of those who thought their development opportunities were good or excellent were disengaged' (Robinson et al., 2007, p. xi).

Having an appraisal or performance review within the past 12 months has been linked to engagement, as has possession of a personal development plan (PDP), having a good induction programme with training (Robinson et al., 2007), and career development opportunities and/or planning (Seijts and Crim, 2006). Kontakos sums this up:

> An Employee Development Programme (EDP) designed for engagement aligns and monitors employees' job and career goals to the organizations' strategic goals. The development plan is customized for each employee, co-designed by the employee and fully supported by the line manager. Through the addition of accountability metrics, engaged employees recognize that their continuing value to the organization increasingly depends on achieving the goals of the plan. Subsequently, the organization secures the talent and skills necessary for operational excellence.
>
> (Kontakos, 2007, p. 76)

Relevant engagement practices range from supporting individual personal and professional development; support for staff to gain professional qualifications; skills development; management development programmes; induction programmes; work shadowing, job rotation and secondments; professional development portfolios and career planning; supporting communities of practice; formal training and on-the-job learning. An 'integrated HR offer' (Brewster et al., 2007) has familiar features associated with a strategic approach to HRD (Walton, 1999; McCracken and Wallace, 2000; Garavan, 2007).

Also of particular significance to HRD is the widely argued-for importance of both line managers and senior management support for EE. This indicates a further management and leadership development role for HRD in order to develop both team leadership and management skills in general, and the particular skills needed to become 'engaging managers'.

Fairlie (2011) suggests that one way that HRD can address engagement is to promote 'human development'. He argues that meaningful work can be shown to link to engagement, as development is a core aspect of meaningful work. In a study involving 574 questionnaire recipients, he found that meaningful work characteristics were the strongest predictor of engagement: 'Given the development theme that is inherent in meaningful work (i.e. self-transcendence), the results would suggest a prominent role for HRD professionals in addressing these issues within organizations' (p. 517). He suggests that meaningful work should be audited on employee surveys, and makes a number of other suggestions as to how HRD professionals could communicate opportunities for meaningful work and enable the development of more opportunities.

Shuck and Wollard (2010) urge HRD to become more involved in the area of EE, arguing that:

> There is a short window of opportunity for the HRD field to take a leading role in fostering EE and to do so, the concept needs to be clearly defined and structured in a way that helps practitioners, scholars, and researchers solve problems and offer solutions through a common language and understanding.
>
> (Shuck and Wollard, 2010 pp. 91–92)

One could agree that there is scope for HRD to become more involved in the whole issue of EE. However, achieving common understanding and reaching agreement on common definitions is more problematic. One could equally argue that what is required is more debate and widening of research rather than seeking more consensus on what is clearly a contested area.

One fruitful line of inquiry is to continue to interpret current models and approaches to EE from an HRD perspective, to establish the implications for HRD in terms of interventions. What might be the significance for HRD in each aspect of a model? For example, Saks' (2006) model examines the antecedents and consequences of EE. Antecedents include job characteristics, rewards and recognition, perceived organization and supervisor support, and distributive and procedural justice. From an HRD perspective, one could assume that the role of training and development at all levels of the model, and recognition of development needs, could be incorporated in this. Distributive and procedural justice should apply in how HRD opportunities are apportioned. And support from supervisors has implications for the training of managers, and links to the notion of 'engaging managers'.

MOTIVATION, COMMITMENT AND EMPLOYEE ENGAGEMENT

Whilst there is not space to go into detail in this chapter, as employee motivation and commitment are important contributors to the concept of EE, some discussion is appropriate to inform our understanding. This section explores the link between EE and these earlier constructs. Meyer et al. (2004) note that the commitment and motivation literatures in organization psychology have evolved independently. Theories of work motivation have evolved out of general theories of motivation, whereas commitment study has its origins in sociology. Both concepts have been difficult to define. They argue that commitment and motivation, although related concepts, are distinguishable, and they suggest that commitment is one component of motivation. Latham (2007) suggests that there is no integrative overarching conceptual framework for motivation.

These points have significance for the study of EE. Commitment and motivation are intrinsic elements in the construct of EE, as well as being multidimensional constructs: so what complexities are added when one suggests that they are part of EE, itself a multidimensional construct? Added to this one needs to take account of the different emphases of research in disciplines such as psychology and sociology.

Organizational commitment describes the employee's involvement and identification with their organization, and there are many similarities between EE and commitment. The concept of 'perceived organizational support' (POS) refers to how the employee views the degree that the organization is committed to them (Ferrer, 2005). Robinson (2003) distinguishes between five types of organizational commitment:

> Affiliative – compatible with organizations interests and values
> Associative – perception of belonging
> Moral – sense of mutual obligation
> Affective – job satisfaction
> Structural – fair economic exchange.
>
> (Robinson, 2003, p. 12)

Meyer et al. (2004) developed an integrative model in which commitment is part of a more general motivational process, which also treats motivation as a multidimensional construct, and distinguishes between nondiscretionary and discretionary behaviour. Basic mechanisms are presumed to be involved in the development of commitment. Other factors (including human resource management practices and policies) serve as more 'distal causes' for motivation. This underlines the importance of not viewing motivation (and EE) as something that can be simply 'switched on' by appropriate HR/D policies and practices. Commitment is influenced by many factors, including 'environmental factors' such as 'leadership, the social milieu, and the work itself' (Meyer et al., 2004, p. 1002).

Meyer et al. (2004) also distinguish between three different elements to commitment – affective, normative and continuance: 'affective attachment to the organisation, obligation to remain, and perceived cost of leaving' (2004, p. 993). Research shows that affective commitment has the strongest positive correlation with job performance, organizational citizenship behaviour and attendance, followed by normative commitment. Continuance commitment tends to be unrelated, or even negatively related, to these factors (Meyer et al., 2004). Since EE surveys incorporate questions related to these aspects of commitment, for example asking if employees intend to stay working in their current organization, it can be seen that they draw selectively on research into organizational commitment. However, there is a danger that such surveys and their interpretations oversimplify complex human processes, and that theories of EE lack robust research of the kind that has been done into commitment and motivation.

Psychological wellbeing has been shown to be correlated with performance. Robertson and Cooper (2010) argue that the current focus of EE concentrates on the organizational benefits of employee commitment, attachment and citizenship, and not enough on employee psychological wellbeing. They suggest that this reflects a focus on 'Narrow Engagement', and argue for an integrated concept of 'Full Engagement', which pays equal attention to the wellbeing of individuals. To focus only on commitment and citizenship may risk employee's psychological health (Robertson and Cooper, 2010).

Engagement also has a link to studies into the psychological contract, which refers to the perceptions of employee and employer of their mutual obligations to one another (Guest and Conway, 2002), and to literature on 'psychological empowerment' (Parker and Griffin, 2011). All the above suggests that we should not ignore research on motivation and commitment in favour of the 'newer' construct of EE.

Focusing on the issue of commitment from an HRD perspective, McCabe and Garavan (2008) suggest that organizational commitment is related to four factors: commitment to the organization, to top management, to immediate superiors and to workgroups (2008, pp. 533–534). In their study of nurses, they noted a range of factors influencing commitment, including shared values; leadership, teamwork and support; training, development and career progression; valuing and staff recognition; and professional, organizational commitment and involvement. These are very similar to some of the suggestions for EE. Chalofsky and Krishna's (2009) reference to 'meaningful work' again echoes much in the EE literature. They identify three themes: sense of self, the work itself and sense of balance. They argue that 'the primary drivers of commitment are identification with the organization's goals and values, congruence between individual and organizational goals, and internalization of the organizational value and mission' (p. 198).

EMPLOYEE ENGAGEMENT AND GROUPS/TEAMS

The focus of much discussion on EE tends to be on the individual's engagement with the organization. However, employees may be engaged with aspects of their work, and not necessarily with the organization as a whole. Research into the 'locus of engagement' has found that employees identify with their team and business unit more strongly than with the wider organization (CIPD, 2011, p. 3). This can be explained by the fact that 'people tend to be engaged with elements of their work environment which they encounter frequently, namely, their job and their immediate colleagues, including their line manager' (CIPD, 2011, p. 19). However, there has been limited research to date into this aspect of EE. Since working in groups and teams is a significant factor in organizations, a useful focus is to locate the level of analysis of EE at the group level. This section examines some of the work in this area and draws out some implications for HRD.

A work team can be described as a group of individuals who work interdependently to solve problems or carry out work (Kirkman and Rosen, 1999, p. 58). There is much emphasis in engagement literature on the importance of the 'engaging manager', but might there also be a role for the 'engaging co-worker'? A range of questions emerge: can teams/work groups contribute to individual EE? Can team management and development practices contribute to the engagement of individuals? Can engaged team members contribute to engagement of others in the team? Can a 'team' be 'engaged'? Can we talk about 'engaging' team leadership and management?

Although there is little in the EE research to date to address these questions, we can draw on the extensive research on motivation and commitment in work groups and teams. Commitment theory recognizes that 'commitment can be directed towards various targets, or foci, of relevance to workplace behaviour, including the organization, occupation, supervisor, team, program, customer, and union' (Meyer et al., 2004, pp. 993–994). The team is an important source of organizational support, one that influences commitment (Bishop et al., 2000), and therefore engagement.

Meyer et al. (2004) introduce the term 'commitment to social foci' as distinct from 'commitment to the goal'. This commitment may be affective, in which case the individual employee will tend to share the values of the particular target of commitment, and is likely to 'experience self-set and assigned goals as autonomously regulated (integrated or identified regulation) and as ideals to be achieved (promotion focus)' (Meyer et al., 2004, p. 1001). This suggests that the work group or team can act as a contributor to engagement.

A strong normative commitment, in contrast to affective commitment, means that individuals are likely to perceive goal acceptance as more of an externally regulated obligation. Normative commitment develops through cultural and organizational socialization and contributes to persistence in motivation (Meyer et al., 2004). This can also happen at the level of the team.

'Perceived team support' (PTS) has been related to job performance (Bishop et al., 2000, p. 1128). Support from the organization and support from the team may impact on employee commitment in different ways. Level of turnover, for example, seems to be more correlated with perceived support from the organization. Job performance, however, seems to be more influenced by a supportive team environment, one that acknowledges and values individual members' contributions (Bishop et al., 2000). This suggests that the team can serve as a 'driver' of engagement. Commitment to organizational goals is mediated through commitment to a supervisor or team. Thus it is not only the action of managers that can support engagement, but also the role of the team.

Commitment may also be to a profession or to customers and client, with the same effect (Meyer et al., 2004). Research has explored the organizational commitment of professionals versus their commitment to their profession. Wallace (1995) in a study of lawyers working in large non-professional organizations found that organizational commitment was subject to a number of factors. These lawyers tended to create a subculture within the company, and shared a common culture of commitment to professional ideals and values. Commitment to the organization evolved through an adaptation of their professional ideology to incorporate the ideals and goals of the employing organization. Thus subgroups can contribute to aspects of engagement.

Exploring the issue of workplace motivation from an HRD perspective, Chalofsky and Krishna (2009) advocate a holistic approach that takes into account contextual and organizational factors. They argue that 'although motivation is an individual and personal process, it is also significantly influenced and shaped by the contextual and organizational factors' (p. 191). One of these is clearly the group/team. Again, as motivation is an aspect of engagement, this research is of interest.

There is evidence that factors associated with EE do focus at the level of work groups/teams. 'Job resources', including social support from colleagues and supervisors, have been positively associated with WE (Bakker and Demerouti, 2008). It has been argued that engaged workers perform better, and that the crossover of engagement among members of the same work team creates a positive team climate, and increases performance in others. Positive emotions experienced by engaged workers transfer engagement to others (Bakker and Demerouti, 2008; Bakker et al., 2006).

The study of motivation on team effectiveness has looked at the way that team members motivate or demotivate one another (Latham, 2007). Processes of 'social identification' occur and people tend to identify with a group that distinguishes them from others. This occurs more with smaller rather than larger groups, as they are more inclusive: 'In larger groups, one's conception of self in relation to others is less informative since this is an identity that "everyone" shares' (Latham, 2007, p. 257). One could surmise an important role for the team as a locus of engagement.

As noted earlier, engagement interventions typically start with some sort of organization commitment survey, which assesses the level of engagement with 'the organization'. However, in the light of Latham's findings, it might be possible for an individual to demonstrate a lack of engagement with organization-level priorities, but to demonstrate engagement at the level of the team, and of the task. This suggests including more of a survey of 'team climate' or 'team commitment', contextualized at work group or team level. Rather than a generalized survey, this should be tied to the function and tasks of the teams being studied. It could focus on aspects such as quality or customer satisfaction, and be linked to methods such as the balanced scorecard approaches (Mathieu et al., 2008, p. 418). Engagement interventions might also usefully take place at the level of the team, in combination with the organizational or individual level. Teamwork competencies themselves can also be improved though training interventions (Mathieu et al., 2008), and this might in turn impact upon engagement.

As we have seen, a particular focus in EE is on the importance of taking an 'engaging' approach to management and leadership. Team leadership may be a useful focus for the study of EE, building on what is almost a century of previous research and theory into leadership research (Parker and Griffin, 2011). For example, transformational leadership behaviours have been positively related to perceived team effectiveness. Shared leadership suggests that leadership functions can be distributed across multiple team members rather than arising from a single formal leader (Mathieu et al., 2008, p. 450). Both these aspects have resonance with the argument around 'engaging managers'. Kirkman and Rosen (1999) looked at leader behaviours and team responsibility in 111 teams from four organizations. They found that external leaders' actions enhanced empowerment experiences. Empowered teams exhibited higher levels of productivity, customer service, job satisfaction, organizational and team commitment. Coaching has also been found to positively influence self-management, team–member relationship quality, member satisfaction, team empowerment and psychological safety (Mathieu et al., 2008).

Srivastava, Bartol and Locke (2006) studied 'empowering leadership' in management teams and its effects on knowledge sharing, efficacy and performance. Although their study focuses on knowledge sharing, they make a number of useful observations relevant to this study. They defined empowering leadership as 'behaviours whereby power is shared with subordinates and that raise their level of intrinsic motivation' (p. 1240). Examples of empowering leader behaviour include: leading by example, participative decision-making, coaching, informing and showing concern. Clearly, the notion of 'engaging leadership' has many similarities.

Kirkman and Rosen's (1999) work on team empowerment has resonance for EE. They define empowerment as 'increased task motivation resulting from an individual's positive orientation to his or her work role' (1999, p. 58). They see team empowerment as having four dimensions:

Potency – the collective belief of a team that it can be effective.

Meaningfulness – team's experiencing its tasks as important, valuable and worthwhile.

Autonomy – the degree to which team members experience substantial freedom, independence and discretion in their work.

Impact – when a team produces work that is significant and important for an organization.

(Kirkman and Rosen, 1999, p. 59)

This notion of empowerment goes beyond the idea of 'engaging leaders' to suggest a significant role for the team itself in facilitating engagement.

As teams become established and legitimate, they participate in networks and gain access to strategic organizational information, and have a greater sense of their impact on overall organization performance (Kirkman and Rosen, 1999). Team empowerment can be impacted from four areas – external leader behaviour, production/service responsibilities, team-based human resource policies and social structure (Kirkman and Rosen, 1999). 'Empowering leaders' are seen to exhibit similar behaviour to the 'engaging leaders' of EE. This includes 'delegation of responsibility to the team, soliciting team input into decision-making, seeking to enhance the sense of personal control of individual team members, encouraging team goal-setting and self-evaluation, and setting high team expectations' (Kirkman and Rosen, 1999, p. 60). Potential problems with multiple loci of engagement need also to be considered. For example, members of teams may experience greater loyalty to the team than to the organization, which may hinder overall performance (CIPD, 2011).

EMPLOYEE ENGAGEMENT – AN EMERGING CONSTRUCT

It seems that EE is here to stay, at least for the present. It is a concept that has evolved in popularity in practice, and for which there is an increasing amount of research being undertaken. Engagement has been heavily marketed by consultancy companies, appears to have a resonance with practitioners and policymakers, and taps into ideas about the meaning of work (Parker and Griffin, 2011). There are questions around whether it really is adding something new, given that definitions and meanings of engagement in the practitioner literature often overlap with other earlier constructs. It is, however, presented as a more distinct construct in the academic literature. Following an extensive critique, Macey and Schneider (2008) conclude that the concept of engagement does have distinctive characteristics, as an integrated set of constructs, interrelated and with relationships to a common outcome. Saks (2006) concurs that it is distinguishable from related constructs such as organizational commitment, organizational citizenship behaviour and job involvement.

However, it is important to recognize the contested nature of much of what passes for research and practice in EE. If it is to be a useful construct, then it needs to be regarded as one that is complex and multi-faceted. We need to draw on the research being done in the various relevant domains within management studies and work psychology. In the urge to discover something new, we should not dismiss the huge body of research and theory in contributory areas such as commitment and motivation.

A special issue of the *European Journal of Work and Organizational Psychology*, online in August 2010, was dedicated to a review of the concept of work engagement (WE). One overall conclusion was that there is sufficient theory demonstrating that engagement is a motivational construct, but no overall agreement on how it is conceptualized, echoing discussion on EE. WE is variously defined as organizational commitment, especially affective commitment, as emotional attachment to the organization and desire to stay in the organization, and with respect to extra-role behaviour (discretionary behaviour) (Bakker et al., 2011a). Two core dimensions of WE seemed to attract most agreement – energy and involvement/identification, which are both included in the Utrecht Work Engagement Scale (UWES).

There is also debate around whether EE is best conceptualized as a broad, generalizable construct (organizational climate) or a more specifically focused construct (service climate), climate for innovation (Bakker et al., 2011b). These different conceptualizations might suggest different levels and foci for engagement interventions. Another question is whether engagement is a stable state, or if there are fluctuations in engagement across the working day. Many studies appear to assume that engagement is expected to be relatively constant, given the presence of specific job and organizational factors. But this simplifies the possibility of engagement as a more temporal ebb and flow (Macey and Schneider, 2008, p. 11).

How engagement develops is another aspect of interest. Shuck and Wollard (2010) propose that cognitive engagement occurs before emotional and behavioural engagement. Cognitive engagement cannot be measured as it is not yet behaviourally manifested. It is a catalyst to the next two levels. A more sophisticated understanding of engagement suggests that prescriptions for organizational efforts to promote engagement may need to be revised.

The costs of driving up EE have received limited consideration, in contrast to attempts to quantify the benefits. For example, over-engagement may have potential unintended consequences. If a worker gets overly involved in work activities, they may experience work/ family conflict, and other negative consequences (Brewster et al., 2007). Possible dangers of over-engagement could also include becoming too internally focused and overreliant on current organizational arrangements, leading to difficulties in coping with major change and contributing to stresses within teams (4-Consulting, 2007).

In Kahn's (1990) research, three psychological conditions necessary for individual engagement emerge: meaningfulness, safety, and availability, and he explores each of these aspects further. For example, he suggests that psychological meaningfulness is influenced by three factors: task character-istics, role characteristics and work interactions. Kahn also notes that work behaviours include both rational and unconscious elements, which are influ-enced by individual, social and contextual sources, including interpersonal, group, inter-group and organizational factors (Kahn, 1990). The implications here are that engagement is not simply something that occurs uniformly under specific conditions, but is more personal and subject to a potentially wide range of contextual factors.

Engagement has been conceptualized as implying 'discretionary effort', defined as extra time, brainpower and energy; something special, extra, or at least atypical. However, 'effort' requires clear definition. Equally, if we define engagement solely in terms of extra effort, this suggests 'just doing more of what is usual. It might equally involve doing something *different* and not just something *more*' (Macey and Schneider, 2008, p. 40).

There is scope for a great deal more focus on HRD and EE. EE also has potential to provide a vehicle for HRD practice to achieve a higher promi-nence in organizations, and provide a focus for HRD to make a more strategic contribution. There is significant evidence that HRD interventions contribute to EE as part of a package of measures. However, there is less evidence on spe-cific HRD interventions and their contribution to EE, pointing to the need for further research. Research from an HRD perspective could examine spe-cific HRD interventions, and their impact on engagement. Indeed, given the prominence of HRD interventions within current EE practices, perhaps HRD is an intrinsic contributor to engagement? Research into the theme of 'locus of engagement' is still in its infancy, and there is scope at different levels to explore HRD's contribution to engagement through working with teams.

The area of groups and teams and EE is of particular interest to HRD, and provides opportunities for research and practice interventions. These could focus on the HRD role in driving and supporting engaged team working, and training and development for team leadership and management.

Evaluation is another area for fruitful research. Developments in HRD theory on evaluation have to a large extent failed to be taken up fully by practitioners, evidenced by the continuing popularity of simplistic evalua-tion measures. Perhaps evaluation could be viewed more favourably in some instances if it is equated with 'measuring engagement'. There is also scope for cross-cultural studies, which has not really been touched on in this chapter. EE is presented as a universalist conception, and there is little examina-tion of culture. But, as Flesher notes: 'a Western definition of a leadership value/competence may not only have no direct language translations into Japanese, it may also have no conceptual translation' (Flesher, 2009, p. 257).

Generally, EE as a construct will continue to encourage further theoretical and empirical research. Whilst it has gained significant popularity, it is ill-defined and conceptually problematic. Yet boundary setting is equally problematic for terms like this that seem to take on a life of their own. Perhaps, as Lee (2001) states for HRD, particular definitions of EE are only valid for particular times and places. EE is indefinable because it is in a continual state of *becoming*, and we can seek to influence this, but it is not helpful or appropriate to seek to finalize a definition.

REFERENCES

Alimo-Metcalfe, B., Alban-Metcalfe, J., Bradley, M., Mariathasan, J. and Samele, C. (2008) The impact of engaging leadership on performance, attitudes to work and wellbeing at work: A longitudinal study, *Journal of Health Organization and Management*, 22(6): 586–598.

Allen, N. J. and Meyer, J. P. (1990) The measurement and antecedents of affective, continuance and normative commitment to the organization, *Journal of Occupational Psychology*, 63(1): 1–18.

Ashman, I. (2007) An investigation of the British organizational commitment scale, *Management Research News*, 30(1): 5–24.

Attridge, M. (2009) Measuring and managing employee work engagement: A review of the research and business literature, *Journal of Workplace Behavioural Health*, 24(4): 383–398.

Bakker, A. B., Albrecht, S. L. and Leiter, M. P. (2011a) Key questions regarding work engagement, *European Journal of Work and Organizational Psychology*, 20(1): 4–28.

Bakker, A. B., Albrecht, S. L. and Leiter, M. P. (2011b) Work engagement: Further reflections on the state of play, *European Journal of Work and Organizational Psychology*, 20(1): 74–88.

Bakker, A. B. and Demerouti, E. (2008) Towards a model of work engagement, *Career Development International*, 13(3): 2009–2223.

Bakker, A. B., van Emmerik, H. and Euwema, M. C. (2006) Crossover of burnout and engagement in work teams, *Work and Occupations*, 33(4): 464–489.

Bishop, J. W., Scott, K. D. and Burroughs, S. M. (2000) Support, commitment and employee outcomes in a team environment, *Journal of Management*, 26(6): 1113–1132.

Brewster, C., Higgs, M., Holley, N. and McBain, R. (2007) *Employee Engagement*. Report from the HR Centre of Excellence Research and Members Meeting, Henley.

Chalofsky, N. and Krishna, V. (2009) Meaningfulness, commitment, and engagement: The intersection of a deeper level of intrinsic motivation, *Advances in Developing Human Resources*, 11(2): 189–203.

CIPD (2008) *Employee Engagement*. CIPD Factsheet.

CIPD (2011) *Locus of Engagement: Understanding what Employees Connect with at Work*. Research Insight, CIPD.

4-Consulting (2007) In association with DTZ consulting, *Employee Engagement in the Public Sector: A Review of Literature*. Edinburgh: Scottish Executive Social Research.

Dicke, C. (2007) Employee engagement: I want it, what is it? *Employee Engagement: What Do We Really Know? What Do We Need to Know to Take Action?* A collection of white papers, Centre for Advanced Human Resource Studies, Paris: 5–17.

Fairlie, P. (2011) Meaningful work, employee engagement and other key employee outcomes: Implications for human resource development, *Advances in Developing Human Resources*, 13(4): 508–525.

Ferrer, J. (2005) *Employee Engagement: Is it Organisational Commitment Renamed?* Working paper series, Victoria University School of Management.

Flesher, J. (2009) The meaning of work: A perspective from practice, *Advances in Developing Human Resources*, 11: 253–260.

Garavan, T. N. (2007) A strategic perspective on human resource development, *Advances in Developing Human Resources*, 9(1): 11–30.

Gatenby, M., Rees, C., Soane, E. and Truss, C. (2009) *Employee Engagement in Context.* London: CIPD Publishing.

Guest, D. E. and Conway, N. (2002) Communicating the psychological contract: An employer perspective, *Human Resource Management Journal*, 12(2): 22–38.

Harter, J., Schmidt, F. L. and Hayes, T. L. (2002) Business-unit-level relationship between employee satisfaction, employee engagement, and business outcomes: A meta-analysis, *Journal of Applied Psychology*, 87(2): 268–279.

Kahn, W. A. (1990) Psychological conditions of personal engagement and disengagement at work, *Academy of Management Journal*, 33(4): 692–724.

Kirkman, B. L. and Rosen, B. (1999) Beyond self-management: Antecedents and consequences of team empowerment, *Academy of Management Journal*, 42(1): 58–74.

Kontakos, A. M. (2007) 'Seeing clearly' employee engagement and line of sight, *Employee Engagement: What Do We Really Know? What Do We Need to Know to Take Action?* A collection of white papers, Centre for Advanced Human Resource Studies, Paris: 72–83.

Latham, G. P. (2007) *Work Motivation: History, Theory, Research and Practice.* London: Sage Publications.

Lee, M. (2001) A refusal to define HRD, *Human Resource Development International*, 4(3): 327–341.

Macey, W. H. and Schneider, B. (2008) The meaning of employee engagement, *Industrial and Organizational Psychology*, 1(1): 3–30.

MacLeod, D. (2010) David MacLeod on employee engagement, *Management Today* 23 March. <http://www.managementtoday.co.uk/news/992265/mt-special-david-macleod-employee-engagement/> (accessed 2 March 2012).

MacLeod, D. and Clarke, N. (2009) *Engaging for Success: A Report to Government.* London: Department for Business, Innovation and Skills.

Mathieu, J., Maynard, M. T., Rapp, T. and Gilson, L. (2008) Team effectiveness 1997–2007: A review of recent advancements and a glimpse into the future, *Journal of Management*, 34(3): 410–476.

McBain, R. (2007) The practice of engagement, *Strategic HR Review*, 6(6): 16–19.

McCabe, T. J. and Garavan, T. N. (2008) A study of the drivers of commitment amongst nurses: The salience of training, development and career issues, *Journal of European Industrial Training*, 32(7): 528–568.

McCracken, M. and Wallace, M. (2000) Towards a re-definition of strategic HRD, *Journal of European Industrial Training*, 24(5): 281.

Meyer, J. P., Becker, T. E. and Vandenberghe, C. (2004) Employee commitment and motivation: A conceptual analysis and integrative model, *Journal of Applied Psychology*, 89(6): 991–1007.

Parker, S. K. and Griffin, M. A (2011) Understanding active psychological states: Embedding engagement in a wider nomological net and closer attention to performance, *European Journal of Work and Organizational Psychology*, 20(1): 60–67.

Robertson, I. T. and Cooper, C. L. (2010) Full engagement: The integration of employee engagement and psychological well-being, *Leadership and Organization Development Journal*, 31(4): 324–336.

Robinson, D. (2003) *Defining and Creating Employee Commitment: A Review of Current Research.* HR Network Paper MP21, Institute for Employment Studies.

Robinson, D., Hooker, H. and Hayday, S. (2007) *Engagement: The Continuing Story.* IES Report 447, Institute for Employment Studies.

Robinson, S., Perryman, D. and Hayday, S. (2004) *The Drivers of Employee Engagement*. IES Report 408, Institute for Employment Studies.

Saks, A. M. A. (2006) Antecedents and consequences of employee engagement, *Journal of Managerial Psychology*, 21(7): 600–619.

Schaufeli, W. and Bakker, A. (2003) UWES Utrecht Work Engagement Scale, *Preliminary Manual* (version 1), accessed 16 April 2012 <http://www.beanmanaged.eu/pdf/articles/arnoldbakker/article_arnold_bakker_87.pdf>.

Seijts, G. H. and Crim, D. (2006) What engages employees the most or, the Ten C's of employee engagement, *Ivey Business Journal Online*, March/April: 1–5.

Shuck, B. (2011) Four emerging perspectives of employee engagement: An integrative literature review, *Human Resource Development Review*, 10(1): 1–25.

Shuck. B. and Wollard, K. (2010) Employee engagement and HRD: A seminal review of the foundations, *Human Resource Development Review*, 9(1): 89–110.

Srivastava, A., Bartol, K. M. and Locke, E. (2006) Empowering leadership in management teams: Effects on knowledge sharing, efficacy, and performance, *Academy of Management Journal*, 49(6): 1239–1251.

Towers Perrin (2008) *Closing the Engagement Gap: A Road Map for Driving Superior Business Performance*. <www.towersperrin.com>.

Wallace, J. E. (1995) Organizational and professional commitment in professional and nonprofessional organisations, *Administrative Science Quarterly*, 40(2): 228–255.

Walton, J. (1999) *Strategic Human Resource Development*. Harlow, UK: Financial Times/Prentice Hall.

Zigarmi, D., Nimon, K. I. M., Houson, D., Witt, D. and Diehl, J. (2009) Beyond engagement: Toward a framework and operational definition for employee work passion, *Human Resource Development Review*, 8(3): 300–326.

FURTHER READING

Albrecht, S. L. (ed.) (2010) *Handbook of Employee Engagement: Perspectives, Issues, Research and Practice*. Cheltenham, UK and Northampton, MA: Edward Elgar.

Bakker, A. B. and Leiter, M. P. (eds) (2010) *Work Engagement: A Handbook of Essential Theory and Research*. Hove and New York: Psychology Press.

Shuck, B. (2011) Four emerging perspectives of employee engagement: An integrative literature review, *Human Resource Development Review*, 10(3): 304–328.

INDEX

Printed and bound by CPI Group (UK) Ltd, Croydon, CR0 4YY